THE BRADMAN YEARS
AUSTRALIAN
C·R·I·C·K·E·T·1918–1948

Recent books by Jack Pollard

The Turbulent Years of Australian Cricket 1893–1917 (1987)
The Formative Years of Australian Cricket 1803–93 (1987)
Australian Fishing (ed., 1986)
The Pictorial History of Australian Cricket (1986)
When Stumps Were Drawn (ed., 1985)
Australian Rugby Union: The Game and the Players (1984)
Tribute to Lillee and Chappell (1984)
Australian Cricket: The Game and the Players (1982)

THE BRADMAN YEARS
AUSTRALIAN
C·R·I·C·K·E·T·1918–1948

JACK POLLARD

ANGUS
& ROBERTSON
PUBLISHERS

Contents

Introduction

Australian cricket prospered in the 40-year period covered in this book. Competitions that had been suspended after the first year of World War I were quickly resumed. State control bodies like the New South Wales Cricket Association, which when the war ended in 1918 had a bank balance of £9 11s, were soon flush with turnstile money.

Some of the animosity of the war years lingered, the patriots bitterly condemning those who had not enlisted, but once the players swapped their khaki uniforms for cricket whites the shame of the shirking cricketers was quickly forgotten. Joe Clayton, the NSWCA president whose two sons had fought in the war, boasted when it ended that 600 of the 900 players under the association's control had joined up, including 11 state players. This compared more than favourably with South Australia's six Sheffield Shield players in uniform and Victoria's three.

Considering the length of the war and the brutality of the fighting, cricket's casualty list was not high. "Tibby" Cotter, whose wonderfully muscled physique had been called a model for any sculptor, had been killed by machine-gun fire while serving as a stretcher-bearer at Beersheba. Johnnie Moyes had been wounded in France, badly enough to be forced later to give up cricket. Bob Massie, the 193 centimetre Adonis Monty Noble had hailed as the best bowler Australia had unearthed since Fred Spofforth, was wounded twice, the first time by a Turk who fired into his trench at Gallipoli. Massie recovered but played no more cricket. Other first-class cricketers who were not so lucky included Norman Callaway, Gother Clarke and John Williams of New South Wales, Fred Collins and Frank Lugton of Victoria, Charles Backman of South Australia, Alan Marshal and Hubert Smith of Queensland, Leo Butler, Ossie Douglas, Keith Eltham, Frank Gatenby and Stan McKenzie of Tasmania, and Ernest Parker, of Western Australia, all of whom died in action or in hospitals. Norman Callaway's death at Villers-Bretonneux left him with a first-class average of 207.00 from one game, a world record. Others such as Bert Oldfield, Bill Trenerry, Austin Diamond and Charles Kelleway were gassed or wounded but were able to continue their careers in the New South Wales side.

Federation was less than 20 years old when peace arrived, and amid the great national surge of patriotism the state cricket associations were among the strongest supporters of British loyalty. The war had vastly strengthened Australia's links with England, burying forever the taint of our convict ancestry, and over the next 20 years the British Empire was at its peak. Bonds of Empire speeches were obligatory whenever England and Australian cricketers dined together. Although short of cash, the state associations did all they could to help the war effort. They staged patriotic matches to raise funds for servicemen, asked clubs to take up collections at matches, and sent cricket equipment to troops in the Middle East and Europe. The NSWCA even organised the construction of a soldier's cottage in Frenchs Forest, which they handed over to a soldier named Eric Milham when he returned from the war. Unfortunately, he was not a cricketer.

When Herbie Collins, a lance-corporal, brought the First AIF team home to revive representative cricket in Australia, the capital cities quickly changed their main grounds from barracks to playing fields and went back to preparing good pitches and painting grandstands, scoreboards and members' pavilions. One had to go out into the bush to find paddocks similar to those on which Australian cricket had begun. The old clashes between administrators and star players simmered but the participants in the 1912 showdown—when six leading players refused to accompany the Australian team to England unless they could appoint their own manager—had either died (Cotter and Trumper) or lost their fervour.

Cricket welcomed the respite from bickering and over the next three decades under review here, the game grew rapidly; those who had served in the war were given preference for cricket's big jobs and there was only an occasional administrative gaffe or official clash with players. This strength enabled cricket to boost its appeal despite the Depression, the Bodyline crisis, and strong challenges from other sports. Cricket never let slip the advantage it had secured by starting earlier than other summer sports, and was able to shrug off the growing support for horse racing, which in 1926 attracted an amazing 118,877 to watch Spearfelt win the Melbourne Cup. Cricket officials were probably right in thinking horse racing—like cricket it had begun in Sydney's Hyde Park—was not really an opposing sport but one cricketers could enjoy.

Other sports produced their heroes, men like "Boy" Charlton, who won the 1500 metres gold medal at the 1924 Olympic Games, Jack Crawford, whose graceful strokes won the 1933 Wimbledon tennis championships, Bobby Pearce, who in 24 years of sculling was never beaten, Hubert Opperman, a world-beater on a bike, and the Kalgoorlie-born billiards wizard Walter Lindrum. Surfing, which virtually began on 1 October 1902, when the Sydney editor William Gocher defied the law by bathing in the sea at Manly, attracted a growing band of enthusiastic devotees. Cricket survived all this opposition by producing an imposing array of celebrities. Players like Jack Gregory, Ted McDonald, Charlie Macartney, Bill Woodfull, Bill Ponsford, Arthur Mailey, Bert Oldfield, Clarrie Grimmett, Archie Jackson, Bill O'Reilly and "Chuck" Fleetwood-Smith not only kept Australia in the forefront of international cricket but did it in a style that gave the public plenty to cheer about.

The most amazing of all Australia's sporting stars, a product of the Depression, was Donald George Bradman, whose feats remain unequalled by any batsman. Bradman averaged a century at better than every third time he batted. Between 1927 and 1948 he scored 117 centuries, including 27 scores of 200 or more, in first-class matches. His 452 not out for New South Wales against Queensland in 1930 is still the highest ever made on a grass pitch anywhere in the world and has only been surpassed on matting. Bradman had to make the transition to Test cricket from beginnings in unenclosed parks on concrete pitches covered by matting. He knew the pleasure of arriving at a country town pitch with one of his team-mates carrying the roll of matting with a stump pushed in either end to prevent the mallet and iron spikes falling out. There was usually a broom available to sweep pebbles from the pitch before the mat was laid and pegged down. Sydney coaches tried to change his grip on the bat and suggested all manner of modifications to his technique, but he knew in his heart that he could make the changes needed for success on grass without radical alterations and he always remained a self-coached cricketer. The same could be said of his great rival and Australian team-mate Bill O'Reilly, who moved to the crease with a flurry of limbs and at the moment of delivery bent his right knee, a movement purists claimed upset his rhythm, but which he absolutely refused to change.

To convey the excitement of this wonderful period in Australian cricket, the feats of its best players, and many of their idiosyncrasies, I have enjoyed hundreds of hours of conversations with old cricketers. This stirred me to long study of the books listed in the Bibliography and numerous sessions in the libraries of all Australia's state capitals, major newspapers and country centres. As usual, I received invaluable help from Cliff Winning, librarian to the New South Wales Cricket Association, Roger Page, Australian co-ordinator of the Association of Cricket Statisticians, Greg McKie, of the Victorian Cricket Society, and Rex Harcourt, chief researcher at the Melbourne Cricket Ground Museum. Bill O'Reilly, Keith Miller, Chris Harte, Phil Wilkins, Ric Finlay, David Frith, Pat Mullins and Sir Donald Bradman answered numerous queries freely and enthusiastically.

I hope the finished product justifies their support.

Sacked by a field-marshal

The Dominions and AIF teams in England 1918–19

William Albert Stanley Oldfield was a corporal in the 15th Field Ambulance Brigade in France when the Germans began a heavy bombardment of Polygon Wood in 1917. The whining of the German shells and the accompanying explosions ended with Oldfield being buried under a mess of splintered timber and mud. Several hours later when they dug him out, he was close to death from suffocation. The three other stretcher-bearers and the patient were killed. Invalided back to England, Oldfield, after five months recuperating in Gloucester Hospital, was on leave in a dingy boarding house not far from the Australian Imperial Forces (AIF) cricket team's headquarters in Horseferry Road, London, when the team captain, Herbie Collins, found him. It was a strange interview, Oldfield said, for Collins did not know his name, only that he was the chap whose skill as a wicket-keeper had all the Australian servicemen-cricketers talking.

The AIF team had only just been established and in one of its first matches a fiery

Australian soldiers playing cricket on Shell Green, Gallipoli, 17 December 1915. Major Macarthur Onslow lost his wicket while shells passed overhead.

delivery from fast bowler Jack Gregory had gashed the cheek of the side's only keeper, Ted Long, who had kept for New South Wales back in the 1911–12 season. Collins offered Oldfield the job as Long's replacement because Hammy Love, the only other good keeper available, wanted to return home immediately. Oldfield at first scoffed at the suggestion that he was capable of first class performances but finally agreed to join the team and that night was on the train to Oxford. He had no flannels and boarded the train with a battered assortment of inners and wicket-keeping gloves and torn pads all tied up in brown paper. Team-mates lent him the gear he needed.

By the end of the first over of the Oxford match Collins saw that all the reports about Oldfield were true; by the end of the innings he realised that a new Australian cricket star had arrived. Ted Long said he was no longer needed but stayed with the team as the reserve wicket-keeper, aware that there was in Oldfield's keeping a near-genius he could never match. There was style and polish inherent in the little man's every movement, a subtlety of control in his hands and in the neat small steps he made to change ends. Oldfield was destined to become one of a group of great Australian cricketers developed by those services matches, and his team became the front-runners in reviving cricket in England, South Africa and Australia.

Bert Oldfield was born in the Sydney suburb of Alexandria in 1894, and was educated at Cleveland Street and Forest Lodge public schools. William Bardsley, father of cricketer Warren Bardsley, was then headmaster of Forest Lodge school. Oldfield was in the Glebe club's third grade team as a batsman when the regular wicket-keeper did not turn up and his captain asked him to take over. He had had only two matches in Glebe's first grade team when he enlisted in the First

AIF. He served in the Middle East and played in services matches with "Tibby" Cotter and his other Glebe team-mates Charles Kelleway and Warren Bardsley before going to France. In London he played for an AIF Second XI.

Kelleway and Bardsley were two of the most taciturn men in Australian cricket, monosyllabic characters with impeccable manners, noted for their careful grooming on and off the field. They had a great influence on Oldfield, who developed a similar approach in his clothes and behaviour. He seldom appealed unless the batsman was out. He would stump a batsman by removing a single bail and if the batsman regained his crease would never trouble the umpires by bashing down the stumps. When the Australian slips fieldsmen all appealed, umpires looked at Oldfield, who was invariably silent if the batsman was not out. Nobody ever saw him fall down or somersault to take a catch and it was unheard of for his shirt-tail to come adrift.

The signing of the Armistice on 11 November 1918 left service chiefs and governments with the problem of keeping many thousands of worn-out servicemen occupied while they waited for ships to take them home. The flower of the Commonwealth's manhood had been wiped out in the fighting in Turkey, France and Belgium, and it would have been a national disgrace just to have fed and clothed the survivors and let them succumb to boredom and homesickness.

Vast quantities of sporting equipment replaced rifles and grenades in government stores. Inter-battalion, inter-brigade and finally international competitions were organised overnight in rowing, boxing, Rugby, tennis and athletics as well as cricket. Between June and August 1918, big crowds saw three one-day charity matches between an England XI and a Dominions XI, which included the Australians Charles Kelleway, Roy Park, Charlie Macartney, Johnny Taylor, Johnnie

One of the AIF teams: (L to R) (back) S. Winning, E. Long, C. Docker, J. Gregory, C. Willis; (front) J. Taylor, E. Bull, H. Collins (captain), E. Cameron, W. Trenerry, W. Oldfield.

Moyes, Cyril Docker, "Nip" Pellew and "Allie" Lampard. All three matches were drawn.

The Dominions batted first in the opening match on 29 June at Lord's and reached 166. Kelleway (30), Macartney (22), and Moyes (22), failed to exploit promising starts and only 23 from Docker late in the innings helped the Dominions to their modest total. The powerful England batting line-up seemed to face an easy task, but Docker took 4 for 39 and Macartney 3 for 22, six of the England side collecting ducks in a total of 98.

Two weeks later at Lord's, the Dominions XI faced an English side strengthened by the inclusion of George Gunn, Percy Fender and Lord Lionel Tennyson. Sent in to bat, England scored 157, with Gunn (36) and Fry (23) top-scorers. Moyes took 3 for 19. Rain interrupted the Dominions' attempt to pass England's score and they were 8 for 34 when time ran out. The Surrey left-arm medium-pacer Ernest Kirk took 4 for 10 to go with the 7 for 55 he took in the first match.

The third match at The Oval on 5 August was again upset by rain. The Dominions declared at 9 for 194 late in the afternoon. The South African Test star Herbie Taylor made 63, and near the end Docker hit out for a breezy 32. Woolley took 6 for 68. England were 6 for 75 and in danger of heavy defeat as Fender joined Johnny Douglas. When Moyes bowled Fender and stumps were drawn, Fender had made 70 of the 87 runs added in 45 minutes. England had two wickets in hand but were still 28 runs short of victory. King George V watched the cricket and presented trophies for Rugby and rowing contests, personally handing them to the winners.

Back in Australia, at the Australian Board of Control meeting in Sydney on 6 December 1918, the delegates H. R. Rush, E. E. Bean, B. V. Scrymgour, J. A. Riley, J. T. Pope, T. H. Howard, R. A. Oxlade, E. A. Tyler, and F. A. Iredale under the chairmanship of Sydney Smith agreed to play the Sheffield Shield competition in 1918–19 and continue it for a further three years, when the state with the best record would take possession of the Shield. The meeting also agreed to discontinue awarding members of winning Shield teams medallions and to extend overs in Shield matches from six to eight balls, a practice that prevailed until 1979–80. The influenza epidemic prevented Shield matches being played in 1918–19 and they resumed in 1919–20, but the Shield competition was out of favour with Board delegates.

The Victorian Cricket Association meeting on 13 January 1919 learned from Ernie Bean that the VCA had recommended that the Shield competition should end when any state won the Shield twice after the start of the 1919–20 competition. Bean said the other states were tired of the Shield and when it was dropped "some other trophy would be played for". The VCA accepted this recommendation but opposed omission of the medallions for winning teams in the Shield competitions that remained.

At the Board of Control meeting in Melbourne on 17 October, 1919, delegates voted enthusiastically to continue the Shield indefinitely. The reasons for this complete change of heart or delegates' temporary opposition to the Shield competition has never been satisfactorily explained, but it goes down as yet another aberration in the Board's erratic history.

At Australian Corps Headquarters in London, Major Syd Middleton, a great oarsman and a member of the first Wallaby Rugby touring team in Britain (he was sent off against Oxford University for punching), had the task of replacing drill sessions with sport and on 31 January 1919 he had AIF Order No. 1539 issued to all ranks:

> AIF Sports Control Board. *The following proposals for the formation of an AIF Board of Control to encourage sport in all units and supervise organisation and selection of representative teams. The Board to consist of a president, two representatives from units in France, one from AIF depots in the United Kingdom, one from London, and one representative of the Australian Comforts Fund.*

The AIF Sports Board had the support of the Australian Board of Control for International Cricket in forming a team comprised of players still in the services. The Board of Control, at a meeting in Melbourne on 6 December 1918, appointed Major Gordon Campbell, the former South Australian wicketkeeper who had toured America with the unofficial Australian team in 1913, as its representative with the Marylebone Cricket Club in negotiations on the proposed tour. Ronald Cardwell, in his booklet on the AIF team published in 1980, disclosed how the cricket Board's minutes stressed that it should retain complete control of the AIF team and determine the size of the party— 15 players, manager Campbell and scorer Bill Ferguson. The Board set Ferguson's remuneration for the tour at £200, allotted £150 to each player, and proclaimed that the team should be known as The AIF Australian XI.

When the question arose whether the team should play Test matches, the Board declined to agree—the side should only become involved in first-class matches. A selection committee comprising Dr E. P. Barbour, Dr Roy Park and Major Campbell was appointed, with instructions to submit their team selection to the Board in Melbourne for approval before making it public. Thus the Board prevented the Army taking control of the team's tour; it also asked that the MCC should indemnify the Board against loss.

Negotiations between Lord's and the Australian Board of Control were well advanced when a group of outstanding players serving in England and France announced that they would be unavailable for the tour. They were Charlie Macartney, Dr Barbour, Dr Park, Dr Claude Tozer, Major Campbell, Johnnie Moyes and Jack Massie. Moyes and Massie had been wounded—Massie twice, once at Gallipoli and again in France. Massie was one of the great losses of the time to Australian cricket for he had been a handsome and gifted exponent of the game, and he never played cricket again. Macartney withdrew because of the death of his father and returned home to be with his mother. The doctors wanted to get back to Australia to re-establish their medical practices.

When the list of players who had withdrawn was announced, the MCC decided there was little chance of the Australian Army fielding a first-class touring team and withdrew their offer of financial support. The AIF Sports Board then took over organisation of the team and its itinerary. Any chance the players had of forcing recognition of their main matches as Tests went with the withdrawal of MCC support, but history has shown that Lord's erred badly and much later, after World War II, they were to acknowledge their mistake.

A lot of the organisation of the AIF tour was undertaken by the Surrey County Cricket Club, strengthening even further the friendship between the club and Australian cricket, which dated back to the first tour of Australia in 1861–62 by an English team dominated by Surrey players. The Board appointed 65-year-old Irishman Howard Lacy, a wealthy supporter of the Mitcham Club who had or-

ganised many wartime matches for Australians in London, to assist with management of the team. In February 1919 the AIF Sports Control Board began a series of trials to ensure the selection of the best available players.

Captain Cyril Docker, who had been called up from Salisbury Plains to assist, forwarded news of the trials and the tour to Australian units all over England and Europe,

Cyril Docker, who helped organise the selection trials for the First AIF team.

and soon applications for trials poured in, many of them from cricketers with first class and first grade experience back in Australia. A dozen nets were needed to handle the trials at Lord's and The Oval. The army could not find the money needed to finance the operation, but the Australian government, the Australian Comforts Fund, and Australian businessmen in London all contributed generously. Nobody knew how much would be needed to launch the tour but it quickly became clear that the expected MCC contribution of £500 would easily be replaced.

Letters were sent to every English county club informing them that a strong AIF team was being formed, which would tour England "not for the sake of financial gain, but for the purpose of giving soldiers a chance to try their strength against the counties on the best English turf". Only three of the fixtures on the first draft of the team's itinerary were not played; matches in Scotland and Ireland were arranged in their place.

On 14 May 1919 the AIF Sports Board invited 20 players to practise with a view to winning a place in the team to tour England, Scotland and Ireland: C. Kelleway (captain), E. A. Bull, H. L. Collins, R. A. Coogan, C. T. Docker, J. M. Gregory, E. J. Long, G. V. Maidment, W. A. S. Oldfield, W. L. Trenerry, J. M. Taylor (all from New South Wales); R. W. Herring, M. D. Hotchin, A. W. Lampard, Dr N. L. Spiers, C. B. Willis (Victoria); J. T. Murray, C. E. Pellew, W. A. Stirling (South Australia); J. F. Sheppard (Queensland).

After the trials Coogan, Maidment, Oldfield, Herring, Hotchin, Spiers and Sheppard were omitted. When Long, who like Bull had played for New South Wales before enlisting, was injured, "Hammy" Love, a wicket-keeper from the Balmain club in Sydney, was brought in. Love played in only one game and his place was taken by Oldfield, whose skills were to prevent Love winning Test selection for most of his first-class career. Love often wondered if his decision to leave the AIF team gave Oldfield this selection edge.

The AIF Sports Board's aim was to give as many players as possible a chance to play in the matches around London, but this had to be modified when the team travelled. The programme undertaken by the AIF depended a lot on the availability of trains and the goodwill of their hosts. The first match, from 14 to 16 May 1919, was against a side collected by Lionel Robinson on his private ground at Attleborough in Norfolk. The AIF team had to finish when they were only nine runs short of victory with two wickets left because their train was about to go. This match, the last in which teams of twelve were considered first-class, saw the AIF dismiss a side which included ten prominent county players and the South Africans S. J. Pegler and H. W. Taylor for only 147. The AIF made 227 in reply, with Collins contributing 87. Robinson, son of the financial editor of the Melbourne *Age*, saw his team improve and score 8 for 362 in their second innings, leaving the AIF to score 283 to win. Johnnie Taylor (66) and Carl Willis (57) top-scored before the stationmaster beckoned.

The second match of the tour, a two-day affair on 17 and 19 May against Essex at Leyton, resulted in a win for the AIF by an innings and 114 runs. Essex were all out for 169, to which the AIF replied with 434, after Kelleway (126) made the first century of the tour. Essex managed only 151 in their second innings. *Wisden* said that Taylor's brilliant 78 suggested even better things to come.

The third match against Cambridge University from 21 to 23 May saw Collins and Kelleway put on 165 for the first wicket. Kelleway went on to 168 in three hours in one of his brightest knocks and the AIF were 7 for 518 at stumps. Next morning Pellew reached

105 not out and the AIF declared at 8 for 650. Cambridge were 9 for 148 in reply when Rotherham and Naumann added 145 for the tenth wicket. All out for 293 in their first innings, Cambridge made only 118 in their second attempt. Australia's ground fielding was superb throughout and helped produce a win by an innings and 239 runs.

Already it was apparent that in Gregory the AIF had unearthed a bowler of frightening pace, who could bounce the ball into the batsman's body off a good length. Tall (193 centimetres), and solid (89 kilograms), Gregory was a dominant player developed at Shore (Sydney Church of England Grammar School), North Sydney, where he captained the First XI in 1912 and 1913, played Rugby for the First XV, and was the school's athletics champion. He had joined up at 18 before he had a chance to further his family's great cricket tradition.

The team faced their biggest test at Lord's on 26 May in the match against Middlesex and on the first day made a splendid 370, thanks largely to a fourth wicket stand of 187 by Collins and Jack Tinline Murray, a gunner of immense strength who hit the ball very hard. Long and Stirling made 66 for the tenth wicket. Next day Middlesex took a 38-run lead when "Patsy" Hendren made 135 and "Plum" Warner 101, his 59th first-class century. Hendren's speedy running between wickets gave Warner cramp and at 82 he had to leave the field. He returned to reach his century, but finally had to retire because of the pain. The AIF left Middlesex 197 runs to score for victory but Kelleway's astute field placements and a vigorous attack restricted them to 4 for 146 when time ran out. Hendren was 63 not out and the impression lingered that had the AIF been able to dismiss him they would have won. Gregory figured in a sensational dismissal when he struck M. H. C. Doll over the heart and Doll fell into his stumps.

Jack Gregory in action with the characteristic "kangaroo hop" just before he bowled.

The AIF dismissed Oxford University for 152 on a rain-sodden pitch at Oxford on 29 May, and were well placed at 4 for 241 at the end of the day. Kelleway took 7 for 47 with his accurate medium-pace. Next day Johnny Taylor reached 104 and John Murray 133 as the AIF lifted their score to 8 for 391. *Wisden* praised Taylor's attractive stroke play. Oxford fought back splendidly and reached 4 for 247 when time ran out and left the match drawn.

Jack Hobbs, who in the 1914 season had scored 2499 runs at 62.47 in the county championship for an outstanding Surrey batting line-up, played a masterly innings for 205 in the next match, which began on 31 May at The Oval. Before 12,000 spectators the AIF made 230. Bill Hitch, off a run punctuated by

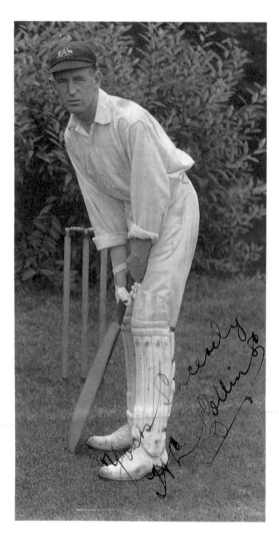

Promising Sydney youngster Herbie Collins who took over the captaincy when Kelleway was sacked from the AIF team.

three hops, showed why he was rated one of England's fastest bowlers by taking 6 for 71. Hobbs' knock then carried Surrey to a 114-run lead, with agile fielding saving countless runs. The AIF recovered to score 8 for 554 in their second innings. Taylor drove brilliantly for 96. Pellew (106) and Lampard (112) added 110 in entertaining fashion for the seventh

wicket. Left to score 440 to win, Surrey were 5 for 128 when play ended.

The AIF Sports Board had nominated Kelleway as captain without the normal election, but after the sixth match against Surrey the GOC commanding the Australian troops, Field-Marshal Birdwood, sent for Herbie Collins and told him that he was to take over the captaincy of the side. Collins was a lance-corporal, Kelleway a captain. Jack Fingleton, in his book *Masters of Cricket*, published in London in 1958, said that Collins was staggered. Birdwood told him: "Kelleway is a good cricketer, but unfortunately he quarrels. I understand that he has already had three arguments, including one with a caretaker. I'm sending him back on the next ship." Kelleway refused to be sacked, however, and went to Brighton with the team for the next match. Collins approached him as he began to unpack his gear.

"Charlie, this puts me in a pretty awkward position," said Collins. "Won't you think it over?"

"I'm playing," Kelleway replied.

The team gathered and after consultation told Kelleway that they would not join him if he took the field. Kelleway gave up and within days was on his way home to Australia. To his credit, he bore Collins no ill-feeling and later played under Collins' captaincy in both New South Wales and Australian teams. Collins said he never had the slightest trouble with him.

The AIF team ignored all considerations of army rank, and Collins, a lance-corporal on seven shillings and sixpence a day, captained a side containing seven commissioned officers without any question of his right to authority. They called each other by their first names, borrowed each other's caps, went quickly to the fielding positions indicated by their leader and through their team spirit gave every side they met a tough match. This was a consider-

Undeterred by his sacking as AIF captain, the enigmatic Kelleway kept playing Test cricket until he was 42, confident to the end in his ability.

able achievement considering the high standards reached by some English county players and the wounds carried by a few of the servicemen.

When Kelleway returned to Australia in September 1919, he told reporters that war injuries had forced him home early. He said he had received "a knock on the head from a piece of shrapnel just before the cessation of hostilities". The *Illustrated Sporting and Dramatic News* said Kelleway had a wound in the leg that still troubled him.

After a fine win over a weak MCC team by ten wickets, the AIF had to hold on grimly to avoid defeat by Sussex at Brighton on 9–10 June. Set to score 180 in 120 minutes in the last innings to win the match, the AIF collapsed and at 8 for 73 Long and S. C. Winning, who had replaced Kelleway in the team, reverted to desperate stonewalling: the last 35 minutes yielded only four sundries. Robert Relf, whose brother Albert played for Sussex and England, scored 64 and 102 for Sussex and took 4 for 23 in Australia's second innings.

The AIF had amazing luck in a rain-affected match from 12 to 14 June at Old Trafford against Lancashire. Willis and Collins put on 117 for the first wicket in the sun on the first day, which ended with the AIF 6 for 310. Collins' second century of the tour (103) took him 195 minutes. Overnight rain converted the pitch into a quagmire, but before it dried out into a "sticky" the AIF took their score to 418. They then dismissed Lancashire for 125 and 136 to win by an innings and 157 runs. Lampard had his career best figures of 9 for 42 in Lancashire's second knock, splendidly exploiting the badly cut-up pitch with his left-arm spinners.

The match against Yorkshire at Sheffield, from 16 to 17 June, was a thriller that put cricket back on the front page of most English newspapers. Yorkshire's openers, Wilfred Rhodes and Percy Holmes, put on 150 before

Gregory blasted Yorkshire out for 224. The last nine wickets added only 74 and Gregory took 6 for 91. Herbert Sutcliffe, in his first season for Yorkshire at the age of 25, made 13 batting at number six. From 3 for 22, the AIF took a first innings lead of 41. Bowling at fearsome pace Gregory then demonstrated what a dangerous bowler he was becoming by removing Robinson, Sutcliffe and Burton, whom he hit in the face. George Hirst, in his thirty-first season for Yorkshire and aged 48, scored 88 to give Yorkshire some hope with a lead of 169. Collins went first ball, and the AIF slumped to 9 for 116, setting up an astonishing finish.

Gregory and Long batted patiently to add 37 in an hour against a classy attack that comprised Rhodes, Hirst, Roy Kilner and William Blackburn. Sixteen runs short of victory, Gregory decided to swing at everything and he hit off the runs required, giving the AIF a highly unlikely victory by one wicket. The last pair remained undefeated with 54 runs in 80 minutes. First man into the Australians' dressing room to congratulate them was Hirst. Although he scored 60 centuries in his career, he never made a hundred against Australia and this time he had been only 12 runs short. Yorkshire were county champions that summer, so the win gave Australian morale a tremendous boost.

Rain forced a draw in the match against Hampshire at Southampton on 20 and 21 June and brought the AIF undone in the important match against the Gentlemen at Lord's from 23 to 25 June. The Gentlemen were 6 for 378 in the first innings when rain started and littered Lord's with puddles. Chasing 402, the AIF batsmen gave a dismal, artless display, allowing Johnny Douglas (4 for 34) and the East Norfolk Member of Parliament Michael Falcon (6 for 41) to dominate proceedings. Falcon was a fine cricketer, who had distinguished himself at Harrow and Cambridge

The great all-rounders George Hirst (left) and Wilfred Rhodes, both born in the Yorkshire village of Kirkheaton and both in the Yorkshire side beaten by the AIF.

and in America on the Incogniti tour in 1913. He played Minor Counties cricket for Norfolk for 40 years, from 1906 to 1946, but his parliamentary duties prevented him from playing first-class cricket. He probably would have played Test cricket had he qualified for a first-class county.

Following on after scoring only 85, the AIF staged a partial recovery, but after Falcon dismissed Taylor for 35 the second innings slumped to 184, giving the Gentlemen a comprehensive win by an innings and 133 runs. The Australians' lack of knowledge of wet English wickets was glaringly apparent.

Gregory underlined his all-round value with a hard-hitting innings of 115 in a total of

297 against Northants at Northampton from 26 to 28 June. Pellew scored a breezy 70. Northants responded with 246 before all the AIF batsmen hit out freely for a second innings total of 314. Gregory took 4 for 74 and Collins 5 for 26 with his left-arm slows in the Northants second innings of 169, the AIF winning by 196 runs.

Four non-first-class matches in Scotland and north-east England followed in the first ten days of July, with the AIF defeating Western Districts of Scotland at Glasgow by an innings and 460 runs, and having draws against the Scottish Union in Edinburgh, against a Scottish XI in Glasgow, and against Durham at West Hartlepool. Rain forced another draw at Leicester against Leicestershire on 11 and 12 July. The AIF made 5 for 551, with Collins (121), Pellew (187) and Willis (156 not out) enjoying themselves. There was no time to dismiss Leicestershire again after they made 224 in their first attempt.

At Derby on 14 and 15 July the Derbyshire right-arm medium pacer James Horsley took a hat-trick to dismiss the AIF for 125 after Derbyshire made 181. Gregory (6 for 65) and Collins (4 for 39) then bowled unchanged to force a Derbyshire collapse for only 112. Needing 165 to win, the AIF slumped to 5 for 26. Derbyshire won by 36 runs, which was the second defeat of the AIF tour.

There were 62 sundries in Australia's innings of 405 in the drawn match against H. K. Foster's XI at Hereford on 16 and 17 July. The home keeper conceded 45 byes. Gregory paved the way to a win by an innings and 203 runs against Worcestershire. He had 7 for 56 in Worcestershire's first innings of 120 and after Australia had declared at 4 for 450— Pellew made 195, the highest score of the tour, and Willis 129 not out—Gregory took a further 4 for 49 in helping Lampard (4 for 46), run through the opposition for only 127.

By now the AIF had proved their crowd

Jack Gregory in his less familiar role of batsman. He never wore gloves when he batted.

appeal and nobody was surprised when 10,000 people turned up for the start of the match against Warwickshire at Birmingham on 21 and 22 July. Warwickshire's first innings of 215 would have been far worse but for a splendid 73 by the former Sydney batsman, the Reverend E. F. Waddy. Collins followed up a five-wicket bowling haul by scoring 110 in the AIF's 321. Warwickshire were then bundled out for only 68 to give the Australians victory by an innings and 38 runs. The Adelaide left-arm medium-pacer Bill Stirling took 5 for 26 for the AIF, "Charlie" Winning 4 for 38.

Oldfield had not only proved his stature as a wicket-keeper but had consistently contributed handy runs with the bat. He did so again by making 80 not out in the drawn match against Nottinghamshire at Trent Bridge between 24 and 26 July. A modest AIF score seemed likely until Oldfield joined Willis at the fall of the eighth wicket. They added 196 before Willis was lbw for 130. George Gunn and Joe Hardstaff batted with expertise in a stand of 173 for Notts, Gunn scoring 131. Collins tried six bowlers but could not stop Notts scoring 391, 20 ahead of the AIF's 371. Oldfield was promoted from number ten to open the servicemen's second innings with Collins. They put on 194 but were very slow, and when the AIF declared at 5 for 242, Notts were left to score 223 in only 25 overs. Collins made 118, Oldfield 80 not out.

J. N. Crawford returned to the Surrey team, after his long exile in Australia, for the match against the AIF at The Oval from 31 July to 2 August. "Nip" Pellew, who had been one of Crawford's pupils at St Peter's College in Adelaide, was in the AIF side. Collins and Trenerry put on 141 in 80 minutes to lift the Australian score to 6 for 369 at the end of the first day. Not long before, Captain Trenerry had led his infantry battalion in the victory parade through London. The AIF reached 436 but Surrey collapsed dramatically to 5 for 26, before Cyril Wilkinson and Craw-

ford rescued Surrey in a stubborn partnership. Wilkinson made 103, Crawford 144 not out, in Surrey's total of 322. The visitors disappointed a large audience by dawdling to 4 for 260 when Collins declared. Surrey were 1 for 121 in their second innings when the game ended in a draw.

The AIF had a splendid win over Sussex on 4 and 5 August before big crowds at Brighton. Sussex, who boasted past and future Test players Joe Vine, Albert Relf, V. W. C. Jupp and Maurice Tate, were dismissed for 120 and 126. The Australians scored 300, of which Willis made 127, his fourth tour century. Gregory bowled extremely fast to take 6 for 38 in Sussex's first innings, Collins with guile and accuracy to take 6 for 27 when Sussex batted again.

An unknown leg-spinner named A. P. Freeman, whom team-mates called "Tich", confronted the Australians in the drawn Canterbury Festival match against Kent, which was played between 7 and 9 August. On a pitch that looked brimful of runs the AIF struggled to 198 in their first innings; Frank Woolley captured the last three wickets in 10 balls for only two runs. Kent replied with 301, Gregory taking 7 for 100. Willis (95) and Pellew (91) appeared certain of centuries in the AIF's second innings of 8 for 419, but Freeman dismissed them both. Kent were in danger at 3 for 30, chasing 317, but Woolley's exhilarating knock of 76 saw them through to 5 for 172 at stumps.

At Southend against Essex from 21 to 23 August Johnny Douglas had the Australians in trouble by taking 7 for 50 in their first innings of 130, but Essex did little better with 151. Johnny Taylor played what was unanimously agreed as the best innings of the tour in the AIF's second innings, scoring 150 in 146 minutes of superb driving, cutting and judicious running. Douglas held no fears for Taylor, who did not play a false stroke.

Murray (82) and Pellew (57) followed Taylor's example and Collins closed at 8 for 447, a lead of 426. Gregory bowled with a strong breeze behind him to take 5 for 34 in Essex's second innings of 117 and the AIF won by 309 runs.

Match figures of 10 for 91 by the outstanding left-arm spinner Charlie Parker compelled the AIF to fight desperately to save the match with Gloucestershire at Clifton on 27 and 28 August. Gloucestershire began with 281, thanks in part to 43 by 42-year-old C. L. Townsend. Bowling with his cap at the customary rakish angle, Parker had 7 for 70 in Australia's first innings of 147. Following-on the AIF were 5 for 64 by stumps with Parker in full flight, but Trenerry, who had opened the innings with Pellew, was undefeated at the close. Like most Australian touring teams who encountered him over the next decade the AIF players were puzzled why Parker did not play more than one Test for England. David Frith may have provided the answer in his book *The Slow Men* when he said that Parker did not help his chances of Test selection by one time grabbing a selector by his coat lapels and demanding an explanation for his omission from the team. Only Rhodes and Freeman ever took more than Parker's career bag of 3278 first-class wickets.

Dismissed for only 85 on a rain-soaked pitch at Taunton on 29 August, the AIF struck back by bundling Somerset out for 70. Then Collins discarded the safety-first tactics that characterised the Australians' approach to wet pitch batting by hitting out boldly for 67. Gregory (32) and Willis (34) copied their captain and this enabled the AIF to set Somerset 169 to win in 90 minutes. A draw seemed certain, but Collins took 8 for 31 in 14 overs for the AIF to win by 95 runs with 10 minutes to spare. Collins' match figures were 12 for 69.

"Charlie" Winning bowled unchanged

Dentist Johnny Taylor was one of the most entertaining batsmen in cricket immediately after World War I. It was unanimously agreed that his score of 150 against Essex in August 1919 was the best innings of the tour.

with Collins throughout the victory over Somerset, and in the next match against a powerful South of England XI at Hastings, from 1 to 3 September, Winning again bowled splendidly. Winning, a noted baseball pitcher, was completely ambidextrous and could change hands without the slightest loss of accuracy. Winning's 5 for 57 enabled the AIF to dismiss a team which included Albert and Robert Relf, Phil Mead, Frank Woolley and Arthur Gilligan for only 183. But by stumps on the first day the AIF had slumped to 6 for 96. They added only 66 the next day, to trail by 21. Woolley took 6 for 74. The

Johnny Taylor in action during a services match in 1919.

South of England made 280 in their second innings, leaving the Australians to score 302 to win. Only Trenerry seemed settled against an accurate, experienced attack and his 54 was full of powerful drives. When he left, the AIF folded to finish 123 runs short of their target, their third loss.

Against a far weaker South of England XI at Portsmouth on 4 and 5 September, the AIF had the best of rainy conditions. Gregory lifted the ball from a full length with alarming persistence and only three batsmen reached double figures in a South of England total of

104. Gregory had 6 for 42. The AIF then took a 102-run lead by scoring 206. Murray contributed 59 and Collins 46 in what proved match-winning displays. Winning's left-arm medium-pace spearheaded the servicemen's second innings attack, the South succumbing in the wet for 115, leaving the AIF the formality of scoring 15 runs for victory.

The last match of the AIF's 34-match tour of England (six of them not first-class) saw the soldiers opposed to C. I. Thornton's powerful side at Scarborough, a fixture that helped establish a tradition for the winding-up of Australian tours and enhanced the high reputation of the festival itself. Thornton was a colourful cricketer who, in popular opinion, hit the ball with a ferocity unmatched by other batsmen. He seldom wore pads and even scorned the use of gloves, and had many of the heaviest hits in cricket history to his credit. Only two of the side he selected to oppose the AIF, Michael Falcon and R. H. Twining, the 1912 Oxford University captain and an efficient Middlesex player, did not at one time play for England.

Collins by then was known as "Lucky" because of his good fortune in tossing, and he did it again and batted first. But at 33 Hitch produced a sustained spell of hostile fast bowling to have the AIF out for 81 in two hours. At the end of the first day Thornton's XI led by 65 but had only two wickets left. Gregory bowled faster than Hitch but his 7 for 83 could not prevent Thornton's side reaching 187. Cardwell makes the interesting point that Oldfield did not concede a bye in this innings, with Gregory at his most fearsome and well-educated bats flashing about. Moist until this stage, the pitch now dried out.

The AIF second innings yielded 296, with Willis dropped several times in scoring 96, and Taylor contributing 71. Gregory's 26 took him past 1000 runs in all matches for the tour. He had passed the 100 wicket mark against Kent a month earlier. Hobbs carried Thornton's XI to within sight of victory with an innings of 93 before Oldfield snapped him up. The ninth wicket fell with Thornton's XI still 10 short of the mark. Michael Falcon did not score a run, but he stayed there, and although the Australians fielded stoutly, Rhodes calmly made 23 runs to give the Englishmen the game by two wickets. The excitement of the finish, and the manner in which the Australians refused to accept defeat, did their team and Australian cricket proud.

The long way home

The AIF team in South Africa 1919

The AIF team's spin around England had produced some new cricket heroes, helped to revive the game at the first-class level and provided entertainment for a public devastated by war losses. While the AIF First XI toured, a Second XI played against lesser sides, but probably just as important from the standpoint of rehabilitating social cricket, winning 37 of their 55 matches, losing 11 and drawing 7. The AIF Second XI's appearance against major schools and colleges was particularly valued by the English authorities.

Although they had not played a Test, the prestige of the AIF team was so high that the Sports Control Board received a cable from the South African government, requesting a visit from the team on their way home. The players had done more than was asked of them and they longed to get home, but when the South Africans presented their invitation to the Australian Minister of Defence, Senator

The AIF team photographed in London just before their departure for South Africa: (L to R) (back) S. Winning, C. Docker, J. Gregory, E. Bull, J. Murray, E. Long, A. Lampard; (centre) W. Stirling, C. Pellew, H. Collins, H. Lacy, C. Willis, W. Trenerry; (front) W. Oldfield, J. Taylor.

Pearce, the team agreed to his request to spend six weeks in South Africa. Sir Abe Bailey, the millionaire vice-president of the South African Cricket Association, guaranteed the tour against loss, and Ernest Cameron, a former rover with the Essendon Australian Rules club, was named manager. Cameron had acted as an assistant to Howard Lacy in handling the AIF's English affairs.

The AIF began their English tour with only Collins and Kelleway established in first-class cricket, but they were able to go to South Africa for ten matches with a side full of players whom spectators wanted to see. Gregory surpassed them all, relishing the sun and the fast pitches, refreshed by the sea voyage from England. He was a gawky athlete who had won the AIF 100-yard sprint and the 120-yard hurdles, and was tennis champion of his artillery unit. He only went to field in the slips when he damaged a finger in the outfield and Herbie Collins put him there to recover. "He was so ungainly he spiked his own finger," said Collins. Gregory never again moved from the position and took 195 catches in the slips in his first-class career.

The Australian servicemen arrived in Cape Town aboard the SS *Ascanius* on 13 October 1919, and were met by the mayor and Mr Van der Byl of the South African Cricket Union. Unlike previous Australian visitors they were given a week to practise and recover from travelling before the first match at Cape Town against Western Province from 18 to 21 October.

Gregory could not get the ball to bounce or fly, but Collins took 4 for 55 and Lampard 5 for 29 to confine Province to 160. Test right-hander Philip Hands, who had won a DSO and MC in the war, made 63, and George Hearne 41. Lampard scored 55 in the dismal Australian reply of 141 and next day captured 7 for 71 in the South Africans' second innings of 179. The AIF stumbled to a two-wicket win by scoring the 199 needed.

The drawn match against Transvaal at Johnnesburg from 25 to 28 October produced outstanding batting from several of the AIF players and virtuoso displays of all-round skill from Collins and Gregory. The Australians were 8 for 343 at the end of the first day. Gregory scored 50, Collins 51. The remaining two wickets took the total to 392 on the second morning, with Lampard 68 not out.

Charles Frank, badly gassed in the war, made 108 in his first-class debut when Transvaal batted and although captain "Billy" Zulch made 60, Transvaal reached only 245. From 4 for 208, Transvaal lost 6 for 37 as Gregory tore their batting apart, mopping up the last three wickets inside an over. He then turned on a spectacular exhibition of powerful hitting and there was general disappointment when he was out for 86. Collins declared the AIF's second innings closed at 4 for 222 after Trenerry contributed a bright 74. Chasing 370, Transvaal were 2 for 44 when rain washed out play.

Natal appeared to have opened the way to victory in dismissing the AIF for 158, but Gregory swung the balance of the match at Durban on 1 to 4 November by taking 9 for 32, the best figures of his career. He ruined his chance to take all ten wickets when he ran out the last batsman. In one over, he had three wickets with his first four balls. Natal made only 83. The AIF's second knock yielded 341, Taylor scoring a stylish 81. Gregory went to work again in Natal's second innings, his 5 for 54 giving him 14 for 86 in the match. Natal's 106 gave the AIF victory by 310 runs.

In the return match with Natal at Pietermaritzburg on 7 to 10 November, only two of the home side reached double figures in Natal's first innings of 45. Gregory took 7 for 21, bowling unchanged with Collins. The AIF made 282 in reply, with Pellew 62 and Taylor 78. Natal's second effort produced a total of 195, Field top-scoring with 70. Collins ensured the AIF's win by an innings and 45 runs by taking 6 for 55. In a one-day match against Natal Colleges XV on 11 November, the Australians interspersed cricket with instruction. The Colleges made 143, while Stirling bagged five wickets in each innings. The AIF then made 238 in light-hearted style, with Collins leading the way with 78.

The return match against Transvaal at Johannesburg, from 15 to 18 November, appeared to hang on whether the locals could handle Gregory's pace, but he did not take a wicket in the first innings. Bill Stirling was the destroyer with 5 for 29 from his left-arm medium pace. Transvaal were out for 165 and then had to watch Gregory compensate for his fruitless bowling spell by hammering the South African bowling all over the ground for a fast 73. Pellew chimed in with 61 and the AIF innings ended at 352. Transvaal failed again in their second innings, only Zulch staying long in an innings of 173. His 95 could not prevent an AIF win by an innings and 14 runs. Docker had 5 for 20.

These six matches ushered in two internationals which the South African officials gave the same treatment as Tests and some South African newspapers described as Tests. The *Cape Argus* said the AIF were an admirable mixture of youth and experience: "As a fielding side and in the art of fielding placing, they have little to learn. Stars of the first magnitude are absent from the batting, but there is a compensating evenness of skill that makes them all the more formidable."

Heavy rain for two days before the first international from 21 to 25 November did not deter Zulch from batting when he won the toss. But his batsmen could do nothing with the bowling of Collins (5 for 52) and Gregory (5 for 72), who bowled unchanged and had South Africa out for 127. Gregory's pace was awesome and the ball with which he bowled Philip Hands knocked a bail 42 metres past the stumps. Collins made a masterly 235 in the AIF innings of 441. Jimmy Blanckenberg

A South African newspaper cartoonist's version of how batsmen felt when facing Gregory's thunderbolts.

sustained a lively, accurate medium pace for hours to take 5 for 114.

Zulch justified his status as the best South African batsman with a stylish century when his side batted again. He made 135 in 195 minutes, meeting Gregory's pace and Collins' guile with an impressive assurance. Wicket-keeper Tom Ward made 62 not out, but South Africa's 359 was not enough to prevent an easy AIF win. Blanckenberg dismissed Trenerry and Pellew before the AIF made the 46 runs required. Collins' 235 in this match was the highest by an Australian against South Africa, surpassing Trumper's 214 not out at Adelaide in the 1910–11 series.

South Africa did not recover from the loss of 9 for 99 on the first day of the second international, at Johannesburg, from 29 November to 3 December. Zulch contributed 42 of the 117 total. Gregory's 6 for 46 on a good batting pitch was further evidence of his remarkable striking power. The AIF made 456 in their first innings, Lampard 73, Willis 71 not out, Gregory 69 and Collins 61, in a fine show of team batting.

South Africa's troubles multiplied when Zulch and Philip Hands were involved in a car smash on their way to the ground, and could not bat in the second innings. Without their captain and their sheet anchor, the Springboks resisted stoutly, however, with 48-year-old Dudley Nourse making a defiant 62, Tancred 50 and Blanckenberg 53. Gregory had to bowl 27 overs for his 4 for 60. South Africa's 210 left the AIF winners by an innings and 129 runs.

The *Cape Times* praised the AIF for their deserved success in both internationals and said the team's fitness, keenness and combination made them a very difficult side to beat. "The tour has served its purpose," the paper said. "The Australians have given us good, honest, clean cricket and have revealed our weaknesses."

The South African part of the AIF tour ended with a drawn match against Western Province at Newlands on 6 to 9 December and a one-day encounter with a Schoolboy XV at Cape Town on 12 December. Willis (94) and Trenerry (52) helped their side to 269 at Newlands and Docker, whose bowling throughout the tour was restricted by a knee injury sustained in France, took 5 for 37 in Western Province's first innings of 153. The AIF declared their second innings closed at 6 for 164 but rain on the last day enabled Western Province to hold out. They were 7 for 141 at stumps.

The AIF team sailed for home a fortnight before Christmas 1919, and while they were at sea the Australian Cricket Board completed arrangements for them to play matches against the teams who were competing for the Sheffield Shield. But there was a mix-up and when their ship arrived in Adelaide on 2 January

The Governor-General Lord Forster (centre) with leading New South Wales cricketers in 1920 at Government House in Sydney. Jim Kelly and Monty Noble are at front left, Charles Turner and Frank Iredale at front right.

1920, it was found that the South Australian side were in Melbourne. So the AIF players went on by train to Melbourne to practise for their match against Victoria from 16 to 19

every batsman ducking. Only Armstrong, Mayne, Ryder and McDonald reached double figures and even these four sustained heavy bruising. The AIF responded with a sound display of calm batting that took their first innings total to 311; Willis made 111, Lampard 45 and Gregory 44. Liddicut was the only Victorian bowler to trouble the servicemen in an innings interrupted by the playing of the Last Post, in memory of those killed in the war, while 18,000 spectators and both teams stood in silence.

Victoria scored 270 in their second innings, thanks to 54 from Mayne and 52 not out from Jack Ellis, but Armstrong, Ryder and Cody all failed. Lampard took 7 for 99. The AIF was unconcerned and hit the 77 runs needed to win by six wickets. Even the phlegmatic Collins could not resist a smile, for he had sent the Victorians in to bat first when he had won the toss. The pitch looked ideal for batting and the Victorian line-up was very strong, but Collins knew that they had never experienced bowling of Gregory's speed. The Victorian Cricket Association made special presentations to Gregory and Willis for their performances in this match.

At Brisbane, in the game against Queensland from 24 to 27 January, the AIF began with 215 in their first innings, to which Queensland replied with 146. Chasing quick runs, all the AIF batting stars enjoyed themselves in a swashbuckling second innings—Collins made 130 in even time, Taylor 67. Set 388 to win, Queensland lost 6 for 144 before a thunderstorm swamped the ground. The rain unquestionably deprived the soldiers of an easy win. Oldfield, unknown in Australia until these three matches, caught the eye by dismissing six batsmen in the match.

A triumphant tour ended with a superb victory in Sydney over the crack New South Wales side between 31 January and 3 February 1920. Matched against the team that was to win the Sheffield Shield later in the season, the

January. The Australian Board of Control agreed to pay them half the gate takings for three matches, with the state associations involved paying their hotel bills and £1-a-day incidental expenses.

Gregory made a dramatic debut in Australian first-class cricket by taking 7 for 22 in the first Victorian innings of 116. On a wicket that favoured pace he bounded up to the stumps and with his characteristic kangaroo-style hop let fly a battery of fireballs that had

One of the great stalwarts of New South Wales cricket, Austin Diamond, who played in the state side against the touring AIF team in 1920.

AIF removed all doubts about their overall strength, and made certain their high place in Australia's cricket history. Considering that they had been on tour for ten months after weeks of protracted trial games and that many of them carried war injuries, this was a remarkable achievement.

Gregory paved the way by scoring 122 in the AIF's first innings and 102 in the second, and taking 8 for 130 in the match. He also held three fine catches in the slips. New South Wales fought dourly but were outplayed, unable to get on top of the opposition bowling in the absence of Charlie Macartney, Charles Kelleway and Jim Bogle, the new batting sensation from Sydney University. Bogle, born at Mossgiel, a tiny hamlet near Hay in western New South Wales, where his father owned the only store, had won Blues in five sports while studying Arts and Medicine. He made 1000 runs for Sydney University in club cricket during the 1918–19 season and in his debut for New South Wales made 145 against Victoria.

The AIF made only 265 in their first innings, saved by Gregory's 122. New South Wales replied with 279, Bardsley (60) and Hendry (85) combining to add 121 for the New South Wales second wicket. Collins followed his first innings duck with a typically courageous 129 in his side's second innings of 395. Arthur Mailey, his leg-spinning skills improving with every outing, took 7 for 122, and only Collins and Gregory played him with any confidence. The sustained accuracy of the AIF bowlers was too much for the New South Wales batsmen and they were all out for 178, leaving the AIF victors by a 203-run margin. In a memorable match, Cyril Docker opposed his brother Keith, and Bill Trenerry his brother Ted. In the AIF's second innings Ted bowled Bill and in the New South Wales second innings Cyril bowled Keith.

The AIF team won 25 of their 47 matches in three countries and lost only four. Their batsmen scored 32 centuries and their bowlers dismissed 648 batsmen. They made a major contribution not only to Australian cricket but to first-class cricket wherever it was then played. Their sparkling play was precisely what the game and the crowds needed after war's devastation, and the emergence of Collins, Gregory, Taylor, Pellew and Oldfield from their ranks also provided ready-made Test players for post-war competition. No cricketer should complain of the demands of an arduous tour after studying what these men did. Only the 1868 Aboriginal team to England has undertaken anything comparable.

Clean sweep for Australia

England tour Australia 1920–21

Australian cricket was given an enormous boost by the AIF stars, who all appeared to be Test material. However, only Gregory and Collins were automatically selected in the Test side, although four others, Oldfield, Pellew, Lampard and Taylor, pressed strongly, and it took supreme effort from other contenders to keep them out of the Australian team in the years immediately following the First World War.

Oldfield had to serve an apprenticeship as deputy to Hanson Carter, Pellew and Taylor had to challenge established batsmen for Test spots, but only Lampard failed to make frequent Test appearances. Kelleway and Love, who had been involved in the formation of the AIF team, continued to figure prominently in Australian first-class cricket for years after their discharge. Most of the others took part regularly in grade cricket, Eric Bull for the Mosman club in Sydney, Ted Long for North Sydney, "Oke" O'Connor for Waverley, "Charlie" Winning for Paddington, and Carl Willis for Prahran, in Melbourne. Willis play-

Herbie Collins doing what he did best — demonstrating his skill at tossing — in a two-up game for English and Australian players at the Melbourne Domain, during the 1920–21 series.

Undertaker Hanson Carter, whose wicket-keeping skills kept Oldfield out of the Australian team in 1921.

ed for Victoria until 1928. Jack Murray had 17 matches for South Australia, Bill Stirling one match for South Australia and several seasons with the East Torrens and Kensington clubs. Only Cyril Docker, who suffered frequent injury during the AIF tour, was not seen again on an Australian cricket field. Cyril was content to concentrate on his work with a Sydney bank, leaving his brother Keith to continue the Docker family's involvement with New South Wales cricket, which stretched back to the 1860s.

Jack Gregory was the superstar of the AIF side, a natural right-hander who had been kidded into batting left-handed by his brothers, Alban and Warwick, in backyard games as teenagers in the Sydney suburb of Strath-

field. They were the sons of Charles Smith Gregory, and cousins of the Test batsman Syd Gregory, captain of the 1912 Australian side at the Triangular tournament in England. They had three sisters, Edith, Mena and Claire. Alban and Warwick knew left-handers liked to club the ball to the leg side and they persuaded Jack to change hands to they could gather apples from a neighbouring orchard when they fielded his biggest blows.

Charles Gregory believed in educating his sons competitively, and sent each boy to a different school. Alban went to Sydney Grammar, where he played in the First XI and First XV, Warwick to The King's School, Parramatta, where he became a first rate sprinter and Rugby player, and Jack went to Shore, the Sydney Church of England Grammar School at North Sydney. Jack was five years younger than Alban, who worked as a telegraphist at Sydney's GPO and was later responsible for the installation of the first telephone links between Australia and New Zealand. While Jack served in England and France with Australian artillery units during the war, Alban was on Cocos Island in the Indian Ocean, and he was one of the radio operators who brought HMAS *Sydney* into position to sink the German cruiser *Emden*, with a signal to the Navy in Fremantle.

Jack Gregory remains the only Australian to take 100 wickets in his debut season, 1919. He took six wickets or more in an innings six times for the AIF; his best figures in England were 7 for 56 against Worcestershire, 7 for 83 against C. I. Thornton's XI, and 7 for 100 against Kent. On the South African leg of the AIF tour he took 9 for 32 against Natal at Durban and 7 for 21 against Natal at Pietermaritzburg, and when the side played in Australia he took 7 for 22 against Victoria. In all matches on that tour he took 198 wickets (131 in first-class games), and made 1727 runs including three centuries. Australian cricket could be eternally grateful to that finger injury

The remarkable reach that enabled Jack Gregory to score runs at an amazing rate. He still holds the record for the fastest century in Test history.

which prompted Collins to send Gregory to the slips for the first time—he held 66 catches there on the AIF tour alone. All remarkable statistics for a cricketer who had not progressed beyond North Sydney third grade when he joined up, and who probably would not have got a chance to open the bowling if Cyril Docker had not injured his back.

Curiously enough, while Gregory was regularly producing his displays of all-round excellence for the AIF, Australian Frank Tarrant was doing much the same thing for the Maharaja of Cooch Behar's XI in India. At Poona, in the 1918–19 season, Tarrant took all 10 wickets for 90 runs against Lord Wil-

lingdon's XI and made 182 not out in the same match. Representing Middlesex, he had already achieved the double of 100 wickets and 1000 runs eight times in England, where he was regarded by some as the best all-rounder of his generation, but had long since decided against trying for a place in the Australian Test team.

None of Jack Gregory's schoolmates and friends were surprised when he followed the traditional path of a Great Public Schools sporting champion to international celebrity: they felt it was all predictable, given his special gifts and his family background. By 1919–20, the Gregory family boasted seven members who had played cricket for New South Wales and four for Australia.

The emergence of Herbert Leslie ("Horseshoe") Collins as an outstanding captain and Test cricketer, however, was not predictable.

Collins was an introverted enigma of a man, a gambler who made impulsive bets and could not resist a card game in any dismal dive, two-up in Flanders trenches, or a hand of poker in the back of an army transport truck. He suffered from arthritis and aimed at setting himself up as a bookmaker because he considered regular employment was for mugs. Collins' luck in all forms of betting was legendary—but even when he lost his face remained impassive.

His patience as a right-hand opening batsman was limitless and although at first glance he appeared stolid and strokeless, he made seven centuries and a double century on the AIF team's tour, averaging 38.45 on the English part of the tour, 50.58 in South Africa and 48.5 in Australia, with an all-up total of 2514 runs. He also took 150 wickets at less than 20 runs apiece and most critics rated him the best bowler in the side, even more valuable to the AIF than Gregory.

Collins was born in 1889 in the Sydney suburb of Darlinghurst, the son of an accountant. He was the friend of touts and racecourse urgers, but nobody could say he lacked steadfastness of character. In fact, he lacked the technical gifts most Test cricketers are blessed with, and he owed everything to his own stable temperament and the ability to assess opponents' weaknesses and pick teammates who could expose them. Few men have ever thought as deeply about the game. Arthur Mailey always claimed Collins was a born night owl, who could see better at night than by day. Mailey vowed Collins' eyes glowed at night. Chain-smoking was his main vice, and his only encounter with alcohol was an occasional glass of champagne. He scorned playing cards with team-mates on trains or in dressing-rooms because there was little fun in an expert winning money from novices.

Jack Gregory first met Tasmanian-born fast bowler Edgar Arthur ("Ted") McDonald in the AIF's match against Victoria. Over the

Tasmanian-born pace bowler Ted McDonald, who formed a formidable opening attack with Jack Gregory just after World War I.

next two seasons they developed into one of the finest opening bowling partnerships in the history of Test cricket. McDonald had been regarded chiefly as a batsman in his two seasons in the Tasmanian side and in his appearances for Victoria just before the First World War. But by 1920 he had become a magnificent bowler and his Test debut, when he opened the attack for Australia in the third Test against Johnny Douglas' England team in the 1920–21 season, was a sight for connoisseurs.

From the start of Test cricket in 1878, Australia had usually had one pace man to spearhead the bowling, players like Spofforth,

Ernie Jones or "Tibby" Cotter, but this was the first time they went into a Test with a genuine fast bowler ready to operate from either end. The success of the Gregory–McDonald combination altered the tactical approach to Test bowling line-ups and ever since most cricket nations have tried to start with two pace men.

They were completely different in style. Gregory did not make the ball deviate much in the air but depended on his terrifying speed to beat the bat; he presented an awesome spectacle as he leapt high to hurl the ball down and was a bowler whose threat derived from an immensely powerful physique. McDonald, from Launceston's Charles Street Public School, approached the crease with a beautifully balanced 15-pace run, devoid of strain, in which his weight was so well distributed that even on the softest of grounds he left barely a footprint. His action at the moment he released the ball was as high as he could reach, his arm-swing completely controlled. He moved the ball both ways and occasional deliveries could match Gregory's fastest. There was no respite for batsmen who survived Gregory's fiery frontal assault when they then faced McDonald's swing and subtle changes of pace, and they always had to watch for the one he let go like a whiplash.

Gregory became a famous fast bowler almost overnight; McDonald's fame came gradually. In 1914–15 he took 5 for 33 and 5 for 22 against Queensland; in 1918–19 he had 8 for 42 against New South Wales, and 6 for 11 and 6 for 69 against South Australia, but he did not win a Test berth until the last three Tests of the 1920–21 series against Douglas' side in Australia. In the high-scoring Adelaide Test he finished with 1 for 78 and 2 for 95. By the end of that series McDonald's six Test wickets had cost 422, or 70 runs each.

The 1920–21 English team were in quarantine at Fremantle for 10 days before the start of the tour because a passenger on their ship, the *Osterley*, had died of typhus. Ernie Jones was on the staff of the customs office at Fremantle at the time and he went through his customary routine, circling the ship in his rowing boat and shouting, "I'll lay 5-to-1 you don't win a Test!" Jack Hobbs was used to this greeting from Jones, but some of the other English players were affronted by Jones' no-nonsense expression of his loyalties.

The English players included seven men who had toured previously: Hobbs, the younger Jack Hearne, Frank Woolley, Wilfred Rhodes, Herbert Strudwick, Bill Hitch and Johnny Douglas, who had taken over the captaincy when Reggie Spooner declined to tour. Rhodes was on his fourth trip at the age of 43, and had been playing Test cricket since 1898. The rest of the side comprised the London right-hand batsman and star soccer wing-forward (for Brentford, Queen's Park Rangers, Manchester City and Coventry), Elias Henry ("Patsy") Hendren, who was expected to score heavily if he could overcome his usual nervous start; the Essex right-hander Charles Albert George Russell, known as "Jack" after the famous little English terriers; and the Lancashire opening batsman and Everton right-half, Joseph William Henry ("Harry") Makepeace. Then there was the right-hand batsman and versatile bowler Percy George Herbert Fender, who in 1920 made 100 in 35 minutes for Surrey against Northants; the Yorkshire all-rounder Evelyn Rockley Wilson; the lively Yorkshire left-arm fast-medium bowler and Bradford City goalkeeper, Abram Waddington; Warwickshire right-arm bowler Henry Howell, who bowled very fast off a long run and played soccer for Wolverhampton Wanderers; and the reserve wicket-keeper, Yorkshireman Arthur Dolphin. Sydney Barnes had declined.

The surprise selection was a Lancashire mystery bowler, Cecil Harry Parkin, who had won a place after only five county matches in 1920. Parkin, nicknamed "Ciss", was an

*Jack Hobbs, master Surrey batsman, who, initially
with Yorkshireman Wilfred Rhodes, had the
daunting task of opening against Gregory and
McDonald.*

eccentric who bowled off-breaks at a cleverly
varied pace. He had been called up by Yorkshire in 1906 but after a single county game it
was found that he was born 6 metres over the
border in County Durham. He headed the
bowling averages for Lancashire in 1920 with
39 wickets at 14.5, including 13 wickets
against Kent at Old Trafford and eight wicket
against Yorkshire at Bradford. Parkin was a
humorist and one of cricket's great talkers,
accustomed in League cricket to playing to the

gallery and entertaining the spectators with
his conjuring tricks. He had never been on a
ship before going aboard the *Osterley* and his
team-mates mercilessly pulled his leg throughout the voyage. He slept for three nights with
a life-buoy around his neck, rushed to the
engine room to put out non-existent fires, and
had to clean out of his cabin fish which, he
was told, had flown through the port-holes.

Yet again the professionals in the England
team travelled second-class, the amateurs first-
class, a practice that continued to bemuse
Australians but was strongly defended at
Lord's by Lord Hawke who said the professionals preferred to be on their own off the
field. "I know that some of our professionals
would prefer to have second-class passages
rather than dress each night for dinner," said
his Lordship.

England started their tour in Perth against
Western Australia on 30 October 1920, a one-
day match designed to provide practice for the
visitors after their long voyage. Makepeace
took the chance and batted for almost three
hours without a mistake to score 117. Hobbs
made 63, Hendren 60, and England declared
at 8 for 276. Harry Nurse took 5 for 82 for
Western Australia, who were 7 for 119 when
time ran out.

At Adelaide in the first important match
of their tour, from 5 to 9 November, the
Englishmen virtually clinched a win on the
first day. Parkin mesmerised the South Australians by taking 8 for 55, raising hopes that
were not realised as the tour progressed. With
South Australia out for 118, England went to
1 for 201 by stumps and next day took their
total to 5 for 512 declared. Russell batted for
four hours for 156, Hearne with great polish
for 182, but Hendren excelled them both for
brilliance after taking 50 minutes to get his
first eight runs. Only a fine stumping by
Albert Ambler, when Hendren was on 79,
deprived Hendren of his century.

The weakness in England's bowling became apparent in South Australia's second innings. From 1 for 51 at stumps on the second day, South Australia progressed to 7 for 315 by keeping England in the field throughout the third day. Bespectacled Arthur Richardson, who used a bat others had trouble lifting, scored 111, his first century for South Australia, unleashing some fierce drives. His bat had a piece of greenhide wrapped round the handle and in Richardson's hands dealt out some heavy punishment for all the English bowlers. Percy Rundell made 75, "Nip" Pellew 64, and South Australia reached a creditable 339 to lose by an innings and 55 runs.

The Englishmen's match against Victoria in Melbourne from 12 to 16 November followed a similar pattern. Victoria batted well in their first innings, scoring 274 after Allie Lampard made 111 and Arthur Liddicut 56 before knocking over his own stumps. England replied with 3 declared for 418, Hobbs scoring 131 and Hendren 106 not out. Heavy rain then ruined the match and the Victorians floundered in the mud against Rhodes and Woolley, who bundled them out for only 85. Rhodes, a master of wet pitch bowling, took 6 for 39, Woolley 4 for 27, and England won by an innings and 59 runs.

The Victorian selectors, Ernie Bean, Matthew Ellis (a gutsy former State leg-break bowler) and the board-room pugilist Peter McAlister, tried to persuade the Victorian team that Armstrong was too old for the captaincy. Armstrong treated this notion with disdain and he proved his point a fortnight before the first Test by scoring 157 not out and 245 against South Australia, thus becoming the first man to score a century and a double century in the same game. This clinched the Australian captaincy for him, but the fact that he was among the six players who rebelled in 1912 against the Board of Control was not forgotten.

At Sydney in the match against New

Warwick Armstrong in 1920. His fine performances at the start of the 1920–21 season assured him of the Australian captaincy despite opposition to his Test selection.

South Wales, from 19 to 23 November, England got a taste of what was to come. The state side included ten players who would later tour England. England made 236 thanks to another fine century by Hobbs (112), and an entertaining knock from Hendren (67). The tourists did well to restrict the New South Wales first innings to 153, with Douglas (3 for 41) and Fender (4 for 26) bowling well and England holding her catches. New

South Wales went in to bat early on the third day, requiring 334 to win after England's second innings of 250. It looked a very difficult task but Collins and Macartney humbled the English bowlers by putting on 244 for the first wicket in 184 minutes. Macartney made 161 in brilliant fashion, Collins 106. Macartney hit 16 fours, Collins 12, and New South Wales won by six wickets.

Three matches followed in Queensland. England won the first against a Queensland XI, between 27 and 30 November, by an innings and 41 runs, after Rhodes made 162 on a day of intense heat to lift England's first innings score to 419. Rhodes and Douglas added 147 before Douglas was out for 84. Queensland made 186 and 192. Only George Moore, the Sydney-born right-hand batsman who scored 85 in Queensland's first innings, and Jack O'Connor, who made 66 in the second innings, showed any resistance for Queensland. The match against an Australian XI on the same ground from 3 to 6 December was left drawn. Macartney top-scored with 96 for the Australian XI in a first innings of 255. MCC replied with 357, with Hendren this time making 96. The Australian XI were 5 for 182 in their second knock when time expired.

Parkin enjoyed a light-hearted match at Toowoomba on 8 and 9 December. England declared at 9 for 208 and then had Toowoomba out for 62 and 27. Waddington took 7 for 29 in Toowoomba's first innings and Parkin 5 for 5 in Toowoomba's second innings. Not one batsman reached double figures in the second knock, with 9 the top score and the Queenslanders made eight ducks in the game.

Back in Sydney for a match against New South Wales Colts, on 14 and 15 December, England were content to grab some batting practice. After dismissing the Colts for 84, with Waddington taking 8 for 33, England made 702. Jack Hearne and Hendren were involved in a long stand. Hendren hit 8 sixes and 25 fours in his 211 and Hearne was at the

crease for 170 minutes for his 144. The match was left drawn with the Colts 4 for 148.

England's captain Johnny Douglas irritated some of his players with his curt habit of handing out instructions. After clapping his hands and pointing to the position where he wanted Waddington to field, Douglas found Waddington reminding him across the SCG that he did have a name. For veteran scorer Bill Ferguson, Douglas' big drawback was that he took his family with him throughout the tour. Ferguson often had to ignore his duties to look after Douglas' mother and father.

Although Douglas' problems in hiding so many elderly players in the field were clear, England had a splendid first day when the first Test began in Sydney on 17 December, the first Test for eight years. From 2 for 80, Australia crashed to 267 all out. Collins, Kelleway and Ryder, one of seven Australians making their Test debuts, were run out and Armstrong was beautifully stumped down the leg side by Strudwick off Woolley, all of this on a perfect batting strip.

England's batsmen, however, failed against the attack headed by Gregory's pace and Mailey's spin, and they were dismissed for 190 in their first innings. Facing a low total on a good wicket, the English batsmen appalled their supporters. Only Hobbs (49) and Woolley (52) showed Test match calibre. Mailey's ability to quickly get through the English batting line-up and the particular problems he provided for Douglas were noted by all the critics in a now-crowded press box.

On the third day Australia batted with admirable poise and took their second innings to 5 for 332; England dropped several catches that should have been caught. While Collins went to 104 on the fourth morning, Armstrong, padded-up, had a whisky in the Members' Bar with his mates. Then he went out and pressed home Australia's advantage by blasting all the English bowlers in a mem-

Jack Ryder, the idol of Collingwood, as he looked when he first came into Test cricket in 1920–21 against Johnny Douglas' England side.

their romance and marry another woman. Mrs Mort shot him twice and then tried to shoot herself. The next day the Australian players wore black armbands as a mark of respect for Dr Tozer. After a long trial Mrs Mort was acquitted of his murder on the grounds of insanity. Dr Tozer, several times wounded in France, had been hailed as a Test prospect and in 1919–20 had a first-class average of 52.00.

England needed 659 for victory and with such an advantage Armstrong could afford to bowl Mailey, who obliged by taking the wickets of key men Woolley, Douglas and Rhodes. The tourists fought well to reach 5 for 228 on the fifth day, but about an hour after tea Australia clinched the match by 377 runs. All the Australian bowlers did well, but Mailey was the one the Englishmen watched with the utmost attention. Mailey's power to bowl a googly that their batsmen could not pick obviously perturbed the visiting team. An even bigger bother was England's failure to hold catches, and over the next few weeks their fast bowler Harry Howell and Cecil Parkin suffered terribly from dropped chances.

After a holiday match against Bendigo and District at Bendigo on December 27 and 28, which England won by an innings and 264 runs, the Englishmen bowled and fielded poorly in the second Test at Melbourne. This was held between 31 December and 4 January. Australia had plenty of batsmen to exploit the great start provided by Bardsley (51) and Collins (64), who opened the match with a stand of 116. Popular Dr Roy Park, batting at number three, was out first ball clean-bowled by Harry Howell. The MCG crowd cheered him anyway, to and from the wicket. Dr Park's wife said she bent to put her knitting under her seat and missed her husband's entire Test career. Later it was discovered that Park, a GP who seldom sent bills to hard-up patients, had been up all night caring for a maternity case. Taylor made 68, Armstrong

orable driving performance. Even the master cover fieldsman Jack Hobbs had to retreat to the outfield as Armstrong hammered out 17 fours in his 158.

After watching this in the stand with Percy Kippax, Alan's father, the prominent New South Wales batsman Dr Claude Tozer visited one of his patients, Mrs Dorothy Mort, with whom he had been having an affair. Dr Tozer told her he wanted to end

Rival captains Johnny Douglas (left) and Warwick Armstrong consult with Melbourne Cricket Ground curator Bert Luttrell in 1920.

39, Pellew 116 and Gregory 100, including 12 fours.

Rain flooded the pitch throughout the Sunday rest day, but spirited efforts by the ground staff made play possible on the Monday morning. Hobbs carried his score from the Saturday night on to a handsome 122, and in the conditions England's supporters were justified in naming it the best innings of the tour. Hobbs had batted for 3½ hours. Hendren (67) also batted cleverly but England's 251 left them well short of avoiding the follow-on. Armstrong's straight breaks or top-spinners continued to deceive and England were only able to make 157 in their second innings. Armstrong's 4 for 26 made it unnecessary for him to ask Mailey to bowl. Australia won by an innings and 91 runs. Mailey did not bowl a single ball.

Two–nil down in the Test series, England went to Ballarat for a match on 7 and 8 January 1921 against a local Fifteen, who batted well on a poor pitch on the first day to score 211. England made 9 for 384 declared in their first innings, Woolley (159) and Fender (106) thrilling the spectators with powerful hitting. The Fifteen managed only 30 in their second innings. Waddington hit the stumps nine times with match figures of 10 for 46.

The great resilience that had become a characteristic of Australian cricket was dramatically demonstrated at Adelaide from 14 to 20 January, in the third Test. Australia was outplayed for three days, but played themselves back into a winning position on the fourth day and they grimly hung on. Cricket historian Irving Rosenwater labelled it a classic in which Australian batting "displayed a depth of unparalleled power".

Ted McDonald played in his first Test for Australia, Percy Fender his first for England, in an astounding match which produced 1753 runs and six centuries. Collins, dropped at 53 and 60, made 162 in the Australian first innings of 354. Rhodes was run out early in England's innings and Mailey brilliantly caught and bowled Hobbs. Makepeace (60) and Woolley (79) scored steadily and Russell held on until loose balls appeared and hit a six and 12 fours to take his score to 135 not out in 4 hours and 10 minutes.

England's 447 gave them a first innings lead of 93 runs, but it was again noticeable that the main English batsmen floundered against Mailey, with Douglas particularly puzzled by his variations of spin, pace and flight. England dismissed Bardsley, Collins and Ryder for 71 runs and, still 22 ahead, must

have hoped for victory. Only two Australian wickets fell on the fourth day, however, and the English attack laboured.

Kelleway, missed in the slips before scoring, took his score to 147 to put on 194 with Armstrong before tea. Armstrong made 121, and Kelleway took all day to reach his hundred, but when "Nip" Pellew hit a fast 104 and Gregory 78 not out, only Rhodes' skill in clean-bowling the last three Australian batsmen confined the Australian score to 582.

John Harold ("Nip") Pellew's performance in this Test, where he made a century in thrilling style, and all his fielding in the deep excited spectators. He was the most successful of four Pellews to play for South Australia, a batsman who flayed tiring attacks, and an outfieldsman of such vigour he sometimes tore the heels from his cricket boots as he stopped and turned to throw the ball in. In 1920–21 he had a moustache and heavy-browed handsomeness that had columnists comparing him with D'Artagnan.

England were set 490 to win, and despite a superlative 123 from Jack Hobbs seldom looked like reaching the target. Hendren and Russell raised a glimmer of hope but after Mailey bowled them both an Australian win was inevitable. Mailey took 5 for 160 and 5 for 142 from his 61.3 overs.

The margin of 119 runs flattered Australia and would have been much closer if England had held comparatively easy catches. The English players' failure to take chances even when they had two hands on the ball, aroused questions about Australian sunlight and the difficult background provided by Australian grandstands, issues that have dogged poor fielding sides ever since.

The rout continues

Tours by England and Australia 1920–21

Despite his success in regaining the Ashes in three Tests, Armstrong's 15-year-old feud with influential VCA secretary and national selector Ernie Bean moved towards a show-down. This culminated with the announcement in 1920–21 by the Victorian right-arm fast-medium bowler Jim Kyle that he had been frequently approached by two Victorian Cricket Association executive members to propose another player to replace Armstrong as state captain. Kyle said he had always been satisfied with the way Armstrong led the side and had no complaints about Armstrong's use of his bowling.

"If this is the sort of thing that's going on in big cricket I don't care if I ever play for Victoria again," said Kyle.

By the end of the war Warwick Armstrong was 40 years of age and had put on a lot of weight, but his skills on the field remained

The Australian team chosen for the 1921 England tour: (L to R) (back) W. Bardsley, J. Ryder, H. Hendry, J. Gregory, E. Mayne, T. Andrews, S. Smith (manager); (centre) A. Mailey, E. McDonald, H. Collins, W. Armstrong, C. Macartney, H. Carter, J. Taylor; (front) C. Pellew, W. Oldfield.

intact. Ray Robinson wrote that no ball he drove and no deckchair he sat on was ever the same again, and his square cut continued as a blow of stunning force. Not the right shape at 22 stone (140 kilograms) to hunt down spin bowling, he often coped with such balls by planting his huge boots well down the pitch and resourcefully presenting his buttocks.

While England played two leisurely matches against odds at Hamilton and Geelong, the cream of Australia's cricket talent gathered in Sydney for the 100th match between Victoria and New South Wales, from 25 to 28 January. Armstrong intended to play but his leg had been badly bruised by fast bowler Howell in the third Test and he withdrew from the match. He was reportedly seen at Randwick racecourse, not far from the Sydney Cricket Ground, and, as Ray Robinson wrote, the odds were against mistaken identity with a man of his dimensions. When the Victorians returned to Melbourne after New South Wales had won by four wickets to retain the Sheffield Shield, the selectors did not ask for the reasons behind Armstrong's withdrawal. They dropped him from the Victorian side to play England from 4 to 8 February. Bean refused to give any explanation.

One of those who temporarily replaced Armstrong as state captain was the Rhodes Scholar and Oxford Blue, John Arnold Seitz, later Victorian Director of Education and a president of the VCA. Feeling ran so high that Dr Albert Hartkopf was not allowed to vote for Armstrong in a players' ballot for Victoria's captain on the grounds that he was the side's twelfth man and not a member of the eleven who played.

There was an immediate public outcry over the dropping of Armstrong and a meeting of his supporters was called at the Athenaeum Club, where the convenor, H. D. Westley, said this most dastardly outrage in the history of Australian cricket was the worst of a series of oppressive acts against players.

Westley's motion, condemning the Victorian selectors for omitting Armstrong without giving him a chance to explain his withdrawal in Sydney, was passed and the meeting agreed to stage a large protest outside the Melbourne Cricket Ground at 3 p.m. on the Saturday Victoria would be playing England.

Hearing of this, the VCA refused to issue the customary pass-out checks to those who wanted to leave the ground to attend the protest: all protesters would have to pay again to re-enter the ground. Despite this, about 8000 of the 17,000 who watched the game left a majestic "Patsy" Hendren innings at 2.55 p.m. to go out and join the dissenters. Those who stayed inside the ground heard tremendous waves of cheering for a succession of speakers; those outside heard cheers for Hendren as he passed 200 on his way to a score of 271.

Westley told the protesters: "I wish to apologise to the English players for the indignity heaped upon them by staging this meeting of indignation outside the ground where they are playing. But the Englishmen are true sports and I am sure they will sympathise with the objects of the meeting." Inside the ground there were cries of "Put Armstrong on!" and "Why don't you give Ernie Bean a bowl?".

England defeated Victoria by seven wickets despite a splendid 108 in Victoria's second innings by Jack Ryder and Ted McDonald's match figures of 9 for 177. Douglas supported Hendren's outstanding innings with a patient 133 not out, giving England some hope that they would be able to muster greater depth than hitherto in the fourth Test.

Forced to respond, the VCA held a full meeting the following week at which they learned the facts their selectors had failed to consider. Armstrong said that the Adelaide Test bowling had caused his left leg to be bruised from ankle to thigh. He had hoped the leg would recover so that he could play in

Warwick Armstrong, at 22 stone the largest of all Test cricketers, caricatured in the Cricketer *by Charles Crawe. His players called him "The Big Ship", believing gunboat diplomacy was his specialty.*

wicket-keeper Carter, but, from 2 for 61, England recovered to score 284 by the second morning. At 38 years 173 days Harry Makepeace (117) became the oldest player to score a maiden Test century.

In the Australian dressing-room Armstrong was suffering from a recurrence of malaria and decided not to bat unless it was absolutely necessary. He sent for a couple of stiff whiskies, thinking his early batsmen would bat out the day and that he would have the benefit of the Sunday rest day. But Australia, handicapped by the absence through illness of Macartney, slumped to 5 for 153 and Armstrong was compelled to bat. Ray Robinson recorded in *On Top Down Under* how, as Armstrong walked to the crease, he saw among the sea of faces the countenance of Bean, wearing, besides his waxed-end moustache, an expression that seemed to say, "I've got him now!". Robinson said the sight of the teetotal Bean, gloating, sobered Armstrong to such an effect that he made 123 not out. The punchline of the story, according to Robinson, was that when Armstrong came off the field, with Australia leading by 105 at the end of their first innings, Bean was drunk.

Armstrong had dismissed Hobbs with a top-spinner in the second Test and now, tossing the ball to Mailey to open the attack in England's second innings, he instructed him to try the same delivery. At 13, Mailey had Hobbs lbw and the batsman walked disconsolately away, realising England had little chance again of making a score of 500 which might enable victory. Mailey was punished occasionally, but three stumpings by Carter, as the Englishmen moved down to stifle the googly, helped him to end the innings with 9 for 121, the first time an Australian had taken nine wickets in a Test innings. His match figures were 13 for 236. Gregory did not have great success with the ball, but his 77 and 76 not out played a big part in Australia's fourth straight win, this time by eight wickets.

Sydney and spent a day in a hot water baths at Coogee, but when the Victorian vice-captain, player-physician Roy Park, looked at the leg he agreed the bruising was too bad for Armstrong to play. "One decent knock and you will be out of the fourth Test," Park told the meeting, which reinstated Armstrong as Victorian captain.

On 11 February Armstrong received a standing ovation as he led the Australians out on to the Melbourne Cricket Ground to start the fourth Test, and the English batsmen Hobbs and Rhodes had to wait until the cheering for the Australian captain subsided. Gregory induced a snick from Rhodes, and McDonald one from Hobbs, both taken by

England's return match against New South Wales in Sydney, from 18 to 22 February, was left unfinished after only 31 wickets fell for 1406 runs. Only Mailey and Douglas made any headway bowling on a perfect pitch. Mailey took 7 for 172 in England's first innings of 427. Douglas had his best match of the tour, scoring 128 runs for once out and taking 7 for 98 in New South Wales' first innings of 447, which he finished with a hat-trick. Macartney made 130 and Taylor 107 not out for New South Wales. Hendren, a failure in the Tests, made 102 and 66 in sparkling style, and Woolley scored 138 in England's second innings.

On the field Douglas approached Mailey and asked him to show him his bowling hand. Mailey held it out. Douglas examined it closely and said, "Arthur, you've been using resin. I'll report you to the umpire." In his book *10 For 66 and All That*, published in 1958, Mailey confessed that he always carried resin in his pocket and when the umpire was not looking, made it his job to lift the seam on the ball to help Gregory and McDonald. The ball was larger in 1921, the legal circumference being between 9 and 9¼ inches, and became easier to grip in 1927 when the circumference was reduced to between 8³⁄₁₆ and 9 inches. Mailey said he was unrepentant, because wicket-keepers were allowed to use bird-lime on their gloves, and retaliated by asking Douglas to show him his bowling hand. The thumb-nail was worn to the flesh on the outside. "Johnny, you've been lifting the seam," said Mailey. Douglas laughed and the issue was dropped.

Armstrong's team won the fifth Test in Sydney, played from 25 February to 1 March, by nine wickets, thus completing a clean sweep of the Tests, the first time either country had achieved this. Mailey took his total of wickets for the series to 36—at the time an Australian record—and Gregory set a record for a non-wicket-keeper by holding 15

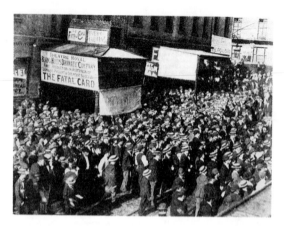

A crowd outside a Sydney newspaper office watch scores from the Tests being posted during the 1920–21 England–Australia series.

catches in a Test rubber.

England were without Hearne, Hitch and Howell through injury and Hobbs and Russell played despite injuries. Macartney returned to the Australian team after missing three matches because of illness and proved the match-winner. England disappointed again with a first innings of only 204 in perfect conditions. When Australia batted, Macartney (170) and Gregory (93) added 198 in only 135 minutes for the fourth wicket, treating all the England bowling contemptuously. Only a tidy spell of bowling by Fender, who took 5 for 90, prevented a complete rout.

England were 188 behind when they returned to the crease and at 6 for 91 seemed unlikely to force Australia to bat again. Then Douglas put on 69 with Russell and 64 with Fender, leaving Australia to score 93 to win. They did so for the loss of Collins's wicket on the fourth morning. England's woeful catching continued to the end of the series, and their bowling lacked the wonderful variety that Armstrong had at his disposal. Nobody in the visiting team could unsettle batsmen like Gregory, and certainly no Englishman in the series could catch like him.

Australian spectators at the fifth Test misbehaved by loudly making fun of Hobbs' lameness, apparently ignorant of his strained thigh muscle. Both Fender and Rockley Wilson condemned the crowd's ribaldry in accounts of the match cabled to English newspapers. By the third day, when these comments were telegraphed back to Australia, the crowd turned their wrath on Fender and Wilson, demonstrating the folly of allowing Test players to comment on matches in which they were currently playing. One wonders if the spite Fender later showed towards Australians had its origins in the coarse chiacking he received that day in Sydney.

When Wilson went in to bat, there was sustained jeering and booing and shouts of "Liar", "Squealer", from spectators intent on unnerving him. He returned to the pavilion after early dismissal looking "profoundly aggrieved". Monty Noble intervened when Wilson objected to a comment from the Members' Stand and menaced the man he thought responsible.

England played a draw against Albury and District on 4 and 5 March at Albury, where Russell made 146 in England's 6 for 326 declared; and then overwhelmed Benalla and District on 7 and 8 March at Benalla, Victoria. England declared at 6 for 348 and dismissed the Benalla Sixteen for 69 and 178. Waddington took 16 wickets for 100 runs in the match, Howell 11 for 94.

This took them to Adelaide for the last match of the tour, against South Australia, from 11 to 15 March. England made their highest score of the tour, 627, after Rhodes and Russell put on 368 for the second wicket in 260 minutes. Rhodes finished with 210, Russell 201, and Douglas completed the triumph with 106 not out. Fender also played a big part in England's win by an innings and 65 runs, taking 7 for 75 in South Australia's first innings of 195, and 5 for 109 in the second innings of 369. Percy Rundell saved the locals from complete disgrace by scoring 121 in South Australia's second innings.

Macartney, who played in only two matches, headed the Australian Test averages with 86.66 for the series; but Collins made most runs with 557 at 61.88 and was the first batsman ever to score more than 500 runs in his first Test series. Kelleway topped the Australian bowling averages with 15 wickets at 21.00 apiece and Mailey took most wickets with 36 at 26.27. Hobbs led England's batting averages with 505 runs at 50.50, and also made most runs for his country. Fender's 12 wickets at 34.16 headed the England bowling averages. Parkin took most wickets in the rubber, 16, but they cost 41.87 each. Parkin drew the biggest laugh of the series after Kelleway batted 420 minutes for 147 in the Adelaide Test by remarking, "He might make a good player in the next world—where time doesn't matter." Kelleway made only 24 between lunch and tea on the third day.

One of the surprises of this Australian summer was that gates for interstate competition did not suffer because of the presence of the English team. Takings for the Victoria *v.* New South Wales match in Melbourne, which was held over Christmas, were a record £2462. New South Wales' win enabled them to retain the Sheffield Shield. In a season of amazing scoring, Bardsley twice made 235, and a remarkably versatile sportsman named Victor York Richardson made 66 in his first appearance for South Australia. William Harold Ponsford was not as fortunate in his debut for Victoria—he made six runs in his first innings and 19 in his second, but made amends with 162 in his third and 429 in his fourth.

Successful with both bat and ball and the source of several tactical master-strokes in a series that saw England humiliated, Warwick Armstrong should never have been in doubt as captain for the 1921 tour of England, but Ernie Bean worked like a demon to get the votes to unseat him. When the vote was taken, author Johnnie Moyes, who was a VCA officer-bearer close to the inner circle, said Armstrong scraped in by the narrowest possible margin. Bean's hatchet had failed.

Kelleway's persistent refusal to join the Australian team on the 1921 tour of England probably helped all-rounder Henry Scott Thomas Laurie Hendry make the tour. Kelleway gave pressure of business as his reason for withdrawing, but relatives said he still agonised over his sacking as the AIF captain. Hendry had borne the nickname "Stork" since Monty Noble took a look at the exceptional length of his legs and neck. He was a right-hand batsman who could drive and cut effortlessly, a right-arm fast-medium bowler, and an outstanding slips fieldsman. He had first played for New South Wales in 1918–19.

Another newcomer to England in the 1921 team was Jack Ryder, the idol of the Melbourne suburb of Collingwood, who had been playing for Victoria since 1912–13. Ryder was predominantly a front-of-the-wicket right-hand batsman with an array of punishing drives, a splendid field, and a useful fast-medium change bowler, who occasionally could get surprising lift and movement away towards the slips. Bowling had been his strength before the war, but it was his batting that clinched his place in the 1921 side.

The team virtually picked itself following the 5–0 drubbing of England and the emergence of the talented and disciplined players of the First AIF team. Ernie ("Sacco") Mayne had played in all four Tests of the disastrous 1912 tour of England. Tommy Andrews had been in the team for the abandoned 1914 South African tour, though he had no Test experience. Andrews had caught the selectors' eyes with a century for New South Wales against South Australia in 1919–20, which he followed up with 247 not out against Victoria.

The full team, managed by Sydney Smith, and facing a programme of 38 matches on level terms, comprised W. W. Armstrong

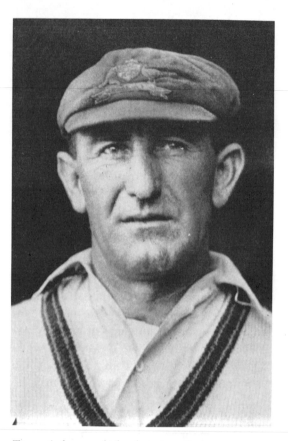

Tommy Andrews caught the selectors' eyes for the 1921 England tour though he had no Test experience.

(captain), C. G. Macartney, W. Bardsley, J. Ryder, E. R. Mayne, J. M. Gregory, T. J. E. Andrews, H. L. Collins, J. M. Taylor, H. S. T. L. Hendry, C. E. Pellew, W. A. Oldfield, H. Carter, A. A. Mailey, and E. A. McDonald. Eleven of the 15 players had captained their state or district teams, so Armstrong knew they were well versed in cricket strategy and would automatically take their right places in the field whatever the circumstances.

The team played a one-day game against a Goldfield XV, a heavy-drinking affair at Kalgoorlie, where they quickly established a high standard of sociability, before they went on to Perth to play Western Australia from 19 went out to toss, local newspapers said the turf was badly bruised, for their combined weight was about 280 kilograms. More than 10,000 people attended the first day when Ryder made 102 of the Australian team's 396. Two days were lost to rain, with Western Australia scoring 88 in a drawn match.

While the Australian team were sailing to England, Vernon Ransford, whose Test career ended with the 1912 dispute between the Board of Control and leading players, took a second-string Australian side to New Zealand. Ransford's team members were A. E. Liddicut, A. W. Lampard, H. Ironmonger, E. L. Waddy, J. M. Bogle, A. Kippax, E. B. Forssberg, A. Ratcliffe, P. M. Hornibrook, O. P. Asher, V. Y. Richardson, Lance Pellew, Nip's brother, and Tom Howard as manager.

Ransford and his players won 11 of their 13 matches in New Zealand and left three drawn. The first of the main matches, against a New Zealand XI at Wellington, was labelled a "Test", as was the New Zealand custom to drum up a crowd, and produced a draw. Australia won the second big match by an innings and 227 at Auckland. The Melbourne right-hand batsman Arthur Liddicut scored most runs and headed the tour averages with 727 at 60.58, top score 143, handling the damp conditions and heavier atmosphere with an ease that suggested he would be suited to cricket in England. Ransford (158), Lampard (132) and Richardson (112) also made centuries. The crew-cut Queensland left-arm spinner Percy Hornibrook topped the bowling figures with 81 wickets at 8.91.

The Australians in New Zealand only had to bat twice in seven of their matches, but this impressive performance was all but lost on the Australian public who were interested only in the team Armstrong was taking to England.

Vernon Ransford, one of the six great players who refused to tour with the 1912 Australian team because they could not pick their own manager, took a second-string Australian side to New Zealand in 1921.

to 22 March 1921. When Armstrong and the ex-New South Welshman, Harold Evers,

Armstrong's last hurrah

Australia retains the Ashes 1921

At a meeting on the way to England the 1921 team decided to risk breaking their contracts with the Australian Board of Control and change the tour itinerary. The team's schedule was rigorous, and the Board, in its first attempt at arranging a full tour program, had made no provision for rest days before Tests. The team were expected to finish matches against strong counties late in the afternoon, travel overnight to the Test venues, and field all next day if they lost the toss.

The players knew the risk of upsetting the Board while the bitterness of the 1912 showdown—in which six players refused to tour on the Board's terms—remained, but, as Armstrong pointed out, they had signed contracts for a deplorably organised program. "I'd have signed anything to get away on this trip," Tommy Andrews said.

To help his players get a break before Tests, manager Syd Smith sent off letters and secured the agreement of Oxford University, Gloucestershire and Warwickshire to drop the third day of their matches. This way the Aus-

Warwick Armstrong leads the Australians out for the first Test of the 1921 series at Trent Bridge, with Herbie Collins on his right.

tralians could rest before the Tests at Nottingham, Lord's and Leeds. Yorkshire refused to give up the third day, but agreed to curtail the match so that the Australians could arrive in Manchester by 7 p.m. the night before the Test.

Ever since the 1921 tour, pre-Test rest days have been an accepted part of tour itineraries, as have many other privileges won for his players by the gruff, boastful, unequivocal Armstrong. Even the teetotallers he scornfully referred to as his "lemonade brigade" respected him. At 42, he proved the strong man of the tour. Only Jack Gregory, at 192 centimetres, was taller than the "Big Ship", but even Gregory looked up to him.

England's selectors spurned tactical planning, and would not bring their best players together to discuss techniques to adopt against Gregory and McDonald, who repeatedly demoralised England's batting in the first half hour. All the leading England batsmen tried to combat the fast rising ball by hooking their way out of trouble until Lionel Tennyson showed them how to play straight. Worst of all, England relied far too heavily on the players who had just lost the rubber in Australia. The organisation of the English team was so appalling that players did not know until the morning of a Test match whether they would be required. In all, 30 players appeared for England in the series.

Matched against Armstrong, who fought for every tactical advantage he could give his team, England's selection body were further rattled by the loss of an injured and ill Hobbs, and only two men, Douglas and Woolley, played in all five Tests. They made it easy for Australia by switching captains after two Tests and failing to settle on a pair of opening batsmen until the fourth Test. Poor Frank Woolley batted everywhere from number one to number five.

The Australians began with a handsome victory over Leicestershire at Leicester from

Frank Woolley, a stylist whose expertise was put to the test in 1921 when he batted everywhere from No. 1 to No. 5.

30 April to 2 May 1921. They had the match won by the end of the first day. After dismissing Leicestershire for 136, they declared on the second day at 7 for 430. They then got rid of the home side for 142 in their second innings to win by an innings and 152 runs at tea on the second day. McDonald took 8 for 41 and 4 for 63, Mailey 5 for 55, in Leicestershire's second innings. Bardsley (109), Macartney (177) and Gregory (78) thrashed all the Leicestershire bowlers.

A change to wet, cold weather produced a poor display from the Australians in the second match against Lionel Robinson's XI on

4 to 6 May at Attleborough. Only Armstrong (51 not out) showed any application on a damp pitch, and Australia were dismissed for 136 in their first innings. Douglas was at his accurate and subtle best in taking 6 for 64. Robinson's XI were rushing runs on at an entertaining rate when tragedy struck. Hobbs was batting superbly on 85 not out when he badly strained his thigh, aggravating the injury that sparked the bad crowd reaction in Australia, and he was out of action for six weeks, missing the first two Tests. Rain ended the match after Robinson's XI declared at 7 for 256 (Jupp, like Hobbs, was off hurt), and the Australian second innings stood at 1 for 25.

Australia overwhelmed Surrey from 7 to 10 May at The Oval by an innings and 55 runs. They were in a strong position by the end of the first day, scoring 6 for 325 despite showers. Collins and Macartney added 136 for the second wicket and at stumps Collins was 158 not out. The Prince of Wales and more than 16,000 spectators watched all the Surrey bowlers take a hammering as Australia's score reached 9 for 357 declared. Armstrong and manager Smith upset the Surrey

committee by insisting that the hours of play should be noon to 6 p.m. Surrey had to give way when Armstrong threatened not to play, although they had wanted a longer match.

Early on the second morning the pitch was under water, but it dried enough for three hours' play in late afternoon. Armstrong took 6 for 38 and McDonald 4 for 29, as Surrey collapsed for 79. Following on, Surrey did better in their second innings, but further excellent bowling from Armstrong (6 for 39) gave Australia a big win. Only Fender (57), Hitch (52) and Peach (42) could cope with Armstrong's spin and he finished the match with 12 for 77.

The drawn match against Yorkshire at Bradford, from 11 to 13 May, gave the Australians one of their few experiences of a really slow, sodden pitch. They were lucky to bat first before rain, but scored 263 only because of Gregory's 104 not out, including 17 fours, of the 181 added while he was at the crease. Heavy overnight rain took the pace from the

Jack Gregory demonstrates his formidable driving technique during the 1921 tour, reaching well out of the crease to club the ball for four.

pitch and Yorkshire took a day and a half to make 224. Australia were 3 for 77 in their second innings when play ended. More than 30,000 people watched Rhodes' triumph over three days, as he took 5 for 87 and then scored 63 in the Yorkshire innings.

Bardsley made a century and Gregory took 11 wickets in a 198-run win against the Services at Portsmouth from 14 to 17 May. Then Gregory took eight more wickets when Australia beat Essex by an innings and 75 runs at Leyton on 18 and 19 May. With the wind behind him, Gregory bowled at a tremendous pace and he and McDonald tore through the Essex top-order batting. Mailey was only needed to dismiss the tail-enders.

The Australians had their first real battle in the match against MCC at Lord's from 21 to 24 May and were lucky to bring off a three-wicket win. There was another unpleasant dispute over playing hours, Armstrong and Smith insisting the times be changed again and the MCC were compelled to apologise to the public for the change. MCC led Australia on the first innings and only a dismal display in their second innings stopped them making the finish even closer.

MCC scored 284 and had Australia out for 191. Fred Durston, a right-arm fast bowler from Middlesex, bowled 25 overs in which the ball moved both ways, for his 7 for 84. None of the Australians reached 50. The MCC failed to press their advantage against excellent bowling from Gregory, McDonald and Mailey, who took 4 for 25. Left to score 270 in the final innings, Australia seemed set when Bardsley made 106. With seven wickets in hand, Australia wanted only 63, but with seven men out they were still 14 short. Armstrong and Carter defended stoutly until the runs were scored. Durston's 4 for 65 gave him 11 wickets in the match.

Batting first on a splendid wicket, Oxford University should have made more than 180 in the match at Oxford on 25 and 26 May, but Mailey's spinners puzzled all the students. The Oxford team included the burly Australian Reg Bettington and the right-arm fast-medium bowler R. C. Robertson-Glasgow, later a distinguished writer on the game. Mailey had Robertson-Glasgow stumped for 12, and took 7 for 108. At the end of the first day Australia were 37 runs ahead and they extended this to 114. Douglas Jardine, the Indian-born son of a former Middlesex amateur, batted pugnaciously for 96 not out in Oxford's second innings of 1 for 174.

There were many disgruntled spectators when, after two days' play, stumps were drawn because of the Australians' insistence on a rest day. Armstrong's players had to accept the complaints over finishing an exciting contest early, a position they were forced into by the Australian Cricket Control Board's ineptitude. Armstrong's major aim, to take his strike bowlers, Gregory and McDonald, into the Tests fresh and rested paid off, however, for they were never collared.

For the first Test, the 100th match between the countries, England brought in five new players, Percy Holmes, V. W. C. Jupp, D. J. Knight, Tom Richmond and Ernest Tyldesley. Australia's newcomers were Tommy Andrews and "Stork" Hendry, whose selection ahead of Mailey caused a sensation. Armstrong and his co-selectors reasoned that the damp Trent Bridge pitch would prove more responsive to Hendry's medium pace than Mailey's spin. It was a view that was never tested, as Australia only needed Saturday 28 May and until just after 6 p.m. on the second day to inflict another humiliating defeat on England. Hendry made 12 not out batting at number 10, and his nine overs produced 2 for 18.

Gregory and McDonald practically clinched this Test in the half hour after Douglas won the toss for England and batted. The Australian openers bowled very fast, with Gregory bouncing the ball menacingly. He

Warren Bardsley, one of the mainstays of the Australian team, finished the 1921 tour with nine centuries to his credit.

had Knight caught behind by Carter and hit the stumps of both Tyldesley and Hendren to rock England at 3 for 18. England were 78 before Armstrong rested Gregory by bowling himself. His three overs were maidens and produced one wicket when Douglas was caught by Gregory. Woolley was out for 20 to a wonderful catch by Hendry in the slips off McDonald. Gregory (6 for 58) was the destroyer in England's innings of 112, but most commentators said that McDonald (3 for 42) bowled equally well.

Bardsley made a dour 66 before he was lbw to Woolley. This innings lifted Australia to a 55-run lead with four wickets left by the end of the first day. On the second morning, Australia raised their score to 232, a lead of 120, with only two Australians failing to reach

double figures despite a difficult pitch. When England batted Gregory's bouncers flew about and Tyldesley was out when Gregory hit him on the head and the ball deflected on to his stumps. It was a long hop which Tyldesley should have avoided, but Gregory was booed as Tyldesley was helped off the field. Happily the injury was not serious.

Armstrong cautioned Gregory not to bowl until the crowd quietened but Gregory ignored both his captain and the spectators. Hendren calmly faced a succession of bouncers but then erred in calling the stylish Donald Knight for a run and sending him back too late. Knight had batted skilfully for 38 and his unfortunate dismissal ended England's resistance. McDonald had 5 for 32 in the England second innings of 147. Australia hit off the 28 runs required to win without loss and the capacity crowd left the ground frustrated that the English players had been unable to extend the match.

The incompetence of England's Test team

was further demonstrated on 1 to 3 June when the poorly rated Cambridge University side produced the first batsman to make a century against the Australians. Hubert Ashton, an attractive right-hand batsman, made 107 before a ball from McDonald injured his hand. He took no further part in the match but he had shown that sound technique could master the most hostile bowling. Ashton batted for 140 minutes and hit 19 fours. Dismissed for 220, Cambridge followed up with some exceptional ground fielding, which saw Bardsley, Macartney and Ryder run out. Sadly for them, their catching did not match their fielding, and dropped chances allowed Australia to make 362. Pellew made 146 of these in 130 minutes. With Ashton unable to bat and Mailey mesmerising every batsman, Cambridge's second innings yielded only 128 and they were beaten by an innings and 14 runs.

The Australians were now in peak form and defeated the champion county, Middlesex, by eight wickets in two days at Lord's on 4 and 6 June. Rain fell before play began and Armstrong, reasoning that the pitch would dry out later, sent Middlesex in. Gregory and McDonald made the Middlesex batsmen duck and weave, but it was the infrequently seen left-arm spin of Macartney (2 for 19) and Armstrong (5 for 15) that bundled them out for 111. Only Hendren (35) stayed long.

Australia went to a 60-run lead by scoring 171, although all the batsmen laboured in the damp conditions. The pitch had rolled out firm and hard and Middlesex were expected to score heavily on it at their second attempt. Only Hearne, dropped before he scored, lasted long in a session of magnificent Australian bowling. The Australians hit the stumps eight times as Middlesex collapsed for 90, and they could afford to rest Gregory after he took 2 for 6. McDonald seldom bowled better. His 5 for 25 made it unnecessary for Armstrong to use either Macartney or Mailey. Hearne's 45 was half his team's score. Australia lost two

A charming photograph of the 1921 Australian team in the garden of a Bristol home. The host, the ladies and the little boy are not known, but the bearded man in front is the legendary team supporter Dr Rowley Pope: (L to R) (standing) T. Andrews, E. McDonald, J. Gregory, the host, J. Ryder, E. Mayne, H. Hendry; (seated) W. Ferguson (scorer), W. Oldfield, W. Bardsley, S. Smith (manager), A. Mailey, C. Macartney, C. Pellew.

running between wickets. Mayne made 79, Bardsley 132, Macartney 149, and Gregory 78 in the Australian total of 8 for 533 declared.

Accepting that the team did not have time to dismiss Gloucestershire twice, Armstrong experimented with his bowlers. Gloucestershire made 179 at the first attempt and in the follow-on, Andrews, Pellew, Mayne and Bardsley, who usually did not bowl, were all given a turn, enabling Gloucestershire to reach a flattering 1 for 140 when time ran out. Wally Hammond appeared in this match but was bowled by Hendry after scoring a single.

England made six changes for the second Test at Lord's from 11 to 14 July. Forty-eight-year-old Charles Fry was invited to play but declined, saying he was disappointed with his form. The Hon. Lionel Tennyson, who was noted for his free thinking and who became a baron in 1928, was not in the original side but came in when Phil Mead was unfit. The noted lawn bowler Alfred Dipper, Fred Durston, Alfred Evans and Nigel Haig all made their first appearance in a Test. Only Haig, Lord Harris's nephew, played Test cricket again. Australia's sole change was to leave out Collins, who had not played since badly damaging a thumb in the first Test. Reliable Tommy Andrews opened in his place and Mailey joined the side to replace Collins.

Just as they underestimated the playing strength of the Australians, the English authorities underestimated their immense crowd appeal. On the Saturday the match began, regular patrons had difficulty getting through the gates and the crush was so bad the MCC issued an apology. This was greeted with boos from some of the stands.

England made another disastrous start but fought much harder than in the first Test and were not disgraced. Their first three wickets fell for 25. Even the Australians sympathised with Hendren, whose stumps were knocked over before he scored by an almost unplayable delivery from McDonald. The rest of the

wickets as they knocked off the 31 runs needed in the last innings.

The match against Gloucestershire, from 8 to 10 June at Bristol, was drawn when the Australians again arbitrarily restricted the hours of play, despite an enormous crowd turning up to watch. The tourists provided a batting feast in their only innings, mixing superb strokes with big hitting and clever

English innings was in the hands of Woolley and Douglas, who put on 83 for the fourth wicket. After Douglas went for 34, Woolley went on to 95, playing some delightful strokes off the back foot and hitting out while the tail-enders kept failing him. Missed twice in the slips at 87 off Gregory, he was stumped chasing a Mailey leg spinner. No man ever deserved a century more, as he made more than half England's 187.

The tourists batted with expected confidence and after an hour were 2 for 116. The fielding was ponderous and fumbles frequent, and maiden overs were applauded noisily. By the end of the first day Australia were already six runs ahead with only three wickets down.

Seamers Douglas and Durston struck back on the second day by dismissing Bardsley and Armstrong for only one run, but Gregory (52) restored Australia's supremacy with lusty hitting, exploiting his long reach again. Carter made 46 invaluable runs in his unpretentious manner in a last-wicket stand of 53 with McDonald. Australia's 342 gave them a lead of 155.

In England's second innings, Woolley went in after Knight had gone with the score on three, and played a wonderful series of drives and square cuts. With Dipper, he put on 94 in such commanding style that the crowd cheered almost every run. On 93 Woolley hit a long hop from Mailey straight to Hendry at forward short leg. Hendry, who had earlier dropped Woolley, juggled the ball but held an exciting catch. The elegance of Woolley's stroke play made his second dismissal close to a century particularly poignant.

Lionel Tennyson, grandson of the poet, survived a series of nasty blows from Gregory and McDonald, but thereafter drove boldly to take England to 8 for 243 at the end of the second day. Apart from technical improvement, shown by using the full length of the bat, the bulky Tennyson's aggression gave England a quality it sorely lacked. He was no athlete, but his defiance showed why he had been given the captaincy of Hampshire before he was 30. On 11 September 1922, Tennyson took the dramatic step of ordering one of his own players from the field in the Hampshire *v.* Notts match. He objected to medium-pacer John Newman bowling round the wicket and to Newman's language when he raised the question. Newman kicked the stumps down as he retired.

England's total of 283—Tennyson 74 not out—left Australia needing 129 to win on the third morning. Parkin, the only English bowler to consistently trouble the Australians, had Andrews lbw to break the Andrews–Bardsley opening stand, but the 101 runs they put on made Australia's task easy. Durston bowled Macartney for 8, but Bardsley's 63 meant Australia won by eight wickets.

England's seventh successive Test defeat since the First World War raised unprecedented criticisms in Fleet Street. The English county system was condemned, as was the reliance on blue-blooded amateurs, and the selectors, justifiably, took a battering. One critic considered that the trouble was that the only Yorkshireman in the match, Hanson Carter, played for Australia. The easy-going pre-war approach to big cricket was thus replaced with a more militant treatment of failure. Only two English Test cricketers, Colin Blythe and Kenneth Hutchings, had been killed in the war, but to read London newspapers in 1921 one could believe the Germans had wiped out every first-class county team, the minor counties and the Lancashire and Bradford Leagues.

The Australians encountered Lionel Tennyson again in the drawn match with Hampshire at Southampton on June 15 to 17. Tennyson brought along his butler, Walter Livesy, an experienced county cricketer, to be wicket-keeper. Australia gave an extraordinary display of hitting to score 5 for 569 on the first day and next morning declared at 7 for

The Prince of Wales and his father King George V talking with the Australian team at Lord's.

708. Bardsley hit 31 fours in his 209, scoring his second 100 in under an hour. Macartney scored 105 in 85 minutes. Taylor made 143 before he was caught and bowled by Tennyson and Ryder did some prodigious hitting on the way to 76 not out. Hampshire scored 370 in reply, Phil Mead making 129 in such a confident fashion the Australians could scarcely believe he did not have a permanent place in the England team.

Bardsley and Macartney had to miss the match against the strong Surrey side at The Oval, from 18 to 21 June, because of injury, and for the first time the Australian batting failed. Gregory saved the tourists with an innings of 101 after 5 wickets fell for 65. Surrey should have had Australia out for less than 213, but dropped easy catches, the worst

example a dolly to Tom Shepherd at mid-off when Gregory was 45.

Surrey's 175 gave Australia a lead of 38. The Australian second innings yielded only 158 and Surrey required 165 to win on the final day, with nine wickets left. Gregory met the challenge with a series of overs of such alarming pace that the Surrey top-order batsmen looked helpless against him. Crawford, in his final season of first-class cricket after patching-up his quarrel with Surrey, made a brave effort to save his side, but after he was unfortunately run out the last five Surrey wickets fell for 28 runs, leaving Australia victors by 78 runs.

Macartney returned for the match against Northamptonshire at Northampton, on 22 and 23 June. After Mayne was out first ball, he batted brilliantly, making 193 out of the 318 scored while he was at the crease, in only 135 minutes and hitting 31 fours. Gregory was dropped on 86 before he went to 107, his second century in succession, and Australia's total was boosted to 621 by fierce hitting from Armstrong (43) and Ryder (93). Northants' first innings of 69 lasted just two hours (Armstrong 6 for 21), the second innings of 68 even less (Mailey 6 for 46), and Australia won by an innings and 484 runs.

Nottinghamshire got away to a splendid start in their match at Trent Bridge on 25 and 27 June, when Tom Richmond clean-bowled Bardsley for a duck, but for the rest of the match Notts were completely outplayed. Australia ran up another massive total, 675. Macartney was dropped in the slips after scoring nine and went on to 345, the highest score of his career, in 240 minutes. He reached 300 in 205 minutes, which in 1988 remained the fastest triple century by an Australian. He hit 47 fours and 4 sixes, one of which went right out of the ground. Pellew made 100 in even time and added 291 runs in partnership with Macartney. Notts made 58 and 100, giving Australia its biggest-ever win, by an innings and 517 runs. Mailey's six wickets cost just over six runs each.

Australia played Warwickshire at Birmingham on 29 and 30 June, aware that a result was improbable as Warwickshire had agreed to drop the third day. In the end Warwickshire only narrowly earned a draw, despite the absence of both Gregory and McDonald, whom Armstrong preferred to rest for the next Test. Warwickshire batted entertainingly for a first innings total of 262 in 225 minutes. For the Australians Bardsley was twice dropped in the slips on his way to 60, Armstrong hit some thundering drives to reach 117, and Bert Oldfield made 123, adding 124 in 40 minutes in a last-wicket stand with Mailey (46 not out). At 6 for 58, Warwickshire looked defeated, but William Quaife held on with Norman Partridge.

England's selectors appointed Tennyson as captain for the third Test at Headingley from 2 to 5 July, replacing Douglas after seven

Pipe-smoking captains Lord Lionel Tennyson (left) and Warwick Armstrong about to toss before the third Test in 1921, in which Tennyson remained captain for only one hour.

successive defeats but retaining him in the side. They also brought in George Brown to keep wicket. England's middle order was strengthened by right-hander Andrew Ducat, the England soccer player who in 1920 had captained Aston Villa to win the FA Cup, Harold Hardinge to open the batting with Hobbs (now recovered), and the Somerset all-rounder Jack ("Farmer") White. Durston, who had travelled to Leeds thinking he would play for England, was left out. For Ducat and Hardinge, it was to be their only Test. Australia retained the same team that had won the second Test, since Collins' thumb injury was still mending.

Within an hour Douglas found himself England's captain again. Australia had lost Bardsley and Andrews to astonishing slips catches by Woolley, off Douglas, but at 2 for 45 Macartney became involved in a 101-run stand with Pellew. Early in this partnership Tennyson split a finger trying to stop a tremendous drive at extra cover. Hallows fielded for Tennyson and, after Pellew was out for 52, Macartney had another exciting stand with Taylor, who made 50. Macartney's 115 was a subdued innings for him but it saw Australia reach 407 after some fierce driving from Armstrong, who made 77. England's misfortunes continued when Hobbs did not return after tea on the first day—he had appendicitis and took no further part in the match. Woolley, who had to open with Hardinge, was bowled in the first over, and Hearne went at 13, when bad light ended England's miserable day.

England's position worsened to 5 for 67 before Brown and Douglas put on 97. After Brown was fooled by Mailey, White was clean bowled by a snorter from McDonald. Tennyson went to the crease with his hand heavily bandaged, accompanied by wild cheering, and despite his handicap scored 50 in an hour and helped Douglas add 88.

Going in at 3 for 30, Douglas guided England to within five runs of saving the follow-on, before he was eighth out at 253. Douglas's 75 came from four hours' brave batting that was faultless until Armstrong beat him. Parkin, amusing the crowd with his clowning, helped Tennyson (63) get the five runs needed, but Australia strengthened her position by scoring 2 for 143—291 ahead—by the end of the second day.

Douglas could not field on the third morning because of his wife's sudden illness—she had appendicitis, like Hobbs—but when Australia declared at 7 for 273 at lunch he was

The Lion Tamer. British lion (to Mr Warwick Armstrong): "I KNOW A GOOD MAN WHEN I SEE ONE. SIGN, PLEASE."

London Punch *tribute to Armstrong's feat in winning the Ashes from a below-strength English team.*

able to bat. Left to score 422 in 260 minutes to win, England never appeared likely to avoid defeat, although Brown and Tennyson again batted with admirable pluck. The Australian bowling had too much penetration and variety and Armstrong's placement of a brilliant fielding side allowed no easy runs. Australian's victory by 219 runs gave her the Ashes and her eighth successive Test win. Tennyson's one-handed scores of 63 and 36 against the Australian pace attack remain a proud feat in English cricket history.

Gregory took 5 for 41 and 5 for 59 to set up the defeat of Lancashire in two days at Old Trafford on 6 and 7 July. All the Lancashire batsmen were caught behind in the slips in the first innings of 92. Bardsley's 71 lifted Australia's reply to 284. Barnes was hit on the head by a very fast delivery in Lancashire's second innings but escaped serious injury. Lancashire failed by eight runs to force Australia to bat a second time.

Four light-hearted matches followed, three two-day games in Scotland, and one at Sunderland against Durham. The home sides were so completely outclassed that *Wisden* later suggested the opposition for such matches should include at least 15 players, and regretted that the old habit of playing matches against odds had lost support. The pleasure of watching the Australians still drew big crowds when they played Scottish XIs in Glasgow, Perth and Edinburgh between 9 and 15 July. Collins played himself back into form with two centuries, 100 in the second match and 113 in the third. Ryder (129), Bardsley (112) and Andrews (125) also made centuries. James Kerr, the best cricketer in Scotland at the time, batted all day to become the third batsman to get a century against Australia, 53 of his 147 coming in singles in the Edinburgh match.

Armstrong wanted to curtail the next match against Yorkshire at Sheffield to 20 and 21 July, but finally a compromise was reached and Yorkshire agreed to draw stumps at 4 p.m. on the third day, 22 July. The fourth Test, at Old Trafford, Manchester, was set for 23 to 26 July. Australia defeated Yorkshire, with eight minutes to spare, by 175 runs. Gregory showed his thoughts about resting before a Test by scoring 68 runs in Australia's first innings and taking 3 for 42 and 4 for 10. Yorkshire should have saved the game but they could not get the bat near Gregory's faster deliveries.

Despite the debate on the hours of play, there was a warm friendliness between all the players. At 5 p.m. on the second day, when manager Smith and his opposite number, Frederick Toone, checked the Bramall Lane turnstile they saw several thousand people outside the ground, apparently unable to afford the entry fee. Smith suggested they be

allowed in free for the last hour and Toone agreed. The crowd surged in and watched every ball in grateful silence. Toone was knighted after the 1928–29 tour of Australia, which he managed.

Australia again preferred Hendry to Mailey for the fourth Test, but England brought in the Lancashire opener Charles Hallows, and the Gloucestershire left-arm spinner Charles Parker, with Tennyson still captain. The first day was washed out, converting the match to a two-day fixture. England did well to reach 4 for 341, thanks to a fine 101 by Charles Russell, who was missed in the slips at 6 and 86 by Armstrong.

At this point Tennyson declared the England innings closed and called his batsmen in. Hanson Carter immediately informed Armstrong the declaration was illegal and Armstrong told his players to stay on the field while he went off to discuss Tennyson's blunder. The rules clearly said no closure was allowable in matches restricted to two days unless 100 minutes' batting was available to the fielding side. The issue was argued out by the captains and umpires, and finally the Australians went off. Twenty-five minutes' play were lost before England resumed batting.

The crowd, deprived of any cricket the previous day, knew nothing about the rule and blamed the Australians for the interruption. They gave Armstrong's team the most hostile demonstration an English crowd ever gave Australians. Tennyson crossed the ground with umpire Alfred Street and tried to explain to spectators that the delay was England's fault, but the hooting continued. This gave Armstrong an excuse to sit down on the grass. He remained there until the noise subsided and then—for the only time ever in Test history—bowled a second over in succession. Amid all the wrangling Armstrong overlooked the fact that he had also bowled the last over before the players went off. No-one realised that he also had unwittingly broken the law.

Ernest Tyldesley took his score on to 78 not out, Percy Fender to 44 not out, and England's total moved to 362 in the 20 minutes remaining. Heavy rain fell overnight but the Manchester pitch remained firm. The Australians won further friends by proposing that ticket-holders who had seen no play on the opening day be allowed to attend either the second or third days. They then saw Collins, who had missed the previous two Tests, bat cleverly for 4 hours and 50 minutes on a damp pitch. He made only 40 but he ensured Australia were never in danger of defeat.

After Collins had been in for four hours in what became one of cricket's classic match-saving stonewalling innings, a voice in the crowd shouted, "Tennyson, why don't you recite him one of your grandfather's poems". The taunt was capped on the instant by another spectator, who called, "He has done. That's why Collins has gone to sleep".

Parkin again proved the best of England's bowlers with 5 for 38 as the Australians scored 175. There was so little time remaining Tennyson did not enforce the follow-on and England were 1 for 44 when time ran out, the match drawn.

Australia defeated Essex by an innings and 88 runs at Southend from 27 to 29 July. Collins scored 119 in his steady style, but Gregory was quite spectacular in taking 5 for 44 and 3 for 59. Bad weather robbed the Australians of an easy win over Glamorgan at Swansea between 30 July and 2 August, when they held a huge advantage. Australia were 8 for 461 (Bardsley 122) in reply to Glamorgan's 213 when rain flooded the ground. Rain again deprived Australia of a win over Lancashire at Liverpool on 3 to 5 August. McDonald bowled magnificently to take 8 for 62 in Lancashire's first innings of 100. Bardsley made 124 in Australia's first innings of 5 for 317 declared. With Lancashire again in trouble at

Yorkshire's stalwart amateur Lord Hawke. When he said there was no betting on English cricket, Armstrong offered to put bets on for him.

2 for 31 in the second innings—both falling to McDonald—rain prevented play for 90 minutes. McDonald's 10 for 78 in this match later won him a contract to play Lancashire League cricket and, after two years' residential qualification, to join Lancashire permanently.

At an Imperial Cricket Conference Armstrong proposed that Test umpires should not be appointed until the morning of the match. "They are paid very little for their services and there is heavy betting on Tests," Armstrong said, "so it would be wise to remove them from temptation." Lord Hawke could not believe there was betting on cricket and adjourned the meeting while he made further enquiries. Next day he said he had found no evidence of betting on big cricket matches. Armstrong was unimpressed. "If you'd like me to get £500 on the next Test I can get it for you, my Lord," he replied.

Warwickshire were overwhelmed by an innings and 61 runs at Birmingham from 6 to 9 August. Armstrong took 5 for 33 in Warwickshire's first innings of 133, McDonald 6 for 52 in the second innings of 118. In between Australia declared at 7 for 312, Bardsley hitting 12 fours in an innings of 75 in 60 minutes.

At Canterbury, three days before the fifth Test, Australia played Kent and made 676 in the first innings. Macartney scored 155, Armstrong 102, and Mayne 157 not out. They dismissed Kent for 237, but on the third day, with Australia holding an enormous lead, Armstrong refused to close. Amid catcalling he sent his batsmen in for more practice, saving his bowlers for the next day's Test. Years later "Nip" Pellew told how he complained to Armstrong that he couldn't bat again. "Can't I?" replied the Big Ship. "You put the pads on!" Pellew made only two and when he was out Armstrong went in to bat out time. The Kent captain Lionel Troughton retaliated by refusing to bowl Woolley.

The England selectors continued their practice of fielding experimental sides by finding places for Andy Sandham and Bill Hitch for the fifth Test at The Oval from 10 to 12 August. Australia used Mailey instead of Hendry, but there was no chance of a result, because of rain. The crowd did not take kindly to the delay on the first day and gathered in front of the pavilion, yelling for the players to come out. The Australians added to their annoyance by arguing that the pitch was unfit for play.

In between the breaks England took the score by the end of the first day to 4 for 129.

England had her best day of the series when play resumed on Monday after the Sunday rest. Mead took his score to 182 not out, a record for England against Australia at home, before Tennyson declared at 8 for 403. The runs had taken 400 minutes to get and cut heavily into the time available. Australia were in some trouble at 2 for 54, but Andrews (94) and Macartney (61) put on 108 for the third wicket to make a draw inevitable. Australia batted on to 389, with Taylor, McDonald and Oldfield, who had replaced Carter, helping themselves against some loose bowling.

Only three hours' play was left when England batted a second time and Armstrong made a farce of it by spelling Gregory and McDonald after a few overs and giving batsmen Andrews, Taylor, Pellew and Collins a bowl. Armstrong took himself out of the slips and lumbered into the outfield. He took one catch there, plodding about carefully for fear of falling down, and had difficulty picking up a newspaper that blew across the field. When he finally caught it, he started to read it, much to the chagrin of the crowd. Years later Mailey asked him why he had done such a thing during a Test match. Armstrong laughed. "I wanted to see who we were playing," was his answer. The truth was, however, that Armstrong's cherished ambition was to go through the tour undefeated and he chose to rest his best bowlers when there were still six matches to go. Given the easy bowling he faced, Russell's 102 not out was regarded by London critics as a presentation by the Australians.

Two more big wins followed the last Test, bringing the chance of an unbeaten tour tantalisingly close. At Cheltenham against Gloucestershire on 20 August Bardsley (127) and Macartney (121) added 218 runs to help Australia to 438. After Mailey took 3 for 21 in Gloucestershire's first innings of 127, Armstrong took the ball himself in the second innings, telling Mailey "I'm going to get

*The 1921 Australian team backstage with the cast
after watching "Ghost Train" at a London theatre.*

some of these cheap wickets myself".

Charles Barnett and Richard Keigwin, a noted authority on Hans Christian Andersen, hammered Armstrong's bowling and amid laughter from his players, Armstrong handed the ball to Mailey. Armstrong had not taken a wicket in conceding 54 runs but now Mailey, bowling unchanged, took 10 for 66. Humorists in the Australian side claimed that he could have had Gloucestershire out for less than 175 and for a better bowling analysis, but he wanted the innings to continue until he got a good title for the book he was always promising to write.

Following this win by an innings and 136 runs, the Australians whipped Somerset at Taunton on August 24 and 25 by an innings and 58 runs. Collins made 101, Ryder 124 not out, of Australia's 331. Somerset were then bundled out for 123 and 150. McDonald had 7 for 31 in Somerset's first innings, Armstrong 7 for 55 in the second.

Throughout Australia's unbeaten run Archie MacLaren had told English cricket followers he could pick an all-amateur side to beat them. He had his chance when he was asked to choose an England XI for the 34th match of the Australian tour to be held at Eastbourne from 27 to 30 August. This was an astounding game, when Australia paid a high price for taking their task too lightly, after dismissing the England XI for 43 in 75 minutes in the opening innings. Gregory injured a thumb and had to be taken off after bowling two overs, but McDonald (5 for 21) and Armstrong (5 for 15) were irresistible.

Australia went to 1 for 80 with only Collins out, but the last eight wickets fell for only 91 runs due to splendid bowling by Falcon. Bardsley made 70 in two hours, without a mistake. Australia's total of 174 was disappointing but appeared to be more than enough.

Trailing by 131 runs on the first innings, the England XI were 4 for 60 when Hubert Ashton joined George Faulkner and brought about a dramatic transformation. Batting tenaciously against tight bowling and excellent fielding, they put on 154 runs. Ashton went for 75, lbw to Armstrong, with the score at 214, but Faulkner carried on to 153, eighth out at 307. Faulkner hit a six and 20 fours and did not make a mistake in 195 minutes. McDonald took 6 for 98 in the England XI innings of 326. Gregory's nine overs cost 51 runs, Mailey's 22 overs 76 runs, and neither took a wicket.

Australia needed 196, and had reached 21 for the loss of Collins' wicket by stumps on the second day, with nothing to suggest they would not get the remainder on the last day. But Bardsley, and then Carter, were dismissed with the score on 52. A wonderful delivery from Falcon bowled Macartney and at lunch Australia had lost five wickets with 87 still to get.

Andrews and Ryder took the score to 143, when Ryder left. Gregory lasted two balls, and at 152 Andrews had his stumps flattened by Faulkner. Amid mounting excitement Armstrong was ruled lbw and the last man, Mailey, went to the crease with Australia needing 42. Thirteen runs were added before the Cambridge University and Sussex fast-medium bowler Clem Gibson removed him.

There was elation in the crowd as the England XI players mobbed MacLaren. The England XI fielding had been magnificent throughout the match and neither side dropped a catch. Gibson's 6 for 64 in the last innings did not include one loose ball, and sealed his side's 28-run victory.

At Brighton four days later the Australians again batted poorly against a lively medium-pace attack from Sussex. Arthur Gilligan moved the ball into and away from the batsmen and dismissed Collins, Bardsley, Gregory and Ryder. Vallance Jupp, an example of that puzzling English cricketer, the professional-turned-amateur, gave invaluable assistance by taking 4 for 41 and only a stubborn 72 from Taylor took Australia to 209.

Sussex's wicket-keeper Richard Young, an England outside-right amateur soccer international, survived two chances in one of the best innings of the season. He batted for 240 minutes and hit 15 fours and a five in his 124. None of the other Sussex batsmen impressed against Gregory, whose figures were 6 for 89 in a marathon 31 overs. All the Australian top-order batsmen did well in the second innings of 9 for 332 declared and Sussex only had to bat out the last hour and a half, but succumbed for 62 runs. Australia's 197-run win came after Mailey took 5 for 13 off 52 balls.

Stimulated by this unexpected coup, the Australians went to Hastings for a match against a powerful South of England XI from 3 to 6 September. They won by an innings and 44 runs after a first innings total of 444. From 5 for 72, Andrews and Armstrong took the score to safety by adding 248 runs. Andrews hit a six and 17 fours in his 132, Armstrong going on to his best score of the tour, 182 not out. Only Hubert Ashton (65) and Henry Lee (64) offered more than brief resistance in the South of England innings of 199 and 199. Gregory, still thirsting for wickets, took 5 for 77 in their first innings.

Arthur Gilligan had a chance to run out Andrews during Andrews' long stand with Armstrong, but as he was about to throw the ball to wicket-keeper Herbert Strudwick, his arm was struck by Armstrong's bat as Armstrong hustled in at the bowler's end. Armstrong was contrite, "You don't think I did that on purpose, do you, Arthur?" Gilligan grunted, but the next ball he bowled at Armstrong knocked his cap off.

Armstrong, in his last appearance in England, finished with a pair of ducks against C. I. Thornton's XI at Scarborough from 8 to 10 September. Thornton's XI scored 280 in their first innings, compared with Australia's 231, and by the second afternoon had a lead of 135, with eight wickets in hand. Mailey bowled the Australians back into the game by taking 6 for 56 and confining Thornton's players to a second innings of 146.

Requiring 196 to win in 210 minutes, the Australians let their chance slip to some outstanding spin bowling by Woolley, who took 5 for 36. A draw appeared certain and with 20 minutes to go Australia had three wickets left, with Hendry and Oldfield well set. But Oldfield was foolishly run out, Hendry bowled and Mailey given out lbw to allow Thornton's XI to snatch victory by 33 runs right on stumps. Defeat meant the Australians had matched the feat of the 1902 team in England by incurring only two losses.

The Australian Board of Control paid all 15 players in the team a bonus of £300; as one of Australia's finest teams, they deserved every penny of it. They retained the Ashes by winning their eighth successive Test by five o'clock on the third day of the third Test. In four months they had won 22, drawn 14 and lost only two matches. Of the 15 teams that had toured England only the 1902 team had a comparable record, with 23 wins, 14 draws and two losses in 39 matches.

Lucky Collins takes over

Australia and England in South Africa 1921–23

In February 1921, George Bradman, a carpenter from a humble house in Bowral in the southern highlands of New South Wales, took his 12-year-old son Donald to Sydney to watch two days of the fifth Test between Australia and England. On the second day, Don, wearing his best knickerbockers, sat in the midst of more than 30,000 people and saw Charlie Macartney score his memorable 170. He was enthralled by the audacity of Macartney's stroke-play and told his father he would never be content until he batted like that and on the same ground.

At the time Don was the scorer for a Bowral team organised by his uncles, George and Richard Whatman, and occasionally when the team was short he was allowed to play. He revelled in all sport but he was so small they made him a cut-down bat, and presented it to him as he rode to one of their matches, sitting on a wooden box in a lorry that ran on solid rubber tyres. After school Don amused himself hitting a golf ball against the brick base of

The teams that appeared in the Frank Iredale SCG benefit match in 1921–22. Iredale, seated in the middle row fifth from the right, received £1741.

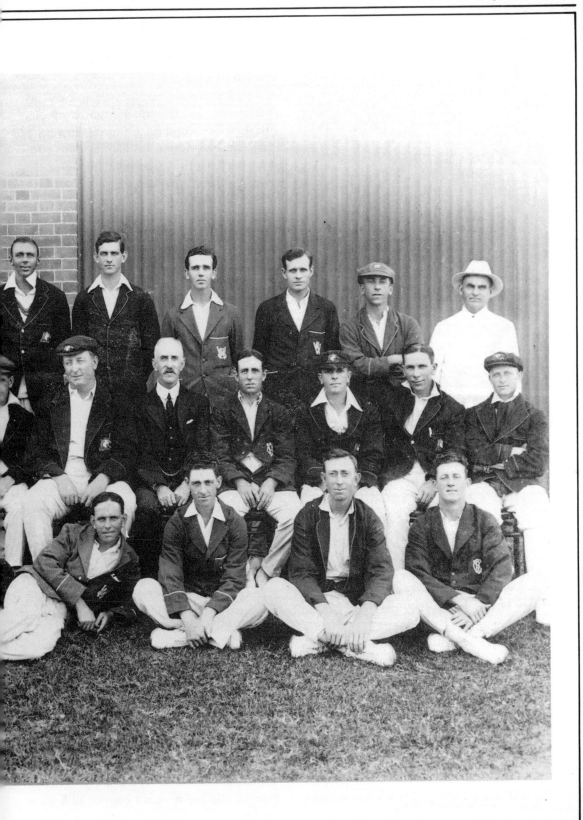

Macartney batting in Sydney in the commanding style that fired the young Bradman's ambition to become a Test batsman.

an 800-gallon water tank with a cricket stump.

Macartney's performances in England later in 1921 only intensified Bradman's ambitions. Macartney headed the tour batting averages with 2317 runs at 59.41 and made eight centuries. Bardsley made nine centuries and was second in the averages with 2005 runs at 54.19. Six of the team scored more than 1000 runs each. They made 37 centuries on the tour and had only eight scored against them. Four of the team's bowlers took more than 100 wickets apiece, Armstrong being the most successful with 100 wickets at 14.44. McDonald took 138 wickets at 16.55, Gregory 116 at 16.59, and Mailey 134 wickets at 19.37.

These were inspiring achievements for Donald George Bradman and for dozens of other Australian teenagers.

Ray Robinson, in his assessment of the 1921 team, said that apart from an opening attack which comprised express bowlers at each end, the Australians had the most effective spinners then operating in the cricket world—Mailey, Armstrong and Macartney. They had the two finest slips fieldsmen in Gregory and Hendry, the two best outfielders, Bardsley and Taylor, and two of the best covers, Andrews and Pellew, while their wicket-keepers, Carter and Oldfield, were superior to any in England. Mailey rated Armstrong a gutsy cricketer who refused to accept any condition that would lessen his side's chances. But he did not rank Armstrong in the same class as Monty Noble as a tactician, while oldtimers like Hugh Trumble claimed Harry Trott more than matched Noble for tactical know-how.

Although not perhaps at the top of the experts' poll as a captain, Armstrong was a formidable cricketer. He made six Test centuries, with a top score of 159 not out and eight scores over 50 in 84 innings, for 2863 runs at 38.68. He took 87 Test wickets at 33.59, and held 44 Test catches, most of them in the slips. He took more than 100 wickets and scored more than 1000 runs on three of his four tours of England, where he scored 5650 runs at 40, and took 409 wickets at around 17 runs apiece. He was also the first Victorian to play in 50 Tests.

On their way home from the triumphant English tour Armstrong's team played six matches in South Africa. Collins took over as captain when Armstrong missed all of these because he had to go into hospital at Durban and receive treatment for damage to his left leg inflicted by England's bowlers. The South African matches also lacked the presence of Pellew, who had broken a bone in his hand in an unscheduled game at Whitehaven after the formal part of the English tour ended.

The Australians beat Transvaal by nine wickets in the first South African match from 22 to 25 October at Johannesburg. Australia had Transvaal out for 173 and were 2 for 112 on the first day, but the following day Eiulf Nupen, a tall 19-year-old fast-medium bowler of Norwegian descent, bowled fast from the mat to take 6 for 68. Ryder (53) and Hendry (57 not out) took Australia to a 100-run lead and from then on Australia had the game under control.

Between 29 October and 1 November in Durban against Natal, Gregory (56) opened the Australian innings with Collins (100), and they put on 105 for the first wicket. The rest of the batting failed, but with a total of 212 they led on the first innings. Herbie Taylor made 66 and Dudley Nourse 39 in Natal's 164. Powerful, almost arrogant hitting from Macartney (135) set up a huge Australian lead and they won by 194 runs, dismissing Natal for 139 in the last innings.

Although South Africa avoided defeat in the first Test at Durban from 5 to 9 November, they appeared outclassed. Australia led on the first innings with 299 against the Springboks' 232, and in the second innings Collins seemed to delay his closure too long. He declared at 7 for 324 after Macartney savaged the bowling for another century, 116. South Africa were 7 for 184, still 207 runs in arrears, when time ran out.

Collins made 203, Gregory 119, in the first innings of the second Test at Johannesburg from 12 to 16 November. Gregory's first 100 runs took only 70 minutes and remains the fastest century in Test history. (Gregory faced 67 balls. When Vivian Richards scored a century from 56 balls for the West Indies against England in April 1986, he took 81 minutes over it.) Gregory hit the ball hard enough to bruise the fieldsmen's fingers and this probably explains why he was dropped

three times. South Africa followed Australia's 450 with 243 and had to follow on 207 runs behind. Charlie Frank batted for 518 minutes to score 152 in South Africa's second innings. Taylor supported him with a bright 80 and Nourse made 111, enabling South Africa to declare at 8 for 472. Australia made seven without loss before an appeal against the light was upheld and the match was abandoned.

Against Western Province at Cape Town from 19 to 22 November, Australia won by eight wickets. They dismissed Western Province for 153 and 191. Mailey captured 5 for 89 and 6 for 88 and Macartney 5 for 40 in Western Province's first innings. Australia made 231 and 2 for 114, the spinners doing so well they scarcely missed Gregory and McDonald, who were rested.

The Australians wound up their South African visit with an easy 10-wicket win in the third Test from 26 to 29 November at Cape Town. The spin of Mailey and Macartney was again the main problem for the Springboks, who only managed scores of 180 and 116. Australia made 396 in their first innings, including Ryder's 18 fours in a fine display of free hitting for 142 Australia needed only one run to win in their second innings. There were cheers all round when Mailey, the least successful batsman in the side, got a single off the edge, depriving his partner. Carter of a strike.

Macartney again headed the batting averages, with 492 runs at 70.29 for this South African part of the tour. Collins made most runs, 548 at 60.89, and Mailey was the highest wicket-taker with 35 wickets at 22.91.

Australia's Prime Minister, Billy Hughes, presented Armstrong with a cheque of £2500, the sum raised at the previous summer's protest meetings, when the Australians reached Melbourne. "When Warwick goes into the field the English team are half beaten; when he takes the ball they are wholly beaten," said Hughes.

Shortly afterwards Warwick Armstrong gave up his job as the pavilion clerk for the Melbourne Cricket Club to take up another he had arranged in England as Victorian agent for Peter Dawson's distillery. The Melbourne Cricket Club elected him a life member and later his old position was filled by "Stork" Hendry, whose cricket undoubtedly improved with the daily practice sessions.

After all the celebratory banquets were completed and his 1921 team had dispersed, Armstrong was asked how the team compared with the 1902 Australians with which he first went to England. Ever the realist, Armstrong said: "The 1902 side could play 22 of my chaps and give them a beating." He knew that in 1902 both England and Australia were at full strength, whereas in 1921 England had not recovered from the First World War and the English selectors had failed to pick a settled, well-prepared side.

On returning home, Armstrong was invited to one of Australia's most remarkable cricket fields on top of a mountain near the old mining town of Walhalla, Victoria. Miners had used many tons of explosives to blow the top off the mountain and they levelled the space created to form a cricket ground. They believed a big hitter like Armstrong would produce a monumental hit at Walhalla, for, once the ball cleared the mountain top there was nothing to stop it rolling for miles. Warwick made several enormous swipes at the ball but could not connect properly before he was dismissed.

The fifteenth Australian team to England returned home too late for the start of the Sheffield Shield competition and a number of the players were reluctant to spend further

---

An unusual studio portrait of Charlie Macartney who continued to top the batting averages for the South African part of the 1921 tour, with 492 runs at 70.28.

time away from their families. New South Wales fielded what was described as a second-string side for the first match of the Shield competition at Adelaide from 16 to 21 December against South Australia. Crafty Sydney University right-hand batsman Ray Boyce captained New South Wales and in a desperately tight finish his nerve and guile triumphed.

Howard ("Mudgee") Cranney made 70, "Billy" Wells 55 and Lyall Wall 61 in New South Wales' first innings of 360. South Australia took a first innings lead, however, by scoring 376. David Pritchard, the Port Adelaide left-hander, contributed a pugnacious 100 and Lance Pellew 77. Cranney followed up his splendid first innings with an admirable 144 in New South Wales' second innings of 439. Hammy Love added 95 to his 43, scoring with a freedom which he thought might get him into the Australian side ahead of Oldfield when Hanson Carter retired to concentrate on his family's funeral business.

South Australia looked like winners when East Torrens right-hander Andrew Smith made 104 and his clubmate Bruce Townsend 117, but calm leadership from Boyce got New South Wales home by just 17 runs. In a New South Wales team that had many heroes, Lyall Wall's effort in taking 11 wickets in the match (7 for 133 and 4 for 123) was an outstanding piece of left-arm fast-medium bowling. Wall bowled more than 60 overs in the game.

New South Wales included seven members of Armstrong's touring side for the match against Victoria over Christmas 1921, but were without key men Bardsley and Macartney. Victoria had Ryder, Mayne and McDonald from the touring team, but were without Armstrong. Victoria had a comfortable win, set up initially by a workmanlike 122 from Dr Roy Park and efficient bowling from McDonald (5 for 65 and 3 for 73) and the fair-haired Melbourne University Club leg-spinner Dr Albert ("German") Hartkopf,

One of Australia's most remarkable cricket grounds, located at the top of a mountain near the Victorian mining town of Walhalla.

who took 5 for 86 in New South Wales' second innings.

This was one of the rare matches in which crowd abuse was directed at a local player. Ernie Mayne, who had been preferred as Victorian captain to Park and Ransford, was jeered every time he touched the ball and frequently advised in obscene and insulting terms about how to run his team. Ryder and McDonald also were noisily heckled. The Victorian Cricket Association called a special meeting to discuss the problem and decided to send extra police to the outer to "repress this evil".

Three batsmen in the New South Wales side offered stout resistance. Andrews stroked the ball all over the field for 115 of New South Wales' first innings total of 254. Hammy Love made 102 and Collins 111 in New South Wales' second innings of 280.

In the end lack of support for their century-makers cost New South Wales a

wonderful match by seven wickets. Ryder made Victoria's final innings task of scoring 233 look easy as he rushed to 85. Such was his power that even on the longest Melbourne Cricket Ground boundaries his drives thundered into the fence. Park made 53 to go with his first innings century and looked good enough to deserve another Test chance. The chance never came.

Ryder sustained his tremendous form in the match between Victoria and South Australia between 31 December and 4 January 1922. Adelaide fans saw a wonderful exponent of all drives, a tall, adventurous batsman to whom half-volleys were gifts. There was nothing fancy or artistic about him, but on his way to 242 Ryder hit the ball with great gusto and good timing. The South Australian side all had sore feet and hands after this onslaught which, with the help of a fluent 87 from Ransford, lifted Victoria to 474.

South Australia struggled against the bowling of McDonald, Liddicut, Hartkopf and Armstrong, who had recovered after a rest, and after scoring 219 had to follow on. Andrew Smith scored his second century of

Edgar "Ernie" Mayne, whose heavy scoring for Victoria was not repeated when he played for Australia in 1921–22.

nings after South Australia had led all the way, ushering in his team's showdown with Victoria.

Receipts for the Victoria *v.* New South Wales match were a record £2257 at a time when you could buy a handsome house in a select suburb for £400. This was also one of the first matches at which the legendary Australian barracker, "Yabba", made his voice heard. "Yabba", otherwise Stephen Harold Gascoigne, was a trader in rabbits who trundled his cart around Sydney's working-class suburbs of Redfern and Balmain. Housewives appeared at the sound of his bell and his "Rabbit-oh!" call and he skinned the bunnies for them on the spot. His father had been a storekeeper in Oxford before migrating to Australia. "Yabba" was blessed with vocal chords Olivier would have envied and his comments from his place on Sydney Cricket Ground's Hill carried right across the field to the Members' Bar. In the days before television and vandalism ruined the Hill's reputation he was the best known regular there and the man who did most for its world-wide reputation.

Victoria and New South Wales shared the honours in their first innings. New South Wales played Jack Scott, a fiery, outspoken fast bowler with a long record of defying authority, and he took 5 for 74 in Victoria's first innings of 265, with Mayne, Ryder, Ransford and Liddicut among his victims. New South Wales made only two runs more against McDonald and Ryder, and Ryder had the match-winning score of 95 in Victoria's second innings of 348.

Chasing 347 to win, New South Wales were humbled by some devastating bowling from McDonald, who took 8 for 84 in 21.2 eight-ball overs. Six of his victims were clean-bowled. Victoria's winning margin of 154 runs gave Ryder and McDonald all the headlines the next day, which was an injustice to O'Keeffe, whose first innings 87 saved

the season (122) in a 162-run stand with Eustice ("Bunny") Loveridge (94), but their plucky seventh-wicket effort only reduced the Victorian winning margin to six wickets.

The key match in a season that produced a significant array of talented new cricketers took place in Sydney from 26 to 30 January, with the return clash between Victoria and New South Wales. This followed New South Wales' remarkable win over South Australia by six wickets after being 104 behind on the first innings. Andrews won the match with an aggressive knock of 129 in the final in-

The notorious barracker from the Sydney Hill, Harold Gascoigne, known as "Yabba", with the cart from which he sold rabbits during the week.

Victoria when they had lost cheap wickets. O'Keeffe made 79 before he was run out in Victoria's second innings.

O'Keeffe's wonderful run continued between 24 and 28 February, when he took 180 runs off the South Australian attack in Adelaide. Vernon Ransford also scored 129 in this match, which Victoria won by an innings and 227 runs. Andrew Smith's second innings 72 looked impressive coupled with his earlier centuries.

Victoria won the Sheffield Shield in 1921–22, but the real winner was the Australian Board of Control, who found themselves with a competition thousands were eager to watch, state teams oozing with talent, and state associations busy planning better grounds and larger grandstands. Club cricket competition was booming, with often tense matches between outstanding teams attracting large crowds on Saturday afternoons.

From 3 to 7 February 1922, an Australian XI, made up entirely of the 1921 team to England, played a match against the Rest of Australia on Sydney Cricket Ground for Frank Iredale's benefit. The cricket provided was fascinating and Iredale received £1741, a sum that would have been larger if the match had been played to a conclusion. Despite the presence of the world's finest bowlers, 1358 runs were scored and only 29 wickets fell.

Gregory bowled right up to the best form he had shown in England in the Rest's first innings and took 7 for 95, but this did not prevent the Rest scoring 393—Frank O'Keeffe made 177 and the AIF star Carl Willis scored 133. The Australian XI countered with 403, Armstrong top-scoring with a powerful 77

Frank O'Keeffe made a brilliant start to his career with New South Wales but tragically died at the age of 27, in 1924, just after qualifying for the Lancashire county side.

innings of 63 by Hammy Love. Hornibrook clean-bowled Collins for 117, Macartney for 9, and had Gregory caught for 4 before time ran out.

The intense competition for places in state teams was typified by the fate of Bill Woodfull, who first played for Victoria just after Christmas 1921, against South Australia in Adelaide, earning his place the hard way after consistently high scoring for Carlton in Melbourne's district contest. Woodfull had to bat at No. 8 after Mayne had made 85, O'Keeffe 180, Ransford 129 and Cody 107, and only had time to accumulate 22 not out.

Bill Woodfull was born in 1897 in the small Victorian town of Maldon, from which he got his second name, and had had rheumatic fever as a boy, which caused doctors to declare him unfit for service in the First World War. He played against Douglas's English tourists at Ballarat in 1920–21 but could not win a regular place in the Victorian team until he was 24. When he did, he became known as "The Unbowlable".

Armstrong dropped out of the Victorian team after his two appearances in the 1921–22 season to concentrate on selling Scotch whisky. He played an occasional match to help old team-mates, and in 1927, bulkier than ever, went to New Zealand in a Victorian team. In 1935 he was appointed to run the entire Australian operation of whisky distillers James Buchanan and when he died in 1947 he was regarded as Australia's wealthiest cricketer, leaving an estate valued at £90,000. Since then a number of Australian Test players have done a lot better.

Armstrong's retirement left Herbie Collins with a clear mandate on the Australian captaincy. Apart from his skill in tossing, Collins' qualifications included his discovery of a big baccarat school opposite the 1921 team's London hotel. He had an implacable trench-warfare approach to cricket, best summed up by Ray Robinson:

not out and Hornibrook taking 4 for 107 from 30.3 overs. The Rest closed their second knock at 4 for 302 after O'Keeffe hit a second dazzling century (144), which dwarfed a fine

Bill Woodfull showing the concentration and determination that won him the nickname "The Unbowlable".

Collins' bat never knew it was in the hands of a gambler. It was never urged to take a risk. Any ball pitching near a length was watched mistrustfully from earth to blade or allowed to pass. Instead of an array of strokes which a Test average of 45 would imply, a lot of his runs came from anonymous nudges and indefinable dabs made at the last moment. He brought off some of the best-placed pushes and prods in the game. An over-the-shoulder hook was the one bold shot in his deft on-side range of taps and glances.

Collins played for the Paddington club in Sydney district cricket, which by the early 1920s had developed into an outstanding competition among teams studded with fine cricketers. At Paddington, which centred on Trumper Park (named after its greatest club member), Collins' team-mates were Oswald Asher, Les Cody, Edmund ("Chappie") Dwyer, Fred Gow, "Billy" Wells, George Garnsey, Charles Lawes, Stan McCloy, Rex Norman, Frank O'Keeffe, Lyall Wall and the Trenerry brothers, Ted and Bill. All of them were state players and all were keen to somehow scrape together their annual subscription and weekly ground fees toward the council curator's salary. Test players Jim Kelly and Monty Noble usually went along to Friday afternoon net practice to offer advice.

But Paddington were by no means the dominant club in the district contest. Waverley won the Percy Arnott Shield outright by winning the Sydney premiership for the third time in four years in 1922–23. Western Suburbs, Marrickville, Mosman and Glebe were very strong. North Sydney's Austin Punch headed the first grade run-scorers in 1919–20, with 827 runs at 63.61 and in 1920–21 with 894 at 67. Charlie Macartney drew big crowds to Chatswood Oval whenever he turned out for Gordon, and Sydney University club's Harold Owen ("Tommy") Rock regularly made more than 500 runs in a season. The rivalry was so intense between grade clubs many people preferred district cricket to state matches. The time allowed for grade games was limited to two Saturday afternoons, with an occasional all-day match thrown in, which meant batsmen could not afford to linger; the action was as exciting as it was colourful, with rule books frequently taken out while players argued a point.

Ted Adams, the Petersham fast bowler, once jumped the fence to exchange blows with a spectator he felt needed disciplining. Tom Moore, the Paddington swing bowler who played for the club for 50-odd years, had to rush from the field for money to pay for a woman's smashed chamber pot when an opposing batsman hit Tom into a house adjoining Trumper Park. Jack Scott, the

Herbie Collins, who took over the Australian captaincy, was a gambler who died a pauper, but he never took risks with Australia's cricket prestige.

Petersham fast bowler who later umpired Test matches, was barred for an entire grade season after a show of bad temper.

Johnnie Moyes played for Gordon in these years before his war wounds and journalistic duties forced him to give up. He told me of the time Gordon dismissed the opposition for just over 100 with a little more than an hour to play on the first Saturday. Gordon captain Charlie Macartney said: "We had better get them tonight. It might rain next Saturday." Gordon had a lead by six o'clock, after Macartney hit three fours back over the bowler's head in the first over. Moyes wrote:

When Macartney went to drive it was as though he had been wound up by a spring and someone had suddenly released the coil. He always looked for fours. "Attack" was his motto, and

he believed that if you got on top, the bowler did not come back. He always liked to open up so he could dominate for his entire innings. I walked out to bat with him and he told me to keep my eyes open for the first ball. I thought what he meant was a quick single, but instead the first delivery came hurtling back and crashed into the fence. I met him in the middle as they went to retrieve the ball. "It's always a good idea to aim the first ball right at the bowler's head," he said. "They don't like it. It rattles them. You can do what you like after that."

Melbourne's club cricket in the 1920s was just as exciting as Sydney's, with all the main clubs attracting large, ardent followings. Jack Ryder's eagerness to bludgeon all bowling made him the king of Collingwood. Jack ("Nana") Ellis became a legendary figure in the Prahran district by topping the club's averages in 1919–20 with 68.00. He was a wicket-keeper renowned for his ungentlemanly comments about batsmen, umpires, and even his own bowlers, as he stood behind the stumps.

Clarrie Grimmett, disgruntled by the raw deal he felt he had received from the Sydney Club, bobbed up in Melbourne after the First World War and switched from South Melbourne to Prahran in 1920–21 when he married a Prahran girl.

Grimmett, bowling his subtle mixture of leg breaks, top spinners and googlies, with Ellis waiting to stump those batsmen deceived by them, was rich fare. Grimmett took 67, 39, 68 and 54 wickets in his four seasons with Prahran, and the club won three successive premierships in the years from 1920 to 1923. Dismissals he made while Grimmett was with the club helped lift Ellis's stumpings for Prahran to 80 and his catches to 71. Prahran celebrated their third premiership in 1922–23 by opening a new press-cum-score-box, which Grimmett, a painter–signwriter by trade, had a hand in designing.

Armstrong continued to play club cricket for Melbourne Cricket Club in those years simply because he enjoyed it so much. He was not amused though, when Prahran's Heinrich Schrader hoisted his deliveries out into the street, with one of them landing in St Alban's Church, in Orrong Road. By 1922–23 the St Kilda Club had the great slow bowlers, Don Blackie and Bert Ironmonger, bowling in tandem most Saturday afternoons, an awe-inspiring attack coming on the heels of Bill Ponsford's batting. Blackie took 502 wickets altogether for St Kilda at 13.69 apiece, Ironmonger 502 at 13.7, remarkably similar figures for a joyful, if incongruous, partnership.

Blackie bowled right-arm off spinners from a run that started near mid-off, which in the early 1920s was considered a joke, but was copied by bowlers in many countries in the 1970s. He was lucky to have the support at St Kilda of former Test keeper Barlow Carkeek and benefited from regular coaching by the Rush brothers. Ironmonger, who bowled left-arm slows, had lost the tops of two fingers as a result of his work at a timber mill in his native Ipswich. "Dainty", as he was known because of the clumsy way he plodded to pick up the ball when fielding, was a bowler of astounding accuracy, destined to worry the finest batsmen of his time, but undeniably the worst batsman in club cricket. Clubmate Allie Lampard offered "Dainty" a beer for every run he scored but he seldom had to bother the barman.

In 1923 a series of conferences in Brisbane resulted in the affiliation of the Warehouse Cricket Association and the Brisbane Junior Cricket Association with the Queensland Cricket Association. The Warehouse competition had 834 registered players at that time and within five years totalled 99 clubs, controlling grounds at Marchant Park—Brisbane's equivalent of Sydney's Moore Park—and at Kianawah Park, Victoria Park and Finsbury Park. The Junior Association's numbers leapt

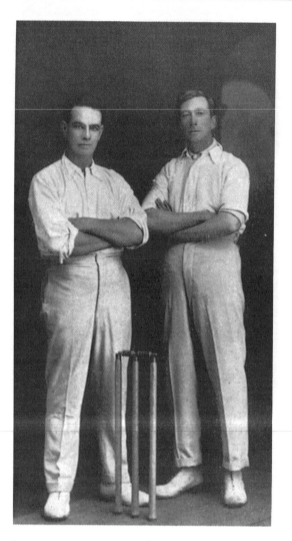

Bert Ironmonger, left, and Don Blackie who bowled together for the St Kilda club from 1922 to 1935, and represented Victoria and Australia. Ironmonger bowled left-arm spinners, Blackie right-arm off breaks.

to 99 clubs by 1929–30. Warehouse cricket attracted brewery sponsorship, keen betting, and made heroes of big-hitters.

After losing eight Tests in a row to Australia, England embarked on a ten-Test schedule against South Africa, the first five in South

Africa in 1922–23 and the second five in England in 1924. England's miserable run continued in the first of these when South Africa won by 168 runs in Johannesburg from 23 to 28 December 1922, but in the second Test at Cape Town from 1 to 4 January 1923, England finally secured a win, defeating South Africa by one wicket with her last pair at the crease. Two draws followed before England wrapped up the series 2–1 with a 109-run win at Durban, where they played between 16 and 21 February 1923. At home, in 1924, England won the first three Tests and finished the series with a 3–0 advantage.

Thirteen players made their debuts in Tests for England in those ten internationals, providing the nucleus of a new-look England team to tour Australia in 1924. F. T. Mann had led England in South Africa but had been replaced by genial Arthur Gilligan for the rubber at home. Gilligan had not only proved a fine captain but also a right-arm fast bowler of the highest quality by taking 17 wickets, including 6 for 7 at Birmingham between 14 to 17 June 1924, when South Africa were dismissed for 30. This was the match in which George Parker, a Bradford League cricketer who was not a member of the touring party, was called up to assist the Springboks and took six wickets. Parker died at Thredbo, New South Wales, in 1969.

Apart from a leader who commanded a place in the Test team through skill alone, England discovered promising Test prospects in Arthur Carr, George Macaulay, Percy Chapman, Roy Kilner, Herbert Sutcliffe, Maurice Tate, George Duckworth, George Geary and Richard Tyldesley, one of four brothers who played for Lancashire but not related to Ernest and John Tyldesley, also of Lancashire, who had already played against Australia. Undoubtedly the most important development had been the arrival of Sutcliffe as a partner for Hobbs. They became one of the most successful opening pairs in the

history of cricket, and were a combination that gave Australian bowlers long hours in the field and caused many a late-night conference among Australian Test teams.

While the leading English players toured South Africa in 1922–23, Archie MacLaren took a party made up of twelve amateur and two professional cricketers to New Zealand, and they also played matches in Australia at the beginning and end of the trip. The tour did not make money, and the Marylebone Cricket Club, which had guaranteed half the expenses, lost £1000 on the venture. The team consisted of A. C. MacLaren (Lancashire), A. P. F. Chapman (Berkshire), G. Wilson (Yorkshire), the Hon. F. S. G. Calthorpe (Warwickshire), T. C. Lowry (Cambridge University), C. H. Gibson (Cambridge University), W. W. Hill-Wood (Derbyshire), C. H. Titchmarsh (Hertfordshire), J. F. MacLean (Worcestershire), Colonel J. C. Hartley, A. C. Wilkinson (Army), D. F. Brand (Hertfordshire); and the professionals A. P. ("Tich") Freeman (Kent) and Harry Tyldesley (Lancashire). Freeman's leg spinners and Tyldesley's right-arm slows were expected to be the mainstay of the side's bowling, leaving the blue-blooded amateurs to enjoy themselves.

The team played 22 matches, won 11 and lost 3, with 8 draws. The three defeats were in Australia, as were five of the draws. The Australian leg of the tour began in Perth on 3 and 4 November 1922. Western Australia held them to a draw, with the MCC scoring 190 and 3 for 132 to Western Australia's 234. South Australia beat them by six wickets at Adelaide from 10 to 13 November. South Australia made 442 and 4 for 60, MCC 205 and 294. Arthur Richardson scored 150 and Vic Richardson 118 in South Australia's first innings, putting on 256 together for the first wicket.

Victoria beat them by two wickets in Melbourne between 17 and 20 November thanks to an amazing display by Hartkopf.

A. P. "Tich" Freeman delivers a googly. He joined Archie MacLaren's second-string touring team in 1922–23, but achieved his greatest successes in English county matches.

MCC scored 210 and 231, Victoria 278 and 8 for 164, with Hartkopf taking 5 for 23 and 8 for 25 as well as scoring 86 and 14 not out. New South Wales then beat them by five wickets at Sydney between 24 and 27 November. MCC made 360 and 121, New South Wales 201 and 5 for 283.

The Englishmen then went on to New Zealand, where they were unbeaten, winning two of the three matches described as "Tests", and nine of the 11 against provincial sides. MacLaren, in his 52nd year, played an astounding innings of 200 not out in the first of the alleged Tests between 30 December and 2

January 1923 in Wellington. The ball hit the fence as if fired from a rifle when he drove, and his batting was full of delicate dabs and robust pull shots, but in the process he injured a knee so badly he played no more first-class cricket. His career total was 22,237 runs at 34.15, with 47 centuries.

England showed vastly improved form in their four matches in Australia after the New Zealand jaunt. They had the best of a drawn match in Sydney with New South Wales from 2 to 5 March 1923. The scores were MCC 275 and 296, New South Wales 314 and 5 for 102. At Melbourne on 7 and 8 March, against Combined Universities came another draw— MCC made 258 and 5 for 135, Combined Universities 332. Universities' Otto Nothling, already a noted athlete and Rugby player, brought his rich personality to this game by taking five wickets and scoring 56 from the bat.

Three days later, on the Melbourne Cricket Ground, came the sensation of the tour. Faced with fiery bowling from Percy Wallace and Arthur Liddicut, the MCC players collapsed for 71. Wallace had 6 for 50, Liddicut 4 for 16. Victoria then hammered the English bowling all over the field and closed at 6 for 617. Hammy Love (192), Roy Park (101), Vernon Ransford (118) and Liddicut (102) were merciless in their humiliation of the MCC bowling. Outclassed and in danger of a bad defeat, the English players sat in the pavilion all the last day as Geoffrey Wilson (142 not out) and Wilfred Hill-Wood (122 not out) batted without error to save them. The end came with the Marylebone Cricket Club on 0 for 282, and the Victorian bowlers shaking their heads in disbelief.

Arthur Richardson made the first century before lunch in Australia on his way to 280 for South Australia in the MCC's last tour match. This was at Adelaide, where 1319 runs were scored between 15 and 17 March while only 20 wickets fell in the drawn game. Richardson was dropped three times and hit 2 sixes, a five and 34 fours. For the MCC, the Hon. Frederick Calthorpe (96) and Percy Chapman (134 not out), both future England captains, finished the trip in splendid form.

From England's viewpoint, the rewarding feature of the tour was the captivating all-round cricket of Percy Chapman, a broad-shouldered giant well over 182 centimetres tall, with boots like small cruisers. Chapman played with a light-hearted charm, but also with a grim determination. He was a startlingly acrobatic close-in fieldsman for his size, could bowl left-arm medium pace or slows, and the Adelaide knock was his fourth tour 100. He had had an impressive record in schoolboy cricket, made a century for Cambridge in the 1922 University match, but was languishing in second-class county cricket with Berkshire, where he was born, before MacLaren took him to New Zealand. He went home straight into the England Test team against South Africa, and in 1924 began a long career with Kent.

Australia, too, had a large number of highly promising newcomers. After failing for three years to win a regular place in the Victorian team, pudgy Bill Ponsford, the powerful youth with the enormous calf muscles and bulky backside, forced his way into the side with a historic innings against Tasmania, which broke the world record for a first-class knock. In his fourth innings in first-class cricket, Ponsford made 429 in 477 minutes, with 42 fours, at Melbourne in February 1923. Only Archie MacLaren, with 424 for Lancashire against Somerset in 1895, had previously made more than 400 in a first-class match. Victoria made 1059 and beat Tasmania by an innings and 666 runs!

Happy years at home

Domestic cricket 1922–24

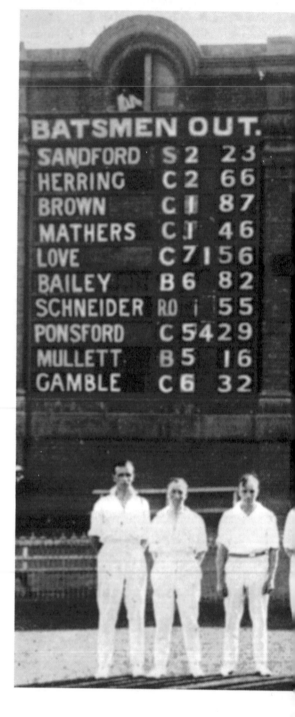

BATSMEN OUT.

SANDFORD	S 2	23
HERRING	C 2	66
BROWN	C 1	87
MATHERS	C J	46
LOVE	C 7 1	56
BAILEY	B 6	82
SCHNEIDER	R.O. 1	55
PONSFORD	C 5 4	29
MULLETT	B 5	16
GAMBLE	C 6	32

Charlie Macartney opened the era of very high individual scores in 1921, when he flogged the Nottinghamshire bowling to make 345, but Ponsford's 429 really got it rolling. Within a few years, top-class batsmen all over the world discarded Victor Trumper's habit of throwing away their innings after reaching a century. Ponsford, whose first eight innings in first-class cricket yielded 1051 runs, made it a practice to take a fresh guard after he passed the 100 mark, a habit he justified by compiling 13 scores over 200, five of them over 300. After a knock of 352 in Melbourne, he steered a ball outside the off onto his stumps. He looked back like a man whose ears played him false. "Cripes, I *am* unlucky!" he exclaimed.

Macartney was a freakish cricketer who improved as he got older. Adept at hitting threatening bowlers out of the attack, at times dazzlingly unorthodox, he was yet able to middle the ball with that cocky bravura which

The Victorian players pose in front of the scoreboard in Melbourne after they became the first side to score more than 1000 runs in first-class cricket, in February 1923. Ponsford's 429 against Tasmania was a world record which Bradman later lifted to 452 not out.

The driving power of Charlie Macartney. Although he had a comparatively quiet season in 1922–23 he was an inspiration to many younger players.

made him look profoundly safe. Robertson-Glasgow said of him:

> No other Australian batsman, not even Bradman, has approached Macartney for insolence of attack. He made slaves of bowlers. His batting suggested a racket player who hits

winners from any position. Length could not curb him, and his defence was lost and included in his attack.

He had a comparatively quiet season in 1922–23, without a century in the Sheffield Shield, but his influence on the younger players in the New South Wales side was a big factor in regaining the Shield for the state. Alan Kippax said he was helped tremendously by Macartney's boosting of his, Kippax's, self-confidence.

Kippax, then 25 years old, made remarkable advances in 1922–23. He began with 170 against South Australia at Adelaide between 15 and 19 December. Taylor (159), Hendry (146) and Oldfield (118) also made centuries in a New South Wales total of 786, but it was the elegance of Kippax that stood out. His late cut was despatched with exceptional power and nobody in Australia could hook as well as he did that summer. New South Wales won by an innings and 310 after dismissing South Australia for 274 and 202, Mailey taking nine wickets.

At Melbourne against Victoria from 23 to 27 December, Kippax showed he could get runs under difficult conditions by scoring 68 in a total of 160 when New South Wales were caught on a sodden pitch. Macartney recalled his best bowling efforts in England by taking 5 for 8 in Victoria's response of 125. New South Wales' second innings, with the pitch still wet, produced only 142, leaving Victoria 177 to win. On a pitch that had dried out, Woodfull paved the way for a Victorian win with a plucky 84 not out.

Victoria beat South Australia by 268 runs in Melbourne between 30 December and 2 January 1923, and New South Wales defeated South Australia by nine wickets in Sydney playing from 6 to 10 January, leaving the Sydney match of 26 to 30 January to decide the Shield. Takings for this game—£2988—were a Sheffield Shield record and demonstrated how avid was the public's interest in their cricketers.

Victoria started with 353 in their first innings, and looked to have an advantage when the sixth New South Wales wicket fell at 250. Collins had contributed 106 to this score. Kippax, who had been batting magnificently, was joined by Hendry and they completely mastered the Victorian bowling by taking the score to 418. Kippax's dismissal for 197 left Hendry and the New South Wales tail free to attack every ball and they lifted the total to 560. Hendry's 93 was full of heavy

drives and cuts, but for grace of strokes and artistry was overshadowed by Kippax's performance. Mailey's spin and Jack Scott's pace overcame the Victorians in their second innings of 179 and New South Wales won by an innings and 28 runs.

New South Wales and Victoria won three matches and lost one each in a season which saw South Australia, very weak in bowling, lose all its four matches. New South Wales took the Shield for the sixteenth time on averages, which was twice as good a record as Victoria's. The southern state had won the Sheffield Shield only eight times. Both Gregory, who was unfit, and McDonald, who had gone off to play in the Lancashire League, were sorely missed.

Jack Scott had a golden opportunity to press his claim for a place in the Australian team during the 1923–24 season. Scott's pace worried all the batsmen, but his temperament let him down. With Gregory struggling to get fit and unable to play for New South Wales for the second year, Australia's attack for the approaching Tests with England suddenly looked inferior.

New South Wales began the season with a spectacular 170-run win over South Australia in Adelaide, fought out over 14 to 18 December 1923, after being caught on a sticky wicket and dismissed for a paltry 98. South Australian medium-pacer, the Reverend Henry Heath, who had made one appearance for the AIF against Oxford in 1919, took 5 for 43. Kelleway matched this with 5 for 40 for New South Wales and South Australia were out, at their first attempt, for 116. With the pitch still difficult, all the New South Welshmen struggled with the batting until Oldfield (84) and Mailey (53 not out), put on a match-winning stand of 135 for the last wicket. New South Wales bundled South Australia out for 145 in their second innings.

There was high drama all the way in the clash between New South Wales and Victoria, in Melbourne from 26 December to 1 January 1924, before Victoria won by 43 runs. The pitch was slow because of rain when play began, but quickened later and 1351 runs were scored in the six days. Victoria made 285 and 412, New South Wales 268 and 386. Collins took five hours for his 108 in New South Wales' first innings and Woodfull hit only 3 fours in his 117 in Victoria's second knock. Mayne's 106 on the first day was the best batting of the match.

At Melbourne, between 2 and 5 January, husky Bill Whitty, the former Sydney left-arm fast-medium bowler who had moved to Mount Gambier in South Australia, bowled with the lovely fluent action which allowed him to swing the ball either way. He took 5 for 49 in Victoria's first innings against South Australia. This enabled South Australia to set up a lead of 98 runs on the first innings when Victor Richardson (100) and Arthur Richardson (144) scored contrasting centuries. Victor batted for 105 minutes, Arthur for five hours.

Ponsford and Love guided the home side to victory with handsome stroke-play in Victoria's second innings of 357. Ponsford made 159, Love 105. Hartkopf had 5 for 56 in South Australia's second innings, but Ryder did the important damage and reduced the total to 171 by clean-bowling both Victor and Arthur Richardson. Victoria won by 98 runs.

At Sydney, from 11 to 14 January, New South Wales defeated South Australia by an innings and 104 runs, despite a fighting first innings 135 by Vic Richardson. South Australia had the game in hand, at 4 for 360, but Mailey and Hendry destroyed the six remaining batsmen to have South Australia out for 383. Mailey took 7 for 133. Bardsley (144), Kippax (248) and Austin Punch (84) then flayed the South Australian bowlers to take New South Wales' score to 684. Sam Everett's 6 for 54 was the main reason for the South Australian collapse for 197 in the second innings.

Left-arm pace bowler Bill Whitty originated from New South Wales but played all his first-class cricket with South Australia, bowling with a lovely fluent action that earned him a berth in fourteen Tests.

With pitches uncovered, the judgement of captains after winning the toss often decided matches. Ryder proved this by sending New South Wales in and then dismissing them for 217 in the vital match at Sydney from 26 to 30 January. Victoria, with the advantage of batting on a strip that had dried out well, led by 128 on the first innings after Mayne made 154, Ponsford 110. New South Wales improved in their second innings to reach 321, but another century by Ponsford (110 not out) made Victoria's scoring of 195 to win look easy.

Ponsford failed, but Victoria still made 454 in their last match of the season against South Australia in Adelaide from 15 to 20 February, 1924. Victorian captain Jack Ryder gave Clarrie Grimmett 22 overs and the little gnome gratefully responded with nine wickets in the match, South Australia scoring only 191 and 256.

Ponsford's domination of the Shield competition was compared in that 1923–24 season with Dr E. P. Barbour's feat in taking 111 wickets at 9.9 and scoring 1154 runs at 88.2 in Newcastle (NSW) first grade. But both these senior players' performances paled against the record of 16-year-old C. Sheriff, of Melbourne, who made 1004 runs in seven innings in school cricket without being dismissed and thus finished that same summer without an average.

At the end of the season the New South Wales Cricket Association sent a team to New Zealand captained by Charlie Macartney; the team, which included six Test players, was W. Bardsley, T. J. E. Andrews, A. A. Mailey, W. A. S. Oldfield, A. F. Kippax, R. Bardsley, A. T. E. Punch, A. T. Ratcliffe, D. A. Mullarkey, S. C. Everett and H. S. T. L. Hendry. They played 12 matches, 6 of them first-class, and seven times made more than 400 runs in an innings.

Warren Bardsley averaged 124.00 on the trip, Kippax 92.20, Macartney 91.57, and Mailey took 37 wickets at 16.30 apiece. The New South Welshmen won eight and left four matches drawn. They won both matches against New Zealand XIs, the first at Christchurch by eight wickets, the second at Wellington by an innings and 126 runs. Hendry was ruled run out in one match when he was six paces (about 18 metres) past the stumps. When he asked the umpire to explain the decision, the umpire said, "You were well outside the wide mark."

Meanwhile at Castlemaine, Victoria, there was a curious incident involving the identical twins Lisle and Vern Nagel. Thinking his team had their innings under control, Lisle went off for a game of tennis. Before he returned his side collapsed, so Vern went on in his brother's place. Nobody watching the match knew it was Vern Nagel, and not Lisle. Vern hit a series of sixes to save the team.

Arthur Mailey had left his job at the Water Board and become a full-time cartoonist and newspaper columnist. Instructed by Dr Roland Pope, he had learned to tie a bow tie and use a fish knife and scheme out opposing batsmen. He had a philosophic attitude, essential in a slow bowler, towards being hit for four and could lull the finest batsman into a feeling of false security before striking. Gifted with incredibly strong fingers, he could impart so much spin on the ball opposing batsmen could hear it. Mailey deliveries fizzed.

He was a tremendously observant bowler, always searching for weaknesses in the batsman's armoury, keen to work out special ploys with his wicket-keeper, Bert Oldfield, and even with his slips fieldsman, who sometimes moved to fine leg on an agreed signal. His understanding of various breaks would have done credit to an atomic scientist. He wrote in *10 For 66 and All That*:

> *The sensitivity of a spinning ball against a breeze is governed by the amount of spin imparted, and if the ball bowled at a certain pace drops on a certain spot, one bowled with identical pace, but with more top-spin, should drop eighteen inches or two feet shorter. For this reason, the difference in the trajectory and ultimate landing of the ball produces uncertainty in the batsman's mind.*

Mailey's niche in big cricket was secure, but a large number of players worked hard in the 1920s to join him. Bill Ponsford, Vic Richardson, the Nagel twins, Archie Jackson, Alan Kippax, and the bush cricketers, Don

Arthur Mailey soon after he forsook his job as a Water Board labourer to become a newspaper cartoonist and columnist.

Bradman and Bill O'Reilly, all made rapid advances. At that time, too, a youngster named Leslie O'Brien Fleetwood-Smith, whose family owned the newspaper at Stawell in Victoria's Wimmera region, was discovering that he could fool his schoolmates at Melbourne's Xavier College with his peculiar left-arm spinners. He had been forced to experiment with this style when he broke his right arm.

The main hazard for these aspiring players was that Australia boasted only three Shield teams. In the belief that he would play more cricket in England than the Sheffield Shield competition could offer, Frank Aloysius O'Keeffe went off to play in the Lancashire League in 1922, but found the wetter, colder weather a formidable hurdle. O'Keeffe, who at 27 was one of the best batsmen in Australia, also found he had to fulfil a two-year qualifying period before he could play for Lancashire; he died of peritonitis three months before he qualified.

Another disgruntled cricketer, Clarrie Grimmett, moved to Adelaide in 1923, taking with him the dog he had taught to fetch balls in the Melbourne suburb of Prahran. He decided he would always bowl in a cap, to disguise his bald head, and every day he rolled his backyard pitch and worked at perfecting his length and deceptions.

Mailey could not understand Grimmett, because he had a round-arm rather than an over-the-shoulder delivery. Grimmett's action upset Mailey's sums. Clarrie Grimmett went back to the days of round-arm bowling and introduced a deception dependent on the arc of his arm, rather than on the spin from his fingers or wrist.

This produced the classic confrontation between Mailey and Grimmett in which Grimmett accused Mailey of misleading him. "Hey, Arthur, you told me wrong about the bosey," said Grimmett, which, as the English cricket writer Robertson-Glasgow observed, "was rather like Virgil had tricked Horace on the number of feet in a hexameter".

These were happy years for Australian cricketers. Interstate matches took the players on long, leisurely train journeys. There was no gaggle of radio reporters thrusting microphones in the team's faces, no television vans in the street outside their hotel. The state associations seldom lodged their sides in luxury hotels, but they usually enjoyed the intimacy of comfortable rooms, where they could gather round a piano at night and join in singing songs like "Rose Of Washington Square".

Kippax was one of the most enthusiastic vocalists, a baritone who rarely missed a beat. Bill Woodfull was often persuaded to put down his book and render a few choruses.

Jack Ryder found Jack Ellis a willing partner in "The Desert Song" and even Bill Ponsford sometimes stopped brooding over the weather to join in. Ponsford hated wet pitches, and it was said that the merest sprinkle of rain during the night was enough to wake him and keep him tossing and turning at thoughts of a sticky wicket next day. Going down to breakfast on tour the players never asked if it had rained, but simply, "How did 'Ponny' sleep?"

Victoria had hit pay dirt when, after Ernie Mayne retired, Woodfull and Ponsford were given the job of opening the batting. At Adelaide in February 1923, they showed the promise of what was to come when they put on 133 together for the fourth wicket. In October 1924, on the same ground, they added 109 for the second wicket. They enjoyed batting together, each man a model of concentration completely lacking in showmanship, concerned only with keeping the runs flowing. But even their most ardent admirers were surprised when they eventually shared 23 century partnerships—including 18 for the first wicket—and five stands over 200.

The player most cricket lovers preferred to watch, however, was Alan Falconer Kippax, the right-hander educated at Bondi Beach Public School, whose style so closely resembled Victor Trumper's. Kippax's supple-wristed elegance was not as forceful as Ponsford's, nor as arrogant as Macartney's, nor so rock-solid as Woodfull's, but his batting had what Ray Robinson called a "silken moonbeam" quality not seen in any player of his time or since. He was at his prime between 1921 and 1926 as he passed through his twenties, but sadly had to wait far too long for recognition.

Kippax was the victim of interstate rivalry and suffered because the men around the selection tables descended to bargaining to force players from their home states into the Test team. By the 1920s positions on state

Alan Kippax, who was so shabbily treated by Australian selectors early in his career.

associations had begun to attract successful businessmen with social ambitions. They had to start as one of the two delegates to the state associations appointed by district clubs; the associations in turn elected members to the Board of Control. The first priority was to satisfy club members at the annual general meeting and woe betide the delegates who did not fight for local players.

The system had little attraction for distinguished international players who found they had to struggle through a barrage of annual meetings, monthly association meetings and sub-committee meetings, as well as hobnobbing at matches with fellow officials and their wives, to gain a position where their experience would be useful. The board and association lunches were always more lavish than those given the players and players were heavily outnumbered by officials' guests at big matches.

Some of these hangers-on put round the story that Kippax's style was too delicately tuned for the tough business of winning matches. He was such a mild-mannered, self-effacing person he helped fan these absurd notions, for he looked almost apologetic as he walked to the crease to take guard. Everything about him was unhurried and polished, and he was too much of a gentleman to brandish at his critics the mountain of runs he had scored.

Throughout the cricket world newspapers had dramatically boosted their coverage of the game. The first radio commentary on cricket anywhere in the world had been tried in Sydney in 1922–23, during a match between teams captained by Herbie Collins and Charlie Macartney, for Charles Bannerman's benefit. Now a radio station announced the first commentaries on Tests would start in the approaching 1924–25 rubber against England in Australia.

In England, most of the main newspapers appointed full-time cricket writers, and famous players often wrote weekly columns. Among these was the Lancashire "comedian" Cecil Parkin, who had headed England's bowling in the 1921 series against Australia with 16 wickets at 26.25 from four Tests. Parkin regularly headed the bowling averages for Lancashire. In 1922, he took 172 wickets at 16.50, in 1923 176 at 14.90, and in 1924 169 at 13.37, a record which stamped him as a certainty for the 1924–25 tour.

But after England defeated South Africa by an innings and 18 runs at Birmingham in June 1924, an article appeared in a Sunday paper, under Parkin's name, headed "Cecil Parkin refuses to play again for England". It said that Parkin was humiliated at being asked to bowl only as fifth change in the second innings. Implicitly, it criticised Arthur Gilligan's captaincy. Parkin claimed the piece was the work of a reporter who had not referred it to him, but it ended both his Test career and any chance he had of visiting Australia for the second time. The Lancashire committee asked Parkin to apologise to Gilligan.

Not long afterwards Parkin was in further strife when he wrote a piece—this time his own work—in which he suggested that if an amateur with the required qualifications could not be found to captain England, Jack Hobbs or Herbert Sutcliffe should be given the job. This was too much for Lord Hawke, who, as chairman at Yorkshire's annual meeting, made the famous speech which included the words "Pray God no professional will ever captain England".

Not everybody shared Lord Hawke's view and at a luncheon in Adelaide, the Australian Governor-General, Lord Forster, a former Oxford University and Kent player, pressed Hobbs' claims for the England captaincy. The furore that resulted forced Lancashire to gag Parkin, and drastically reduced the proceeds from his benefit match in 1925. He collected only £1880. Dozens of prominent Lancashire businessmen refused to contribute as they normally did for Lancashire players. The following year Parkin left Lancashire and returned to League cricket.

Gilligan captained England in four of the five 1924 Tests against South Africa, establishing himself as a courageous batsman, one of the finest mid-off fieldsmen, and a genuinely hostile fast bowler. But a few weeks after taking 6 for 7 and 5 for 83 in the Test match at Birmingham, he suffered a savage blow over the heart while batting. His doctors advised him not to bowl fast again. Despite this warning he agreed to captain England on the 1924–25 tour of Australia and New Zealand. The team was A. E. R. Gilligan (captain), H. Sutcliffe, E. Hendren, J. B. Hobbs, A. Sandham, F. E. Woolley, J. W.

Hearne, J. L. Bryan, A. P. F. Chapman, R. Kilner, J. W. H. T. Douglas, M. W. Tate, R. Tyldesley, A. P. Freeman, H. Strudwick, H. Howell and W. W. Whysall.

The players the MCC gave Gilligan were much more judiciously chosen than those in 1921, but the team would have been improved by Parkin's inclusion. The batting was strong, with Hobbs and Sutcliffe to open and high calibre stroke-makers like Hendren, Sandham, Woolley and Jack Hearne to follow. Kilner, Chapman and Douglas also looked capable of plenty of runs. High-scoring Cambridge University and Kent left-handed batsman John Bryan was restricted by his academic commitments to one month a year in county cricket. The selectors obviously regarded him as a batsman capable of brilliant innings who might surprise everybody, but the gamble did not pay off.

The bowling depended heavily on Maurice Tate, Kilner and Freeman, while Strudwick was an experienced, craftsmanlike wicket-keeper at his best against pace bowling. England's lack of an opening bowler who could break through the early Australian batting was exacerbated by Gilligan restricting himself to medium-pace, on doctor's orders. He drove himself hard, however, and appeared in more matches than any of his team, fielded with enthusiasm, chasing everything, but against some of the most resolute top-order batsmen Australia has ever fielded he must have often felt frustrated.

England's lack of a pace bowling partner for Tate might have been solved had C. H. Gibson agreed to tour. Gibson, born at Entre Rios in Argentina, bowled at a brisk fast-medium for Sussex and Cambridge University but did not play first-class cricket regularly. His selection was challenged by English critics who considered him ineligible and he tactfully withdrew for business reasons.

The twentieth England team to tour Australia were under no illusions about the enormity of their task to get back the Ashes. On the way out the team were discussing problems the bowlers faced with the heat, the spectators and the hard, dry pitches. "You don't try to hit the wicket out there," said the droll Lancastrian Dick Tyldesley. "What you do is to keep on bowling at the bat and hoping against hope that you will miss it." Everybody laughed, but they all knew that when bowling to an in-form Charlie Macartney it *was* about the only hope they had.

Australia's bowling wanes

England in Australia
1924–25

The normally meticulous Australian captain Herbie Collins did not bother to inspect the Sydney pitch before the first Test of the 1924–25 series, which began on 19 December 1924. He won the toss, with his renowed luck, and batted, knowing there had been no rain for a week. But as he marked his guard with his boot-sprig, moisture came out of the ground and Collins knew then there would be plenty of early life in the strip.

In a series in which the Tests were to be played to a finish, with eight-ball overs, the first ball from Maurice Tate whipped off the pitch and hit the wicket-keeper Herbert Strudwick hard on the neck. Strudwick immediately moved back several metres, the only time he ever did so for Tate. For most of the first hour the ball zipped off the ground, but thanks to dropped catches Australia did not lose Bardsley's wicket until the score was 46.

Ponsford came in for his first Test innings

*The Australian team that played England at
Melbourne in the second Test of the 1924–25 series:
(L to R) (back) A. Hartkopf, V. Richardson,
C. Kelleway, J. Gregory, A. Richardson,
W. Bardsley, T. Andrews; (front) W. Oldfield,
A. Mailey, H. Collins, J. Taylor, W. Ponsford.*

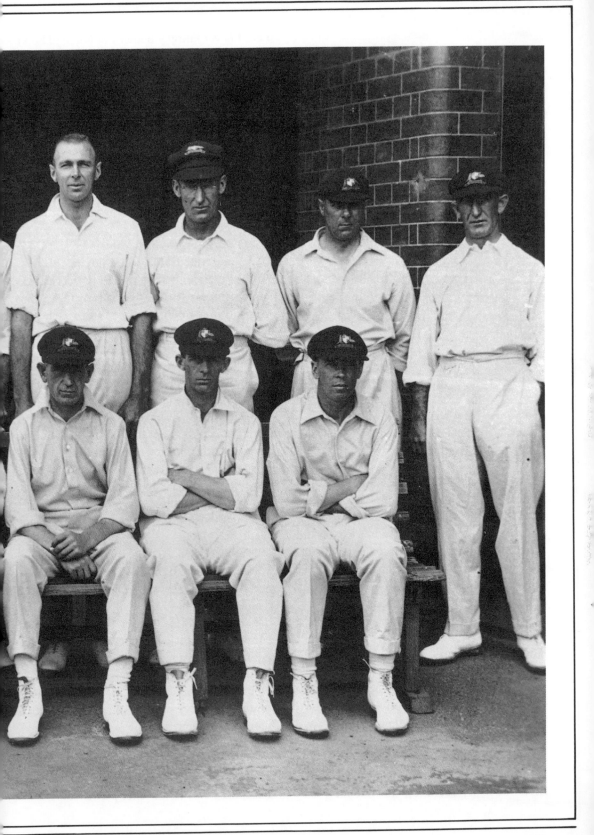

Bill Ponsford, who first played for Australia in 1924.

and was morally bowled three times in Tate's first over. Twice the ball swung late and shot from the pitch, rocketed through Ponsford's defensive stroke, eluding Strudwick too, and smacked into the fence for four byes. Strudwick was relieved to get a glove on the other delivery, for he was having as much difficulty as Ponsford predicting Tate's late swing.

Collins walked down the strip and told Ponsford, "Don't be afraid of Tate. He can't bowl." Collins was aware it was a stupid thing to say but he wanted to lift Ponsford's confidence. The truth was that Collins, too, was being made to look a novice by Tate, so he decided to try a little gamesmanship.

"It's no good bowling me that inswinger, Maurice, I can pick it a mile away."

Tate looked at Collins and grinned. "Well, Bert," he said, "you know more about it than

I do. I never know whether I'm going to bowl a ruddy inswinger or a ruddy outswinger."

Collins and Ponsford added 190 for the second wicket. Collins made 114 in one of his most agonising knocks and Ponsford started his Test career with 110. Collins shielded Ponsford from Tate with masterly skill for most of the day and when team-mates surrounded Ponsford to congratulate him in the dressing-room, he went across to Collins and shook his hand. "This chap deserves all the credit," Ponsford said.

Former Australian captain Clem Hill came into the room and told the players: "That's the toughest bowling I have ever seen on the first day. If Tate had had any luck, your whole team could have been out twice before lunch."

This account of play by Jack Fingleton, in his book *Masters Of Cricket*, typified the ebb and flow of luck in a desperately close rubber. By holding out to reach 3 for 282 on the first day Australia was able to make 450 in the first innings. Tate had one spell of 4 for 9 on the second day. On the third morning Hobbs (115) and Sutcliffe (59), in their first opening stand in Australia, took the score to 157, but the last nine English wickets fell for 141; Hendren finished on 74 not out, and England made only 298.

Bespectacled Arthur Richardson opened with Bardsley in Australia's second innings and had the misfortune in his first Test to be dismissed for 98. Taylor, dropped down the order to No. 8 by Collins, put on 127 with Mailey, the best-ever last-wicket stand for Australia against England. Taylor made 108, Mailey 46 not out, and Australia scored 452. Hobbs (57) and Sutcliffe (115) had another century opening stand (110), but the task of scoring 605 to win in the last innings always looked beyond England, despite Sutcliffe's century and 123 from Woolley. Australia won by 193, and 189 of those runs had come in Australia's two last-wicket partnerships.

Six great players from the past photographed during the 1924–25 series with England: (L to R) (back) Clem Hill, Warwick Armstrong, "Nip" Pellew; (front) Ernie Jones, George Giffen, Jack Lyons.

Gilligan's team had gone into this Test with high hopes, following an impressive build-up of strength in a spin round the Australian states. They had four matches in Western Australia early in October 1924, beat South Australia by nine wickets in Adelaide from 7 to 11 October (despite an innings of 200 not out by Arthur Richardson), lost to Victoria in Melbourne by six wickets between 14 and 19 November, and had won a keen tussle with New South Wales in Sydney from 21 to 25 November by three wickets. This was a splendid win, as Bardsley, with 160, and Andrews, with 86 not out, in the New South Wales first and second innings respectively, appeared to have mastered England's bowling.

Two drawn matches in Brisbane, where Hendren made 168 and 100, were followed by an innings and 126-run victory over a local thirteen in Toowoomba early in December. Then Hobbs made 114 in Sydney playing against an Australian Junior XI captained by Monty Noble, between 13 and 16 December. Noble had to defend grimly for 41 not out to save the Juniors from defeat.

Tate had by then taken 30 wickets and looked in outstanding form for the first Test. Freeman had 41 wickets and appeared likely to give England's attack variety and Tate valuable support. Hobbs and Sutcliffe were in awesome touch and the England fielding was a class above that shown by any England side since the First World War. It turned out that Collins' luck with the toss and the Australian survival of the hectic first morning thwarted England once again, despite Tate's wonderful display in sending down 89 eight-ball overs to take 6 for 130 and 5 for 98.

Bob Crockett returned to umpire the second Test in Melbourne from 1 to 8 January 1925 with a record 28 Tests and 38 years of first-class umpiring behind him. The only other Australian who came near Crockett's

Herbie Collins takes the New South Wales team onto the field for the match against England in November 1924.

record was "Dimboola Jim" Phillips, who stood in 13 Tests in Australia between 1885 and 1898, and 29 Tests in all, before going to North America and making a fortune from mining. Crockett was a stony-faced, unemotional man, whom players knew could not be bluffed. He gave his decisions without fuss in a soft voice. At the end of a day's play he retired to his room at the back of the Melbourne Cricket Ground to discuss events over drinks with a few friends.

"Stork" Hendry, who had taken 3 for 36 in the last innings of the first Test, was left out in favour of Dr Albert Hartkopf, a crowd-pleasing mixture of furious hitter and leg-spin bowler. "German" Hartkopf was a reliable, stubborn batsman, but was included to give Mailey bowling support. England brought in Dick Tyldesley for Freeman and Johnny Douglas for Andy Sandham.

Collins won the toss again and Australia batted for the first two days, but not without setbacks. Collins, Bardsley and Arthur Richardson were out for 47 before Taylor and

Ponsford batted with rare confidence, Taylor driving handsomely on either side of the wicket, Ponsford cutting freely. At 208, a bad call by Ponsford led to Hobbs throwing Taylor out from cover. Ponsford went on to his second Test century and at stumps Australia were 4 for 300, Victor Richardson aggressive in all he did.

Next day Tate bowled Ponsford for 128, but in the heat all the England bowlers suffered heavy punishment. Richardson, tall, straight-backed, with the grandeur of a guardsman, hit 21 off one over from Douglas. Chapman finally ran him out for 138 while he was attempting a fourth run. Australia again batted well right down the order, Hartkopf chiming in with a ninth-wicket stand of 100 with Oldfield before he was out for 80.

Chasing Australia's 600, England had a night's rest before Hobbs and Sutcliffe went out and batted all day for 283 runs without offering a chance. At lunch Collins instructed Ponsford to move from fine leg to a position 30 metres closer to square leg and in from the fence before Gregory bowled the fourth ball after the interval. Ponsford was told to move only if Sutcliffe had strike. It was important, Collins said, that Ponsford should move

Bert Oldfield at the peak of his powers, a wicket-keeper of style and rare polish who seldom appealed unless batsmen were out.

without any signals from Collins which would alert Sutcliffe.

The trap was sprung. Gregory bowled the fourth ball to Sutcliffe, who was unaware that Ponsford had moved, and Sutcliffe hooked the deliberately short-pitched delivery straight into the hands of Ponsford—who dropped it. Ponsford spent the rest of the day apologising to Collins and Gregory.

Ponsford's missed catch did not affect the result. Hobbs was out without addition to the score on the fourth morning for 154. The England innings closed for 479, with Sutcliffe (176) fifth out at 404. Four of the batsmen who followed Hobbs and Sutcliffe failed to reach double figures.

Australia batted again with a lead of 121, but Tate grabbed three quick wickets, and although Taylor and Collins added 79, Australia were in jeopardy at 5 for 139 at lunch on the fifth day. When Taylor went for 90, Gregory made an invaluable 36 not out in a ninth-wicket stand of 71 with Oldfield. Left to score 372 to win, England were 3 for 200 at tea on the sixth day, but at stumps were 6 for 259. Sutcliffe had batted through the day, for the second time, completing his second Test hundred and third century in succession.

On the seventh morning Mailey had the vital wicket of Sutcliffe for 127 and finished with the match-winning figures of 5 for 92. The last four English wickets fell in 45 minutes for 10, three of them for ducks. Yet again, England's tail-enders had failed to back up good top-order batting, and England, out for 290, were defeated by 81 runs. Apart from his 154 in England's first innings, Hobbs gave a memorable display of fielding in the covers, toying with the batsmen who drove the ball towards him, daring them to run as he hung back, always ready to swoop.

After the sometimes unpleasant relations between the teams when Armstrong led Australia during the 1921 series, the sportsmanship of both teams conveyed itself to spectators. Gilligan had a remarkable personal triumph leading a beaten side, inspiring in the field but sadly unable to bowl at his fastest. He even decided against taking a rest in the match between the second and third Tests against Fifteen of Ballarat on 10 and 12 January.

Collins, of course, won the toss before the third Test at Adelaide, which was held from 16 to 23 January. The pitch had sweated under tarpaulins and Tate gave England a fine start by bowling Collins and having Taylor lbw. However, Tate was then in such pain with an injured toe that he had to go off. From 3 for 22, Australia recovered somewhat, and at 4 for 114 Gilligan strained a leg muscle and had to leave the field. Freeman took a nasty blow

Arthur Gilligan watches as "Lucky" Collins tosses at the start of the third Test at Adelaide, in the 1924–25 series.

on the wrist in fielding and went off next, leaving only Woolley and Kilner of England's regular bowlers. The last four Australian wickets put on 370 and Australia made 489. Ryder's 201 not out equalled Syd Gregory's record score against England in Australia, and included a stand of 136 with Andrews, who made 72. The tail wagged splendidly, the last three batsmen contributing 90.

England had to bat for half an hour before stumps on the second day, so Gilligan changed the batting order to protect his stars. Whysall and Strudwick were lost before play ended that evening for 36 runs and next morning Tate and Chapman were soon out. At 4 for 69, Hobbs and Sutcliffe came together for what everybody sensed was the crucial part-

nership of the match. They added 90 without a mistake before Sutcliffe was caught behind off Ryder.

Woolley, who had had a 43–over bowling stint, made only 16. A determined 117–run stand by Hendren and Hobbs ended when Hobbs was out for 119. Hendren bravely chased the runs but lacked support from the last three batsmen, and when he was out for 92 England remained 124 behind.

Australia at 3 for 211 were going well at the end of the fourth day, then rain delayed play for 45 minutes next morning. When the match resumed Kilner and Woolley took the last seven Australian wickets for only 39 runs, Ryder making 88 to complete a fine double. This fighting comeback meant England needed 375 to win. Hobbs and Sutcliffe put on 63 and with Whysall and Chapman batting splendidly, England now looked like winners.

Whysall was out to an extraordinary caught and bowled by Jack Gregory for 75, Chapman to a dazzling catch by Ryder for 58. With 63 needed and eight wickets down England seemed finished, but Gilligan and Freeman put on 45 comfortably.

The tension in the teams as England neared their target was too much for Andrew Sandham, who went across the road from the ground and sat alone in a church. He returned when England still had 27 runs to get, with two wickets left. "The idea was a failure," he said. "The noise from the crowd could still be heard in the church and as it was empty, it seemed to echo round the walls."

Further rain gave the weary Australian bowlers the chance of an overnight rest. Refreshed, they grabbed the last two England wickets next morning to win by 11 runs and retain the Ashes.

Takings for this thrilling game were £10,794 and the total attendance 103,617. Given any luck with injuries or the weather England might easily have reversed the result. Australia had clinched the rubber in only three

An elated Gregory throws the ball in the air after taking a brilliant catch to dismiss Hobbs for 119 in the third Test at Adelaide.

matches, but England's cricket prestige had been revived and Gilligan had restored the friendliness to England–Australia clashes.

Two matches in Tasmania at the end of January gave England the chance to rest their injured. They beat Tasmania by 119 runs at Launceston thanks to Sandham's first innings 116 and Hendren's 101 not out in the second innings. Geoffrey Martin drove powerfully for 121 in Tasmania's second knock. England won the second match in Hobart, where Sutcliffe made 188 and put on 161 in less than two hours with Sandham, setting up victory by an innings and 136 runs.

Back in Melbourne for a tough match against Victoria from 6 to 10 February, England caught the opposition on a wet pitch. Kilner took 10 for 66 in the match, Hearne 8 for 69. Hearne also made 193, the highest score of the tour, to play a major role in Eng-

land's victory by an innings and 271 runs. Ironmonger bowled 39 overs for 93 runs in the England total of 500, finishing off the innings with a hat-trick and a personal bag of five wickets.

At Melbourne in the fourth Test between 13 and 18 February, England won the toss at last and with it a change in luck. They batted for all of the first two days to score 548. Hobbs and Sutcliffe put on more than 100 for the fourth time in seven opening stands and Sutcliffe batted right through a day's play for the third time in the series. His 143 was his fourth century of the rubber and a record for England–Australia matches.

Australia began confidently but at 38 lost two wickets in one over to Tate. Hobbs then ran out Bardsley with an underhand throw and Richardson was bowled by Hearne. After rain the Australians were 5 for 168 at the end of the third day, and although Gregory helped Taylor (86) add 72 for the eighth wicket they had to follow on 279 behind. Another excellent display from Taylor was all that delayed England's win by an innings and 29 runs on the fifth morning, when Tate took 4 for 21 to finish with 5 for 75 in all. It was Australia's first defeat for 13 years after a run of 16 Tests without loss.

At Sydney in the return match against New South Wales, from 21 to 25 February, England made their best total of the tour, 626, after leading by only seven runs on the first innings. Sandham batted for 235 minutes for 137, Woolley for 150 minutes to score 149 and Hendren for 190 minutes for his 165. Collins and Andrews both surpassed these scores. Collins took 235 minutes for 173, Andrews 300 minutes for 224, and they put on 270 for the second wicket. There was no time for a result after such heavy scoring but Sandham managed to make a second century (104) in England's second innings of 8 for 296.

Clarrie Grimmett began his Test career at the age of 33 by taking 11 wickets in the fifth Test at Sydney between 27 February and 4 March, a performance that sealed victory for Australia by 307 runs. Kippax also made his Test debut in this match, scoring 42 and 8. Australia started with a first innings of 295 before Grimmett's 5 for 45 helped bundle England out for 167. With a lead of 128 all the Australian batsmen could afford to bat aggressively. At 6 for 156 Kelleway and Collins steadied the innings by adding 53. Kelleway (73) received further help from Oldfield (65 not out), and by scoring 325 Australia set England 454 to win. Tate took nine wickets in the match, which made his aggregate for the series 38, another record.

Sutcliffe, who also had set a series record with 734 runs at 81.55, finished with a duck when he was bowled by Gregory. Hobbs, who had been superbly caught down the leg side by Oldfield in the first innings, this time was stumped by Oldfield off Grimmett and the rest of the England batting collapsed. Grimmett had 6 for 37 and provided Oldfield with four stumpings in the match.

This was Bob Crockett's last Test and

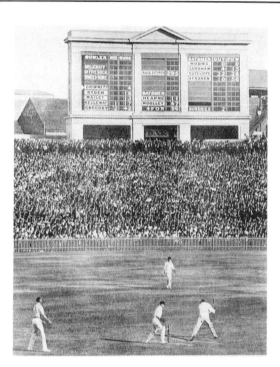

Clarrie Grimmett clean bowls Frank Woolley in Sydney to claim his first Test victim. Grimmett was to dismiss 215 more Test batsmen.

took his total to 32, a record no other Australian umpire has approached. He kept going in state and grade matches until 1926, but at 63 finally gave up because of failing eyesight. During the tea interval of a Melbourne match, his admirers gave him a cheque for £1043. He thanked them, looked at his watch, then announced it was time for play to resume and returned to the field, showing no sentiment, precise to the end.

England's failure to find an opening bowling partner for the magnificent Tate cost them dearly, but in the end it was the Australians' ability to bat right down the order that swung an enthralling series. The failure of England's spinners, Hearne, Freeman and Tyldesley, to emulate the deeds of Mailey and Grimmett for Australia puzzled all the experts.

The tour ended with England heavily

The great Australian umpire Bob Crockett, who set a record when he stood in his 32nd Test in the 1924–25 series.

them they made 24 centuries, and had 13 centuries scored against them. Sutcliffe, suave, neat, and his hair always in place, headed England's tour batting averages in all matches, with 1626 runs at 73.90, but Hendren (1317 at 62.71), Hobbs (1077 at 56.68) and Sandham (1024 at 44.52) all scored more than 1000 runs. Tate bowled 524.5 eight-ball overs on the tour and took most wickets (81 at 17.66). His 38 wickets remained the best for any series in Australia until 1978–79 when Rodney Hogg took 41 in six Tests.

Maurice Tate in that summer was a great bowler, setting a standard by which all other medium-pacers have since been measured. He combined swerve and whip from the pitch with alarming late swing, avenging his father Fred's sad fate at Manchester in 1902 when England lost by three runs, with Fred Tate last man out. Maurice bowled with a body-rock he could vary to change the speed and movement of the delivery, bustling his 182 centimetre, 95 kilogram frame to the bowling crease in half a dozen strides in his size 12 boots. At a time when *Wisden* advertised horse boots, which "would not damage beast or pitch", for the horses that pulled the rollers to flatten the wickets, Tate's boots were the delight of cartoonists.

Off the field he looked uncoordinated and ponderous, lumbering up to shake hands with a fist like a wharfie's, but he went through the delivery stride with a smooth, rhythmical union of arms and body. In his 25-year career in first-class cricket he conceded only 33 runs from every 100 balls he bowled and took a wicket every 53 balls.

Johnny Douglas again insisted on taking all his close relatives with him on the tour and scorer Ferguson often felt England could have fielded a reserve team of Douglases. "In addition to J.W.H.T., we were blessed with his wife, his parents and their daughters," wrote scorer Bill Ferguson in *Mr Cricket*. "What a time I had with that lot." Douglas

beaten by South Australia at Adelaide from 13 to 15 March. England were without Hobbs and Sutcliffe and were dismissed for 179. Arthur Richardson took 5 for 52 and Sandham top-scored for England with 59. South Australia made 443 in reply, the left-hander Jack Rymill helping himself to 146 after David Pritchard (87), Vic Richardson (43) and Percy Rundell (90) had softened up the attack. Grimmett shattered English hopes of saving the game by taking 7 for 85 in their second innings of 264 and South Australia only had to get one run to win. Whysall took 150 minutes for his 101 in England's second innings.

Gilligan's men won 8 of their 23 first-class matches, lost 6 and had 9 draws. Between was England's major failure, scoring only 239 runs in 12 matches at 23.90 and taking only seven wickets at 63.00.

Jack Ryder, tall, energetic and always out to enjoy himself, topped the Australian Test batting averages for the series thanks to his 201 not out in Adelaide, his six innings producing 363 runs at 72.60. Fleet-footed Johnny Taylor, the boundary fieldsman who could cover 100 metres in even time, was the most consistent and stylish, however, with 541 runs at 54.10. Grimmett's 11 wickets at 7.45 in his sole Test dominated the bowling averages, but Gregory, 22 wickets at 37.09, and Mailey, 24 wickets at 41.62, did most of the work.

The new scoreboard at the back of the Hill at the Sydney Cricket Ground, where it did not obscure the view of as many fans as the old board, proved one of the wonders of the cricket world in the big matches of 1924–25. Spectators were delighted with the comprehensive information it provided and commended the 20 men inside who worked the numbers and put up players' names and identified the fielder of every ball. "Patsy" Hendren made himself an idol of the Hill's patrons by jumping the fence and sharing their beer when a wicket fell.

"Stork" Hendry had left Sydney to take Armstrong's old job as ground secretary at the Melbourne Cricket Ground in the middle of 1924. In Hendry's first match for the Melbourne club, Armstrong had an altercation on the field with Vernon Ransford, who he claimed should not have appealed against the light when a dust storm swept the ground. Armstrong resigned the Melbourne Club captaincy in a huff and Hendry replaced him, holding the job for five of his nine seasons in Melbourne.

Although overshadowed by England tour matches, the 1924–25 interstate contests produced captivating cricket, with teams cons-

Stubborn England batsman Johnny Douglas whose initials earned him the tag "Johnny Won't Hit Today".

tantly changing because of the absence of players in Tests and young replacements seizing the opportunity to establish themselves. New South Wales introduced Harry ("Tommy") Rock, the Sydney University right-hand batting star, the Manly right-hander and noted coach Les Gwynne, and Jack Scott, who had joined the recently established Marrickville club. Frank Tarrant, on leave from Middlesex, returned to the Victorian side, which included a dashing young left-hander named Karl Schneider. South Australia picked big-hitting grazier Jack Murray, whose enormous sixes for the first AIF side were not forgotten; the Adelaide University left-handed batsman and right-arm fast-medium bowler Lance Gun; and a left-hander called Jack Rymill, who hailed from a grazing property beyond Broken Hill.

Victoria retained the Sheffield Shield by winning three of their four matches, twice defeating South Australia and winning one of the two matches against New South Wales. South Australia had beaten New South Wales in Adelaide after New South Wales had easily won their earlier match in Sydney.

Victoria's win over South Australia, in the first match of the season in Adelaide from October 31 to 6 November, was impressive, considering they trailed by 175 runs on the first innings. South Australia made 518. Murray and Gordon Harris put on 205 for the second wicket, Harris scoring 98 and Murray 126. Vic Richardson followed up with 123—a fine start. Grimmett's 5 for 97 restricted Victoria's first innings to 343, Tarrant contributing 86. South Australia reached 233 in their second knock, but Victoria made the task of scoring the 409 needed to win look easy, Hendry finishing on 109 not out.

Victoria won the return match at Melbourne, from 21 to 27 November, by eight wickets, despite a resolute 115 from David Pritchard, the consistent Port Adelaide left-hander, in South Australia's first innings. South Australia made 288 and 202, Victoria 357 (Ponsford 166) and 2 for 134. Tim Wall, a right-arm pace bowler from the Adelaide Colts club, could get no response from the MCG pitch in his first-class debut, taking 2 for 96 and 1 for 20.

Vic Richardson made 100 in each innings of the South Australia versus New South Wales match in Sydney, from 28 November to 2 December, but, apart from Pritchard (71 and 85), the rest of the South Australians failed badly. New South Wales started with a score of 510, Rock scoring 127, Andrews 99 and Kippax 127. South Australia followed on after making only 248 in reply (Richardson 100). Scoring 314 (Richardson 125) in their second innings, South Australia left New South Wales with 53 to win in their second innings. Rock made 27 not out.

Despite that impressive debut Rock was dropped from the New South Wales team for the second match against South Australia from 9 to 14 January. Pritchard hit another century (101) and Gun remained 136 not out in South Australia's first innings of 389. New South Wales appeared to have the match under control when Gwynne's 138 in his first Shield match was followed by a typically graceful Kippax knock of 122. With New South Wales 19 runs ahead on the first innings, South Australia made 406 in their second try. This time Rymill (110), Pritchard (61) and Rundell (69) did most of the scoring. Needing 387 to win in the last innings, New South Wales managed only 226. Grimmett's nine wickets in the match (3 for 43 and 6 for 103) proved to be the decisive factor.

The first of the crucial matches between New South Wales and Victoria was an extraordinary affair. New South Wales looked to have only a moderate side but they went out onto the Sydney Cricket Ground on 24 January 1925, and put together a total of 614. Rock and Kippax scored double centuries, Rock 235 after an opening stand of 202 with the Glebe club's right-hander Gordon Morgan, Kippax an undefeated 212. Seven New South Wales batsmen failed to reach double figures, and Hartkopf's 5 for 121 was an admirable effort.

Victoria replied with 502, to which Liddicut contributed 132, Willis 100. Hartkopf and

Hendry then caused a New South Wales second innings collapse, only Rock (51) looking comfortable in a total of 152. This gave Victoria the task of scoring 265 to win, which they made with the loss of only two wickets. Woodfull, run out for 81 in Victoria's first innings, ended on 120 not out, and Hendry complemented his tight bowling with an innings of 85.

This victory allowed Ernie Bean to retire after eight years as secretary of the Victorian Cricket Association and a far longer period as a wheeler-dealer for the Australian Cricket Board with Victoria in possession of the Sheffield Shield. According to one of his successors as VCA secretary, Jack Ledward, Bean was always "paranoid" about the Melbourne Cricket Club, Warwick Armstrong's employers.

New South Wales dropped Rock for the return match in Melbourne on 30 January despite his 440 runs in four knocks, preferring Test openers Bardsley and Collins. Victoria led by 17 runs on the first innings, Ponsford scoring 80 of their 295. After New South Wales struggled to make 278 they rushed Victoria out for only 155 in the third innings. Left to make 172, New South Wales lost seven wickets achieving their target because of accurate bowling by Hawthorn speedster, Bert Gamble, who finished with 4 for 38.

New South Wales reasserted her supremacy before record crowds in the 1925–26 season, twice defeating Victoria by an innings, and beating South Australia by an innings and 99 runs in Adelaide and by 541 runs in Sydney. The New South Wales totals included 708, 705, 642, 593 and 554, and 11 of their 13 players averaged more than 40. Helped by an innings of 271 not out against Victoria, Kippax's average was 112. Woodfull played an innings of 236—following 97 in the first innings—against South Australia in Melbourne. Charlie Macartney made a century in both matches against South Australia and was

"Stork" Hendry, Warwick Armstrong's successor as organiser of the Melbourne Cricket Club's daily practices.

the best of the regular bowlers.

To help selectors pick the team to tour England in 1926, a match between Australia and the Rest was held in Sydney from 4 to 8 December 1925. The Rest won by 156 runs, with only Collins (102 and 81), Gregory (25 and 100), Kelleway (99 not out and 34), and Macartney (84 and 28) of the regular Test batsmen showing any form; the selectors disregarded the event by sending nine of the losing side to England.

The Board of Control foolishly announced the team for the trip in batches, a procedure that has never been repeated. English cricket historian Harry Altham called it "a domestic blunder difficult either to justify or comprehend". Instead of allowing the most recent Sheffield Shield form to determine who made the team, the Board announced the names of 12 "certainties" months before the side was due to sail. Although the Board added an extra player, so that 16 toured instead of the previously planned 15, they could not plug the gaps left by poor performances of some of the 12 named early and completely failed to bolster Australia's unmistakable batting strength with a balanced attack.

Interstate bargaining for places in the touring team clouded the selectors' judgement as much as their lack of knowledge of English playing conditions. Players whose form did not justify a trip, such as Jack Ellis, Sam Everett, Arthur Richardson and "Stork" Hendry, were included and in-form players like Percy Hornibrook, Charles Kelleway and Don Blackie discarded. "Hammy" Love's far superior batting skill should have clinched him the role of Oldfield's wicket-keeping deputy instead of Ellis, but Love's seven first-class centuries were somehow forgotten.

The worst blunder in a team comprising nine players from New South Wales, five from Victoria, and two from South Australia, was the omission of Alan Kippax, the form batsman in Australia for the two seasons preceding the 1926 tour. Kippax was then at the peak of his powers and in his 29th year was scoring centuries almost every weekend in Shield or club cricket. To pass him over in favour of Arthur Richardson, who was 38, was unforgivable, and justly labelled the worst piece of selectorship since Albert Trott was left out of the 1896 tour of England. Monty Noble called it "a crime against the cricketing youth of Australia".

No reprimand for Arthur

Australia in England 1926

For gaunt, chain-smoking Herbie Collins, the omission of a bowler capable of lessening the work-load carried by Jack Gregory was an even more disastrous selection than the dropping of Alan Kippax. Gregory's fitness was at best highly suspect. Deprived of his old ability to spread apprehension among England's top-order batsmen, Australia's bowling had the power of a pop gun.

This was puzzling as Collins, who selected the 1926 team with Clem Hill and Jack Ryder, had always been an advocate of fielding balanced teams with the specialist positions adequately filled. He supported the dropping of Rock from the New South Wales side, although Rock had an average of 118.50 from five games, because Rock was a poor fieldsman whom he could not hide.

The underlying strength of Collins' captaincy was the care he took in studying the make-up of every player in his side and in the opposition. His judgement of players who would fail or succeed in England was un-

The 1926 Australian touring team: (L to R) (back)
J. Ellis, H. Hendry, J. Gregory, J. Ryder,
A. Richardson, S. Everett, S. Smith (manager);
(centre) A. Mailey, C. Grimmett, W. Bardsley,
H. Collins (captain), C. Macartney, T. Andrews,
J. Taylor; (front) W. Woodfull, W. Ponsford,
W. Oldfield.

Herbie Collins at the nets during Australia's preparation for the 1926 England tour.

before he was called on to bowl. Jack Scott may have been wild, but he was strong and genuinely fast and could bruise even good batsmen.

The selectors' mistakes were temporarily forgotten, however, when the team manager, the great survivor, Syd Smith, disciplined Collins on the voyage to England. Collins had agreed to write a series of articles for the Beaverbrook newspapers for the sum of £1000, a handsome fee at the time. Smith informed him that publication of the articles, written in collaboration with an English journalist who was on the ship, would breach his contract with the Board. Collins believed the contract referred to events on the tour and that sober, considered comment on past events did not conflict with his Board agreement, but he was forced to cancel the Beaverbrook deal.

"What I should have done, of course," said Collins later, "was to allow the articles to be printed, then accept the fine for the nominal sum of £50, which is what happened to Bradman, Miller and Lindwall."

The 1926 tour was carefully arranged, with long journeys avoided and rest days before Tests, but 40 matches had been fitted in between April and September without over-taxing the players. Apart from the unbalanced composition of their side, the Australians' main problems came from an unusually wet summer, the general strike in May and industrial unrest, illness in normally robust men, and appalling luck with injuries in games.

It soon became clear that aside from leg spinners Mailey and Grimmett, Australia lacked bowlers who could dismiss strong counties or Test opponents quickly enough to win in three days. With the first four Tests restricted to three days and only the fifth Test to be played to a finish if necessary, no fewer than 27 tour matches were drawn.

The aggression that had characterised Australian sides in England for so long was missing. In the major encounters of the tour

erring. He was able to discount what they did on Australia's hard pitches and look for the skills required in England conditions. Collins must have known that Sam Everett had neither the pace nor the deviation to make a dangerous opening bowler in England and that when pitted against batsmen of the calibre of Hobbs, Sutcliffe, Woolley and Hendren, the supporting bowlers, Richardson, Hendry and Ryder, would be found lacking. As it was, he was forced to bat Gregory too high in the order to give him an opportunity to rest

Collins was often compelled to use Gregory to attack at one end while he tried different bowlers to keep the runs down at the other. Little wonder that Australia was left with a mere 12 wins from six months' endeavour, and that English critics complained that many of the matches were used simply for practice, exhibition games in which spectators who paid to see a conclusion were defrauded.

The Australians left Sydney by train on 25 February 1926, for Melbourne, and travelled on to Tasmania by ship. They played against Northern Tasmania in Launceston and a Tasmanian XI in Hobart. They went back to Melbourne on the *Otranto* and caught a train for the four-day journey across the Nullarbor to Perth, where they easily defeated Western Australia. They rejoined the *Otranto* in Fremantle and sailed to Colombo for a one-day match against a local side.

Steamships like the *Otranto* had transformed overseas tours for Australia's cricketers. Instead of wild, arduous trips when seasickness worried even the hardiest sailors and players took to their bunks, the tourists enjoyed deck cricket against the crew, fancy dress parties, clay target shooting, cards and a variety of games. At night there was dancing in the moonlight after a first-rate meal. For the nine bachelors in the team it was a delight.

Collins ran a book on a ribbon-cutting contest in which a grazier's daughter named Nancy quickly emerged as hot favourite. He stood to lose heavily on the final, and he joked that he would have to jump overboard if she won. As it turned out her enormous backing made Nancy so nervous she dropped her scissors and was out of the race, leaving Collins a winner yet again.

After sailing through the Suez to Cairo, the *Otranto* went on to Naples, where the cricketers disembarked for an eleven-day journey across the Continent, visiting Pompeii, Rome, the Vatican, Florence, Milan and on through Switzerland to France. The

Frank Iredale, whose death in 1926 saddened cricket lovers. He had been a popular secretary of the NSWCA for four years and often left his desk to bat in the nets with the state side.

weather was wretched when they arrived in London and very little practice was possible before the first match. Disputes that finally culminated in the general strike were rampant and even short journeys proved troublesome. Understandably, with rain interrupting all their games for the first two months, a lot of the Australians took weeks to find form. There was plenty of time to read the bombardment of articles in London newspapers by Monty Noble, Clem Hill, Charles Kelleway, and team member Warren Bardsley, whose explanation to Syd Smith was that he had posted his stories to England before the team left home.

The first match, against the Minor Counties, was played at Maidenhead on 28 and 29 April and was drawn after rain on the first day. Michael Falcon, then in his twentieth season with Norfolk, took 7 for 42 in the Australian innings of 179. On Monday 3 May Jack Gregory scored the first century of the trip, 120, in Australia's total of 336 against Leicestershire at Leicester. Rain again prevented a result after Leicestershire made 96 (Macartney 5 for 9) and 1 for 15.

Bill Woodfull made 201 and Charlie Macartney 148 in Australia's innings of 9 for 538 declared against Essex. This match was held at Leyton from 5 to 7 May, and Essex had lost 2 for 5 when rain ended play.

The rain followed the tourists to the drawn match with Surrey at The Oval from 8 to 11 May, but despite the general strike, 10,000 spectators attended on the first day. Woodfull scored 118 in the Australian total of 9 for 395 declared, despite some magnificent fielding by Hobbs. Sandham made 84 in the Surrey innings of 265 and Macartney took 6 for 63. To the Australians who had not seen him field before, the manner in which Hobbs gathered and threw in even the hardest drives was a revelation. He covered the ground within ten paces on either side of him with ease, swooping in on the ball and returning it with such speed that nobody accepted when he baited them to attempt a run.

When Hendry complained of a high temperature and a sore throat, doctors discovered he had scarlet fever and he was taken on a stretcher to the London Fever Hospital. The team doctor did not go to see him and over the seven weeks he spent in the hospital Jack Ellis was his only visitor. Hendry was recuperating on a farm near Taunton, in Somerset, when he received a letter from Syd Smith saying Smith intended to send him home. Hendry ignored it, and simply replied that he would be fit for the match against Worcestershire in the first week in August. Meanwhile Ponsford had recurring bouts of tonsillitis and

Collins, an undernourished contrast to the overfed Armstrong five years earlier, suffered attacks of neuritis which eventually put him out of action for the whole of July.

A more serious problem for the team than these illnesses was the injury to Gregory, who developed shin soreness from the start of the tour. He was under constant treatment but had to be carefully watched. At no time could he indulge in long spells of bowling, although he continued to score splendidly with the bat.

Gregory was largely responsible for the first win of the tour, in the match against Hampshire between 12 and 14 May, at Southampton. He hammered the Hampshire bowling to the far corners of the ground to score 130 not out and at one stage helped put on 160 in 100 minutes. Taylor contributed 73. Mailey took 11 wickets in the match, Macartney 7, and Australia won by 10 wickets. The scores were Australia 371 and 0 for 33, Hampshire 152 and 248.

Then came a controversial match against a strong MCC XI, which aroused the ire of regulars at Lord's. Australia fired the MCC out for 199, the last seven wickets falling for 27 runs. Australia quickly established a lead, but continued batting, using the chance to get practice before they declared at 9 for 383. Ponsford scored 110 not out, Richardson 50 not out, Macartney 61. MCC then lost 5 for 83, the Australians sacrificing a win for the sake of Ponsford's hundred.

Further rain forced a draw against Cambridge University from 19 to 21 May after Grimmett took 6 for 28. The Australians then beat Oxford University by an innings and 13 runs between 22 and 25 May. All the Australian batsmen except Ponsford got runs and Arthur Richardson had an outstanding double by taking 6 for 28 and 5 for 36 with his brisk medium-paced off breaks. Oxford University made 131 and 177, Australia 321. Spectators applauded Bardsley, who captained Australia, when he recalled Oxford's John Stephenson.

Arthur Richardson, who was 38 years old when he scored a century at Headingley in 1926. He remains one of the few Australians to play Test cricket wearing glasses.

The umpire had ruled Stephenson run out by a Ponsford throw, but Bardsley explained that Stephenson had been accidentally obstructed by the bowler in his follow-through.

A 21-year-old student, Kumar Sri Duleep-sinhji, nephew of the great Ranjitsinhji and already hailed as a right-hand batsman of skill and elegance, failed in the Cambridge match and only made 28 for South of England against

the Australians at Bristol. Ryder was unbeaten at Bristol on 108 and Andrews was 74 not out when rain again washed out play.

The match against Middlesex at Lord's from 29 May to 1 June disclosed Australia's bowling frailty when faced with a strong side. Australia batted well, with Andrews scoring 164 and Collins 99 in the first innings of 489, and Woodfull made an even 100 in the second innings of 5 for 239. But Middlesex also scored freely and the former schoolboy prodigy Greville Stevens made 149 and Jack Hearne 59 in Middlesex's innings of 349.

At Birmingham on 2 June, the North of England dismissed the Australians for 105 on a wet pitch. Fred Root, the medium-pace swing bowler, showed why he regularly took 100 wickets a season for Worcestershire, by claiming 7 for 42. Root, tall and exceptionally strong, had survived being shot in the chest while serving as a dispatch rider in the First World War. He made the ball dip into the batsmen's toes with unpleasant late swing. Rain caused repeated interruptions. The game ended in a draw, with flags at the ground at half-mast following the death of the legendary Australian demon bowler, Fred Spofforth. Harold Larwood, aged 21, played against Australia for the first time in this match, and in Australia's second innings narrowly missed a hat-trick. He dismissed Woodfull and Taylor with successive deliveries and Andrews just stopped the hat-trick, Larwood finishing with 2 for 18.

The rain followed the Australians to Bradford for the match with Yorkshire between 5 and 8 June, and delays spoiled an exciting Australian attempt to snatch a win. The Australians, disappointed that they were not opposed by a full-strength Yorkshire side, due to the absence of Kilner, Holmes, Macauley and Sutcliffe, began with 177 and had Yorkshire out for 155 when Grimmett took 6 for 87. The touring batsmen hit out freely and Collins was able to declare at 3 for 243. Set to score 263 to win, Yorkshire were 0 for 25 when play ended.

Australia picked Woodfull and England Fred Root to make their debuts in the first Test at Nottingham from 12 to 15 June. England won the toss and opened with Hobbs and Sutcliffe against the bowling of Gregory and Macartney, on a pitch that had only been cut just before play began, on a ground without sight-screens. England were 0 for 32 when rain drove the players from the field after 50 minutes; not another ball was bowled.

The miserable weather continued in the return match against Yorkshire at Sheffield. This was to be played between 16 and 18 June. Australia had lost 6 for 148 when the rain came and play was washed out. The tourists were grumbling about wanting to go home, but Mailey revived their spirits with an inspired bowling display at Old Trafford that gave Australia victory in their first match against Lancashire, the County champions. This was perhaps Australia's best performance of the tour. Lancashire were dismissed for 149 and 148, and by scoring 374 Australia won by an innings and 77 runs. Mailey's figures were 7 for 74 and 4 for 91. Macartney gave him wonderful support, scoring a chanceless 160 in 195 minutes. Ted McDonald (3 for 115) opened the bowling for Lancashire with "Ciss" Parkin (3 for 85) in this match.

At Chesterfield, in the match against Derbyshire on 23 and 24 June, Bardsley returned to his sparkling best, playing all his strokes freely in an innings of 127 out of Australia's 5 for 373 declared. Collins was very sound in a knock of 93. Derbyshire scored 146 and were 2 for 55 when rain produced another draw. Indeed draws had become so frequent that by 1930, when the Australians were next in England, a few county administrators, aware of the cash the Australians attracted, discussed postponing the County championship matches to ensure the Australians' games could be played out.

The second Test, from 26 to 29 June, drew huge crowds to Lord's and on the first day more than 10,000 people were turned away. The batting by both teams reached a very high standard, but neither had enough bowling strength to defeat the other within three days. This was Harold Larwood's first Test, the selectors reasoning that Larwood, in his second full season, would be more threatening with his searing pace than Jack Hearne with his leg breaks.

Larwood, born in the Nottinghamshire mining village of Nuncargate on 14 November 1904, worked in the pits looking after the underground ponies when he left school at 13. He was captivated by the sight of the Nottinghamshire fast bowler Fred Barratt smashing stumps and dismissing Jack Hobbs, and set out to emulate him. Blessed with a powerful physique, he progressed from cleaning boots for the Notts players to opening the bowling for England at the age of 22. He whitened the boots worn by Maurice Tate, with whom he later opened the English bowling, and received two shillings for his work from Tate.

Collins, like the rain, was consistent, and won the toss. He spent the padding-up period trying to stop Bardsley looking so glum. "Cheer up, Bards," he said. "It can't be that bad." To which Bardsley replied, "Can't it? Wait till we get out there."

With the score at 11, Collins did not offer a stroke to a ball from Root which swung in late and hit his leg stump after hitting the back of Collins' left leg. Australia recovered steadily from this disaster, with Bardsley, at 42 years and 201 days, dominating the innings by becoming only the third man to bat through an innings. Macartney was caught in the slips from a lifting ball by Larwood, who also clean-bowled Gregory. These were Larwood's only triumphs and he finished with 2 for 99 in Australia's innings of 383. Bardsley was slow and methodical, scoring mainly off his legs.

Collins (left) and Bardsley going out to open for Australia. They proved a successful opening pair for Australia until Collins fell ill and was replaced by Woodfull.

His 193 not out owed much to Strudwick, who dropped him three times, the first time at 112.

With Australia 8 for 338 overnight, it was discovered early on the third morning that a section of the pitch had been flooded. This produced one of Test cricket's first scare stories, a piece of exaggerated nonsense alleging the pitch had been tampered with, when in fact a careless member of Lord's staff had left a tap, connected to a hose, half turned on. Fortunately the water did not reach the creases or the area where the ball pitched.

Hobbs and Sutcliffe soon showed that Gregory was no longer the bowler of disturbing pace that he had been in 1921, and he was replaced by Mailey. To the crowd's delight both batsmen skipped metres down the pitch to drive Mailey, or waited for him to drop them short so that they could cut and hook. Only when the gnarled figure of Richardson came on bowling at the middle and leg stump,

with four short-leg fieldsmen, did the run rate slow down. Hobbs went for 119, after spending 40 minutes in the nineties, Sutcliffe for 82 after tea, then Hendren and Woolley rushed the score ahead. Next morning England added 178 in 150 minutes to declare 92 ahead at 3 for 475. Woolley made 87, Hendren, who took half an hour to score his first run, finished unbeaten on 127, and Chapman made a swinging 50 not out.

Collins surprised spectators by opening Australia's second innings partnered by Gregory, apparently hoping the big man could savage the England bowling. But Gregory was dismissed for a duck by the first ball he received from Root. Now, while Collins plugged away at one end, shrugging off the numerous deliveries from Tate that he missed, Macartney played an amazing knock, defying all the efforts of England captain Arthur Carr to curb his scoring. There was impudence in the way Macartney delayed his shots, experimentation in the way he hit the ball to impossible parts of the field, but every stroke came from the middle of the bat.

Collins took 2 hours 25 minutes to make 24, and although three more Australian wickets fell cheaply Macartney was still there on 133 not out when the match petered out. Macartney's innings took 200 minutes. The other six Australian batsmen contributed 44 runs between them.

England cricket fans, accustomed to captains calling the names of fieldsmen they wanted to move, were fascinated by Collins' silent captaincy. There was no clapping of hands or shouting. Collins simply moved or waved a hand near his hip, usually with his back to the fieldsman he wanted to shift, and every Australian remained alert for his signals, moving without noise and often surprising the England batsmen.

The Australian batsmen now began to show more urgency. At Northampton, between 30 June and 2 July, they quickly ran up

*Hobbs sweeps a ball from Mailey to the leg
boundary for four, watched by Australians Jack
Gregory and 'keeper Bert Oldfield.*

a total of 397, leaving Mailey to take 10 wickets and help dismiss Northants for 125 in both innings. Australia won by an innings and 147 runs. At Nottingham from 3 to 6 July they repeated this form, defeating Nottinghamshire in two days by an innings and 136 runs. Woodfull made 102 not out and Bardsley 87 in Australia's 468 and Mailey had 15 for 193 in Notts' innings of 193 and 139. At Worcester, on 7 and 8 July, the tourists scored 197 and 4 for 182 to beat Worcestershire, 120 and 83, by 176 runs.

Collins did not take part in any of these wins because of his neuritis. So the invariably pessimistic and mournful-faced Warren Bardsley, just turned 43, entered the record books as Australia's oldest captain in the third Test at Headingley. The match ran from 10 to 13 July and for once England won the toss. Carr, an aggressive captain, sent Australia in before 30,000 spectators. This decision appeared justified when Bardsley was caught by Sutcliffe

low down in the slips off the first ball of the match from Tate. Macartney came in and audaciously cut his first ball for two. Tate's fifth ball forced him to hurry his stroke and the ball flew off the edge straight to Carr at third slip. Carr, usually an efficient slips fieldsman, got both hands to the ball but his right hand knocked away his left and he dropped the ball, one of the most famous of all missed catches.

The next Australian wicket did not fall until 235 was on the board. Macartney struck out boldly on both sides of the wicket and in an unforgettable display, reached his century in 103 minutes and was 112 not out, in 116 minutes, at lunch on the first day. He was the second Australian to score a Test century before lunch—Victor Trumper had been the first in 1902 at Old Trafford, when he made 103 in 108 minutes. Some of Macartney's off drives in this innings were so powerful only the keenest eyes could follow the ball to the fence. After lunch Macartney took his score to 151, including 21 fours, in 172 minutes before he was caught by Hendren off a George Macaulay medium-pacer. The only blemish in his innings was that he missed a few cuts.

Woodfull (141) and Richardson (100) went on to centuries, Richardson being the ideal man to flog a tired attack, and Australia made 494. Macartney and Woodfull had put on 235, Woodfull and Richardson 131.

Hobbs and Sutcliffe began England's innings in fine style, putting on 59 in 90 minutes. Australia's spinners then took over and by stumps on the second day England were 8 for 182 and in danger of defeat. But Geary and Macaulay batted determinedly to add 108 in a match-saving stand for the ninth wicket and England followed on exactly 200 runs behind with only two sessions of play remaining. Hobbs and Sutcliffe made certain of the draw for England by scoring 156 for the first wicket.

Ted McDonald, one of Australia's heroes on the 1921 tour, excelled himself for Lancashire against his old team-mates at Liverpool, from 14 to 16 July. He captured 5 for 135 in Australia's first innings of 6 for 468 declared. On a pitch that did not suit him, he remained a wonderful spectacle, a bowler whose action Bob Menzies, later Australian prime minister, described as "silk running off a spool", and who charmed the crowd through 37 overs.

Bardsley made 155 and Andrews 95, batting with a confidence none of the Lancashire players could match when they faced Mailey. From 37 overs Mailey took 9 for 86 and had Lancashire out in their first innings for 234. When Lancashire followed on, Bardsley gave Andrews 34 overs and his leg breaks yielded 6 for 109. Andrews' bowling surprised even his team-mates, but Bardsley remembered that he had twice taken five wickets in an innings for New South Wales.

The Australians had three matches in mid-July in Scotland that provided lavish hospitality and useful batting practice. Ponsford, Macartney and Ryder made centuries and Oldfield polished his stumping skills in Edinburgh against a Scotland XI. Grimmett took 7 for 42 to bundle the Scots out for 94.

A rare picture of Warren Bardsley bowling. He was more at home with the bat than the ball, scoring 53 first-class centuries but failing to take a wicket.

Australia then made their highest score of the tour, 563, before rain caused the match to be abandoned.

The clamour for Tests to be played over four days instead of three intensified after another draw in the fourth Test at Old Trafford on 24, 26 and 27 July. This was the sixth successive draw in a Test in England. Bardsley led Australia again in the absence of Collins, and an oddly self-conscious Ponsford returned after missing the first three Tests through illness to replace Taylor. Charlie Parker, the Gloucestershire spinner who had rushed across England in high glee, was told when he arrived that he would not be playing and cried openly. Ernie Tyldesley took his place on the strength of scoring centuries in seven matches in a row.

Carr, England's captain, developed tonsillitis after the first day and took no further part in the match. Jack Hobbs took over, as England's first twentieth-century professional captain. The previous English professional captain had been Arthur Shrewsbury back in 1887.

Rain permitted only ten balls to be bowled on the first day after Bardsley won the toss and batted. Australia batted all the second day. Macartney scored his third Test century of the series without the impertinence of his Leeds display, and Woodfull showed that despite his short backlift he could hit the ball hard. When Macartney left for 109 and Woodfull for 117 the Australian innings fell apart, and from 3 for 252 they were all out for 335. Chapman, fielding for Carr, made a wonderful running catch in the outfield to dismiss Andrews for eight, but the rest of the Australians simply played foolish strokes. Bardsley indicated that Australia wanted to bank everything on the timeless fifth Test by refusing to declare when the pitch started to wear.

England survived frequent lbw appeals to reach 5 for 305 before time ran out. Mailey and Grimmett bowled in tandem, providing a rare interlude for connoisseurs. Both turned their leg breaks and googlies but the pitch was too slow to help them. Grimmett was the steadier of the two, Mailey the more adventurous but more prone to loose balls. Throughout the tour neither bowled on the fast pitches that suited them. Grimmett returned figures of 1 for 85, Mailey 3 for 87. For Mancunians, the main pleasure from the match came from Ernest Tyldesley's hard-hitting 81.

Australia declared at 9 for 432 in the return match from 28 to 30 July against Surrey. Woodfull was impressive again with his infallible defence in scoring 156, while Ryder was much faster in scoring 104 in 2 hours and 20 minutes. Rain ruined the pitch on which play had begun, and to allow Surrey to bat, the unusual decision was taken to continue on a fresh wicket. Surrey were 6 for 82 when play ended. Grimmett took 4 for 30.

Mailey and Grimmett were far too skilful for Glamorgan's batsmen from 31 July to 3 August at Swansea. Glamorgan relied on the left-arm finger spin of the eccentric Frank Ryan, who bowled 49.2 overs in the game and took six wickets. Ryan, born in New Jersey, USA, took more than 900 wickets for Glamorgan but had some curious habits; he was found one morning asleep under the pitch covers, where he had spent the night. Ponsford handled him comfortably in an innings of 143 not out in Australia's first innings of 283. Mailey then took 5 for 40, Grimmett 4 for 56 to rush Glamorgan out for 139. After Australia declared at 5 for 200 in their second innings, Mailey (4 for 58) and Grimmett (4 for 45) dismissed Glamorgan for 120, Australia winning by 224 runs.

Collins and Hendry reappeared for Australia against Warwickshire at Birmingham between 4 and 6 August. Ponsford and Woodfull had an opening partnership of 117, Ponsford going on to 143 not out, his second successive century, and Australia reached 464. The limitations of the Australian bowling were apparent as they struggled to break a last-wicket stand of 65 before rain washed out play, with Warwickshire on 9 for 363.

Grimmett's 11 for 126 and a stylish innings of 95 by Taylor were the main factors in a nine-wicket win over Gloucestershire at Cheltenham on 7 and 9 August. Gloucestershire made 144 and 178, Australia 287 and 1 for 39. The Australians agreed to play a Public Schools XV at Lord's on 11 and 12 August, but when Australia went out to bat Collins objected to all the Schools' players fielding. Four players went off. After discussions with Syd Smith in the dressing room they were allowed to bat but not field. Australia made

Clarrie Grimmett on the 1926 tour when he topped the Australian bowling averages with 112 at 17.04.

year-old Wilfred Rhodes, then at the head of the English bowling averages, who had already been a Test player in 1900 when Chapman was born. England also dropped Root for Larwood, who looked more suited to the fast pitch at The Oval. Collins' return meant that Ryder had to be left out of the Australian team.

Nothing about this extraordinary match went according to plan. On the first morning, with English newspapers predicting record attendances, thousands stayed away thinking they would not get into the ground and the match started with the stands half-full. Early in the morning Mailey, still in his dinner jacket after an all-night frolic, met manager Smith on the hotel steps. Smith was about to deliver a stinging rebuke when Mailey asked him to postpone it until the close of play.

England were all out on the first day for 280 after Mailey removed six of the first seven batsmen, Hobbs to a high full toss that hit the leg stump. Smith never did reprimand Mailey. Mailey said impishly that he had to take six wickets to earn his reprieve—"five would never have done it".

Australia, however, were 4 for 60 at stumps and it was not until Collins and Gregory added 107 for the seventh wicket that an Australian lead looked possible. Collins, batting at number six so that Woodfull could open with Bardsley, was Larwood's third victim and made 61. Gregory scored 73.

Only a ninth-wicket partnership of 67 by Oldfield and Grimmett enabled Australia to total 302, 22 ahead. By stumps on the second day Hobbs and Sutcliffe had England back in the lead with an unbroken stand of 49. The match stood evenly poised but that night there was consternation among the Australians when heavy rain fell.

Collins made the worst miscalculation of his career when he persisted with Arthur Richardson's off breaks at the start of the third day. Hobbs and Sutcliffe later confessed they

264, the Schools XV 114 and 2 for 105. Australian Bob Crockett, on his first visit to England, was given the honour of umpiring this match and received a standing ovation from Lord's members as he took the field. He spent the rest of the season umpiring in England, the first Australian since Jim Phillips, at the turn of the century, to stand in England.

After four drawn Tests the first ever Test in England without a time limit began on 14 August amid unprecedented public interest. This increased when England selectors dropped Carr and replaced him as captain with the 25-year-old Percy Chapman. Many thought Percy Fender should have been given the job. Carr was officially "ill" but he played for Notts during the Test. There was no room for Carr once it had been decided to recall the 48-

Although attendances were down from those predicted by the English newspapers, crowds still queued up outside The Oval to see England regain the Ashes in 1926.

deliberately made Richardson's bowling appear difficult so that Collins would not replace him with Gregory, who they considered would have been a spiteful proposition on such a pitch. It was very subtly done, with Hobbs and Sutcliffe steadily building up the score in the absence of wind and sun. Hobbs cleverly shielded Sutcliffe from Richardson's bowling whenever Sutcliffe was in trouble.

They were well set when the sun came out and the wind stirred and the pitch became genuinely unpleasant. The ball bit and kicked viciously, rising sharply as it turned. Hobbs and Sutcliffe countered with the last-minute dropping of the wrists, at which they were masters. Harry Altham in his *History Of Cricket* described the classic confrontation:

No tenser scene could be imagined as, over after over, the duel continued. Richardson, bowling round the wicket, pitched his off-breaks persistently on the leg and middle stumps. His accuracy was exceptional, but the fatal misjudgement of length, the mistiming of stroke would not come. Where a Blythe or a Rhodes must surely have induced an error with the left-hander's ball that leaves the bat at the blind spot, Richardson could not succeed against such superlative technique with the ball coming on to the bat.

After lunch Hobbs reached probably his finest century against Australia before Gregory came on and bowled him for an even 100. On such a pitch how Collins must have yearned for Ironmonger, who was 21,000 kilometres away. Woolley made 27 and Tate 33 not out, but compared with the artistry of Hobbs and Sutcliffe their batting looked clumsy. Sutcliffe had batted without blemish for seven hours for 161 when Mailey deceived him in the last over of the day, leaving Australia to score 415 to win on a ruined pitch.

Further rain hastened the end. Making the ball fly, Larwood removed Woodfull, Macartney and Andrews for 31 runs in the first 50 minutes of Australia's innings. In dismissing Woodful and Macartney, Geary took two catches off Larwood's bowling of such force that they bruised the *back* of his hand. Then Chapman threw the ball to Rhodes, who turned it sharply from the start and accounted for the rest of Australia's leading batsmen. Rhodes had given up bowling to concentrate on batting and only returned to bowling to help Yorkshire out. He had Ponsford caught low down in the slips, Collins and Bardsley to easy slips catches, and clean-bowled Richardson. After his twentieth over, Chapman took Rhodes off, a decision which drew some well-chosen words from the Yorkshireman. Chapman said he wanted to "share the wickets round a bit".

Gregory, whose low grip on the bat handle restricted his mis-hits, lashed out at Tate and for once skied the ball straight to mid-off. Oldfield and Grimmett held out for half an hour but the innings ended at 125, with England winners by 289 runs. Collins and Mailey, both in their last Tests, were cheered all the way to the crease.

Mailey and Grimmett grabbed stumps and bails for souvenirs as thousands of spectators swarmed across the field and, standing in front of the pavilion, roared their approval of the Australians as loudly as they applauded the England players. England had bowled with hostility throughout and had not dropped a catch or given away a single unnecessary run,

Wilfred Rhodes of Yorkshire and England, from a painting by Ernest Moore. The picture shows him in action during the later part of his career, in the 1920s. Rhodes was one of the greatest all-rounders in cricket.

but it was the Hobbs–Sutcliffe second innings partnership that had swung a memorable match and regained the Ashes after 14 years.

No champagne for losers

The aftermath of the 1926 tour; domestic cricket 1926–27

Defeat at The Oval was to change Herbie Collins' life. He played in six of Australia's seven matches after the fifth Test and left England at the end of the tour expecting to continue his cricket career. Arthur Gilligan, the former England captain, wrote that at 37 Collins was batting and bowling as well as ever and all Englishmen looked forward to seeing him play again in England.

Back in Australia, administrators' displeasure over Australia's failure brought swift retribution. Collins found himself replaced as captain of the Waverley club and of the New South Wales team by tour discard Alan Kippax. Collins was blamed when Australian newspapers revived criticism of selections for the tour. The masterly wet-wicket batting by Hobbs and Sutcliffe was ignored. "The best thing to come out of Australia's defeat was that it demonstrated that the pursuit of practice instead of victory in county matches

Queensland's first Sheffield Shield team before they met New South Wales in Brisbane: (L to R) (back) H. Noyes, E. Bensted, N. Beeston; (centre) F. Gough, F. Brew, R. Higgins, R. Oxenham; (front) W. Rowe, F. Thompson, L. O'Connor (captain), A. Mayes, L. Oxenham. New South Wales won by only eight runs.

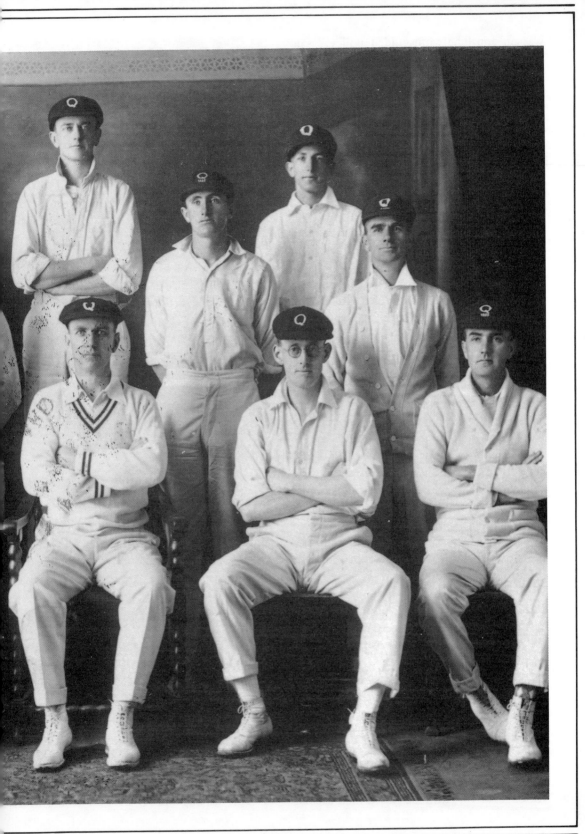

was an appallingly misguided policy," said the Melbourne *Argus*.

Loss of the Ashes also brought a severe check to the ambitions of team manager, Sydney Smith. He had to fight for survival when the Gordon club, still incensed by the omission from the tour of local favourite Charles Kelleway, dropped him as its delegate to the New South Wales Cricket Association, effectively stripping him of his position on the association and as secretary of the Board of Control. Kelleway had gone to England as a commentator for the *Daily Express*, at a big fee.

Clem Hill had taken his wife to England to watch the team he had helped Collins and Ryder select. At Headingley, when Hobbs reached 60, he waved his bat to the place where the Hills were sitting with his wife Ada. Hobbs had just passed Hill's record of 3412 runs in 49 Tests. After The Oval defeat Hill was never again asked to select a touring team.

Collins retired, giving ill-health as his reason, but those close to him said he would have continued had he not been so callously cold-shouldered when he returned home. There had been none of this bitterness in England in the matches that followed the fifth Test, only expressions of sympathy and admiration for the manner in which Australia had lost a wonderful game.

At Taunton, three days after the Test, Somerset put up a stirring fight against the Australians, who appeared certain of defeat at tea on the third day but recovered to win another thriller by 56 runs. Australia made 225 in the first innings, thanks to a gutsy last-wicket stand by Jack Ellis and Sam Everett. From 9 for 127, they took the score to 225 before Everett was stumped for 59. Ellis was 42 not out. Somerset found the tricks of Grimmett too much for them in their first innings of 153. Grimmett took 5 for 64, Richardson 4 for 18. Australia closed their second

The talkative Victorian wicket-keeper Jack Ellis, who could not oust Bert Oldfield from the Test berth, remained a popular tourist.

innings at 4 for 229. Taylor, the unlucky man of the tour, made 75, Collins 60. Set to make 302 in 220 minutes, Somerset were only 106 short with five men left, but the last five wickets fell for 49 runs.

Australia and Kent then played a draw between 25 and 27 August at Canterbury, where Ryder drove ferociously on his way to 109 and Mailey had 5 for 133. Bardsley scored 118 not out in another draw at Brighton on 28 to 31 August, time running out with Sussex on 5 for 157, chasing 231 to win. At Folkestone, in the opening match of the Festival, continual interruptions through rain forced a draw against a powerful England XI. Larwood took 7 for 95 in Australia's innings of 274 and the England XI were 75 behind with nine out when play was abandoned.

After weeks of disappointment Taylor played a glorious innings of 201 against a Civil Service XI at Chiswick on 4 to 7 September. Everett was on 100 not out when Australia declared at 7 for 454. Collins took 6 for 17 in the Civil Service's first innings of 59 and had 2 for 23 in the second innings of 3 for 93 before time ran out.

Two tame draws on rain-sodden pitches wound up the tour, the first against C. I. Thornton's XI at Scarborough on 8 to 10 September and the second against an England XI at Blackpool on 11 to 14 September. Grimmett took 5 for 68 at Scarborough and Mailey 5 for 58 at Blackpool, where Woodfull batted through the first innings for 116 not out, his eighth tour century, and one more than Charlie Macartney. The Australians made 35 centuries on the tour and had only six scored against them.

The first-class figures for the tour told some fascinating stories. Woodfull on his first tour scored most runs, 1766 at 58.87, closely followed by Macartney with 1561 at 53.83, and Bardsley with 1495 at 48.23. The only other batsmen to score more than a thousand runs were Andrews with 1248 at 37.82 and Ryder with 1071 at 36.93. Collins, clearly affected by his illness, managed only 779 runs at 29.96 without a single century, and took just 6 wickets at 28.17.

Mailey took most wickets, with 130 at 19.10, but Grimmett topped the bowling averages with 112 at 17.04, a remarkably economical cost for a spinner. None of the speedsters came close to taking 50 wickets. Sam Everett, sent as the pace bowling backup for Gregory, took only 17 first-class wickets at 34.35. Gregory had his worst tour with 36 wickets at 32.16. Grimmett, Macartney, Richardson, and Mailey all bowled more than 500 overs on the tour.

The Australians scored seven individual centuries in Tests, compared with four by England batsmen. Macartney topped both sides' Test averages with a personal series best of 94.60 from six innings, with only two other Australians Bardsley (57.75) and Woodfull (51.00) averaging more than 50. Hobbs topped England's Test averages with 81.00 from seven innings, but had three team-mates over 50, Sutcliffe (78.66), Hendren (62.00) and Chapman (58.33). Neither side set any records with the ball, Tate topping England's Test averages with 13 wickets from five matches at 28.94, Grimmett taking 13 wickets at 31.84 to top Australia's bowling performances.

Years later Dame Pattie Menzies, widow of Australia's cricket-fanatic prime minister, described how her husband forced her to watch the Test at The Oval in 1926.

I'd only been to one Test in Australia. When I arrived Hobbs and Sutcliffe were batting, and after watching them for a couple of hours, I became bored and went home. Then in 1926, when we went to London, Bob said I should see at least one Test. So I went to The Oval, and what do you think? There they were again— Hobbs and Sutcliffe. They were still batting.

Collins quit first-class cricket with 1352 runs at 45.06 in 19 Tests to his credit. In first-class matches he scored 9924 at 40.01 and took 181 wickets at 21.38, only four of them in Tests at a high 63.00. He had worked as a stipendiary steward at pony club races when he was Australian captain and after he retired he took out a bookmaker's licence. He had some big wins, one day clearing £4000, but there were too many bad days and he gave up bookmaking to become a commission agent, punting with his fees and what he could win in poker schools.

Five years after he relinquished the Australian captaincy he had to seek help from the Cricketers' Fund, set up in 1922 by the New South Wales Cricket Association to aid famous players down on their luck. The association's treasurer, E. A. Tyler, who recommended assistance for Collins, was the man Collins had abused years earlier for the failure to produce iced drinks for Collins' players during a Sheffield Shield match. Philip Derriman, in his history of the association, *True To the Blue*, gave this as the text of Tyler's submission:

> *I have to report that I interviewed Mr H. L. Collins in regard to his present financial position. He informs me that he has been right up against it for a considerable time, has tried in every way to get employment or means of earning a living, but has failed almost completely. He has an invalid mother who has no hope of recovering. So short has he been of money that on occasions he has not been able to buy the necessary medicine, and more infrequently they have been short of food.*

The Depression and his gambling undoubtedly added to Collins' problems, but he remained dependent on the Cricketers' Fund for years, and even in 1938 drew money from it. He was not the first noted cricketer to seek assistance from the fund but he was certainly the first Australian captain to do so.

Syd Smith was luckier than Collins. Snubbed by the Gordon club, he received what Derriman described as totally unexpected support from the New South Wales Junior Cricket Union. Its delegate to the New South Wales Cricket Association, Jack Durham, stood down, and Smith was elected in his place. After a year as the Union's delegate, Smith was elected a vice-president of the Association and thereafter his membership of the NSWCA was never challenged. Durham resumed his place as the Union delegate.

Smith, born in 1880 and the son of an Australian member of parliament, had been in cricket administration since the age of 10, when he was secretary of a boys' cricket club in Annandale, an inner Sydney suburb. At Bathurst Superior School he was secretary

of the cricket club for three years, and at Hawkesbury Agricultural College he was the cricket club's secretary for two years. He first went into the NSWCA's minutes in 1902, when he wrote for permission to play for Petersham second grade. He was said to have been responsible for Petersham achieving first grade status a few years later.

Sydney Smith was a fluent speech-maker, impressive at social functions, but extremely brusque with subordinates, a non-smoking teetotaller who was never heard to swear. He worked in a series of important New South Wales government jobs and at one time was chairman of the Western Lands Board. He looked to have the manager's job in Australian touring teams for as long as he wanted it until the Gordon club withdrew their support. He became president of the New South Wales Cricket Association in 1935 and held the job for 30 years. He died in 1972, aged 92.

The graceless inhumanity with which New South Wales officials greeted the loss of the Ashes thankfully did not spread to Victoria, where five members of the beaten Australian team were allowed to continue their careers without a hint of criticism. There seemed a greater awareness that after years of recovery from the horrors of war and the disruption of a general strike, England was entitled to some good fortune.

Woodfull, one of the surprise successes of the English tour with 1672 runs at 57.65, took over the Victorian captaincy from Edgar Mayne. This was a controversial appointment because the most popular cricketer in Melbourne was Jack Ryder, whose big hitting for Collingwood, Victoria and Australia had won him a huge following. Ryder, seven years older than Woodfull, had been captain of Collingwood since 1917 and was renowned as a bold, aggressive leader.

Bill Woodfull had learnt to play cricket on a wicket laid down by Jack Ryder's brother, Jim, for his father, the Reverend Thomas

Sydney Smith (left), manager of the 1921 and 1926 Australian teams in England, with Sir Frederick Toons, manager of the 1920–21, 1924–25 and 1927–28 England teams in Australia.

Staines Brittingham Woodfull. The pitch was behind their home, the Collingwood Methodist Church parsonage, and Jack Ryder often practised on it. Woodfull's father had enclosed the wicket with wire netting to protect his neighbours' property.

All Ryder's sixes were driven, and he seldom cut. He gripped his long-handled bats high and took a long back lift, swinging through a long arc with a heavier bat—2 lb 6 oz (1077 grams)—than his team-mates used. His drive reminded Ray Robinson of a slamming gate and with it he hit more sixes around the Melbourne suburbs than any other batsman. "Ryder rampant was a sight to bring out the best in barrackers," wrote Robinson. "No bowler could dictate to him. Not even Larwood."

He bunched his hands on the bat handle and waited restlessly for bowlers, forever hitching up his pants, wriggling his shoulders and tapping his bat in his blockhole. He had a long record of run-outs and never could master the art of good calling. His running was full of second and third thoughts, and he had a habit of advancing several metres down the pitch following his drives, which made many of his partners think he was on his way, only to see him turn back when somebody like Hobbs intercepted the shot.

The Australians visited North America on the way home from their 1926 tour. They visited the famous Brockton Point Ground at Vancouver, which rates among the world's most beautiful grounds, but had no time to organise a match.

Queensland entered the Sheffield Shield competition in the 1926–27 season, after years of pressure at Board of Control meetings from their delegates Roger Hartigan and Jack Hut-

cheon. Both excellent debaters, they exploited every win in the field by Queensland to convince fellow Board members that Queensland pitches were of first-class standard and that the high cost of sending players all the way to Brisbane was justified. The frustration of Queensland cricket fans was expressed at a public meeting, in the 1926–27 season, to try and secure a Test for Brisbane. The anger of the northern fans at being continually ignored finally filtered through to the south, but instead of a Test Queensland was given a place in the Shield competition.

Queensland was admitted to the competition on the condition that they played only one match against South Australia, but such was their performance that this condition was dropped after only one season. But the chance was missed to adjust Queensland's unfair share of Board of Control profits. The Board had always distributed profits on the basis that New South Wales, Victoria and South Australia were entitled to more (three-thirteenths) than the other states because they were foundation members. In fact, Queensland (two thirteenths) became a member of the Board 17 months before South Australia, but the falsely based disbursement of funds has continued.

Queensland had built up a strong side after the First World War around players like Leo O'Connor, the right-hand batsman and wicket-keeper from the Valley club; F. C. Thompson, known as Cecil, the South Brisbane club's all-rounder; Percy Hornibrook, the slow left-arm bowler from Toombul; and the Oxenham brothers, Lionel and Ron, both at that time also with Toombul Club.

For one of Queensland's finest players since 1906, Charles Barstow, Shield recogni-

The 1926 Australian team with the Vancouver cricketers, at the picturesque Brockton Point Ground. Unfortunately time did not permit a match.

tion came too late. Barstow was the supreme grade cricketer, with the unique record of playing in 16 premiership teams in 25 seasons of first grade with the Woolloongabba, South Brisbane, North Brisbane and Toombul clubs. In all, he took 1073 wickets in club cricket. His best season was 1913–14, when he captured 101 wickets for Toombul at 8.80 each. He twice took 10 wickets in an innings and in 1908–09 had 8 for 1 for South Brisbane against Toombul. He played 22 matches for Queensland, taking 78 wickets at 28.12. When Ernie Mayne first played against Barstow he said, "I was amazed! I did not know Queensland had a bowler of such class. He flights the ball better than anybody in Australia and makes one hang in the air that is a beauty." Barstow was 43 and frustrated by years of unsatisfactory Test trials when Queensland made her Sheffield Shield debut.

In their first Shield match, which began on 26 November 1926, Queensland went within eight runs of bringing off an astounding upset against the powerful New South Wales side, which was without the nine players they had provided for the 1926 touring team. Only a fighting 127 by Kippax allowed New South Wales to reach 280 in the first innings. Queensland took a handy lead by scoring 356 in reply. Harry ("Bob") Steele, a left-hander from the Marrickville club in Sydney, who opened, scored 130 in New South Wales' second innings of 475, but was overshadowed by another majestic knock from Kippax for his second century in the game. Archie Jackson, a 17-year-old right-hand batsman from Balmain, was run out for 86, and Albert Scanes, the Petersham right-hander, made 47.

Left to score 400 to win, Queensland started badly, losing three wickets cheaply, before O'Connor played the innings of his life to reach 196 before being run out. The crowd at the Brisbane Exhibition Ground were ecstatic as Queensland edged closer to the target. Dr Alex Mayes hung on grimly while runs were added and lost his wicket hitting out when victory for Queensland looked assured. With nine wickets down and eight runs needed, O'Connor drove powerfully towards Gordon Amos at cover point. Last man Bill

Queensland players and officials show their enthusiasm by combining to pull the roller across the pitch before their first Shield match in 1926–27.

Noyes started to run, but hesitated. O'Connor was left unsure of whether Noyes would run, and a lightning-fast throw from Amos, who later migrated to Queensland, ran him out.

James Campbell, a right-arm, leg-break bowler from the Gordon club in Sydney, took 10 wickets in this match, which confirmed Queensland's right to a regular place in the Sheffield Shield games.

At Adelaide in early December, South Australia beat Victoria by two wickets, despite a typically sound innings by Ponsford, who made 214 out of 315. Only Ponsford was at ease against the Port Adelaide leg-spinner Norman Williams, who had 6 for 88. Vic Richardson made 137, and left-hander Jack Rymill 142, in South Australia's reply of 481. Blackie bowled 51.7 overs to finish with 7 for 159. Woodfull (84) and Ponsford (54) put on 104 for the first wicket in Victoria's second innings, a start Hendry followed up with a hard-driving 177. Spinner Williams this time had 6 for 146 in an innings of 430.

South Australia lost eight wickets in scoring the 265 to win. Vic Richardson completed a match-winning double by scoring 92. Blackie took a further four wickets to make his match total 11, a display which made enthusiasts wonder how on earth he missed being a 1926 Test tourist.

Queensland won their first Shield match when they defeated New South Wales by five wickets in Sydney in December 1926. Charlie Macartney and Tommy Andrews returned to strengthen New South Wales but Bardsley and Taylor confirmed their retirement by dropping out. New South Wales' first innings was a curious effort, Macartney scoring 114 out of the 287 total. As Queensland ran up a score of 577 it was announced that Macartney was ill and would take no further part in the match. O'Connor made 103 and Ron Oxenham 134 not out through sound, unspectacular batting.

Facing a 290-run deficit, New South

Don Blackie, whose omission from the 1926 English tour puzzled experts and ended all chance of this wonderful bowler getting an overseas trip.

Wales were off to a fine start when openers Norbert Phillips (144) and Bob Steele (78) plundered all the Queensland bowling. Kippax chimed in with an entertaining 182 and Archie Jackson resisted a tendency to hang the bat outside the off stump to make an even 100. Jackson was on 99 when last man Ray McNamee went in. Four times Jackson drove the ball straight to fieldsmen until he pushed the ball slowly to mid-off and got the vital single for his initial first-class century.

Queensland had to make 299 to win, and they did it thanks to another exciting century by O'Connor, who was unbeaten on 143 when the winning hit was made. Elated at Queensland's five-wicket win, spectators jumped the fence and carried O'Connor shoulder-high from the field. The Queensland dressing-room resounded with joy as delighted players and officials congratulated each other. Their celebrations continued well into the night.

Just before Christmas 1926 New South Wales went south for matches against South Australia in Adelaide, and Victoria in Melbourne, where the Victorian Cricket Association had been defying the Laws of Cricket —and the Board of Control—by covering pitches for Shield matches. In Adelaide they overcame an immense hurdle to win after South Australia scored 500 (Vic Richardson 157). New South Wales replied with 341. Colin Alexander, a right-hander from Adelaide University, made 104 in South Australia's second innings of 286, which left New South Wales 446 to win, facing the classy spin bowling of Arthur Richardson and Clarrie Grimmett.

New South Wales lost six wickets in the chase. Andrews made 126, Phillips 52 and Kippax 42, but the crucial contributions came from Gordon Morgan (116) and Archie Jackson (56 not out), who put on 130 for the sixth wicket. Then with 20-year-old Sydney University right-hander, Jim Hogg, as his seventh-wicket partner, Jackson calmly tapped Richardson through mid-off for the winning run.

The euphoria caused by this victory was short-lived. While the arguments raged over the Victorian intention of covering the wicket if it rained, New South Wales were dismissed for 221 and then had to field for ten and a half hours while Victoria scored 1107, a world record.

Woodfull and Ponsford began the slaughter with an opening stand of 375 in 225 minutes. Ponsford and Hendry then put on 219 in 120 minutes for the second wicket. Ponsford was out, 13 runs short of Clem Hill's Shield record score of 365, cursing his luck when he dragged the ball onto his stumps for 352. Hendry and Ryder then set about

The Melbourne Cricket Ground scoreboard showing Victoria's world record total of 1107 in December 1926. Mailey, 4 for 362, said he was sorry the innings ended when he was just finding his length.

demoralising the opposition bowlers. Hendry made an even 100 but was completely overshadowed by Ryder, who hit 6 sixes and 33 fours in his 295 in 245 minutes.

On 29 December 1926, wicket-keeper Jack Ellis took Victoria's score past 1000 with a pull shot off Tommy Andrews. "Come on, there's three in it!" he yelled. "Three to me and 1000 up. Long live Victoria!"

While this was going on, the New South Wales wicket-keeper Andy Ratcliffe could only reflect that the two chances he had dropped had probably cost 300 runs. Fifty thousand people cheered as the thousand came up.

Bowling into the wind, Mailey continued to float the ball up, probing for mis-hits that were all too few. He bowled 512 balls in all and his four wickets cost 362 runs. In his newspaper column Mailey bemoaned the fact that Ellis was run out at 1107, and claimed he 'was just striking a length'. His figures would have been better, said Mailey, if a chap in the crowd in a dark suit had not dropped four catches from his bowling.

Run ragged in the field, the New South Wales batsmen managed only 230 in their second innings, with Archie Jackson unbeaten on 59. Hartkopf's spinners took 6 for 98 and Arthur Liddicut's fast-medium right-handers 4 for 50.

Queensland did not fare much better in their trip south, where the giant Melbourne Cricket Ground and the narrow Adelaide Oval were quite strange to them. Ron Oxenham, one of several players who could not get leave to tour, was badly missed. In the end, they found the combination of Blackie's spin and South Melbourner Frank Morton's pace bowling too much for them and were beaten by an innings and 169 runs between 18 and 22 December. Woodfull and Ponsford had a partnership of 115 and Ponsford and Hendry a stand of 237. Ponsford scored 151 and Hendry 140 in Victoria's innings of 533.

The following week in Adelaide, the Queenslanders suffered a sustained onslaught from Arthur Richardson's heavy bat. Queensland made 251 and 379, Grimmett taking five wickets in each innings; but Richardson's 232 in 225 minutes in a total of 579 was the decider, and South Australia won by 10 wickets. Back in Brisbane, the badly mauled Queensland team were all too aware of southern misgivings about their entry into the Shield.

To compensate for the lack of experience among Brisbane groundsmen, the Queensland Cricket Association had asked the curator of the Sydney Cricket Ground, Bill Stuart, to advise on the Exhibition Ground pitch. His dislike of the local soil persuaded the QCA to import 50 cubic yards of the Merri Creek soil used at the Melbourne Cricket Ground. Apart from supplying the Exhibition Ground, the QCA made an allocation of this Victorian soil to senior clubs to top-dress their pitches to a depth of about 10 centimetres. The worry was whether all this would satisfy the southern sceptics.

Meanwhile Victoria had proved far too strong for South Australia in Melbourne from 1 to 6 January 1927. Morton, tall, strapping, worked up a lot of pace to take nine wickets in the match. Blackie got seven with his subtle off-spin. Ponsford made 108 and 84, Hendry 68 and 85, and Hammy Love (188) had a 217-run sixth-wicket stand with Hartkopf (126), Victoria winning by 571 runs. Grimmett had the satisfaction of taking nine wickets against the state which had dropped him, but at a cost of 281 runs.

On New Year's Day 1927, a team of New South Wales stars, captained by E. L. Waddy, engaged in a run-orgy against Northern Tasmania at Launceston. Waddy scored 112, Kippax 132, "Magic" Sullivan 124 and Jackson 160. At the tea interval an official asked Kippax if he or Jackson, who were batting together, could wear a coloured sash so spectators could tell them apart. They were a similar lean build, and Jackson had modelled his batting style on Kippax's. Kippax agreed, and Jackson wore the sash.

Batting with his sleeves rolled down to protect his sensitive skin, Jackson continued in outstanding form a week later in Sydney. However, his artistic second innings 104 not out was not enough to prevent a South Australian win by 340 runs. Arthur Richardson made 189 in South Australia's first innings of 344, Karl Schneider 146 in the second of 399, leaving New South Wales to score 547 to win in the last innings. They were all out for 206, off spinner "Perka" Lee finishing with 5 for 36. Only Kippax (52) and Jackson, who went in with the score on 4 for 37 and finished on 104 not out, offered real resistance.

E. L. "Gar" Waddy was one of three big hitting brothers to play cricket. None of them played in Tests, but "Gar" and "Mick" both played for New South Wales.

Only a few weeks after conceding more than 1000 runs in Melbourne, New South Wales dismissed Victoria for only 35 runs in Sydney. New South Wales began with an innings of 469, Kippax scoring 217 not out without offering a chance. Handicapped by the absence of Woodfull, Ponsford, Ryder, Love and Hartkopf, Victoria would not have scored 30 runs had a catch not been dropped. Macartney took 3 for 10 and McNamee, who at one stage had five wickets without conceding a run, took 7 for 21. Victoria lost by an

innings and 253 runs after their second knock produced 181.

The upset of the season came in February at the Brisbane Exhibition Ground when Victoria, strengthened by the return of Ponsford, were out for 86 and were beaten by 234 runs by Queensland. Supported by some brilliant fielding, Ron Oxenham, Percy Hornibrook, Les Gill and Dr Mayes bowled splendidly. Oxenham had 4 for 18. Queensland made 399 and 439, Eric Knowles scoring 40 and 144, Ron Oxenham 104 and 73. Victoria made a wonderful effort to achieve the 753 required to win after Ponsford (116) and Hendry (137) gave them a start of 225, but they finished on 518, an impressive score for a fourth innings.

Queensland's second win of the season deprived Victoria of the Sheffield Shield and proved Queensland's worth to the competition. The Shield was decided on the basis of percentages of matches won. South Australia, which had last won the Shield in 1912–13, had a percentage of 60, Victoria and New South Wales 50, Queensland 40.

Queensland's performance caused the rules of the Shield to be altered for the 1927–28 season, so that the outcome was decided on a points basis. All four states involved had to play each other twice, whereas Queensland and South Australia had previously met only once. Points were awarded thus: four for an outright win, three for a first innings win, two each for a tie, and one for a first innings loss. To fit in the 24 matches involved, each was limited to four days, with a portion of the fifth day available if a result was possible.

In the last match of the 1926–27 season, staged for Charlie Macartney's benefit, the 1926 Australian team defeated the Rest by seven wickets. Ponsford scored 131, his sixth century in a row, Woodfull 140 (they began with a stand of 223 runs) and Andrews was not out for 115. This set up the Australian XI total of 533, in reply to the Rest's 305, of which 100 were contributed by Kippax. Jack-

Bill Ponsford (left) and Fred Yeomans after they created an Australian record for any wicket in a second wicket stand in 1926–27 against South Melbourne.

son made 32 in the Rest's second innings before he was caught and bowled by his mentor, Arthur Mailey. This gave Jackson 500 runs for the season at an average of 50.00, a wonderful effort for a lad not yet 18. Jackson also scored 870 runs that summer in 12 innings for the Balmain club, for whom he made five centuries and a 96.

O'Connor capped a satisfying season with 101 in the Rest's second innings, but the Australian XI needed only 117 to win and lost just three wickets scoring them. Ponsford completed the season with 1229 runs from 10 innings. In club cricket, Ponsford (295) playing for St Kilda created an Australian record by putting on 472 for the second wicket against South Melbourne with Fred Yeomans (186).

Macartney received £2598 from the match. Herbie Collins had to wait until 1933–34 for his benefit, which produced £500, Arthur Mailey and Johnny Taylor until 1955–56 for their joint benefit match which raised £3591. They had missed out on various ballots, had their benefits postponed several times, and endured long debates over suitable dates and venues. Their sad financial returns clearly showed the need for a better system of rewarding distinguished players.

The boy from Bowral

Bradman's first seasons 1926–28

At the start of the 1926–27 cricket season the New South Wales selectors started a concentrated search for bowling talent. The selection panel were worried about the lack of promising young bowlers and, at their suggestion, the executive committee of the New South Wales Cricket Association adopted a scheme called "Coaching For Young Bowlers", which enabled the selectors to go anywhere in the state to view youthful aspirants. The young finds would then be sent to Sydney Cricket Ground nets for special coaching by an array of former bowling greats. Mailey was seen giving Bill O'Reilly advice on his grip, which O'Reilly refused to accept.

Somebody changed the original draft, scratching out the word "bowler" and replacing it with "player". The change allowed the Association to write to 18-year-old Don Bradman in Bowral and invite him to the nets in Sydney. Bradman's bowling figures in the

RIGHT: Don Bradman at the age of 17 when his huge scoring for Bowral first started to attract the attention of cricket administrators.
FAR RIGHT: The letter that first brought Bradman from Bowral to demonstrate his batting skills in Sydney. It was sent to Alf Stephens because officials did not know Bradman's address.

NEW SOUTH WALES CRICKET ASSOCIATION

Address all Communications
to The Secretary.

Telephone: B3541.

HH/IM

254a GEORGE STREET,

SYDNEY.

5th October, 1926.

D. Bradman, Esq.,
C/o A. Stephens, Esq.,
Boolwey Street,
BOWRAL.

Dear Sir:

      The State Selectors have had under consideration
your record in cricket in the past season, and in view of
such record they particularly desire to see you in action.

      For this purpose I would like you to attend
practice at the Sydney Cricket Ground on Monday next, 11th
instant. Practice commences at 4 p.m. and continues through
out the afternoon. Should you be able to attend as requested,
please let me know in order that I may inform the Selectors
who will be on the watch for you and in order that I may
advise you as to the further particulars. My Association is
prepared to pay your fare from Bowral and return and should
you deem it necessary to remain in Sydney overnight you will
be reimbursed to the extent of your accommodation.

      I sincerely trust that you will give this matter the
consideration its importance warrants and hope that you will
realise that this is an opportunity which should not be missed.
If you will be able to attend, let me know immediately and
state the time you hope to arrive in Sydney. Should you find
it impossible to attend on the 11th, please inform me if any
other Monday in the near future would be suitable, and I will
have arrangements made accordingly.

      Yours faithfully,

SECRETARY.

1925–26 season for Bowral included 5 for 5, 5 for 10, 5 for 11, 4 for 9 and 5 for 13, so he probably would have been worth a trial anyway, but the change in the Association's minutes made it certain.

The letter, dated Tuesday, 5 October 1926, and sent by the NSWCA secretary Harold Heydon, said in part: "The State selectors have had under consideration your record in the past season, and in view of such record ... desire to see you in action."

Don Bradman regularly made centuries for Bowral, but it was his big scores which won him special attention, including 234 against Wingello and 300 against Moss Vale. In Berrima District matches in 1925–26 he scored 985 runs at 109.44 and took 51 wickets at 7.8 with his leg breaks.

Bradman travelled to Sydney with his father and went into the nets watched by state selectors A. G. Moyes, Harold ("Mudgee") Cranney, and R. L. ("Dick") Jones, who in turn conferred with Jimmy Searle. Searle was the coach who devoted himself to helping youngsters in the nets from the time he ruined his own career smashing into the fence while fielding back in 1889. C. T. B. Turner, Harry Donnan, and Dr "Ranji" Hordern were on hand to watch all the young bowlers, but immediately Bradman took strike they devoted their attention to him. There was something about the way he carried himself that suggested special talent.

"Mudgee" Cranney, who had played for New South Wales as far back as 1909–10, asked Bradman to join him in the Central Cumberland first grade side. Bradman accepted but before he could play in a match discovered that he could afford neither the time nor the expense of playing in Sydney every Saturday. Central Cumberland had no funds to pay Bradman's fares from Bowral so they had to let the invitation lapse.

On 10 November 1926, Bradman returned to Sydney to play for Possibles versus Probables. This was a one-day trial match organised by the NSWCA to help select a state side to play Queensland in Brisbane, and to uncover more bowlers. Bradman made 37 not out for the Possibles and Archie Jackson, a year younger than Bradman, scored 53 for the Probables, who won by 65 runs. This match on the main Sydney Cricket Ground pitch was the first time Bradman set foot on a first-class ground.

The *Sydney Morning Herald* was particularly impressed by the way Bradman left his crease to deal with the leg spin of J. N. Campbell, and called his display "one of the successes of the day". Bradman was not included when the state team to play Queensland was announced, but one of the selectors, "Dick" Jones, recommended to the St George club that they invite him to join the club.

Bradman returned to Sydney at the end of November to play in the annual Country Week carnival, and by that time St George had told "Dick" Jones to go ahead and arrange for him to play for the club. Without going back to Bowral, he turned out for St George at the end of the Country Week matches. On 27 November 1926, he scored 110 in 110 minutes against Petersham on Petersham Oval in his first appearance in grade cricket. The next day he made 98 for Country against City and with his 110 this earned him a place in the New South Wales Second XI.

At Bowral, in the last week in December 1926, Bradman took 8 for 36 and scored 103 (retired) for the locals against a visiting Sydney team. On New Year's Day, 1927, he made 43 for the New South Wales Second XI against Victoria's Second XI before he stepped on his own stumps, pulling a ball to the boundary from Hans Ebeling, the future Test player. On 21 and 28 May 1927—successive Saturday afternoons—he broke his own local record by scoring 320 not out for Bowral against Moss Vale in the final of the Picard Cup. He finished the season with an average

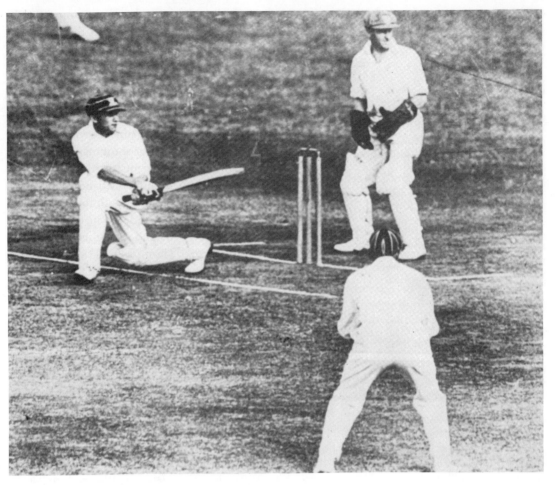

A youthful Don Bradman batting for the St George club against Gordon in the Sydney grade competition in 1926–27.

of 188.66 in the Picard Cup and the Berrima District competition.

Bradman travelled to Sydney each Saturday to play for St George at the start of the 1927–28 summer, but when the state squad was announced he was not among the 29 chosen. He also missed selection in the New South Wales side which went to Brisbane in mid-November to play Queensland in the first Shield match of the season. Rain interrupted this game and it was left drawn after Queensland scored 419 and had New South

Wales out for 167. Bill Rowe, a left-hander whose career with Queensland spanned 18 seasons, made 128 and shared in a stand of 91 with Otto Nothling (46). Eric Bensted made 44. Alec Hurwood, a medium-pace off-break bowler from the Valley club, took 5 for 50 in his initial first-class match, to give Queensland first innings points.

On 30 November came news of George Giffen's death in an Adelaide private hospital, aged 68. Until 18 months before he died Giffen, regarded by some as Australia's greatest all-rounder, appeared every morning at 6 a.m. in the Adelaide Parklands to coach small boys. He lived on his letter sorter's pension from the Post Office and on the £2020 raised from his benefit match between South Australia and

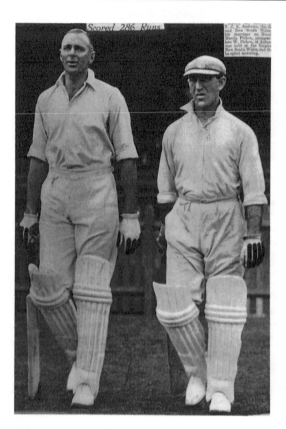

Scored 286 Runs

Before Australia toured New Zealand later in the 1927–28 season New Zealand played one match in Sydney against New South Wales. Andrews (134) (right) and Gregory (152) batted in great style to secure the match for New South Wales.

Victoria in 1922–23.

The prolific Victorian batsmen over-whelmed South Australia in Adelaide from 2 to 6 December. Victoria were 2 for 361, and declared at 8 for 646. Ponsford made 133, Hartkopf 111 out out, Hendry 168, in perfect conditions, but South Australia had to bat on a damaged pitch and made only 177 and 159. Ironmonger's left-arm slows were particu-larly effective after rain. Woodfull, surprising-ly appointed to captain Victoria ahead of Ryder, handled his bowlers skilfully.

Queensland captain Leo O'Connor sent Victoria in when he won the toss on 16 De-

cember, hoping to exploit the customary early life in the Melbourne pitch. At the end of the first day Victoria were 2 for 400 and they carried on to 793. Ponsford batted for almost two days to beat his own world record and score 437 in 621 minutes. He gave difficult chances at 162 and 239, but was always master of an attack that used nine bowlers, making his runs without fuss or showmanship, rebuk-ing himself when he mistimed a slower ball and gave Amos a caught-and-bowled oppor-tunity. Hendry's 129 went almost unnoticed.

Otto Nothling made 66 in Queensland's first innings of 189 and in the second innings of 407, Frank Thompson (118) got useful support from O'Connor (66) and Gough (54). Blackie took 6 for 46 in Queensland's first innings but could not bowl in the second because of injury. It was left to Ironmonger to do most of the work and 40.6 steady overs yielded 5 for 88, giving Victoria victory by an innings and 197 runs.

Bradman was not in the original New South Wales line-up for the southern tour, but when Hammy Love and Jack Gregory drop-ped out he and his St George clubmate Albert Scanes, a Sydney cake-maker who had first played for the state in 1921–22, replaced them. The team travelled to Adelaide on the newly opened railway line to Broken Hill, where they stopped for a match against a local side. Bradman shared in a fourth-wicket stand of 97 in his first appearance for New South Wales, scoring 46 before he was stumped. Bradman was expected to be twelfth man in Adelaide on 16 December 1927, but when Archie Jackson developed a boil on his knee he went into the side, batting at No. 7.

By scoring 118 in his first Shield match Bradman became the sixteenth Australian cricketer to score a century in his debut match. The previous 15 were Gordon-Stewart, C. Rock, O'Halloran, Pye, Morton, McPetrie, Moyes, Gooden, Hyett, Callaway, Bogle, Forssberg, Mullarkey, Wootton and H. Rock.

Don Bradman at the nets soon after he began his first-class career with New South Wales.

have New South Wales out for only 150 in their second knock. Left to score 180 to win, South Australia lost 7 for 131, thanks to fine bowling by McNamee, but Grimmett made 32 and Lee 27 not out to see them home by one wicket.

Queensland were again without Ron Oxenham when they played South Australia in Adelaide between 23 and 27 December. Their bowling failed badly against a side which included four youngsters: Albert ("Bulla") Ryan, Colin Alexander, Chris Sangster and Alf Hack, the eldest of Fred Hack's sons. South Australia made 471, Ryan top-scoring with 86, with fine support from Alexander (84), Hack (65) and Sangster (54). Queensland made 256 and had to follow on 215 behind. They managed 315 in their second attempt but could not get on top of Grimmett, whose ten wickets in the match cost less than 19 runs apiece. South Australia scored the 101 needed to win for the loss of two wickets.

At Melbourne, from 23 to 27 December, Victoria defeated New South Wales by 222 runs, largely because of Ponsford and Woodfull. Ponsford made 202 in Victoria's first innings of 355, Woodfull 99 and 191 not out in the second innings of 7 for 386. Andrews scored 110 in New South Wales' first innings of 367 but the New South Wales batsmen succumbed to Blackie in their second innings of 152. Blackie took 6 for 32. McNamee caused a dramatic Victorian collapse in Victoria's first innings by taking 7 for 77 after the opening pair had put on 227.

A week later Ponsford's big scoring continued when he made 336 in Melbourne against South Australia. Woodfull helped him put on 236 for the first wicket but hit only two boundaries in scoring 106. Ponsford hit 33 boundaries and batted for just over six hours. His only chance occurred after he had made 90. Harris, Grimmett and Lee all batted pugnaciously but South Australia never looked

Surprisingly few of these players went on to greater things.

Phillips (112) and Kippax (143) also scored centuries to take New South Wales to 519 in their first innings. Karl Schneider (108) had a partnership of 140 with Gordon Harris (77) and 128 with Vic Richardson (80) to lift the South Australian reply to 481, 30 behind. From then on the bowlers took charge of the match. First Grimmett took 8 for 57 to like avoiding the follow-on as they confronted Victoria's 637. They made 319 in their first attempt and 283 in the second to give Victoria victory by an innings and 35 runs.

Ponsford's 336 proved the climax of the most phenomenal sequence of high scores in Australian cricket. After returning from a moderately successful tour of England, he made centuries in ten successive matches. His scores in six matches in 1926–27 were 214 and 54, 151, 352, 108 and 84, 12 and 116, 131 and 7. In 1927–28, he began with 133, 437, 202 and 38, and 336, a scoring spree no batsman has matched.

Recovering magnificently after following on 363 in arrears, Queensland went close to victory when they played New South Wales from 31 December to 5 January 1928 in Sydney. Kippax compiled his highest first-class score of 315 not out and Gordon Morgan was 121 in New South Wales' first innings of 639. Queensland replied with 276, but in their second innings Rowe made 147, Thompson 68 and Roy Higgins 179. The last five wickets added 255 and Queensland reached 590. New South Wales lost eight wickets scoring the 100 needed to win, with Nothling almost causing an upset by taking 5 for 39. Bradman made his first duck and took his first wicket in first-class cricket in this match, scoring 0 and 13 and taking 2 for 49.

Archie Jackson had the distinction of scoring a century in each innings of New South Wales' match with South Australia from 6 to 10 January in Sydney. New South Wales won by 118 runs, after scoring 291 and 368, with Jackson making 131 and 122. South Australia replied with 248 and 293. Nicholls, a 192 centimetre tall bowler, captured 5 for 115 and 4 for 84 for New South Wales. Bradman contributed a handy 73 in New South Wales' second innings.

Queensland's champion Ron Oxenham started in the match against South Australia at Brisbane on 14 to 18 January, but had to retire

A young Bradman, at the time he worked as a real estate clerk in Bowral and sang in the church choir.

with pleurisy after scoring 26 in the first innings. Queensland made 143 and 351, but South Australia scored 505, to win by an innings and 11 runs. O'Connor made 133 in Queensland's second innings.

The return match between New South Wales and Victoria in Sydney from 26 to 31 January produced eight individual centuries and in four and a half days 1513 runs were scored. But Ponsford had no part of this run-riot, failing in both Victoria's innings. New South Wales began by scoring 533, which included 134 from Kippax, 110 from Morgan, 101 by Oldfield and 110 from Nicholls. Victoria replied with 422, with Hendry scoring 138 and Ryder's 106 the innings of the match.

Bradman made 134 not out in New South Wales' second innings of 8 for 353 declared. Keith Rigg ended the excitement with 110 not out in the last innings, Victoria reaching 1 for 205, still 159 short of the New South Wales two-innings total when the match was declared a draw. Ted a'Beckett took 6 for 119 in New South Wales' first innings, Don Blackie 6 for 101 in the second. Even his victims enjoyed Blackie, who had the familiar failing of never remembering people's names. He called everybody "Rock" to compensate and this became his nickname.

A feature of the match was the return of Jack Gregory, who opened the batting in both innings for New South Wales and had 4 for 81 in Victoria's first innings. Gregory was the cause of Ponsford's failure, scattering his stumps in the first innings and catching him in the slips off Nicholls in the second.

Victoria had already won the Shield when they went to Brisbane for the last match of the season against Queensland, from 3 to 7 February. Victoria made 300 in the absence through injury of Woodfull. Rowe made 134 of Queensland's first innings of 384. Rain washed out further play and the match was declared a draw, Queensland taking first innings points.

Ponsford's batting dominated the season. He scored a total of 1217 runs at an average of 152.12. Grimmett took 42 wickets and with Blackie (31 wickets from his old-fashioned finger-spin) stood out among the bowlers; but for artistry Kippax took all the honours. His 26 first-class knocks since his omission from the 1926 tour of England had yielded almost 2000 runs at an average of 85 and there appeared to be no likelihood of his remaining on the sidelines when the Tests came round again.

Ponsford developed into a complex, reticent character, suspicious of reporters. For him the most difficult part of every innings was getting past the photographers who gathered round the gate through which he went out to bat. He even pulled his bulky cap down over his face to spoil their shots and they took few good photographs of him. The cap became an indicator to his progress through his long innings. He began with the peak well down towards his brown eyes. The longer he batted, the further round the cap worked itself until it reached a rakish angle above his left ear, by which time he would be on his way to a second hundred.

Ponsford's high scoring over-shadowed everything in the 1927–28 season, including the emergence as batsmen of rich potential of Archie Jackson and Don Bradman. They were often compared because of their youth and the fact that they appeared at the same time, but they had little in common in either batting technique or temperament. Their only link was that they both came from British migrant stock, but in their own way they were to win unique niches in Australian cricket, which had officials queueing up to claim the honour of having discovered them.

Jackson, born at Rutherglen in Scotland, was the son of penniless migrants who settled in the Balmain district of Sydney. He was always a slight figure who looked in need of a good meal. Dr H. V. ("Doc") Evatt paid Archie's annual club subscription and weekly ground fees, and those of his school-mate Bill Hunt, so they could turn out for the Balmain district club. Jackson was an unashamed admirer of Alan Kippax's graceful style and many were reminded of Kippax when they saw him bat. Within two seasons of winning a place in the New South Wales side, Jackson's shot-making had old-timers comparing him with Victor Trumper.

Bradman had the same lovely foot-work as Jackson, but his strokes were more controlled and predictable. He found gaps in the field with unerring accuracy, but did not have to produce anything unorthodox to do so. On that first trip to Adelaide he had fallen victim

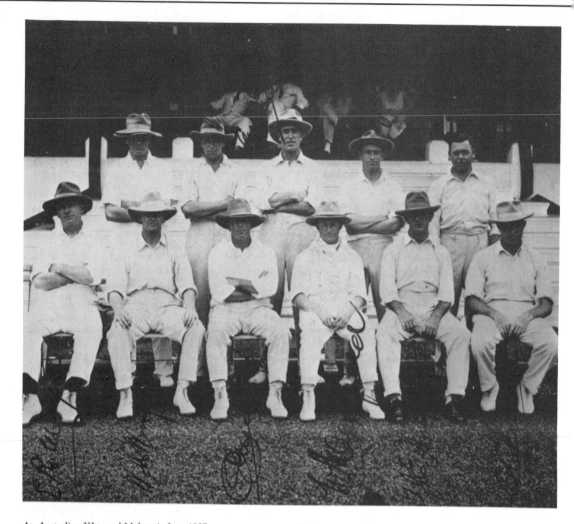

An Australian XI toured Malaya in June 1927 playing only two matches, the first at Kuala Lumpur where they lost by 39 runs, and the return match at the Singapore Cricket Club where they won by an innings and 136 runs. The team included six Test players: (L to R) (seated) E. Mayne, W. Woodfull, C. Macartney, W. Oldfield, T. Andrews, S. Everett.

to the noted prankster Halford Hooker, who kidded him into playing the piano to build up his back muscles. Once Hooker had Bradman at the piano at the team's hotel he challenged the young leg spinner Hughie Chilvers to dance as fast as Bradman could play.

Don Bradman showed the same con-fidence at the piano as in his batting. There was something bright and infectious about him which excited hardened cricket watchers. People who saw him and Archie Jackson chasing the ball at practice said they were like a pair of playful puppies.

There was another remarkable teenaged prodigy in action in 1927 and 1928— Richard Terry, who captained the First XI at The King's School, Parramatta. Terry, a right-hand opening batsman, had innings of 122 and 106 in 1927, and in 1928 had a sequence of 215 not out, 136 not out, 135, 203 not out, 121, and 101. In the two rounds of the 1928 Great Public Schools' competition, Terry made 1225 runs at an average of 102.10. Unlike

Bill Ponsford with the bat many bowlers thought was wider than the laws of cricket permitted. He made a habit of taking a fresh guard after scoring each hundred.

Bradman and Jackson, Terry chose to forsake his cricket career and went to work on his father's property, Dennistone, at Breeda, New South Wales. A few months after leaving school he was burnt to death in an accident on the property.

Archie Jackson was chosen to go to New Zealand at the end of the 1927–28 season with a team of Australian hopefuls captained by Vic Richardson. The side had a sprinkling of proven internationals in Woodfull, Kippax,

Ponsford, Oldfield and Grimmett, backed by a group of players pressing for places in the Australian team like Jackson, Ron Oxenham, Blackie, McNamee, Morton, Alexander and Karl Schneider, who, at 157 centimetres, was the smallest first-class cricketer in Australia. Bradman was left at home as a possible replacement.

The Australians began by defeating Wellington by four wickets at the end of February. Into March they continued with wins over Canterbury, by nine wickets, Auckland by an innings and 40 runs, Taranaki by an innings and 177 runs, Wanganui by an innings and 213 runs, and New Zealand, at Dunedin, by seven wickets. They played draws with Nelson, North Otago, Otago, Southland, North Island, Poverty Bay and New Zealand at Auckland.

Woodfull headed the batting averages with 864 runs at 86.40, but Ponsford made more runs, 915 at 63.35. Nine of the 13 players on the tour, which was managed by "Billy" Bull, scored centuries. Grimmett was hailed everywhere as a returning hero and was largely responsible for the side's unbeaten record, taking 74 wickets at 13.86. Blackie was the next highest wicket-taker, with 38 at 16.10. Woodfull had partnerships of 184 with Ponsford and 218 with Schneider in the match against a New Zealand XI in Auckland, finishing with 284, the highest individual score of the tour. Woodfull also made 165 against Wellington and 107 against Otago. Ponsford scored three centuries, 148 against Otago, 110 against Southland, and 101 against Wanganui.

Karl Schneider scored 547 runs at 45.58 on the tour, but six months after he returned to Australia he died of leukemia. Towards the end of the New Zealand trip he was horse-riding on the slopes of Mount Cook with a group of players when he began to haemorrhage. Team-mates carried him to a hut, where he revived. Archie Jackson's family believed that Jackson contracted tuberculosis from this incident but there was no substance to the story.

While Vic Richardson's team toured New Zealand, an England team, captained by R. T. Stanyforth, visited South Africa. The team were without established players Hobbs, Hendren, Tate, Larwood, Jardine and Chapman, but it gave England a way to provide experience for rising stars like Wally Hammond, Ian Peebles and Bob Wyatt. England won the first two Tests, drew the second, and surprisingly lost the last two to share the series.

Hammond was one of the English side who failed to show his potential with the bat, but he filled in splendidly when Geary broke down, bowling accurately on the mat with a lot of nip from the pitch. Ernest Tyldesley headed England's batting averages with 1130 runs at 59.47, including four centuries. Tyldesley followed up this good form by scoring 122 in the first Test against the West Indies in the 1928 English summer. He finished second to Hobbs in the batting averages for this series. England won all three Tests, with Hobbs averaging 106.00 at the age of 46.

"Tich" Freeman was England's leading wicket-taker in both South Africa and at home against the West Indies. This undoubtedly won him a place in the team that toured Australia in 1928–29, despite his failure on England's 1924–25 Australian tour. Indeed his taking 22 West Indian wickets in three Tests convinced English critics that they should forget Freeman's form on Australian pitches. Some even hailed him as a potential match-winner, comparing his figures with those of Grimmett, Mailey, Blackie, Ironmonger and Hartkopf.

Percy Chapman, who captained the 1928–29 party, by then had become the most popular cricketer in England, an adventurous spirit whose batting, bowling and fielding could swing a match, and a captain who could cleverly match his resources against those of

The tragic Karl Schneider, star of the 1928 Australian team's tour of New Zealand, who died soon after returning home, aged only 23.

his opponents. Chapman was always worth the price of admission on his own, for he never let a game become dull. He was extremely agile, with a spring in his gait unexpected in such a huge man, a dogged fighter, and responsible for some of the biggest sixes seen in England since the days of Australia's George Bonnor.

With Chapman as England's captain the series in Australia seemed certain to provide thrills galore. To support him, the Marylebone Cricket Club sent W. R. Hammond, D. R. Jardine, E. Hendren, L. E. G. Ames, J. B. Hobbs, H. Sutcliffe, M. Leyland, C. P. Mead, E. Tyldesley, H. Larwood, M. W. Tate, G. Geary, J. C. White, G. Duckworth, S. J. Staples and A. P. Freeman. Ames and Duckworth were the new wicket-keepers, and like Leyland, Mead, Tyldesley, Larwood, Geary, Staples and White were on their first Australian tour.

Before it sailed in the *Otranto*, the England

team was acclaimed as the strongest the MCC had sent abroad in the 1900s, strong in every phase of cricket, and with every specialist Test position filled by a proven performer. The unknown factor was how the side would handle the Australian wickets, which had undergone radical change. The preparation of capital city pitches had been taken to such perfection that batsmen enjoyed a marked advantage and only exceptional bowling, or stupid mistakes by batsmen, could turn a match. As well as the "shirt-front" strips, another daunting prospect for the England bowlers was the thought of long hours in the Australian sun. The only exception to a series which appeared to heavily favour batsmen could be at the Brisbane Exhibition Ground, where the rubber would begin with the first Test ever staged in Queensland.

Most of Queensland's important matches had been played at the Brisbane Cricket Ground at Woolloongabba, but from 1923–24 interstate matches were played at the Gabba and the Exhibition Ground in rotation because crowd facilities and appointments were superior at the Exhibition. A sub-committee comprising Clem Hill, Harry Rush and Syd Smith reported to the Board of Control that they could not find fault with amenities at the Exhibition Ground, but expressed the view that the pitch would not last for four or five days' continuous play.

This adverse judgement delayed the staging of a Test in Brisbane even after the Queensland Cricket Association convened a public meeting to appoint a Test match committee. The committee comprised the Hon. (later Chief Justice) J. W. Blair, J. N. Norton, George Down, J. S. Hutcheon, R. J. Hartigan, A. D. Graham, J. W. Fletcher MLA, A. Faulkner (mayor of South Brisbane), F. L. South, G. W. Ward, W. H. Henley, E. H. Hutcheon, J. R. Lendrum, T. McWilliam, E. J. D. Stanley, H. J. Diddam (mayor of Brisbane) and E. J. Lugg. They all pledged to work unceasingly until Queensland received a Test.

The change from the Gabba to the Exhibition Ground did not help Queensland bowlers such as Percy Hornibrook and Jack McAndrew, who found their nip from the pitch reduced, but visiting batsmen praised the new wicket. Doubts about the Exhibition Ground pitch lasting the extra days of a Test remained, however, even after the committee took delivery of the soil specially selected by the curator of the Melbourne Cricket Ground, Bert Luttrell.

A stranger to captaincy

The Test series in Australia 1928–29

Unlike early Australian tours by English teams preoccupied over tour bonuses, who trusted to luck with hotels, transport and the make-up of opposing sides, the 1928–29 tour was planned like a military operation. No detail was missed. Every hotel which housed the team on the five-and-a-half month, 80,000-kilometre tour was approved at Lord's. An expert masseur went with the team. The manager, Frederick Toone, dealt with a mountain of data before the players sailed, approving social appearances and assessing every offer of hospitality. On a journey which involved spending 30 nights in trains, he became an expert on Australian railway time-tables. Every day he checked on the players' health. No illness nor injury escaped him.

When the important matches came round, England's organisation proved invaluable. Australian administrators, in contrast, were slow to acknowledge the claims of the rising generation of gifted players of which Brad-

The Australian team for the second Test of the 1928–29 series: (L to R) (back) W. Woodfull, W. Ponsford, H. Ironmonger, D. Blackie, O. Nothling, H. Hendry; (front) V. Richardson, C. Grimmett, J. Ryder (captain), D. Bradman, W. Oldfield, A. Kippax. Bradman was twelfth man.

man and Jackson were the outstanding representatives. They were loath to accept that
cricketers who had served Australia well for
years were now past their prime. They may
have been led astray, of course, by the performance of Jack Hobbs, who, in his forty-
sixth year, remained nimble, alert and exciting
to watch, but Hobbs was no ordinary cricketer.

For the first time the MCC departed from
its habit of asking its general committee to
select the players to go to Australia, and instead appointed a panel made up of Lord
Harris (chairman), J. W. H. T. Douglas, P. F.
Warner, A. E. R. Gilligan, F. T. Mann, and
H. D. G. Leveson-Gower, all of them students of Australian conditions. The side they
picked was still criticised. It had only one
proven all-rounder, Tate, and a comparatively
inexperienced captain in Chapman. Woolley,
Hallows and Holmes, who had strong claims,
were left at home.

Advised by his canny professionals,
Chapman was to make fools of his critics.
From the start he set a superb example. Fielding at short mid-off he cut off dozens of firmly hit strokes in every match, and with Hobbs
ready to swoop on anything that got through,
England restricted scoring on the off side.
Inspired by their captain, the England team
produced undreamt-of fielding displays and
did not drop a catch in five Tests. Tips from
Hobbs helped Chapman cleverly judge bowling changes and big-match batting orders.

The Englishman left home in two groups
and almost immediately had a setback. Sam
Staples, the Nottinghamshire off spinner, was
kitted out, photographed with the team, and
sailed with one group in the *Moldavia*, only to
be stricken with back muscle trouble and confined to bed. Within a month he returned to
England at his own request without playing in

*Jack Hobbs as he looked to Australian bowlers,
relaxed and crisis-proof.*

a match, leaving his side a bowler short. Staples, one of the last slow bowlers to occasionally open a first-class attack, would have been very useful, as he took 1331 wickets in his career and made 6470 runs.

Australia had more than one replacement to worry about. Collins, Bardsley, Macartney, Taylor, Mailey and Arthur Richardson were missing from the team that had lost only one match in England in 1926. Taylor had left to concentrate on his dental practice, Arthur Richardson to take up his job as coach to the Western Australian Cricket Association, and Mailey to full-time journalism after a dispute with the Board of Control; the rest had simply had enough.

Most of the officials who had provoked the 1912 confrontation with the leading players had retired from office, but some of those on the Board in 1928 objected when Mailey's newspaper comments condemned Board decisions and questioned the qualification of Board members with no experience as cricketers. Forced to stop writing about matches in which he often starred, Mailey chose a career in journalism, writing and drawing cartoons.

He went out with 99 wickets in 21 Tests. For Australia his best figures were 10 for 66 *v.* Gloucestershire in 1921, and in Tests 9 for 121 against England in 1920–21. For New South Wales his best analysis was 8 for 81 the same season against Victoria. In all first-class matches he took 10 wickets in a match 16 times and five wickets in an innings 61 times. He always regarded his cricket as a bit of fun and said of his bowling: "At times I am attacked by waves of accuracy, and I don't trust them."

Mailey brought to the press box an approach as individual as his bowling. He believed many cricket writers were far too solemn about their work and he once invited his colleagues watching a match to join him in a hymn. For almost three decades the administrators of Australian cricket denied him the testimonial he richly deserved. Finally, in the 1955–56 season, the New South Wales Cricket Association gave him and Johnny Taylor a benefit match in Sydney. During the luncheon interval, these two old men went out to the middle and Mailey, who turned 70 on 3 January 1956, bowled a ball to Taylor which scattered the stumps.

The 1928–29 England team included one wonderful character to whom Mailey responded warmly, the much-battered Leicestershire fast bowler George Geary, one of 16 children of a bootmaker and his wife. Geary, who had been struck by an aircraft propellor during the First World War, had his nose smashed in the first match of the tour, which was held in Perth from 18 to 20 October 1928. Officials did not have a stretcher so they carried Geary off on a kitchen table. He did not play for a month.

Only two days after landing in Fremantle, England did extremely well to score 406 in the first innings of the match. Arthur Richardson, who had just taken up his WACA job, tried seven bowlers but could not stop the flow of runs to Ernest Tyldesley (66), Jardine (109) and Hendren (90). Western Australia replied with 257, thanks to sound knocks by Frank Bryant (61) and the Lancashire-born right-hander, Bill Horrocks (75 not out). Geary was hurt in England's second innings of 1 for 26.

Meanwhile in Melbourne four Queenslanders, Nothling, Oxenham, Thompson and O'Connor, appeared in a Test trial, Australia versus the Rest, designed to help the Australian selectors. Only Oxenham made any impression by taking 10 wickets in the match. The Australian XI won in the three days between 19 to 22 October by an innings and 43 runs. Ponsford's 79 for the Australians was the top score in a desultory affair.

After a four-day train trip to Adelaide, England played a high-scoring draw with South Australia from 26 to 30 October.

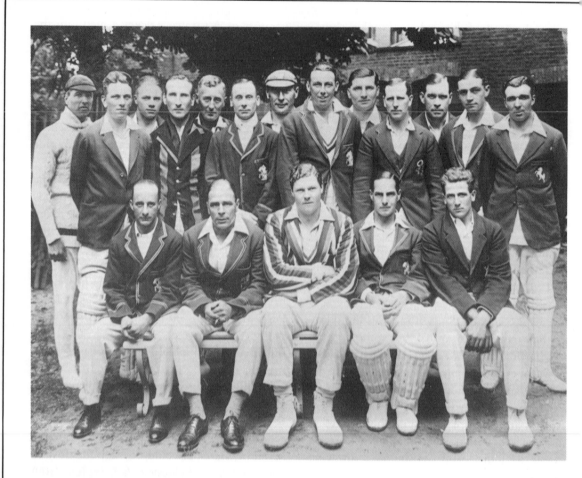

The 1928–29 England team in Australia: (L to R)
(back) masseur (unnamed), M. Leyland,
G. Duckworth, D. Jardine, J. White, J. Hobbs,
C. Mead, M. Tate, S. Staples, E. Tyldesley,
E. Hendren, W. Hammond, L. Ames; (front)
A. Freeman, G. Geary, A. Chapman (captain),
H. Sutcliffe, H. Larwood.

Hammond and Chapman both scored 145, Hammond with splendid strokes all round the wicket, Chapman with lusty hitting that enabled him to take 18 off one over from Grimmett and 16 from an over by Harry Whitfield. Grimmett had the last four England wickets for 39 runs to finish with 6 for 109, England scoring 528.

Critics under-rated the England bowling from the time South Australia made 524 in reply. Vic Richardson batted brilliantly for 231 and was involved in a second-wicket stand with David Pritchard of 255 runs in 180 minutes. Richardson hooked Larwood for six, hit 27 fours, and at one period made 26 in seven strokes. Freeman took five wickets but they cost 180 runs. Hobbs and Sutcliffe hit up 131 in 75 minutes when England batted a second time. In the closing stages of the match Maurice Leyland, who had waited eight years for a place in the England team, scored 114, his first century in Australia, through some glorious driving and cutting. England were 4 for 341 when time ran out, after 1400 runs had been scored for the loss of only 24 wickets.

Larwood found that occasional showers suited his bowling, by helping the ball skid, in the drawn match at Melbourne against Vic-

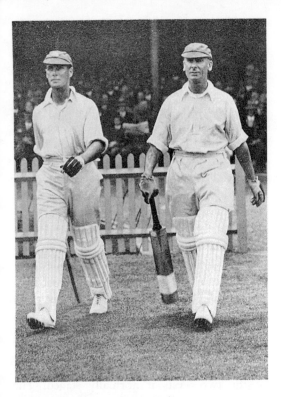

The superb England opening pair, Herbert Sutcliffe, left, and Jack Hobbs, continued their valuable form in the 1928–29 series in Australia, which England won 4–1.

toria from 1 to 5 November. He took the first seven Victorian wickets, including three in four balls, before Chapman took him off. He was bowling so well onlookers thought he might have taken all 10 wickets had he continued. Only Woodfull, who made 67 not out and carried his bat through Victoria's innings of 164, made regular contact against Larwood.

England again proved their run-getting prowess by scoring 486 in reply. Jardine opened with Hobbs and scored 104, showing rare skill off the back foot. Hendren stroked the ball to all corners of the field for an even 100 before he was run out; Chapman (71) hit with tremendous power in a 93-run stand with Larwood, who was out for 79 when a century seemed likely. Woodfull (74 not out)

and Ponsford (60 not out) added 135 in steady rain when Victoria batted a second time.

England's heavy scoring continued in Sydney from 9 to 13 November in the match with New South Wales. Hammond treated fans who had not seen him before to a wonderful display of his talent, top-scoring with 225 in an impressive total of 7 for 734 declared. Jardine and Sutcliffe added 148 for the first wicket and after Sutcliffe was out for 67, Jardine went on to his third successive tour century. Jardine, a cold, authoritarian figure with a stiff, upright stance in which he held the bat well away from his legs, went on to 140. A partnership of 333 between Hammond and Hendren followed, the highest for any wicket against New South Wales.

Hendren hit Bradman twice over the sight-screen for six and was caught trying for a third with his score on 167. Hammond batted for five and a half hours and hit a six and 30 fours; his driving through the covers was so profitable that Herbie Collins said he could not understand why New South Wales captain Alan Kippax did not position a man at deep extra cover to cut off the boundaries.

If Hendren and Hammond had made their hits over the fence in Sydney grade cricket that summer they would have been rewarded with eight for each hit, a rule change the NSWCA tried for one season in an unsuccessful effort to produce brighter cricket. The temptation to score eights failed to increase the number of hefty blows that connected.

New South Wales lost 3 for 38 before Kippax, Bradman and Kelleway rescued the innings with some outstanding batting. Kippax was lbw to Hammond for 64, Bradman bowled by Freeman for 87 and Kelleway remained unbeaten on 93. Following on 385 behind, New South Wales were 3 for 115 at lunch on the last day, but did not lose another wicket. Kippax was 136 not out, Bradman 132 not out, when time ran out. Their stand had yielded 249.

England had their first tour win at Sydney in the match against an Australian XI from 16 to 20 November. The Australian XI was drawn almost entirely from South Australia and New South Wales, with the exception of the Queensland fast-medium bowler Otto Nothling. Tommy Andrews looked promising until "Farmer" White deceived him with his pace and trajectory for 39. Bradman batted well for 58 not out and Reg Bettington, who had returned to Australia in the same ship as the Englishmen after eight fruitful years in England, cut with style for a handy 34. White bowled 28 overs for 47 runs with scarcely a bad ball.

Three English wickets fell for 112 before Phil Mead and Ernest Tyldesley put on 122 in an hour of excellent batting. Mead made 58, Tyldesley 69. Tate and Geary then added 76 and England reached 357. Jackson made 61 in aggressive fashion in New South Wales' second knock before he was out to a magnificent leg-side catch by Duckworth. England required only 118 to win, and with Hobbs scoring 67 in his most entertaining style, got them for the loss of only two wickets.

All the English players were now in splendid form and they took less than three days to defeat Queensland by an innings and

Brisbane's first-ever Test. The scene at the Exhibition Ground during the first Test of the 1928–29 series. Cricket later made its Brisbane headquarters at Woolloongabba.

17 runs between 24 and 27 November in Brisbane. The spinners Freeman and White proved Queensland's downfall, taking 13 wickets between them, and Geary carried on the attack by taking 5 for 47 in Queensland's second innings. Queensland made 116 and 160, England 293. Leyland, missed four times, scored 114 with some splendid cuts and off-drives. John Litster, a right-hander from Townsville, was the only Queenslander to impress with the bat, hitting nine fours in his 59.

England's tour selection committee—Chapman, White, Jardine, Hobbs and Tyldesley—sat long into the night before deciding on the team for the first Test, at Brisbane's Exhibition Ground, from 30 November to 5 December. The decision to hold a Test in Brisbane, passed by twelve votes to one at a Board of Control meeting the previous September, meant that New South Wales lost one of the two Tests it normally staged. The decision aroused angry protests in Sydney, where the NSWCA delegates to the Board were strongly denounced.

In Brisbane, the arrival of Test cricket was seen as a great victory for the state's Board delegates Jack Hutcheon and Roger Hartigan. Not only did they win Test match status for Queensland but they succeeded in having the composition of the Australian selection committee altered. Hartigan urged the Board to rescind a 1907 resolution that said the selection panel must comprise one representative each

FIRST TEST MATCH
PHOTO TAKEN 1·12·28.
ATTENDANCE 24442.
GATE MONEY £1261·0·5.

BIRTH   E   22008

BIRTH in the District of   MORETON WEST   in the Colony of Queensland,

1 882   Registered by   Michael O'Malley

Column 1 Number	5042	2354
CHILD		
2. When and where born	7th April 1882 Pine Mountain	
3. Name	Herbert	
4. Sex	Male	
PARENTS		
Father—		
5 1. Name and surname of father	Francis William IRONMONGER	
2. Profession, trade or occupation	Farmer	
3. Age	48 years	
4. Birthplace	Derby Derbyshire England	
6. Issue—living and deceased	Living years	
	Sarah Matilda 21 Edwards Eli 4	
	Frederick 19	
	Rachel 12	
	Alfred 10	
	Francis Henry 6	
	Deceased	
	1 Male 1 Female	
Mother—		
7 1. Name and maiden surname of mother	Caroline Matilda formerly Norris	
2. Age	40 years	
3. Birthplace	Northampton England	
INFORMANT	Certified in writing by	
8. Signature, description, and residence of informant	F.W.Ironmonger, Father Pine Mountain	
WITNESS		
9 1. Medical attendant		
2. Nurse		
3. Other witness to birth	Mrs Rossiter	
REGISTRAR		
10 1. Signature of Registrar	M.O'Malley	
2. Date 3. Place of registration	22nd May 1882 at Ipswich	
11. Name, added after registration of birth		

I,   Colin James Green   , Registrar-General, do hereby certify that the above is a true copy of an entry in a register kept in the General Registry Office, Brisbane.

Extracted on   14th March 1988

Registrar-General.

Exd. by

N.B.   Not Valid Unless Bearing the Authorised Seal and Signature of the Registrar-General.

CAUTION:—Whosoever shall unlawfully alter any Certified Copy of an entry in any Register of Births, Marriages, or Deaths, whether by erasure, obliteration, removal, addition, or otherwise, is guilty of a CRIME, and is liable to the punishment by law provided in that behalf. (Vide Sections 486 and 488 of the "Criminal Code.")

Bert Ironmonger claimed he was 41 when making his Test debut but as his birth certificate shows he was really 46 years old.

from New South Wales, Victoria and South Australia, and to add Queensland to the list. Thus selectors of the Test teams for the 1928–29 competition were Warren Bardsley (New South Wales), Ernie Bean (Victoria), Dr C. E. Dolling (South Australia), and Jack Hutcheon (Queensland). When they met, Bean ignored visual assessment and instead consulted his little black book which was crammed with statistics.

The Australian team included Don Bradman, who went into the side for the first time three months after his twentieth birthday, and Bert Ironmonger, who claimed he was 41, but was really 46. This made him the oldest Australian cricketer to make a first Test appearance, a record that only lasted for a fortnight until Don Blackie played his first Test at the age of 46 years 253 days. Bradman had won his place after only nine first-class matches. The team was led by Jack Ryder, who looked at his first Test line-up of Woodfull, Ponsford, Kippax, Hendry, Kelleway, Bradman, Oldfield, Grimmett, Ironmonger and Gregory, and immediately began pleading for another fast bowler.

England gambled heavily by going into the match with only four regular bowlers, preferring to strengthen the batting. They failed to find a place for Geary, who bowled impressively in the lead-up matches, and left out Freeman, relying heavily on Hammond to provide support for Larwood, Tate and White.

Luck was with England, and, aided by the weather, a tragic injury suffered by Jack Gregory and the illness of Charles Kelleway, the match created consternation in Australian cricket. Ten of the Australian team looked capable of scoring runs—Ironmonger was the only duffer—but they paid a high price for depending on a side in which 33-year-old Gregory was the youngest bowler.

England won the toss but were slowly into their stride. Sutcliffe was well caught by Ponsford at deep fine leg off a firmly hit shot, Bradman's speedy footwork and throwing ran out Hobbs, and Grimmett fooled Mead lbw. Hammond and Jardine put on 53. Hammond was let off at 155 when Oldfield missed stumping him off Grimmett, but fell six runs later for 44. Jardine and Hendren then added 56 but when Jardine went at 217, England were not well placed on 5 for 217.

Hendren, spirits lifted by the bold hitting of Chapman, batted superbly and through useful partnerships with Chapman (50), Tate (26), Larwood (70) and White (14) was last out with England's score on 521. Hendren's 169 took five hours and included 16 fours. Larwood hit a six, a five and 7 fours. White's

"Patsy" Hendren cover driving in the first Test of the 1928–29 series at Brisbane during his innings of 169.

contribution came out of a stand of 52.

In the first over of Australia's innings Woodfull snicked Larwood between Hendren, at third slip, and Chapman, in the gully. The ball flew at terrific speed off the bat and was next seen in Chapman's outstretched left hand. His leap took him into Hendren's lap, in what Harry Altham described in his book, *History of Cricket*, as one of the finest catches ever seen on a cricket field. "The fear of its repetition had a disturbing effect on the Australians whenever they faced Larwood or Tate."

Larwood made it 2 for 7 by bowling Ponsford with the second ball of his third over, and Tate took it to 3 for 24 by holding a return catch from Kippax. The calamitous first hour of Australia's innings ended with Larwood bowling Kelleway, with the score on 40.

At this stage it became known that Gregory's Test career was over, because of a recurrence of his cartilage trouble. In *Big Cricket*, "Patsy" Hendren described how Gregory limped into the English dressing room "the picture of misery". He looked round at the English players and said: "Boys, I'm finished. Never again shall I bowl you out." The tears were streaming down his face.

With Gregory out of the game Australia scored only 122. Bradman, in a tough Test introduction, was lbw to Tate's slower ball for 18. Ryder, captaining Australia for the first time, tried desperately to hold out but after 83 minutes of sound defence hit out and mis-hit a long hop straight to Jardine. Larwood had taken 6 for 32, his Test career best and Australia were dismissed in just under two and a half hours.

England batted on, despite a first innings lead of 399. Kelleway was suffering an attack of food poisoning, which prevented him from fielding and left Australia a bowler short, and Australia used two substitute fieldsmen, Ron Oxenham and Frank Thompson. Ironmonger bowled 50 overs, 20 of them maidens, to take 2 for 85, Grimmett 44.1 overs to take 6 for 131, but all the England batsmen made runs against the badly handicapped Australian attack. Mead top-scored with 73, Jardine made an impressive 65 not out, and Hendren took his match total to 214 with a solid 45.

Bert Oldfield brilliantly stumps England captain Percy Chapman, at Brisbane in 1928–29, but the dismissal went into the scorebook as caught because Chapman had first snicked the ball.

Chapman's declaration at 8 for 342 was a first for either side in an Australian Test, and set Australia the mammoth task of scoring 742 to win. With only six runs scored, Ponsford was out in the second over of the innings, caught by Duckworth, and bad light ended play for the day with Australia 1 for 17. There was heavy rain overnight and next morning bright sunshine converted the pitch into a classic sticky.

With the two invalids unable to bat, Australia's last six wickets fell in only 50 minutes, and England won by a massive 675 runs. Bradman, who had never seen a sticky wicket before, made only one before he was caught by Chapman off "Farmer" White, who finished with 4 for 7. As Bradman walked off, Tate called to White, "What do you mean by stealing my rabbit?", a comment Tate no doubt regretted when Bradman became better known to England's bowlers.

The arguments about the Brisbane pitch lasting were forgotten with the rain and

ENGLAND 1ST INNINGS.		5 2 1
ENGLAND 2ND INNINGS		3 4 2
FALL OF WICKETS 7 F		6 6

· BOWLERS ·	WKTS	RUNS
1 LARWOOD	2	3 0
2 TATE	2	2 6
3 WHITE	4	7
4 HAMMOND		2
5 JARDINE		
6 HENDREN		
7 CHAPMAN		
8 HOBBS		
9 SUTCLIFFE		
10 MEAD		
11 DUCKWORTH		

AUST. 1ST INNINGS.		1 2 2
AUST. 2ND INNINGS.		
		6 6

· BATSMEN ·		SCORES
1 PONSFORD	C 1	6
2 WOODFULL		3 0
3 KIPPAX	C 1	1 5
4 HENDRY	C 3	6
5 RYDER	C 2	1
6 BRADMAN	C 3	1
7 OLDFIELD	C 2	5
8 GRIMMETT	C 3	1
9 IRONMONGER	C 3	
10 KELLEWAY		
11 GREGORY		
SUNDRIES		1
TOTAL		6 6

The scoreboard for Brisbane's first Test. Australia were dismissed for only 66 in the second innings to lose by 675 runs, Bradman contributing 18 and 1 in his Test debut.

Queensland escaped much criticism of her first Test. The teams were surprised by the barbed wire barriers to contain the crowds, and the fact that they had dressing rooms with partitions so thin they could hear almost every word the opposition said. Facilities for spectators and pressmen remained primitive for years. People who arrived without their own provisions usually went home hungry and thirsty and for the players it was inevitably corned beef and salad every day for lunch.

The only people to be fed and watered in style were the Queensland Cricket Association members and their guests.

It was a big season for Queensland because in February 1929 they beat South Australia for the first time. The win was the result of an overthrow. Grimmett dropped a catch from Levy which would have won the match and he threw the ball away in disgust. Queensland sneaked a run and won by one wicket.

England took only a day and a half to defeat a Combined Queensland Country XI at Warwick by an innings and 169 runs between 8 and 10 December. Tyldesley and Hammond made dashing centuries, Sutcliffe, Leyland and Duckworth hit out freely and effectively, and Freeman sealed the triumph by taking 8 for 32 and 7 for 74. Queensland Country scored 128 and 213, England 510.

These were critical days in Bradman's career. A few months before he had left his family home in Bowral to settle in Sydney, taking a job as secretary to the newly opened Sydney office of his Bowral employer, real estate agent Percy Westbrook. Mr and Mrs Frank Cush generously invited him to stay in their home at Frederick Street, Rockdale, ending any doubts about his eligibility to play for St George under the residential rule that applied for all Sydney grade players. He made 106 not out for St George against Gordon at Chatswood, and followed with 131 and 133 not out for New South Wales against Queensland. His century (132 not out) for New South Wales against England had clinched his first Test spot.

The selectors made Bradman twelfth man for the second Test from 14 to 20 December in Sydney, and brought in Vic Richardson, Otto Nothling and Don Blackie. Gregory and Kelleway disappeared from Test cricket. Warren Bardsley, the only selector with Test experience, said he opposed Bradman's omission, but was outvoted three to one. England did not risk going into a Test again with only three bowlers plus Hammond. Geary, fully recovered from his Perth experience, came in for Mead and played out the series.

In the days preceding the second Test the *Sydney Sun* organised what they called a "Birthday Fund For Hobbs", who was to turn 46 during the match. A world record crowd of 58,456 turned up to see him presented with his birthday cheque. This remained, in 1988, the biggest crowd to watch Test cricket in Sydney. Hobbs went round the outfield to the applause of the crowd who had given a shilling each towards his present, a tribute he never forgot. Before the series was over Australians were to see how richly he deserved the accolade "The Master".

Ryder won the toss and Woodfull and Richardson put on 50 for Australia in the first hour, but when Larwood returned for his second spell he bowled Richardson. Fourteen runs later a ball from Geary cannoned off Kippax's pads from outside his leg stump. With the bails on the ground, Kippax stood firm, believing that the ball had rebounded off wicket-keeper Duckworth's pads. Duckworth denied this. At the bowler's end umpire George Hele called "Over" but umpire David Elder, at square leg, gave Kippax out, believing the ball had curled in off Kippax's pads onto the stumps. Duckworth's stentorian appeals already had aroused the crowd's anger and they gave him the full treatment as Kippax left the field. Larwood said later the barrackers were right, but the *Sydney Morning Herald*'s report said that Elder was right.

There was ill-feeling between Kippax and the English players over the incident, but the happy relations that existed among the players were quickly restored. Australia's ill luck with injuries continued when soon after lunch Ponsford turned his ample backside to a shortish delivery from Larwood. The ball failed to rise as high as he had expected and it broke a small bone in his left hand. He took no further part in the rubber.

Hendry justified his selection with a 77-run stand with Woodfull but when both were dismissed, only a plucky knock of 41 not out from Oldfield enabled Australia to make 253. Woodfull's 68 was a typically unexciting effort that ended when Geary had him lbw. Chapman changed bowlers shrewdly and none of the five men who bowled allowed Australia to dictate the scoring. Geary's 5 for 35 was an outstanding stint.

Grimmett appeared to have the measure of the English batsmen as he and Ironmonger combined well for a long period, but Hammond and Jardine gradually wore them down. An attractive partnership by Hammond and Hendren then added 145. After Blackie had

The second Test incident which caused ill-feeling between the England and Australian teams in 1928–29. Kippax was given out bowled by the square leg umpire, after the umpire at the bowler's end called "Over". Kippax believed the ball came off wicket-keeper Duckworth's pads onto the stumps.

Hendren cleverly caught close in by Richardson, Chapman, Larwood and Geary all gave Hammond great support. Hammond batted for 7 hours 41 minutes altogether and included 30 fours in his 251. Twelfth man Bradman fielded throughout England's innings of 636, and was on the ground for a total of 11 hours during the match because of Ponsford's injury. Years later Don Bradman said he had heard that when the selectors were undecided about who would be twelfth man, Ryder remarked, "Well, the little fellow has a lot of time ahead of him".

Richardson's fielding at silly point and in the covers to the most powerful strokes from Hammond, Chapman and Hendren caused the *Sydney Morning Herald* to run an editorial on him the next morning. Headed "Is Richardson Human?", it went on, "If we were Greeks and staged Test cricket as our Olympics, Richardson would be a demi-god this morning, with precedence over satyrs and other earth gods."

Richardson came down to earth, however, when Australia batted a second time—he was out first ball. With Australia a man short, and one wicket gone without a run on the board, Hendry and Woodfull staged a marvellous fight-back, adding 215. Larwood gave Hendry many anxious moments, but he hung on to score 112. Then Woodfull, who had seen one of his shots rebound onto the stumps without removing the bails, ran himself out for 111. Ryder ensured that England had to bat again with a robust 79, Australia's innings ending at 397. England only had to score 15 to win but lost the wickets of Geary and Tate doing so. Bradman executed a splendid catch to get rid of Tate, who had

Bradman in the unusual role of drinks waiter in the second Test in 1928–29. Later Ponsford hurt his hand and Bradman fielded.

bowled 46 overs to finish with 4 for 99 in Australia's second innings, a wonderful display of accuracy.

Between the second and third Tests, England's team played a light-hearted two-day match against a Newcastle and Hunter District XI in Newcastle. The game was declared drawn after Newcastle and Hunter scored 9 for 350 and England made 281 in

reply. Reg Bettington enjoyed himself, scoring a breezy 53 and taking 4 for 96 with his leg breaks.

Bradman returned for the third Test in place of the injured Ponsford, Ted a'Beckett replaced Nothling as the medium-pace bowler, and Ron Oxenham (twelfth man in Brisbane) played in his first Test instead of Ironmonger. England, holding a 2–0 lead, retained the side that had won the second Test by eight wickets.

Australia won the toss on 29 December and began batting in ideal conditions—a marvellous Melbourne pitch and a near-capacity crowd. Aware now of the superb quality of Larwood and Tate, the audience seethed with excitement as Woodfull and Richardson faced the opening deliveries, and that was the way the cricket continued for seven days, as first one, then the other side, took charge of events.

Larwood was the first to strike. He forced Richardson to edge a ball that made great speed off the pitch to the eager hands of Duckworth with the score on five. Then Tate had Woodfull caught by Jardine in the gully. Hendry stayed briefly, but he too edged a ball from Larwood and Jardine took his second catch.

At 3 for 57 Kippax and Ryder put on 161 at a run a minute, before Kippax also edged Larwood to Jardine in the gully. Kippax had made an even century in his usual eye-catching style, his drives, cuts and that wonderful hook shot defying the English attack for three hours. Bradman joined Ryder and they had an exciting stand until stumps, when Australia were 4 for 276.

The selectors had originally appointed Ryder as Australia's captain for the first two Tests, and when he got the job Woodfull sportingly offered to stand down as captain of Victoria to give Ryder more experience. By appointing what Harry Altham termed in his *History of Cricket* "a stranger to captaincy",

Ryder tossing for Australia while Chapman looks on.

who had not led his state team, the selectors had placed Ryder in a difficult position, which Woodfull's sense of diplomacy overcame. True to form, the selectors told Ryder he would be captain for the third Test just before he went out to bat, so he knew as he took strike that his job as well as the Ashes was at stake in this match.

Ryder was out for 112 on the second morning after batting defiantly for three hours, mixing determined defence with those thundering drives. When he left, Bradman and a'Beckett put on 86. Unhappily for Bradman, when he was within sight of his century and had hit 9 fours he played over a Hammond yorker and was bowled for 79.

The excellent bowling and fielding of the England players and the exceptional fight put up by Bradman and a'Beckett was warmly applauded at the end of every over by the day's record crowd of 62,259. Ted a'Beckett's 41 took 2 hours and 22 minutes and after he left, England swept through the rest of the tail to have Australia all out for 397. England were 1 for 47 at stumps, only 168 runs being scored on this tense second day. White's 57 overs had cost only 64 runs, but the critics agreed that Tate was the best English bowler with 2 for 87 off 46 overs.

Sutcliffe was never comfortable on the third day as he struggled for three and a half hours for his 58. Chapman and Hendren tried to lift the scoring rate but both were out cheaply. Hammond continued doggedly on and at stumps was 169 not out, England 4 for 312. Lacking a genuinely fast bowler, Ryder directed the attack to Hammond's leg stump and this kept him subdued for six and a half hours, when he reached his second successive double century. He was out soon afterwards and although Jardine made 62 the Australian bowlers did a splendid job in restricting England's lead to 20. At stumps on the fourth day Australia were 2 for 118; Larwood bowled Richardson for 5 and Duckworth brought spectators to their feet as he stumped Hendry off White.

Australia all but stopped work to follow the struggle on the fifth day; the Melbourne

The Wally Hammond cover drive was often on view in the 1928–29 rubber when he made three double centuries and two centuries and a total of 1553 runs at 91.35.

Cricket Ground was full and thousands more in the capital cities followed every ball on giant boards erected outside newspaper offices. Kippax and Ryder failed, and with Australia desperate for runs, Bradman came out to a tremendous reception for a slight lad known only for his feats in the bush and his few big-city appearances. From the start he batted with a maturity that belied his inexperience, but after he had made 24 Woodfull was out for 107. Woodfull had batted stolidly for four and a half hours against bowling so accurate he could only hit 7 fours.

Bradman took over, nursing Oxenham and calmly dominating the strike. His confidence was amazing as his strokes radiated all round the wicket. Every run was applauded by a nation glued to their radios or the giant scoreboards as he sped past his 50. This was how Billy Hughes, Australia's prime minister from 1915 to 1923, described the innings:

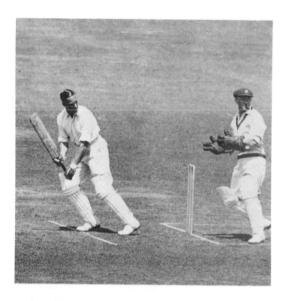

Herbert Sutcliffe in action during the 1928–29 tour. He was lucky once in Brisbane (above), seen here glancing down to fine leg as Oldfield watches in disbelief, but not so in a later test (below) when he is stumped by Oldfield off the bowling of Grimmett.

Bradman's footwork was wonderful, his timing superb, and he was the master of every stroke. The experts around me that day compared him with Trumper, some holding he was not in the same class, others contending he was Trumper's equal. But none denied that he was a wonderful batsman. Indeed, that could not be denied in the face of that flick of the wrist with which he sent the ball like a cannon shot to the boundary.

Oxenham and Bradman added 93 at a run a minute and when Bradman reached his century the vast assembly of people outside the *Sydney Sun* office joyously tossed hats in the air. Women waved handkerchiefs and umbrellas, car drivers tooted their horns, tram bells clanged. When Bradman was caught behind by Duckworth off Geary for 112, Australia had reached 345. He had batted for four hours and hit 11 fours in the first of his 29 Test centuries. He was never dropped from an Australian team again. The gallant Oxenham

went soon after for 39 and the Australian innings closed at 351. White's 5 for 107 came off 56.5 immaculate overs.

The likelihood of England scoring 332 to win appeared remote when heavy rain fell overnight. Play resumed almost an hour late on the sixth day, and straight after lunch, with the score on 10 and his own total 3, Hobbs was dropped in the slips by Hendry, a blunder for which a heavy price was paid. Thereafter Hobbs and Sutcliffe batted in masterly fashion on the difficult pitch. The ball kicked and hit the batsmen's arms and shoulders and even their heads, but far too many deliveries were not aimed at the stumps. Hobbs and Sutcliffe played every ball as late as they could and avoided contact with anything they were not forced to play. This time Ironmonger was in the stands only 150 metres away from a pitch that would have suited him perfectly, one of the two players dropped from Australia's nominated 13.

Only 75 runs were scored between lunch and tea but, by surviving, the batsmen improved England's situation with every over. Just after tea Hobbs signalled for a new bat and took the opportunity to pass a message to Chapman that Jardine should be sent in next. Hobbs was out lbw to Blackie at 105 after yet another remarkable display of clever footwork, faultless concentration and consummate defence on a gluepot made worse by a hot sun. Jardine made what most agreed was his most valuable tour contribution by staying with Sutcliffe until stumps.

Next day the pitch had dried out and caked hard, too brittle to stand the roller. Sutcliffe was completely composed on such a wicket and took the score relentlessly on to 318 before he was lbw to Grimmett for 135. It was one of cricket's finest examples of sustained skill. England were then only 14 runs short of success and lost a further three wickets making them, one to a superb throw by Bradman which ran out Tate. For the second time in five months the matchless craftsmanship of Hobbs and Sutcliffe on a difficult, drying pitch had frustrated Australia, this time by a margin of three wickets. But when Geary pulled a half volley to the fence to score the deciding runs and win the Ashes, all the 262,467 people who had paid £22,561 to see the match considered themselves well rewarded.

Jackson's Adelaide classic

The fourth and fifth Tests 1928–29

Bradman's success in the third Test encouraged the selectors to take a chance with their other gifted young cricketer and invite Archie Jackson, then 19, to play in the fourth Test on 1 February 1929, in Adelaide. Arthur Mailey, the Balmain club's only previous Test player, rushed down from the *Sydney Sun* office to Alan Kippax's sports store in Martin Place, where Jackson worked, to bring the good news.

Balmain celebrated that night and the house at 14 Ferdinand Street, where Archie lived with his father, mother and three sisters, reverberated with joy. Archie slept in a bedroom on the second floor, and his father often tied up the handles on the doors to the upstairs wrought iron balcony to safeguard his sleepwalking son. Another of Archie's minor problems was his name—he felt disadvantaged having only one Christian name, when other Australian team members had

The Adelaide Oval scoreboard for the fourth Test in January 1929 showing Jackson's score of 164, despite which England still won the match by 12 runs.

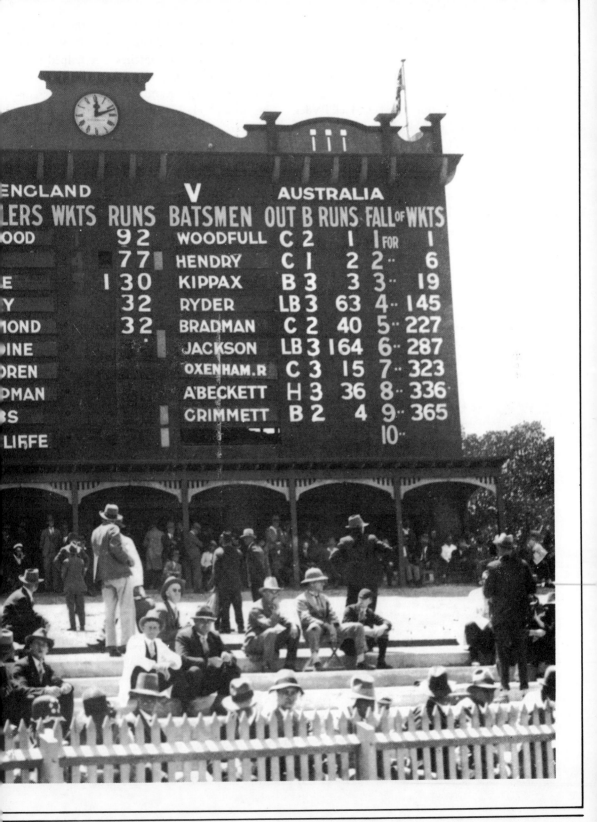

ENGLAND			V	AUSTRALIA				
LERS	WKTS	RUNS	BATSMEN	OUT	B	RUNS	FALL of WKTS	
OOD		92	WOODFULL	C	2	1	1 FOR	1
		77	HENDRY	C	1	2	2··	6
E	1	30	KIPPAX	B	3	3	3··	19
Y		32	RYDER	LB	3	63	4··	145
MOND		32	BRADMAN	C	2	40	5··	227
INE			JACKSON	LB	3	164	6··	287
REN			OXENHAM.R	C	3	15	7··	323
PMAN			A'BECKETT	H	3	36	8··	336
S			GRIMMETT	B	2	4	9··	365
LIFFE							10··	

163

two or more and Hunter Hendry had four. So it was agreed that he should use his father's name, Alexander, as his second given name, and he became known in the cricket world as A. A. Jackson.

In the days preceding the Test, Jack Ryder sought the advice of Jackson's employer and state captain Alan Kippax about the wisdom of Jackson opening the batting. Kippax's reply was "I am sure he expects to open". Even then Jackson was a talker, a batsman who liked to congratulate bowlers who dismissed him with a good ball. However tense the situation, he was invariably friendly to his opponents, and let them know what he thought of their bowling.

This portrait, showing the world record tenth wicket stand of 307 by Alan Kippax (left) and Halford Hooker for New South Wales v. Victoria in 1928, was presented to both players. They batted all Christmas Day.

Jackson fought his way into the Test side with outstanding displays for New South Wales in interstate matches. He helped New South Wales beat Queensland in Brisbane between 27 October and 1 November by scoring 50 and 71, his second innings providing the start required, 121 runs, in the chase for 399 to win. New South Wales won by six wickets after trailing by 76 runs on the first innings. Bradman's knocks of 131 and 133 not out overshadowed Jackson's effort, however, and also that of Cecil Thompson, who made 158 not out in Queensland's second innings.

Jackson made only 19 for New South Wales against Victoria at Melbourne between 22 and 27 December, but nobody in this match could expect any limelight after Alan Kippax and Hal Hooker put on a world record 307 for the last wicket. Chasing 376, after centuries from Ryder (175) and a'Beckett (113), New South Wales were 263 behind when Hooker joined Kippax late on Monday

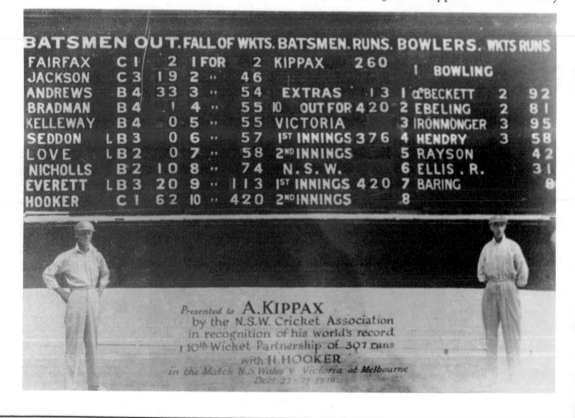

afternoon. They stayed together until midday on Wednesday. Kippax was 260 not out when Hooker went for a big hit and miscued. Hooker's 62 was his highest first-class score and the catch he gave Ryder off a'Beckett was his first attempt to forget defence. "I was counting on you getting a hundred," said Kippax as they walked off, with the total on 420.

Victoria declared at 6 for 251 in the second innings, a'Beckett scoring 95 for a match aggregate of 208. New South Wales made 2 for 156 striving for 207 before time ran out, with Bradman breezing along on 71 not out. New South Wales also took first innings points in the return meeting with Queensland from 31 December to 4 January 1929 in Sydney. Cecil Thompson had put Queensland in a winning position with innings of 143 and 76 and six wickets. Left to score 343 in the last innings, New South Wales had to fight grimly to avoid defeat and were 7 for 304, thanks to Jackson's 53 not out, when time expired.

The superstitious Thompson amazed team-mates when he went into the dressing room and found his bat on the floor. He called Ernie Hutcheon's attention to it and asked him to pick it up. Hutcheon laughed, but obliged, leaving Thompson to describe the evils that would have resulted if he had picked it up himself.

Jackson clearly needed something spectacular to push his Test claims and he supplied it with scores of 162 and 90 in the match against South Australia at Adelaide from 11 to 16 January. New South Wales won by 60 runs, scoring 402 and 313 to South Australia's 304 and 351. Kippax (107) batted with his protege in the first New South Wales innings while 221 was added by a partnership that delighted the spectators. This match had a far-reaching effect on Bradman's career. Tried as an opener, he made only 5 and 2, and was never again seriously considered for the job.

With newspapers advocating Jackson's

Cecil Thompson, one of the mainstays of the Queensland team for 16 seasons. He had probably his finest season in 1925–26 when he had the remarkable average in club cricket of 279.66 for nine innings.

inclusion in the Test team, Victoria went to Sydney for the match that decided the Shield competition between 24 and 29 January. Jackson made a smart 41 to get New South Wales away to a good start, and his opening partner, Alan Fairfax, continued to 104. Bradman then batted for almost eight hours to score 340 not out, enabling New South Wales to declare at 6 for 713. Bradman's score was the highest for New South Wales in a Shield match until then and the highest individual score at the SCG, beating Billy Murdoch's 321 for New South Wales against Victoria in 1881–82.

Hooker capped his grand batting in Melbourne by taking 6 for 42, including four wickets in four balls, and assuring New South Wales of first innings points. Dismissed for 265, Victoria followed on 448 behind, but 131 from Basil Onyons, 91 from John Scaife, 96 from Len Darling and 63 from Tom Bird took Victoria to 7 for 510 and deprived New South Wales of outright points. New South Wales' first innings win still clinched the Shield.

Meanwhile there was little rest for the English tourists following their Ashes-winning victory in the third Test. Two days later they played a draw against Twelve of Geelong, followed by another draw against Thirteen of Bendigo on 9 and 10 January. On 12 January they began a three-day match against Tasmania in Launceston, which they won by an innings and 116 runs because of an innings of 214 by Jardine. At Hobart on 18 and 19 January they again beat Tasmania, this time by an innings and 64 runs. At this match Phil Mead met a Tasmanian fan who said that he had met Mead's father in 1911–12, the season Mead first toured Australia.

Hobbs helped England outplay South Australia in Adelaide from 25 to 29 January.

Archie Jackson in 1928–29, when he was considered more promising than Bradman.

He made 75 in England's first innings of 392, adding 155 in an opening stand with Sutcliffe, who carried on to 122. After England dismissed South Australia for 178 (White 7 for 66), Hobbs went in again and made 101. Jardine also made a century (114) and England declared at 5 for 307. Left to score 522 to win, South Australia were 1 for 75 when rain prevented further play.

In the fourth Test at Adelaide, from 1 to 8 February, Hobbs and Sutcliffe again put on over a hundred, Hobbs' footwork and defence reaching the highest standard. Both were out with the score at 143. Grimmett had Jardine lbw immediately and when Hendren missed a wide off break from Blackie, England were 4 for 179. Chapman helped Hammond add 67 before Duckworth went in to play out time, with England restricted to 5 for 246 on the first day, and Hammond 47 not out. Next morning Hammond farmed the strike cleverly and scored 72 of the last 88 runs, to finish on 119 not out in a total of 334.

Jackson opened the Australian innings with Woodfull, and leaned forward to the first ball he faced from Maurice Tate, an inswinger that finished in line with the leg stump. Tate appealed for lbw, believing the ball had struck Jackson's pads. The ball flashed to the fine leg boundary. Realising Jackson had glanced it, Tate turned to umpire George Hele and said, "This kid'll get a hundred".

Woodfull and Hendry were both caught by Duckworth before the shine left the ball, and when "Farmer" White bowled Kippax, Australia were 3 for 19. Ryder came in and at once began encouraging Jackson. "Stick to it, son, you'll be all right. Take your time." They were still together at stumps with Australia 3 for 131. Next morning Ryder was lbw to White for a plucky 63, but Jackson began to play a succession of lovely forcing strokes, mainly to the leg side. George Hele, in *Bodyline Umpire*, gave his impression of the tension in the match.

Maurice Tate shown in his delivery stride. He bowled 480.6 overs for England in the 1928–29 series, taking 44 wickets at 29.88.

I stole a glance at Jackson. An umpire is not supposed to have any feelings, but I was just as keenly interested to see Jackson succeed as any of the 50,000 spectators. It was with dismay that I saw Jackson was standing there with his face as white as a sheet, nervously trying to moisten his lips. Anybody would have felt sympathy for Jackson. What a position to be in.

Jackson and Bradman remained together until lunch, when Jackson was 97, Australia 4 for 201. Bradman, who had looked far from confident with White bowling his tantalising slows at one end, and Larwood at his fastest,

bowling to a packed leg-side field, tried to reassure Jackson, saying that there was no need to worry about the century, just to relax and it would come. Jackson asked Hele during the luncheon break if England would take the new ball. Hele said that with his bowlers refreshed and the new ball available, Chapman would be crazy not to take it.

First ball after lunch Larwood stepped out his long run, turned and went rushing in, front arm held high in front as he swung his right arm down and let fly with the gleaming new ball. The ball whipped down towards Jackson's off stump, but he moved confidently into it and with a crisp sweep of the bat, struck the ball between point and cover to the fence. He had made 101 and, at 19 years 152 days, remains the youngest player to score a century in Tests between England and Australia. Larwood said later, in David Frith's book *The Archie Jackson Story*,

Having had his back to the wall, he cover-drove me beautifully to bring up his hundred. That ball was delivered as fast as any I had ever previously bowled. That glorious stroke has lived in my memory for its ease and perfect timing. I am sure that few among the many thousands present sighted the ball as it raced to the boundary.

The quality of Jackson's drive, the utter defiance of it, sent the crowd wild. Hats were thrown in the air and the game was held up because of the deafening cheers. Although the Ashes had been decided, the closeness of the struggle attracted enormous numbers of cricket lovers to Adelaide and now Jackson had rewarded them with one of the game's immortal innings. He had the eye, the freedom of stroke, the wrists and the guts of a truly great player, and he went on to 164 before his first mistake had him leg-before to White.

After he scored his century Jackson's timidity disappeared. He drove, cut and glanced with an ease that reminded everyone of Mac-artney, mixing lofted shots into the outfield with late cuts which almost plucked the ball out of Duckworth's hands. Tate banged the ball into the unresponsive pitch for 42 overs and had Bradman caught by Larwood for 40. Bradman and Jackson had added 82 in even time, Jackson's performance over-shadowing even Bradman's finest strokes. Larwood, who had been criticised in the second Test for deliberately bowling at the batsmen, bowled rising balls on the leg stump at both Bradman and Jackson, with five or six men on the leg side, the first time Australians saw what later became known as Bodyline. Then in a final flourish Jackson scored 51 out of a 60-run stand with a'Beckett.

In that last flurry Jackson drew gasps from the audience when he several times chopped over-pitched deliveries with thrilling speed past second slip to the boundary, striking the ball very late with the full face of the bat. P. G. Fender wrote in his London newspaper the *Star* that it was a stroke he had only ever seen Macartney execute. By the end of the day Australia were 9 for 365. Larwood was down to medium pace, Geary was off the field with a strain, and White was left to serve up over after over. Australia's innings ended at 369 on the fourth morning. White had taken 5 for 130.

Facing a deficit of 35, England began their second innings that morning against some excellent bowling by Hendry and a'Beckett. Hobbs went for one and Sutcliffe with the score on 21. Hammond batted slowly, Jardine with a complete indifference to scoring, and for hour after hour they dabbed and scratched about, intent only on keeping the Australians bowling. They were not separated until the fifth afternoon and put on 262. Hammond batted for 7 hours 20 minutes before Ryder caught and bowled him for 177, his fourth century of the rubber and his second in the match. Jardine took 5 hours 45 minutes for his

Archie Jackson plays a classic cover drive during his magnificent innings of 164 at Adelaide in 1928–29.

98. From 3 for 283, England slumped to 383 all out, leaving Australia 349 to win.

After one interval George Hele was about to straighten up the stumps so that play could resume. "Leave them as they are a second, George," called Bradman, who was standing at square leg with the ball in his hand. He hit the one stump standing three times in a row, Hele fielding his shots, then ran off to the boundary, chuckling to himself.

Grimmett was infuriated by an incident when Hammond was in the seventies, with Jardine at the bowler's end. Hammond spooned what looked like an easy catch straight back to Grimmett, but slightly to the leg side. As Grimmett moved to take the catch he ran into Jardine's elbow. The ball dropped to the turf just in front of Jardine. Grimmett swung round and called, "He did that on purpose!" Umpire Hele took no action. At the end of the over Grimmett renewed his protest. "He did that deliberately," he said.

At stumps pressmen surrounded Grimmett as he came through the gate. "Did you appeal for that interference by Jardine?" asked Vic Richardson. Grimmett replied, "No, but it was deliberate." "You bloody fool, Grum," said Richardson, "why didn't you appeal in the correct way?" Percy Fender approached Hele and asked, "Had there been an appeal, George, who would have been out?" Hele's answer was "There was no appeal".

Back in the press box somebody turned up Law 40, which read "Either batsman is out 'Obstructing the field'—if he wilfully obstruct the opposite side; should such wilful obstruction by either batsman prevent a ball from being caught it is the striker who is out." The hundred runs Hammond scored after Jardine prevented his dismissal swung the game.

A section of the crowd misinterpreted Woodfull's action in repeatedly going down the pitch to encourage Jackson at the start of the second Australian innings. Spectators believed Woodfull was trying to curb Jackson's stroke play, and noisily heckled him, and he received further angry catcalls when Jackson was out for 36. Woodfull had made 30 when he too was out and as he came off spectators heckled him again. All he had said at the mid-pitch conferences was "Keep it up, Jacko, you're going well."

Hendry mis-timed a pull shot to be out for five. With Australia 3 for 74, Ryder and Kippax put on 137. Kippax was beautifully caught by Hendren for 51 and Ryder caught and bowled by White for 87. At stumps Australia were 6 for 260, needing just 89 runs to win. Ryder told Bradman, "Play your own game. I think you can pull this off for us." Bradman replied, "I think I can too".

On the seventh morning, with Australia on 308 and four wickets in hand, Oldfield hit a ball straight to Hobbs in the covers and called Bradman for a run that was never possible.

Hele said later that Hobbs deliberately fumbled the ball to dupe Oldfield into calling for the run. Hobbs' throw was wide as he had no time to get full control of the ball, but Duckworth took it easily and flattened the stumps, leaving Bradman out by two metres. He had made 58 and looked in complete control. It was the last time England ever ran him out.

Grimmett stayed for half an hour but at 336 Tate took a fine catch from a hard, low cut. Blackie came in amid intense excitement and played four balls from White. The fifth was shorter and Blackie hooked it high into the outfield, where Larwood, running several yards, held a splendid catch and ended a wonderful struggle. England had won by 12 runs.

Hammond's two centuries, Jardine's obstruction of Grimmett, and White's admirable marathon in bowling 124.5 overs and taking 13 wickets all received wide publicity. In the four innings of the Melbourne and Adelaide Tests, White had bowled 57, 56.5, 60, and 64.5 six-ball overs, which included 87 maidens, at an average cost of 1.7 runs an over. His 19 wickets in that period had cost 22.47 each. But when it was over, Hammond's batting, White's tireless bowling, and England's superb catching faded in the memory. The magic of Jackson's stroke play overshadowed it all.

At Ballarat on 9 and 11 February Les Ames made 127 against Thirteen of Ballarat, which set England on the way to a score of 9 for 493 declared. England then dismissed the crude Ballarat batting line-up for 77 and 176, Freeman taking seven first-innings wickets at less than four runs apiece. "Patsy" Hendren had a delightful trick for these light-hearted matches: he would pretend to pick up and throw from the outfield long before the ball reached him, invariably bluffing the bush batsmen.

England's return match against New South Wales was eagerly awaited, since the Sydney selectors had decided to gamble heavily on youth. Apart from Jackson and Bradman, they had introduced Bradman's club-mate Alan Fairfax to the state side, and an exciting 18-year-old right-hand batsman developed at St Joseph's College, Hunters Hill, named Stan McCabe. After he left school McCabe had become a prolific scorer in northern New South Wales and the story went that when the New South Wales Cricket Association sent a telegram to cricket officials in Grenfell, McCabe's birthplace, the cryptic message said simply, "Send McCabe". Almost 50 years later the cricket buffs of Grenfell clung to the view that the wrong McCabe had gone to Sydney and that Stan's brother Bill was the McCabe intended to go.

None of the young players showed any form in a match ruined by rain, although Fairfax batted for two hours for 40 runs in New South Wales' first innings of 128. Fairfax had 3 for 36 with his right-arm fast-medium swing when rain washed out play with England 4 for 144.

England's bowlers continued in grand style at Bathurst from 21 to 22 February in the match against a Western Districts XI. Larwood, Tate, White and Freeman were too skilful for the locals and bowled England to victory by an innings and 111 runs. Tyldesley made a stylish half century and Ames was bowled by the Rugby Union international Ron Biilmann for 123. England made 319, Western Districts 127 and 81. Larwood took 5 for 17 in Western Districts' first innings, hitting the stumps five times. Freeman had 8 for 31 in Western Districts' second knock.

At Goulburn against a Southern Districts Thirteen, England played a draw on 25 and 26 February. The match provided an opportunity for Arthur Allsopp to display his strong driving and pulling in an innings of 79 not out that included 14 fours, a performance which won Allsopp an invitation to play for New South Wales the following summer. England scored 250 (left-arm pace bowler Bill Lampe 5

Don Bradman (left) with Alan Fairfax and Archie Jackson, the youthful trio selectors gambled on during the 1928–29 season.

for 46) and 5 for 226 declared, Southern Districts 135 and 4 for 135.

England spent all of 1 March chasing the ball around the Melbourne Cricket Ground as Victoria piled up the highest opposition score of the tour. Woodfull was 275 not out, Ryder made a lusty 60, Darling 87 and Victoria were 9 for 572 when trouble began.

Spectators not only objected to Larwood bowling balls that flew past Ironmonger's ears, they felt Larwood should not bowl at all against such a poor batsman. The booing intensified as Chapman tried three times to persuade Larwood to run in and each time Larwood balked. Woodfull and Chapman went to the noisiest sections of the crowd and tried to quieten them but to no effect. When Ironmonger hit successive balls for two runs the crowd could not restrain their glee. To those who knew what a woeful batsman Ironmonger was, it was sheer comedy, but Larwood did not see the joke and threw the ball down. Ryder ended the stalemate when he rushed through the gate and closed the innings. It was the third time on the tour that Woodfull had batted right through an innings against England.

In London the *Daily Sketch* called the demonstration "the outrageous action of churls"; the *Sporting Life* added that it was a blot on the game; the *Daily News* said the protest would have been scarcely credible in a children's match on the sands. Larwood confessed he did not understand the crowd's motives, especially when they stood up and cheered when his turn came to go out and bat.

Ames, who had been in outstanding form, could not bat after fracturing a finger keeping wicket to Larwood. England were thus virtually 3 for 49 when Jardine and Leyland were out and were forced to bat carefully. Hammond hit only 5 fours in an innings of 114. Dismissed for 303, England followed on. Leyland and Jardine put on 98 for the first wicket and when Leyland went for 54, Jardine moved on to 115, his sixth tour century. Tyldesley and Hendren had put on 61 when bad light brought an early end to what had become a dreary match. England were then 3 for 308, 49 ahead.

The Australian selectors finally gave Ryder the fast bowler he wanted by bringing in Thomas Welbourne Wall, the Prospect club's tall, lean right-hander whom everybody called "Tim", for the fifth Test at Melbourne on 8 March. They also included Percy Hornibrook, who could provide a brisk left-arm medium pace before reverting to spin, and Alan Fairfax, who could bat soundly and bowl a lively right-arm medium pace. Hendry, Blackie and a'Beckett were dropped and the critics agreed the Australian selectors had got the team right for the first time. England's captain Chapman had flu and White took over the job. Sutcliffe had an arm injury and was

Alan Fairfax, who went into the Australian team from the St George club with Bradman. He later settled in England.

replaced by Leyland, while Ames' broken finger confirmed Duckworth in the wicket-keeping spot.

The Test was the first to be played over eight days, and once England had batted until lunch on the third day in their first innings it was apparent it would become a marathon. Hobbs opened with Jardine and at the age of 46 years and 83 days scored the last of his 12 centuries against Australia and his fifth Test hundred in Melbourne. The scoring rate was desperately slow but the spectators did not care; they knew they were watching a once-in-a-lifetime event as Hobbs batted for 4 hours and 40 minutes and hit 11 fours in his 142.

Duckworth went in as nightwatchman, and after he was out on the second morning Hendren and Leyland put on 140 in 170 minutes. Hendren hit 10 fours and an eight (four run and four overthrows) in his 95. Leyland completed his century, on his debut against Australia, partnered by last man White and then hit out to reach 137.

Australia scored less than two runs an over but did well to get within 28 runs of England's total of 519. Woodfull made 102, his third century of the series, but was at the wicket five and a half hours and hit only 3 fours. The best batting of the Australian innings came when Fairfax, making his debut, joined Bradman. They put on 183 for the fifth wicket in 210 minutes. Bradman showed an exciting ability to drive into open space, and against accurate, subtle bowling kept the ball down well in hitting 8 fours in his 123. The ninth Australian wicket fell at 432 but Hornibrook and Grimmett added 59 in 95 minutes to take the two-innings aggregate to 1010 runs. Only 14 wickets fell in the first four days. Geary's stamina was fully tapped as he took 5 for 105 off 81 overs in Australia's first innings.

The game turned on England's comparative failure in the second innings. Wall completed an impressive debut by moving the ball about at an uncomfortable pace to take 5 for 66. England never recovered from the loss of Jardine for a duck, although Leyland (53 not out) and Tate (54) added 81 in 55 minutes. Oldfield and Hornibrook did a fine job by holding out for 20 minutes when Australia's second innings began late on the sixth day, and next morning they lifted the score to 51, a great start for tail-enders in a side chasing 286 to win. A voice in the crowd called to Oldfield, "Bertie, if we get the runs, you'll go to heaven."

England's bowlers made Australia strug-gle for every run all through the seventh day. Hammond had a dramatic spell in which he took three wickets, moving the ball in from the off. Oldfield was out at 80, Woodfull at 129 and Jackson at 158. By bowling Woodfull, Hammond became the first to do so for 27 months. Bad light stopped play for the day with Australia 4 for 173.

Leyland cleverly ran out Kippax on the eighth morning, picking up and throwing the ball strongly from the outfield as the batsmen attempted a fourth run. At 5 for 219, Bradman, who was on five, gave Duckworth a stumping chance which was badly missed. One run later Ryder had his wicket thrown down by Leyland, who had fielded behind the bowler after sprinting from mid-off. To the annoyance of the Englishman, the umpire gave Ryder not out. Bradman and Ryder hit the runs required without further incident. Geary's 20 overs in this innings meant he had bowled 101 in the match.

After conceding more than 500 runs in the first innings, Australia had achieved a notable victory by five wickets. Ryder, who had taken charge with Australian cricket at its lowest ebb for 16 years, was deservedly carried shoulder-high from the field. The 39-year-old captain had led a frequently changed team uncomplainingly, if without subtlety, against one of the finest teams England ever had, and after nine Tests without a win, Australia had turned the tide.

After the celebrations in the Australian dressing-room there was consternation when no car appeared to take the four New South Wales players to their Sydney-bound train. Finally somebody found a hansom cab, and the horse and carriage made its slow way through the Melbourne streets with Kippax, Fairfax, Bradman and Jackson and their gear crushed in and outside the cabin.

None of the Australian stars were included in the Australian XI which played England at Perth in the last match of the tour,

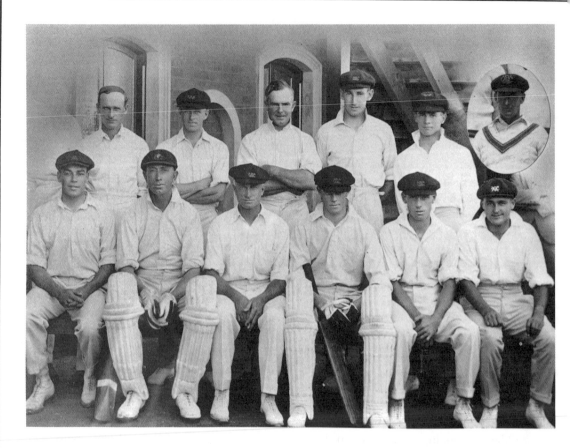

The Australian XI that met England in Perth from 21 to 23 March 1929 included stars from all states. Second from the left in front is Victorian Jack Ryder, two away from local hero Ernie Bromley. Clarrie Grimmett, Jack Ellis, Len Darling and Arthur Richardson were the other interstate players in the side.

from 21 to 23 March. Arthur Richardson made 101 not out in the Australian XI's innings of 310, in which Harold Rowe was unluckily run out for 73. Hammond added 80 runs to his tour aggregate in England's listless innings of 241. Ryder was 81 not out after a fine stand with Bill Horrocks (76), when to the relief of the Englishmen time ran out. Two days later they sailed for home.

The tour had made a profit of £17,968. The third Test in Melbourne drew 262,467 spectators, the fifth Test, on the same ground, 213,464, and altogether 859,009 people paid £73,877 to watch the five Tests.

Hammond took all the honours for batting in an England team which scored 30 individual centuries. He made 1553 runs in first-class matches at 91.35, with eight centuries, three times passing 200. He had a record aggregate of 905 runs in the Tests at 113.12. Jardine surprisingly finished ahead of the professionals by scoring 1168 runs at 64.88, with six centuries. All the leading English bowlers got through massive workloads. White bowled a total of 752.5 overs, 223 of them maidens, and took 65 wickets at 22.63 to top the first-class averages, with 25 of his wickets coming in Tests at 30.40 apiece. The big-hearted Tate bowled 480.6 overs, taking 44 wickets at 29.88. Freeman was the big disappointment of the tour, his 35 wickets costing 32.45 each.

Jackson topped Australia's Test batting

averages with 276 runs in his two Tests at 69.00, but Bradman was not far behind with 468 runs from four Tests at 66.85, figures he was able to improve vastly over the next 20 years. Grimmett took most Test wickets, 23 at 44.52, but Blackie headed the averages with 14 wickets at 31.71. Woodfull scored a double century for Victoria against the tourists and three centuries in the Tests. England played 24 matches, won 10, drew 13 and lost 1.

Bradman scored 1690 runs in first-class cricket in 1928–29, still the record for an Australian season, though his average, 93.88, was to become common in the Bradman story. He averaged 148.83 in 1928–29 Shield cricket, and with almost 1000 more runs in minor cricket, had an all-up aggregate of 2616 runs at 76.94. The St George club gave a dinner for him and Alan Fairfax, at which a Bradman–Fairfax testimonial fund was opened and they were both presented with a gold fountain pen.

In Balmain the mayor called a public meeting to honour Archie Jackson, whose spoils included a travelling clock, rugs and a set of cut glass pieces from the New South Wales Cricket Association, and the proceeds of a "bob-in" fund organised in Sydney factories and offices. Archie enjoyed it all until it came to speech-making, which he loathed, with nobody to come on the stage and whisper encouragement.

The highest innings

Domestic cricket 1929–30

Although defeated for the second time in three years, Australia received a wonderful bonus from the 1928–29 Test series. The success of Archie Jackson and Don Bradman sparked the ambitions of Australian youth. It was the start of a twentieth-century phenomenon, hero-worship fed by the media, then just news-papers and radio, and in every state youngsters set about emulating their idols.

Jackson's influence was tragically brief, but over the next two decades Bradman had a magical effect on attendances at major matches. People who had never thought of going to the cricket, particularly women, went to see him bat, and when news spread that he was at the crease vast audiences swarmed through the turnstiles. Entire grounds were refurbished and new grand-stands built on the money he attracted through the gate.

The legend that had started with Brad-man's initiation in Test cricket during 1928–29 grew during the following season in Austra-lia. Bradman had won over the last of his Australian critics, Warwick Armstrong, with

Bradman captured public imagination to an extent where even at practice big crowds watched his every move. He gave them plenty of thrills as this shot from the nets in Perth in 1930 shows.

his performance in the fifth Test, but there were still some who doubted that his success would continue or that he would succeed in England. Bradman's detractors tried to justify their attitude by finding fault with his technique. His grip on the bat handle was wrong, they said, and that meant he was forced to hit too many shots in the air. Another accusation was that far too many of his forcing shots were played with a cross bat. Reports circulated about New South Wales coaches taking Bradman in hand to correct his "untutored defence", but they were untrue, for Bradman was a self-made batsman who learned by his own remarkable powers of observation.

Sydney Edward Gregory, who at the time held the Australian record for Test appearances—he had made 58—died on 1 August 1929. Gregory, who went on eight tours to England, three to America, and one each to New Zealand and South Africa, scored 15,192 first-class runs at 28.55. His Test career included eight scores over 50, with 201 at Sydney in 1894 his highest. He was only 152 centimetres tall and his work in the covers was an inspiration to team-mates. He made 25 first-class centuries. On the way home from the funeral his uncle, Arthur Gregory, fell from a tram. His injuries caused septicaemia from which he died on 17 August.

When Bradman celebrated his 21st birthday on 27 August 1929, he had an aggregate of 2106 runs behind him in first-class cricket at an average of 78.00. He had made nine centuries, one more than Clem Hill made before he was 21, and the same number that W. G. Grace had scored by the time he was 21. Englishman Dennis Compton later made 11 first-class centuries before he turned 21.

The most acerbic of Bradman's critics was the Surrey captain and England all-rounder

Don Bradman in his New South Wales cap in 1929.

Percy Fender. He covered the 1928–29 series for the London *Star* and *Daily News*, who in turn syndicated his views around the cricket world. Fender did not share spectators' excitement in watching an inexperienced country lad, unaccustomed to big cities or turf pitches, defy three of the best bowlers cricket had known—Tate, Larwood and White. Throughout the tour he belittled Bradman's achievements and repeatedly spoke of Bradman's great luck, uncontrolled strokes, mis-hits that were catches just out of the reach of fieldsmen, and dangerous shots.

Fender did not meet Bradman in Australia and was said to have dismissed him as a batsman who would not get a run in England. None of the other expert commentators on the tour, notably M. A. Noble, Arthur Gilligan and R. W. E. Wilmot, a former Melbourne University Blue and cricket writer for the Melbourne *Argus*, shared Fender's doubts about Bradman's technique, nor did they display the same lack of charity for a young man just starting in big cricket.

Fender's considered judgement on Bradman appeared in his book on the tour, *The Turn Of The Wheel*, published in mid-1929: Bradman, he wrote, "was one of the most curious mixtures of good and bad batting I have ever seen". He spoke of Bradman's inferior shots in Brisbane and said that for the rest of the series Bradman was never able to avoid really bad shots. He contended that Bradman would cram half a dozen shots worthy of the greatest into two or three overs and then two or three times in a row would completely mis-time, mis-judge, and mis-hit the ball. Fender summed up:

Promise there is in Bradman in plenty; though watching him does not inspire one with any confidence that he desires to take the only course which will lead him to fulfilment of that promise. He makes a mistake, then makes it again and again; he does not correct it, or look as

if he were trying to do so. He seems to live for the exuberance of the moment.

Fender's appraisal looked extremely shaky in the 1929–30 season when Bradman scored 1586 runs, averaged 113.28, and played the highest individual innings in the history of first-class cricket. In that innings Bradman somehow managed to keep going for five minutes short of seven hours with the technique that Fender described as unsound.

Young cricketers, keen to play where the best chances of success lay, often evaded the residential qualification for district clubs. When doubts about Bradman's right to play for St George had arisen he had moved into Ellimatta, 172 Frederick Street, Rockdale, home of Mr and Mrs Frank Cush, not far from Hurstville Oval. Cush, a timber merchant, was secretary of the St George club and the club's delegate to the New South Wales Cricket Association. The guidance the Cush family gave to young Bradman helped him enormously in overcoming the problems arising from his sudden fame.

During the Adelaide Test against Chapman's team Bradman was approached by the Sydney sports store chain, Mick Simmons, to join the staff of their main store in Sydney's Haymarket. He made the switch to Mick Simmons when Percy Westbrook, hard hit by the Depression, closed his Sydney real estate office. Bradman spent the 1929 Australian winter travelling round New South Wales for Mick Simmons.

Before first-class matches began in the 1929–30 season, Bradman toured country centres Orange, Dubbo, Parkes and Bathurst with a NSWCA XI captained by Charlie Macartney, attracting audiences that fully tested ground facilities. He scored more runs than anyone on this trip, which went from 21 to 28 October.

Between 8 and 12 November Bradman scored 48 and 66 for the New South Wales team which defeated Queensland by 23 runs in the first Sheffield Shield match of the season. Captained by Oldfield, New South Wales scored 373 and 198, Queensland 273 and 275. McCabe made a fine 77 in New South Wales' first innings. Oxenham scored 117 in Queensland's second innings and had a match haul of 6 for 116. On the way home Bradman made 111 in 90 minutes against Newcastle.

Every promising young Australian cricketer realised that each time he took guard his prospect of touring England with the 1930 Australian team could hang in the balance. There was tremendous eagerness to do well, and when Harold Gilligan's England team stopped off for five matches on their way to a 17-match tour of New Zealand they were surprised by the keenness of their Australian opponents.

Gilligan's team beat Western Australia by seven wickets when they played between 31 October and 2 November 1929 in Perth, after losing 6 for 58 in their first innings and taking a dusting from controversial fast bowler Ron Halcombe. From Perth they went to Adelaide to play from 8 to 12 November. They defeated South Australia by 239 runs thanks to an innings of 146 by veteran Frank Woolley and outstanding bowling by Fred Barratt (5 for 32) and Maurice Allom (5 for 26) in South Australia's second innings of 86. Allom was to take four wickets in five balls, including the hat-trick, in the Test against New Zealand a few weeks later.

Don Blackie put on one of his greatest performances when Victoria beat England by seven wickets in Melbourne between 15 and 19 November. Facing a Victorian team which included seven Test players, England were dismissed for 238 and 114, Blackie taking 5 for 82 and 7 for 25. Woodfull, who was out for a rare duck in the first innings, made an even hundred in Victoria's second innings, to clinch victory. Barratt again looked a splendid

Don Blackie, who with Bert Ironmonger had a big influence on Victoria's Sheffield Shield win in 1929–30. He made his Test debut at the age of 46 years and 253 days.

pace bowler with match figures of 7 for 105 for England.

The match between New South Wales and England was a draw, Kippax twice declaring but lacking the time to dismiss England in their second innings on 26 November. Bradman made 157, Kippax 108, Allsopp 117 and Stan McCabe 90 in New South Wales' first innings of 8 for 629. England replied with 469, Woolley contributing 219, Turnbull 100. Jackson was 168 not out in New South Wales' second innings when Kippax called the batsmen in at 3 for 305. The Leicestershire captain Edward Dawson saved England from any danger of defeat by scoring 83 not out in a total of 2 for 204 in the last innings.

Allsopp's 117 in his first big match at the age of 21 won widespread acclaim for him as a candidate for the 1930 tour of England, but he was not sympathetically handled by officials dismayed by his rough manners. His mother died when he was six and he was brought up by a father who tried to put him to work in the Lithgow coal mines at the age of 12. He went from one relative's home to another until Dr Parsonage took him into his home for delinquent boys at Yanco. His only delinquency was in coming from a poor family, but cricket officials wrongly assumed he must have been guilty of some crime, and failed to encourage a rich cricket talent.

When they reached Brisbane for the match against Queensland between 29 November and 2 December, England had difficulty fielding a team because of injuries, and Andrew Ducat, the 43-year-old Surrey all-rounder who was coach to the Queensland Cricket Association, was called in to complete the side. Queensland won by five wickets with only three minutes to spare, a result that looked improbable when Harold Gilligan and Ranjitsinhji's nephew, Kumar Duleepsinhji, hit out freely to put 109 together in England's first innings. Gilligan made 53 and Duleepsinhji 68, and England were all out for 171, with the Valley club's Alex Hurwood taking 4 for 48. Roy Levy made 86 towards Queensland's 248 in reply. Stan Worthington topscored with 66 in England's second innings of 259 but Queensland hit the 181 runs needed to win, with the loss of five batsmen, because of an aggressive 104 by Frank Gough, who was missed twice.

The selectors brought Western Australian Bill Horrocks, Tasmanian Owen Burrows and South Australian Harry Whitfield to Sydney for a trial match between teams captained by Jack Ryder and Bill Woodfull between 6 and 11 December. Horrocks made only 25 and 5 with the bat, and neither Burrows nor Whitfield did enough right-arm fast-medium

The driving style that made Kippax beloved of Australian cricket fans.

bowling to advance their claims for a place in the team for England. Experts were puzzled why a place could not be found in this match for the right-arm leg-break bowler Bill O'Reilly, who had impressed in his debut for New South Wales in 1927–28.

The truth was that after playing for New South Wales for half the 1927–28 season O'Reilly had been exiled to Kandos, in the central west of New South Wales, by the Department of Education. The department informed O'Reilly that his time belonged to his job as a teacher and not to the Australian Cricket Board, and that he was in the habit of taking too much time off for cricket. While O'Reilly brooded over his treatment and perfected his leg breaks and googlies on concrete pitches in the bush, the selectors had no op-

portunity to assess his form. For O'Reilly, who grew up in the tiny north-western New South Wales opal mining town of White Cliffs, where his school-teacher father established the first school, the satisfaction of spreadeagling a batsman's stumps was matched only by the joy of helping a pupil.

Bradman dominated the trial with innings of 124 and 225, Jackson made an impressive 182, and Ponsford scored 131 in his first big match after recovering from his hand injury. Ryder's XI made 663 and led by 354 when they had Woodfull's XI out for 309. Woodfull's side recovered to reach 541 in their second innings due to Bradman's double century and 170 from Kippax. Left to score 188 to win, Ryder's side lost 9 wickets in getting them on a rain-damaged pitch. Hornibrook, Oxenham and Grimmett were the outstanding bowlers, although nuggety left-hander Alex Marks took the eye in the first innings with a knock of 83 for Ryder's XI.

Bradman had been sent in to open when Woodfull's team followed on. Thus his 124 and 205 not out—the score he reached by stumps—were all scored on the same day. This provoked a lot of research among enthusiasts who had to go back to 1896 to discover that Ranjitsinhji had made 100 and 125 not out in one day.

Two of the oldest players in Australian cricket, Don Blackie and Bert Ironmonger, bowled together for most of the season and had a big influence on Victoria's Sheffield Shield win. They triumphed in an unusually low-scoring match between 18 and 20 December on the Melbourne Cricket Ground, in which Victoria beat Queensland by five wickets. Queensland began by scoring 70 without losing a wicket, before Ironmonger and Blackie caused a collapse. All out for 114, Queensland bundled Victoria but for 107 after Woodfull suffered a broken bone in his hand. This injury kept Woodfull out for the rest of the season. Blackie took 5 for 28 in Queensland's second innings of 158. Victoria lost 4 for 30 before Rigg and Ebeling added 125 to make a win certain.

Bradman's short-lived frailty in running between wickets was again shown in the match between New South Wales and South Australia at Adelaide from 19 to 24 December. After scoring two, he called for a single to mid-on, but his partner failed to respond. Bradman slipped as he turned to go back and was unable to beat a throw from Wall. In the second innings Bradman and Jackson put on 172 for the first wicket before Bradman was out for 84. Allsopp (77 and 73) and McCabe

Outstanding New South Wales Colts: (L to R) Arthur Allsopp, Don Bradman, Stan McCabe and Cassie Andrews. Bradman and McCabe played many Tests together, but Allsopp and Andrews missed Test selection though many considered them good enough.

(69 and 70) completed fine doubles, but New South Wales still lost by five wickets. David Pritchard, with innings of 148 and 75, and Brian Hone, with 126 and 61, turned the game for South Australia. Hone later won a Rhodes scholarship to Oxford University and became a celebrated educationalist.

In the match that followed on Adelaide Oval from 25 to 30 December, however, South Australia only narrowly managed to avert defeat by Queensland. Set to score 209 to win in the last innings, South Australia were 9 for 177 when time ran out. Hurwood took 4 for 81 and 5 for 62 for Queensland and Vic Richardson had a knock of 126 for South Australia.

An exceptional century by "Stork" Hendry (103) supported by sounds innings from Ted a'Beckett (50) and John Scaife (60 not out), allowed Victoria to escape defeat by New South Wales at Sydney from 26 to 31 December. Scaife repeated this form the following week in Melbourne, scoring 69 before he was run out. Ponsford's second innings mastery of Grimmett took him to 110 and Victoria to victory by seven wickets, despite innings of 46 and 106 by Hone.

Bradman had been working hard in the nets to modify strokes designed for matting wickets and make them suitable to turf. He was also trying to play with a straighter bat, as Maurice Tate had suggested, and endeavouring to keep his pull shot down. How well this practice paid off was dramatically demonstrated in the match between New South Wales and Queensland in Sydney from 3 to 7 January 1930. He failed in New South Wales' first innings of 235, scoring only 3 before he was caught behind by wicket-keeper Harry Leeson. After Queensland replied with 227 he went in to bat with the score 1 for 22 in the second innings.

By stumps Bradman was 205 not out. He completed his first 50 in 51 minutes, reached 100 in 104 minutes, 200 in 185 minutes, and at 176 reached his 1000 runs for the season. There was no play the next day, a Sunday, and Bradman was able to rest quietly at the Cushes' home before resuming on the Monday morning. Refreshed, he carried on without the slightest trouble, passing 300 in 288 minutes and 400 in 377 minutes.

An off drive off Alec Hurwood took him to 434. Two scoreless deliveries followed, and then with a savage pull to the square-leg fence he passed Ponsford's world record score of 437 and went to 438. Kippax declared the New South Wales innings closed at tea, with Bradman 452 not out after 415 minutes' batting and still fresh. Ponsford had taken 621 minutes for his 437. At the end of the 1986–87 season, Bradman's 452 not out remained the highest first-class score by an Australian, though it had been surpassed by Hanif Mohammad, who was run out for 499 in Pakistan

Queensland players carry Bradman from the field after he made the world record score of 452 not out against them in Sydney.

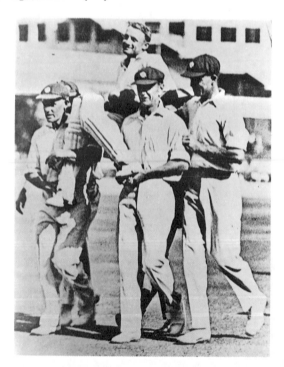

in 1958–59 while trying for his 500th run on a coir matting pitch. Bradman's score remains the world's highest on turf.

Bradman's innings is still the fastest quadruple century in first-class cricket anywhere in the world. He hit 49 fours and made only two mistakes, neither of them a chance. At 264 Queensland's mid-on fieldsman failed to move in quickly enough when Bradman hit a ball up from Bill Rowe's bowling, and at 345 wicket-keeper Leeson obstructed first slip in diving for a snick off Thurlow. Bradman had stands of 272 with Kippax for the third wicket, 156 with McCabe for the fourth wicket, and 180 with Allsopp for the sixth wicket, and was at the crease while 739 runs were scored.

Only Alec Hurwood, the right-arm off-break bowler, gave Bradman the slightest trouble; the other eight bowlers tried were hit all round the field. Hurwood finished with 6 for 179 off 34 overs. Faced with the enormous task of scoring 770 to win, Queensland collapsed for 84 in two hours. Sam Everett's 6 for 23 made the New South Welshmen winners by 685 runs.

In *Don Bradman's Book*, published in 1930, Bradman said that he did not set much store on the making of records and declared that he had never departed from the rule of playing for his side. But there is no doubt that he chased Ponsford's record. He confided to Mrs Cush over the weekend that he was going after the world record and in his book admitted: "On this occasion, however, I set out to establish a record. The highest first-class score was the one record I wanted to hold."

To achieve such a score Bradman not only hit 196 runs in boundaries, but he also gave an exuberant and skilful display of retaining the strike. He went from 391 to 395 with a four, all run, and allowed his captain Kippax an average of only two balls an over. When he passed Ponsford's record, his partner, Waverley wicket-keeper, Hugh Davidson, raced up

the pitch and congratulated him and one by one every Queenslander shook his hand. Then the Queensland captain, "Pope Leo" O'Connor, called for three cheers.

When Bradman walked off the field on 452, a spectator jumped the fence and tried to carry him on his shoulder from the ground. The effort was too much and the man collapsed in a heap with Bradman on his chest. Tired as they were, the Queensland players picked Bradman up and carried him off. Among those who watched this comedy was Charles Bannerman, Australia's first-ever Test century-maker, and that afternoon they were photographed together. Bannerman died a few months later, aged 79.

There were only 3000 spectators present when play began that day, but as word spread about Bradman's batting 2000 more had arrived by lunch time, and when he passed

Charles Bannerman, who hit the first Test century, talking to Bradman in 1929 when Bradman was at the start of his memorable career.

Ponsford's record there were 7848 watching. They saw Bradman clock up his runs at the rate of 65 an hour and allow the Queensland bowlers only one maiden over in the 117 overs they bowled in the innings. The Queenslanders conceded 6.50 runs an over, of which Bradman's share on the Monday morning was 4.25. "The mood to make runs was on me," Bradman wrote later.

This was the innings that changed Bradman's life, for it placed him above all other batsmen and made him a world celebrity. From that day, 6 January 1930, he became a unique sporting hero, and subsequently one of the most hounded men of his time, a cricketer to whom privacy was precious but the achievement of it almost impossible. While he celebrated with a cup of tea in the Sydney Cricket Ground dressing room, the story of his innings was telegraphed round the world, and with it went all chance of Bradman ever again being treated as an ordinary man.

Bowral claimed Bradman but the truth was that he was born at 89 Adams Street, Cootamundra, in the house of the midwife "Granny" Schultz, and spent the first two years of his life in the family cottage at Yeo Yeo, between Wallendbeen and Stockinbingal in southern New South Wales, where Don's father ran a wheat and sheep farm. Don had one brother, Victor, and three sisters, Islet, Lillian and May, and the family moved to Bowral because his father believed the climate in the southern highlands would improve their mother's uncertain health. Don's father turned to carpentry in Bowral, and one of the first people he worked for was Alf Stephens, a builder who happened to be president of the Bowral Cricket Club.

Strangely, in a batsman who was to average a century at a slightly better rate than every third time he went to bat, Bradman did not score another Shield century that season. He was hit on the head by a fieldsman's return before he had scored in the 8 to 13 January

Bradman's parents at their Bowral home.

match at Sydney Cricket Ground against South Australia, and retired hurt. When he resumed, he made 47 in a New South Wales total of 535, which was good enough to win the match by an innings and 220 runs. Allsopp, who made some wonderful drives in his 136, and Chilvers, a cunning leg spinner who had a match bag of 8 for 95, were the New South Wales stars. Chilvers also made 57 going in last.

A Western Australian team toured the eastern states in 1929–30 managed by former state player Alf Randell, who was briefed to secure support in the east for a Western Australian proposal to stage an interstate Second XI competition. Randell explained that the competition would be between Western Australia, Tasmania and the second elevens of the other states; the idea was to lift the standard of the two junior states with the ultimate aim of their joining the Shield competition as full members. Randell conceded that there was a large gap between standards in Tasmania and Western Australia and the senior states.

The return match between Victoria and New South Wales at Sydney Cricket Ground in the last week of January 1930 was ruined by rain, which stopped any play on the first three days. Bradman made 77, Allsopp 65 and Fairfax 64 in New South Wales' score of 330. Victoria was 3 for 222 in reply, through a 177-run stand for the third wicket by Hendry (95) and Ryder (100 not out) when time ran out.

The Australian selectors, Dr Charles Dolling, Dick Jones and Jack Ryder, were due to announce the team to tour England in 1930 on the day after this match ended. Each selector had written down a preliminary list of names, with Ryder's name on all three lists, but while they waited for the rain to clear, Dolling and Jones showed Ryder their final choices and his name was not there. Ryder went out to bat knowing he had missed selection. As his partnership with Hendry prospered, Hendry said, "A hundred should make it certain for you." Ryder's dismal response was "Two hundred wouldn't do any good".

When the team was announced on 30 January, Bradman was out rabbit-shooting in the fields around Bowral with his brother. On the way home they learned that Don had been picked. In Sydney there was high drama as Board chairman R. A. Oxlade announced the team. There had been an alleged "leak" to newspapers, which Oxlade said the Board "viewed with grave concern": Monty Noble and other critics had named the team correctly in newspaper articles during the New South Wales and Victoria match. The source of the leak was never disclosed and officials finally attributed the accuracy of Noble's forecast to his cricket acumen.

The Board of Control refused the selectors' request to send a sixteenth player before it announced the team, only four of whom—Ponsford, Oldfield, Grimmett and Woodfull, who replaced Ryder as captain—had toured England before. The complete team was W. M. Woodfull, D. G. Bradman, A. L. Kippax, W. H. Ponsford, A. Jackson, S. J. McCabe, V. Y. Richardson, A. G. Fairfax, E. L. a'Beckett, W. A. Oldfield, P. M. Hornibrook, C. V. Grimmett, A. Hurwood, T. W. Wall and C. W. Walker, with W. L. Kelly as manager and T. Howard, treasurer.

From the day the team was announced Ryder never spoke another word to Dick Jones nor attended any functions organised by Jones, blotting Jones from his life for 37 years until Jones died in 1967. There was an immediate outcry in Depression-ridden Melbourne over the sacking of Ryder, the incumbent Australian captain, and in Collingwood public protest meetings were called. Queensland had players in the Australian team for the first time, Hornibrook and Hurwood, but in Brisbane the omission of Ron Oxenham was bitterly resented. His rejection was seen as a further example of the ineptitude of the Queensland Cricket Association officials.

The dissatisfaction with the QCA caused some selected players to withdraw from the match against Victoria in Brisbane from 1 to 4 February. Fielding a badly weakened side, Queensland were beaten by an innings and 33 runs. Queensland made 80 and 200, Victoria 313 after a bold innings of 168 by Ryder. Ryder refused to give interviews and all attempts to get him to discuss his displacement as Australian captain failed, but that Brisbane century was cited for years as an example of his indomitable spirit.

Ironmonger had match figures of 10 for 86 for Victoria against his home state. There were theories that he missed selection for England because he was a labourer and socially unacceptable. A more likely reason is that the selectors feared he may have been no-balled for chucking in England.

The last match of the 1929–30 season,

Ted a'Beckett, the Victorian fast-bowling prodigy who played Test cricket after only five first-class matches. He made his debut for Victoria at 15 and in 1929–30 was selected for the Australian team.

between Victoria and South Australia, was played in Adelaide from 14 to 17 February and began with Ryder's supporters clamouring for another century. They were disappointed; he made 37 and 20. The limelight switched instead to the new Australian wicket-keeper, Charlie Walker, who in his debut for South Australia the previous season had dismissed eight batsmen, five stumped and three caught.

Walker's selection as Bert Oldfield's deputy for the 1930 tour was attributed to the expert manner in which he took Grimmett's slow bowling. Back at the start of the summer he had stumped four and caught three for South Australia against Harold Gilligan's England team. With Australia likely to rely heavily on Grimmett and Hornibrook, Walker's expertise in taking spin gave him the

edge over Jack Ellis, and New South Welshman Hugh Davidson.

Victoria appeared to have ended their chances of winning the Shield when they were all out for 118 in their first innings, but they recovered to dismiss South Australia for 110 and then scored 438 at the second attempt. Ted a'Beckett celebrated his inclusion in the team for England by scoring 152, which swung the match. Left to score 447, South Australia failed by 223 runs against the bowling of a'Beckett and Ironmonger, whose eight wickets showed that he, too, was unlucky not to go to England.

Throughout his 23 seasons in first-class cricket, there were accusations that Ironmonger was a chucker, but in 96 matches he was never called. His followers argued that his missing finger top-joints caused players, such as Jardine and Hammond, to claim he threw, but the fear that he would have been harshly treated by English umpires undoubtedly cost him a tour.

McCabe's tour berth was in jeopardy when he was asked to strip for the doctor who examined all the tourists on behalf of the Board of Control. The doctor discovered that he had remarkably high insteps and that when he stood at ease his toes did not touch the floor. One foot, in fact, was size 5, the other size 6, and it was only after carefully quizzing McCabe about balance, muscle strain and bruising of his heels, that the doctor allowed him to tour, which turned out a happy verdict for Australian cricket.

When Don Bradman boarded the *Nairana* in March, 1930, to sail to Launceston with the seventeenth Australian Test team, it was the first time he had been on a ship. He quickly discovered that he was a poor sailor. The Australians dismissed Tasmania for 157 and 158. Stan McCabe scored his initial first-class century, 103, in Australia's innings of 311. Australia won the match by 10 wickets when they scored the six runs required without loss in the second innings. The second match between the same teams at Hobart was drawn, Tasmania scoring 131 and 5 for 174, Australia 4 for 419 after Ponsford made 166, Bradman 139.

There was more seasickness on the trip back to Melbourne before the long haul to Perth and the match against Western Australia from 21 to 24 March. Following his 5 for 30 in the second match against Tasmania, Grimmett took 6 for 75 to help dismiss Western Australia for 167. The Australians responded with 324, Kippax scoring 114. Then the Australian XI had Western Australia out for 132 to win by an innings and 25 runs. Bradman completed the season with 1586 runs in first-class matches at an average of 113.28. McCabe's 844 runs was the next highest aggregate and Woodfull's 77 the next-best average.

The team travelled in the *Orford* via Ceylon, Suez, Italy and France, where they disembarked and went on by train to England. Only McCabe and Walker lacked Test experience in a side with an average age of 27. From the start Bradman set out to bat naturally and score runs as conditions and bowlers allowed, without worrying about the position of his left elbow, whether his bat was

Bradman, packing for his first tour of England in 1930, appears to be in trouble fitting everything into his suitcase.

straight or cross, and if there were purists in the stands. The series clearly depended on how well he succeeded.

A birthday present for Bill

Australia regains the Ashes 1930

Bill Woodfull had to be persuaded to accept the Australian captaincy. When fellow selectors dropped Jack Ryder, Melbourne auctioneer W. L. Kelly, already named as manager of the Australian team to England, telephoned Woodfull at Melbourne High School, where he worked as a mathematics teacher. Kelly sought permission to put Woodfull's name into the Board of Control's ballot for the tour captaincy. Woodfull was then Carlton's captain and had led an Australian side to New Zealand, but he was reluctant to be nominated.

Kelly had to work hard to secure Woodfull's acceptance, which was no surprise to anybody who knew him. Woodfull was the most reserved and modest of men, conservative but disciplined in his approach to cricket, as befitted a clergyman's son. He was 32, a Bachelor of Arts, and he still carried an

The 1930 Australian team to England: (L to R)
(back) T. Howard (treasurer), A. Jackson,
T. Wall, E. a'Beckett, P. Hornibrook,
A. Hurwood, C. Grimmett, W. Kelly (manager);
(front) A. Fairfax, W. Ponsford, V. Richardson,
W. Woodfull (captain), A. Kippax, D. Bradman,
C. Walker; (sitting) S. McCabe, W. Oldfield.

awkwardness of movement ascribed to a boyhood bout of rheumatic fever. Australian cricket was lucky that a man of such instinctive calmness and high principles finally took on the task of leading a comparatively inexperienced team on a 34-match tour of England.

With 11 players new to English conditions, Woodfull set about moulding them into a winning combination, showing an interest in each player's welfare and personal problems which none of his predecessors had shown. Before the Australians reached Britain he knew all about each man's family concerns and aspirations. By personal example he extracted loyalty from his men and a devotion to the team's cause that guaranteed a successful and happy trip. Ray Robinson, emphasis-

ing Woodfull's attention to even the smallest detail, explained how, on the Australians' first night in London, Woodfull, a strong proponent of the Methodist faith, gave 19-year-old Stan McCabe the whereabouts of the nearest Catholic church for next morning's Mass.

The famous English cricket writer R. C. Robertson-Glasgow said of Woodfull: "He reminded me of a master who gets the whole school to and from a picnic without losing a boy or his reason. He was the most calm-browed cricketer I have seen."

By then Australian teams arriving in London spent the first fortnight practising at Lord's, where those staunch royalists, Lord Harris and Lord Hawke, ruled over the game's affairs, and banqueting in splendid settings. Only at breakfast were they spared the speeches. At the dinner at the Merchant Tailors' Hall in their honour, Ranji's speech stressed that cricket was what kept the Empire

Team captain Bill Woodfull accepts a presentation from Board of Control chairman Dr A. Robertson just before the 1930 team departs for England.

together. "How often have I wished that all our political leaders were cricketers," he said.

Australia began the tour at Worcester between 30 April and 2 May with a resounding win. After dismissing Worcestershire for 131, Australia declared their first innings closed at 8 for 492. Woodfull repeated his feat of the previous tour by scoring a century in the first match, throwing his wicket away by swinging at every ball after he reached three figures. His 133 took 190 minutes and included 11 fours and a five.

English cricket fans' first glimpse of Bradman came as he went to the crease, a small, wiry figure who soon showed he was quick on his feet, but to those accustomed to over-coached English amateurs decidedly unorthodox. Jackson, McCabe and Fairfax all mis-timed shots and Richardson was run out, while at the other end Bradman rattled up the highest score by an Australian against Worcestershire, 236, in 280 minutes. He hit 28 fours in an innings that immediately sparked the close scrutiny of his methods that continued throughout his career. Grimmett, who had 4 for 38 in the first innings, took 5 for 46 in the second to help bundle out Worcestershire for 196 and give Australia a win by an innings and 165 runs, but it was the technique of 21-year-old Bradman and not that of the phenomenal 38-year-old Grimmett that attracted attention.

In the second match, against Leicestershire at Leicester on 3 and 5 May, Bradman had a long period on the defensive, but on the second afternoon was on 185 not out when rain washed out any further play. Leicestershire's last nine batsmen made 29 in a score of 148 (Grimmett 7 for 46). Australia lost 4 for 80 before Bradman and Richardson (100) added 179 for the fifth wicket. Bradman and Fairfax (21 not out) had put on 106 unfinished when the rain arrived.

Clever bowling by Percy Hornibrook, whose match figures were 10 for 40 (4 for 11

Queensland left-arm spinner Percy Hornibrook, whom many rated unlucky to miss the England tours in 1921 and 1926, finally made it when he was picked in the 1930 touring team.

and 6 for 29) paved the way for another Australian win, this time by 207 runs over Essex at Leyton on 7 to 9 May. Grimmett overshadowed even this feat by taking 10 for 37 against Yorkshire on 10 to 13 May at Sheffield. Rain and bad light forced a draw after Woodfull had made 121 and Bradman 78. Yorkshire were 2 for 120 but their last eight wickets added only 35 runs. Walker stumped three and caught one of the Yorkshire batsmen. Only Howell in 1899 and Mailey in 1921 had taken all 10 wickets in an innings for Australia.

At Liverpool Grimmett and Hornibrook

gave Australia a chance of a win over Lanca-shire but the batsmen made no effort to score the 227 runs needed in 160 minutes on the final day, using the time for batting practice. Lancashire scored 176 (Grimmett 6 for 57) and 165 (Hornibrook 5 for 38), Australia 115 and 2 for 137.

In Australia's first innings Tasmanian-born Ted McDonald, bowling at great pace, had knocked Bradman's leg stump out of the ground after he had made 9. The London *Sun* correspondent said: "I could see the whites of McDonald's eyes from the pavilion. After he tasted blood he increased his speed and bowl-ed unchanged for an hour and a half, getting rid of Jackson, Bradman and Richardson. The Australians must be pleased McDonald is not English." Bradman wrote in his book *Farewell To Cricket*: "I am ready to argue McDonald's place among the greatest of all fast bowlers. It's hard to visualise a more beautiful action which, coupled with splendid control and real pace, made him the most feared bowler in England at that time."

All the Australians were worried by the cold and found it difficult to adjust to wearing sweaters, blazers and overcoats and sitting before roaring fires before they went out to bat. Against a strong MCC side which in-cluded five bowlers—G. O. Allen, M. J. Allom, I. A. R. Peebles, A. S. Kennedy and G. T. S. Stevens—they played with extreme caution and over the three days of 17, 19 and 20 May on a true Lord's pitch, a result was never likely. Woodfull made 52, Bradman 66 and Ponsford 82 not out in Australia's first innings of 285. Fairfax bowled superbly to take 6 for 54 in MCC's innings of 258. Duleepsinhji gave a masterly display, scoring 92 off an extremely hostile Australian attack. Australia's second innings batting yielded only 213. Time ran out with MCC needing 241 in their second knock.

Hornibrook set up a much-needed victory over Derbyshire from 21 to 23 May at Chesterfield by taking 12 for 143. Stan Wor-thington made 79 and Harry Storer, the famous England soccer player and football club manager, 65 in Derbyshire's first innings of 215. Ponsford put together his first century of the tour (131), adding 127 with Jackson (63) and 106 with Bradman (44) in Australia's reply of 348. Hornibrook, who had 6 for 61 in the first innings, then repeated that form by taking 6 for 82, rushing Derbyshire out for 181. Australia made the 48 runs required to win without loss.

The match between Australia and Surrey, scheduled for three days at The Oval between 24 and 27 May, was restricted to one day by rain, but in that time Bradman made a stinging reply to Percy Fender's criticism of his batting. Going in first wicket down at 11, against a side captained by Fender, Bradman thought it best not to take any early risks. He took 90 minutes to reach 50, reached 100 in 145 minutes and then cut loose, flogging the Surrey bowlers to move from 100 to 200 in only 80 minutes.

Fender was powerless to stop the on-slaught and increased his own embarrassment with clumsy fielding. Bradman had stands of 116 for the second wicket with Woodfull, 113 in 65 minutes with Richardson and 129 unfinished with Fairfax for the sixth wicket. Bradman in one burst made 51 out of 52. He gave no chance until he was 207 and finished with 252 not out in Australia's 5 for 379.

This innings aroused hopes that Bradman would become the first Australian to score 1000 runs in England by the end of May, but in the match against Oxford University, at Oxford on 28 and 29 May, it was Ponsford who produced the batting fireworks. McCabe and Ponsford had an opening stand of 172 before McCabe was out for 91. Bradman then took an hour to make 32 but Ponsford went on to 220 not out, Australia to 2 for 406 de-clared. Oxford University made 124 and 124 to lose by an innings and 158, Grimmett

Bradman and South Australian captain Vic Richardson going out to bat for Australia against Surrey in 1930.

minutes and thereafter he was in his most brilliant form. When he was out for 191 he had not given a chance. His 1145 runs to that stage had come in 11 tour innings.

Grimmett finished off the Hampshire match with seven more wickets for a match bag of 14 for 95, Australia winning by an innings and eight runs. Bradman was the first touring batsman to score 1000 runs in England before June, an exploit he repeated in 1938, when he achieved the 1000 runs in only seven innings. Only four batsmen have made 1000 runs prior to June—Hayward, Bradman, Bill Edrich and Glenn Turner.

There was now tremendous public interest in Bradman, for what happened in Australia now happened in England. Big crowds flocked to wherever he played and wherever he stayed. What they saw was a young man who looked every inch a cricketer, scrupulously neat, a short, broad-shouldered youth who approached his cricket with tremendous zest. He had very small feet and his footwork was magical. He made it a habit to try and score off the first ball he received and thus show the bowler who was boss.

The Australians got off to a fine start against Middlesex on 4 to 6 June at Lord's and never surrendered their supremacy. Middlesex were 8 for 46 after lunch on the first day and all out for 103. Australia made 270 in reply, thanks to Kippax's 102, his first century of the tour. Hornibrook and Grimmett then combined to send Middlesex back the second time for 287, Hendren's 138 proving the only obstacle. Left to score 121 to win, the Australians made them with the loss of five wickets. Hornibrook took 7 for 42 and 4 for 60.

All the Australians were in fine form now and nobody was surprised when they defeated Cambridge University by an innings and 134 runs on 7 to 10 June at Cambridge. Australia replied to Cambridge's first innings of 145 with a massive 8 for 504 declared, Woodfull

gathering a further seven wickets.

The match against Hampshire at Southampton started on the last day of May with Bradman 46 runs short of 1000 for the month. Grimmett gave him the chance to get them by dismissing Hampshire for 151, taking 7 for 39. Bradman went in first at 3.30 p.m., the only time he ever opened in a first-class match in England, and had to wait through two rain interruptions before he took his aggregate to 993. With the rain pouring down, Tennyson spoke to his bowler, who produced a full toss and a long hop, both of which Bradman dispatched for four. Five minutes later the ground was under water. He then joined the other players in a race to the pavilion as the skies opened up again.

Next morning Bradman reached 50 in 90

scoring 216, McCabe 96. Australia then wrapped up the match by dismissing Cambridge for 225. Bowling leg breaks, Bradman had 28 overs in this match, taking 3 for 35 and 3 for 68, the best of his career.

Bradman went into the first Test at Nottingham, from 13 to 17 June, with 1230 runs in 14 tour innings behind him, the most ever by a touring cricketer. It was a curious match which England won by 93 runs, near the end of the fourth day, after all the luck with the weather. Many of those who watched an even struggle believed the result turned on a spectacular catch by a substitute fieldsman.

The Australians stayed at the Black Boy close to Nottingham's Council House, which had a carillon in its clock tower. The noise of the bells booming each hour was too much for the Australians and Woodfull asked for the chimes to be turned off from 11 p.m. to 7 a.m. so his players could get a good night's rest. Meticulous over even the smallest details, he never allowed visitors into the Australian dressing-room and even asked a Board of Control member to leave and wait until he received an invitation to return.

England found themselves in the position Australia had been in during the previous series, with Hobbs at 47 years old, Hendren at 41, White at 39 and Geary at 36 obviously past their prime, while Chapman and Jardine had played very little cricket since the last rubber in Australia. They faced a side that had nine players in their twenties, and six of those were under 23. Most worrying for England's veterans, however, was Grimmett, not Bradman, because his clever mixture of leg spin, top spin, googlies and the occasional straight one was more troublesome than the pace of Tim Wall or Alan Fairfax.

Chapman won the toss for England and on the first day his side struggled to 8 for 241. The lack of confidence against Grimmett had England reeling until Chapman hit out in a partner-

Test cricket's most famous substitute, Sydney Copley. He was a member of the Notts ground staff who went on for an injured England player and swung the first Test by brilliantly catching McCabe when Australia appeared in command.

ship of 82 with Hobbs, who took 215 minutes to compile 78. Heavy rain fell on the uncovered pitch overnight and interruptions for the weather prevented Australia starting the chase after England's 270 until mid-afternoon.

Tate bowled Ponsford at 4, had Woodfull superbly taken by Chapman at 6, and bowled Bradman for 8 with the score on 16. Kippax, so cruelly excluded from the last tour of England, batted intelligently on a drying pitch but could not prevent an Australian deficit of 126. The pitch had now recovered and England began with a stand of 125 by Hobbs and Sutcliffe, and when they left, Hendren's 72 helped England to 302.

Australia wanted 429, and at 1 for 60 at the end of the third day it still looked possible. At lunch the next day they were 3 for 198, with Bradman and McCabe scoring comfortably. Larwood was off the field with gastritis, with Copley, an almost unknown cricketer, fielding as England's thirteenth man at mid-on as his substitute. (Duleepsinhji, the nominated twelfth man, was already substituting for Sutcliffe.) Bradman and McCabe realised 77 in 70 minutes before Copley sprinted and then dived forward a full three metres to just take a catch that removed McCabe. Copley rolled over and over, but he still held the ball. It was the only thing of merit he did in first-class cricket and Notts only gave him one match in their senior side despite eight years on the ground staff.

Copley's catch swung the match. Shortly after McCabe left the field Bradman offered no stroke to a Robins googly and watched it turn in onto his stumps. He had batted for 4 hours 20 minutes and hit 10 fours for 131. Later Bradman explained that he had intended to protect his stumps but he had had gear trouble. "Just as I moved my feet across to put my pads in front, my left boot got stuck in my right pad, with the result that I could not move my feet at all," he wrote later. "I was helpless, and all I could do was to bend my knees and hope the ball would hit my pads. It turned back, kept low, and flicked the off stump. I was heart-broken."

From 3 for 229 Australia slumped to 5 for 267 and England had the match under control. Fairfax stayed for some time and Richardson made a few brave blows, but the Australian innings ended at 335, England winning by 93 runs. Tate's big effort in sending down 50 overs for only 69 runs in Australia's second innings, when Larwood was off the field, prevented Bradman and McCabe exploiting a winning chance.

After taking 10 for 201 in the Test, Grimmett turned on another fine showing in the next match against Surrey from 18 to 20 June at The Oval. Grimmett's 6 for 24 enabled Australia to bowl Surrey out for 162. Sound batting by Woodfull for 141 helped Australia to a big lead and allowed him to declare at 5 for 388. Hobbs rescued Surrey from likely defeat by scoring 146 not out, batting for four hours to force a draw.

Kippax made 120 against a weakened Lancashire attack at Old Trafford where rain caused frequent stoppages between 21 and 24 June. McDonald was unfit to play. Australia's first innings of 427 gave them enough runs to enforce a follow-on when they had Lancashire out for 259, but with only half an hour left for play Woodfull gave his batsmen some batting practice during which they made 1 for 79.

Behind the scenes a political argument had been going on in England for almost two years over the eligibility of Prince Kumar Duleepsinhji to play for England. Duleep, totally supported financially by his uncle, His Highness Shri Sir Ranjitsinhji Vibhaji, Jam Sahib of Nawanagar, scored 2500 runs for Ranji's old county, Sussex, in the 1929 season. He played for England in the first Test against South Africa in 1929 but was left out of the remaining Tests, some said because the South Africans objected to his selection. The South African captain Hubert ("Nummy") Deane denied this, but there was no doubt that Lord Harris and other influential figures at Lord's opposed Duleep's inclusion in the England side.

Duleep was fully qualified under the rules for Test matches set down by the Imperial Cricket Conference and the Australians had no objection to his playing in the Tests. Lord Harris was still treasurer and trustee of the MCC and when it became clear the England team needed strengthening, following the poor performance against Grimmett in the first Test, Duleep was brought into the side

Woodfull leads the Australians out at Lord's in 1930, with Bradman on his right.

for the second Test between 27 June and 1 July at Lord's.

England batted first and Duleep, going in after Hobbs and Woolley were out for 53, made 173 out of 332 in 235 minutes. Bradman was applauded as he took his place in the outfield and he and McCabe proceeded to field with a brilliance that saved dozens of runs and received repeated ovations. Bradman wrote later that many of Duleep's drives off Grimmett were so powerful that he had to bandage his bruised hand at the tea interval. Almost 30 years afterwards Neville Cardus wrote that "Duleep's cutting left even the Australian slips standing. His cricket was as though part of the afternoon's sunshine; it gleams in my mind even as I write."

Ranji was in his box at Lord's for the entire innings and said, "It was nothing but a sheer delight to see him. Through this innings of Duleep I have lived again all my own cricketing days." Ranji told friends that night he was the proudest man in England and that one of the great ambitions of his life had been realised when Duleep emulated his uncle's feat and scored a century in his first Test. Duleep scored 2562 runs that summer to further uplift Ranji, including 125 and 103 not out for the Gentlemen versus the Players, and his highest ever first-class score of 333 for Sussex against Northants.

England were 6 for 239 before bold hitting by Tate and Duleep added 98 and then a 38-run last-wicket stand lifted the total to 425. Ponsford and Woodfull began the Australian innings against the bowling of Tate and G. O. B. ("Gubby") Allen. Allen was the 27-year-old stockbroker son of Sir Walter

Allen, Commander-in-Chief of the London Metropolitan Special Constabulary, who had married the daughter of a Queensland Minister for Lands, and a grandson of Sir George Wigram Allen, a Speaker of the New South Wales Legislative Assembly. "Gubby" Allen was born in Sydney but went to England when he was 9 to be educated at Eton and Cambridge. Allen went into the England side in place of Larwood, who was injured, but he had no luck and at the end of the second day Australia were 2 for 404, only 21 behind.

The Australians batted to a plan. Woodfull and Ponsford steadily wore down the bowling for an attack later by Bradman, Kippax, McCabe and Richardson. Australia took three hours for the first 162, but when Ponsford was out for 81 the next 165 minutes yielded 242 runs. Woodfull was the second man out at 393 after scoring 155, but it was Bradman who dominated the stage with one of the most perfect innings he ever played.

Bradman did not offer a chance nor make a false stroke in contributing 155 of the 231 added with Woodfull. He had just caught up with Woodfull, who had had 78 runs and 170 minutes start when Duckworth stumped Woodfull off Robins. After a day's rest, Bradman carried on to 254 before a wonderful right-hand catch by Chapman at extra cover ended a glorious knock. He made only one false shot in five and a half hours' batting, at 191, when he edged a ball along the ground into the slips. The first ball he hit in the air cost him his wicket, with the Australian total at 585. He had put on 192 with Kippax for the third wicket and hit 25 fours. His 254 was the highest score ever made in a Test match in England to that time (exceeding Murdoch's 211 at The Oval in 1884) and was made 58 days before Bradman's twenty-second birthday.

Kippax continued to 83 and Australia declared at 6 for 729, a lead of 304. Grimmett dismissed both Hobbs and Woolley when England began the long task of saving the

Bradman gleefully raises his bat to acknowledge the crowd's applause after one of his fine performances in 1930.

match, and at stumps on the third day England were 2 for 93. Grimmett got Hammond and Hendren early next day and at 5 for 147 England looked badly beaten, until Chapman and Allen joined in a fighting partnership which carried the score to 5 for 262 at lunch.

Allen was out 10 runs later and with Chapman continuing to hit out at everything Grimmett concentrated on the other batsmen.

Chapman was eighth out at 354 after scoring 121, which included 4 sixes and 12 fours, a wonderful innings in a match full of marvellous batting. A foolish call by Robins ran out White, before Fairfax ended the England innings at 375 by trapping Duckworth leg before wicket.

Australia had only 72 to make and plenty of time to do so, but the excitement was not over. Ponsford, Bradman and Kippax went cheaply before Woodfull cleverly farmed the strike for the rest of the innings, taking most of danger-man Robins' bowling himself. Australia won a memorable struggle by seven wickets.

In Sydney, where the news arrived at 3 a.m., harbour ferries tooted their whistles and as dawn broke thousands of people mingled outside the *Sydney Morning Herald* office waiting for scores to be posted. Although thousands were on the dole, their worries were shelved as they listened to ball by ball descriptions of play on radio. The story of the game was sent from Test grounds to ten Australian broadcasting stations in specially coded messages. Power was supplied to the broadcasters by generating stations which stayed open to meet the demands of thousand of cricket fans across the nation. Those fortunate enough to own a "wireless" held cricket parties for friends and neighbours to hear broadcasts of play.

When the Australians went to Bradford to play Yorkshire from 2 to 4 July, Bradman had a tour average of 99. The cry that went up when local hero Emmott Robinson, a wily 46-year-old, had Bradman lbw for 1 with his first ball was still talked about 50 years later. Those who were there "that day Emmott shifted him" bragged about it proudly, although Australia won the match by 10 wickets. Australia's heroes this time were Ponsford, who made 143 out of 302, and Grimmett, who helped dismiss Yorkshire for 146 and 161. Grimmett took 6 for 75 and 5 for 58. This took him past his 100th wicket for the tour in only the sixteenth match.

At Trent Bridge from 5 to 8 July Nottinghamshire made the highest score of the tour against Australia by hitting 433, following Australia's first innings of 296. The ungainly William ("Dodger") Whysall, who had set a Notts county record the year before by scoring 2620 runs, made 120 and was well supported by team-mates against an attack that looked inept without Grimmett. Jackson (79), McCabe (79), Kippax (89 not out) and Richardson (69), had Australia 223 ahead when time ran out. Whysall died of septicaemia only four months later after he injured an elbow in a fall on a dance floor.

Yorkshire had a longer look at Bradman in the third Test at Headingley from 11 to 15 July. He went in when Jackson, who had replaced the unfit Ponsford, was out in the second over, after almost being bowled first ball by Tate. Bradman reached 50 in 49 minutes and 100 in 99 minutes from only 145 balls. At lunch he was 105 not out, the third Australian to score a century before lunch in a Test—Trumper was the first in 1902 and Macartney the second in 1926. By the tea interval he was 220 not out, having scored 115 in the second session of play, and at stumps he was 309 not out, having transformed Australia's total from 1 for 2 to 3 for 458.

Bradman added 192 for the second wicket with Woodfull, who made 50, 229 for the third wicket with Kippax (77) and after batting for 5 hours 15 minutes, passed R. E. Foster's highest ever England v. Australia Test score of 287. Foster took 6 hours 59 minutes to set his record in Sydney in the 1903–04 season, and it was the highest individual score in all Test cricket to that time. *The Times* said: "To mention the strokes from which he scored most of his runs is to go through the whole range of strokes known to modern batsmen. It was in fact an innings so glorious that it might well be classed as in-

Archie Jackson (left) going out to bat with Bradman during Australia's 1930 English tour. Two years later Jackson died of tuberculosis.

comparable, and how the Yorkshiremen loved it." Watching Bradman bat against Larwood, who had 1 for 139, "Plum" Warner turned to Lord Hawke and said, "This is like throwing stones at Gibraltar."

Next morning Bradman went on to 334 in 383 minutes. He hit 46 fours and gave only one chance, at 273, when Duckworth dropped him off Geary. He hit very hard in front of the wicket, cut and pulled in dazzling style and once again charmed the capacity crowd with his audacious footwork and the ease with which he found the gaps. Every full pitch bowled to him went for four and he lifted the ball off the grass only three times in the innings.

With Australia all out for 566, England were 5 for 212 by stumps on the second day. After Sutcliffe's dismissal the Australian

twelfth man, Alec Hurwood, took a telegram out to Bradman, who again was fielding superbly. The telegram read "Kindly convey my congratulations to Bradman. Tell him I wish him to accept £1000 as a token of my admiration for his performance." It was signed by Arthur Whitelaw, an Australian living in London who had made a fortune from a patent soap-making process. Bradman accepted the money.

English newspapers were ecstatic about Bradman's batting. Trevor Wignall said in the *Daily Express*: "When Bradman exceeded Foster's record, the enthusiasm was so terrific that play had to be stopped until the noise diminished. Bradman acknowledged it by waving his bat. He could not have been more mightily acclaimed in Australia." The *Sunday Times* considered that "Bradman is one of the rare miracles of the game, a player who can beat a side off his own bat." In Australia the *Sydney Morning Herald* reported that famous players at Headingley suggested the revival of lob bowling to combat Bradman. Newspapers in both countries agreed that in the face of such batsmanship only a cloudburst could save England from defeat.

The cloudburst arrived next morning, leaving pools of water across the ground. Play did not begin until 5.30 p.m., although it was clear the Australians were correct in their objection to the long delay, so easily did the pitch play when it was rolled out. Hammond reached his century (113) in 5 hours 25 minutes when there was only a draw to play for, but England followed on 179 runs behind with three hours remaining. Spectators booed when Hobbs and Sutcliffe appealed against the light and went off. There were cheers on the resumption when a spectacular throw from Bradman, at mid-off, ran out Hobbs. At 95 Duleepsinhji was out to a ball he confessed he did not see and another appeal against the light was immediately successful. Australia had to be satisfied with a draw, knowing they had

Bradman making his way through the crowd after his world record Test innings of 334 at Leeds in 1930.

given England's selectors plenty to think about.

Bradman's 334 set numerous records. On the way he became the first Test player to make 300 runs in one day. His time in reaching 200, 214 minutes, remains the fastest by any batsman in Test cricket. At 138, he completed his one-thousandth run in his seventh Test and thirteenth Test innings. At 21 years 318 days, Bradman was then the youngest

player to make 1000 Test runs. George Headley reached 1000 runs when 38 days younger than Bradman the following year, 1931, but Bradman remains the youngest to reach this mark in England versus Australia Tests. His and Kippax's 229 for the third wicket broke the record for that wicket against England, passing the 207 by Murdoch and Scott in 1884.

Two matches in Scotland and one in Sunderland between the third and fourth Tests were all ruined by rain, although Bradman did manage to make another century (140) in the second fixture at Glasgow against a Scottish XI before rain arrived.

The rain followed the Australians to Manchester and made another draw inevitable in the fourth Test from 25 to 29 July. Rain delayed the start, and only 45 minutes' play was possible on the third day and none at all on the fourth. The foothold was so uncertain that Chapman had a whole lot of sawdust put down at silly mid-off to stop himself slipping in the mud.

Woodfull and Ponsford gave Australia a good start against an England team from which Larwood, Geary and Tyldesley had been dropped for Morris Nichols, Tom Goddard and Ian Peebles. When Woodfull was caught at 106, Bradman went in and was beaten three times in an uneasy half-hour against Peebles, who had him caught at slip for 14. Ponsford went on to 83, then 51 from Kippax and 50 from Grimmett allowed Australia to score 345. England were 8 for 251, Sutcliffe scoring 74 and Duleepsinhji 54, when rain washed out play.

Archie Jackson, who had had a quiet tour, scored 118 against Somerset at Taunton. Jackson and Bradman (117) put on 231 for the second wicket. Australia made 360 because of this fine stand and defeated Somerset (121 and 81) by an innings and 158 runs inside two days, 30 and 31 July. Grimmett captivated capacity crowds by taking another 10 wickets, 3 for 38 and 7 for 33.

Three draws in a row followed in rainy weather—at Swansea against Glamorgan, at Birmingham against Warwickshire and at Northampton against Northamptonshire—in the first two weeks of August. Northants had the distinction of dismissing Australia for 99, their lowest score of the tour, and Australia had to follow on. Woodfull and Richardson, who both made 116, ended fears of an Australian defeat.

In the fifth Test England tried to solve their batting problems by dropping their captain Chapman for Bob Wyatt and replacing Nichols with Whysall. Whysall was 42 years old and had not played in a Test for six years. Australia replaced Richardson with Jackson for this Test at The Oval between 16 and 22 August.

Hobbs and Sutcliffe, knowing the match was to be played to a finish, began slowly. Just before lunch Hobbs, playing a pull shot from the pugnacious Wall, was caught by Kippax. Whysall made 13 before Wall had him lbw. Duleepsinhji made a dashing 50, Hammond failed, and Leyland was bowled by a Grimmett leg break. Wyatt went in at 5 for 197 and stayed with Sutcliffe until stumps, when England were 5 for 316. Next morning Sutcliffe took his score to 161, Wyatt was out for 64, and England finished with 405.

Australia quickly demonstrated her batting superiority. Woodfull and Ponsford put on 159 for the first wicket and when Woodfull was out for 54, Bradman helped Ponsford take the total along to 190. Ponsford was bowled by Peebles for 110, and Bradman batted the whole of the third day. Play was interrupted six times by rain or bad light, and Bradman finished on 130 not out as Australia moved to a huge score.

Numerous inspections of the pitch resulted in the captains disagreeing over its fitness, with Woodfull keen to protect his batsmen and Wyatt eager to get at them while the ball was popping. Finally the umpires decided to let play resume five minutes before stumps. The ground was almost empty and only two overs were possible as a result of this farcical decision.

The rain produced a lively wicket on the fourth morning. Larwood and Hammond made the ball fly, and Bradman, frequently hit, appeared inclined to draw away and spar at it. On 175 he received a nasty hit on the chest from Larwood. At the other end Jackson stood his ground, taking painful blows on the jaw, hip, ribs, shoulder and elbow. Bradman reached his third double century of the series in 6 hours 23 minutes and helped Jackson add

Australia's familiar foe, Herbert Sutcliffe, cutting a ball through the gully during his knock of 161 in the fifth Test at The Oval in 1930.

243 for the fourth wicket, another record for England versus Australia Tests. Jackson was out for 73, and soon after Bradman wrongly timed a square cut and was caught behind by Duckworth for 232; it was the first time Larwood had taken his wicket.

McCabe (54), Fairfax (53 not out) and Oldfield (34) continued the humiliation of England's bowlers and Australia's score reached 695, 44 of which were sundries. The 22 byes vindicated those who had urged the selection of Ames ahead of Duckworth behind the stumps, but the big loss to England was Chapman's inspiration in the field. Apart from his brilliant catching and throwing, Chapman had the knack of changing his bowlers at precisely the right moment.

England began batting 45 minutes before stumps, 290 in arrears. The great batsman

Jack Hobbs came to the wicket with Sutcliffe for his last Test innings and the Australians immediately surrounded him and gave him three hearty cheers. Hobbs was out for nine when the score was 17 and when bad light stopped play early, England were 1 for 24, and needed 266 to avoid an innings defeat.

The fifth day was washed out by rain and when the sun shone on the sixth morning it created conditions ideal for Hornibrook's left-arm spin. Sutcliffe (54) and Duleepsinhji (46) batted well and Hammond hit out boldly for 60, but when Leyland was bowled by Hornibrook, England were 5 for 189 and all hope had gone. Hornibrook finished with 7 for 92 in an innings in which Grimmett's 43 overs only yielded 1 for 90. England's second innings total of 251 meant that Australia had won by an innings and 39 runs. Against all the odds the Australians had regained the Ashes.

King George V immediately sent a message of congratulations to the Australian players through his private secretary: "I am directed to convey to Mr Woodfull His

Majesty's hearty congratulations on their success and their remarkable exhibitions in the Tests. It was a great pleasure to meet them and to watch them play." *The Times* praised Woodfull for the way he managed his bowling and encouraged his young players, and the big scores he made himself. "No praise is too high for Woodfull. The length of his stay at the wickets prepared the way for the rest of the side, and wore down the English bowling. He showed all the qualities of a great captain."

A controversial homecoming

The 1930 Australians return; the first West Indies tour 1930–31

The excitement of Australia's Ashes win by two Tests to one had barely subsided when the Australian players were involved in a remarkable finish in the match against Gloucestershire at Bristol between 23 and 26 August 1930. The Australians approached the match in a celebratory mood, which appeared justified when they bundled Gloucestershire out for 72, after they had asked for the start to be delayed. On a rain-affected pitch the Australian spinners achieved amazing break and the ball beat the bat more often than it was hit.

The last wicket fell just late enough to save the Australians from batting that night, which was probably fortunate, since the London *Sun* said "they were much under the influence of their Test-winning jubilations".

Hordes of people troop across Moore Park to see Bradman in action after his 1930 tour. Usually if Bradman was still in at lunch the crowds would increase dramatically, as they were almost sure of seeing him reach a century during the afternoon session.

Australian singer Harold Williams, who played Hiawatha, shaking hands with Bradman after a performance at the Royal Albert Hall in 1930.

and then bowled him. Goddard twice appealed unsuccessfully for lbw against Jackson and had a third appeal accepted. Parker then had Richardson, who as captain lacked Woodfull's disciplinary ability, stumped. But at 3 for 67 at lunch Australia still appeared in no danger.

However, Parker next had Kippax lbw, and then Sinfield picked up the ball and threw smartly from mid-on to run Ponsford out. Bradman and a'Beckett stayed for a time but could not get the ball away. At 81 there was a tremendous roar as Parker bowled Bradman, taking his wicket for the second time in the match. This elation in the crowd increased when Parker had a'Beckett caught in the slips five runs later. Australia looked in dire trouble with the seven top-order batsmen out and 32 runs still required.

At 96, with Grimmett on 6, Lyon, in the leg trap, dived impetuously and got a hand to a ball which would have carried to him had he remained where he was—and dropped it. Twice Grimmett was almost run out scampering for singles, but he put on 22 with Hurwood to take Australia within 12 runs of the target. Goddard appealed every time the ball hit the pads but it was Parker who had Hurwood lbw to end the stand.

Ten runs were needed, with eight batsmen out, as Hornibrook joined Grimmett. Hornibrook withstood two appeals for lbw, but with only three runs to win Parker dismissed Grimmett. Last man Charlie Walker came in and two singles brought the scores level. Hornibrook survived an over from Goddard without touching the ball. Walker played his second successive maiden, then Goddard appealed for lbw against Hornibrook and up went the umpire's signal of agreement. The scores were level, with Australia all out for 117 on a pitch that had been just about unplayable for the last hour. It was the first time in 17 tours of England that Australia had played a tied match. Parker took 7 for 54.

Bradman celebrated his twenty-second

Hornibrook carried on the destruction he had wreaked in the Test and took 4 for 20, and Grimmett caused great amusement by imparting spin that made the ball curl round the batsmen's legs, as if he had it on a string.

Taking the match quite easily, the Australians managed only 157 in their first innings. When Hammond made 89 (mainly boundaries off Grimmett), Gloucestershire reached 202 in their second innings, leaving Australia to score 118 to win on a pitch which was helping the bowlers.

Charlie Parker was erratic early and could not find the worn patches to exploit with his left-arm spinners. McCabe and Jackson made 59, half the runs needed, for the first wicket, in only 40 minutes. Then Parker found the right spots, twice completely beat McCabe birthday on the first day of the match with Kent at Canterbury, which ran from 27 to 29 August. He went in at 1 for 39 but was lbw to "Tich" Freeman for 18 in an Australian total of 181. After Tim Wall took 5 for 60 to help get Kent out for 227, Bradman went in again just before tea on the second day and was 205 not out when Australia declared at 3 for 320. Bradman batted for four and three-quarter hours without a chance. It was his sixth double century of the season and included 28 fours.

Kent batted out the remaining two hours to force a draw and the large crowd went home happy that they had seen Bradman at his best. His footwork against Freeman's leg spin often took him metres down the pitch but he never appeared likely to miscue. His partnership with Jackson (50 not out) was worth 195 unfinished.

Although the struggle for the Ashes was over, big crowds continued to watch the Australians as they wound up the tour, most of them eager to catch a glimpse of the phenomenon, Bradman. At Brighton against Sussex between 30 August and 2 September it was Kippax, however, who gave most entertainment. Maurice Tate, making the ball dart about in a helpful sea breeze, took 6 for 18 and Australia were 7 for 79. But the ever-nimble Kippax, with the help of three tail-enders, took the score to 367 with a marvellous 158. When Kippax was out, Hurwood flung the bat at everything in a hectic knock of 61, adding 100 for the last wicket with Hornibrook, who went on to 59 not out, highest score of his career.

After Sussex had responded with 269 (Hornibrook 5 for 51), Kippax made his second century of the match. He scored 102 not out in Australia's second innings of 9 for 233 declared. Play was delayed while the players had tea with the famous English pilot, Amy Johnson, who had just become the first woman to fly solo from England to Australia. Sussex had no time to get the 331 which

would have given them the game and were 1 for 93 when time expired. Tate's match aggregate of 9 for 121 earned him a collection from his home crowd, spectators showering a huge blanket with coins.

Another draw followed at Folkestone from 3 to 5 September against an England XI, with the Australians trying to enliven proceedings after dreary batting by all the Englishmen except Chapman. The England XI took all the first day to reach 5 for 249 in what was intended to be a carefree festival match. Ames reached 121 and Chapman made 40 in half an hour on the second morning for the England XI to declare at 8 for 403 before the Australians produced some champagne batting. Bradman and Jackson added 100 in an hour, Bradman striking Wyatt for 3 fours in one over. Ponsford made 76, Bradman 63, Jackson 78, a'Beckett 53 and Hornibrook maintained his fine record at number ten with a sparkling 43. Australia's 432 gave them a 29-run lead.

At Lord's on 6 and 8 September in a match against the Club Cricket Conference (CCC) players, the Australians scored 278 in their first innings, but it was enough to win by an innings and 41 runs. For the first and only time on the tour the wider and higher stumps were used, but they had little to do with the collapse of the CCC batsmen for 133 and 104. The bowling was just too classy, Hurwood having first innings figures of 5 for 14, a'Beckett 3 for 1 in the second innings.

Rain prevented any chance of a result in the final match of the tour against H. D. G. Leveson-Gower's XI at Scarborough on 10 to 12 September. Bradman could have been out first ball but Wyatt was slow to move to a catch off Rhodes at mid-on. Rhodes was then 52 years old. Bradman made 96 before he was bowled by Charlie Parker and Hornibrook's eight wickets for the match took him past 100 tour victims. Hobbs, a disappointment in the last four Tests, in which he showed signs of frayed nerves by quarrelling with spectators and umpires, passed his 2000 runs for the season by scoring 59 in the second innings.

Despite a wet summer Bradman scored 2960 runs at an average of 98.66 in 36 tour innings. This was a far higher aggregate than the previous record by Victor Trumper, who made 2570 at 48.49 in 1902, and better than the previous best average of 58.37 by Charlie Macartney in 1921. In seven Test innings he made 974 runs at an average of 139, with a century, two double centuries and a triple century.

Grimmett also broke all previous tour records by taking 144 wickets, four more than the previous best by Hugh Trumble in 1902. But Grimmett's wickets, four more than the previous best by Hugh Trumble in 1902. But Grimmett's wickets cost 16.85 apiece, whereas Trumble's were slightly cheaper at 14.27. In Tests the cost of Grimmett's 29 wickets jumped to 31.89 each.

The Australians lost only one of their 34 matches and made history by playing a tie. They had 12 wins and 19 draws. In all, they scored 27 centuries and had only eight scored against them. Bradman's 10 centuries were four more than the next best Australian, Woodfull, and six more than Kippax and Ponsford scored. Six of the Australians, Bradman, Kippax, Woodfull, Ponsford, Jackson and McCabe, scored more than 1000 runs on the tour. Only Grimmett (144) and Hornibrook (103) took more than 100 wickets in all matches.

In the 12 months from 1 November 1929, to 31 October 1930, Bradman scored 4546 runs in first-class matches, the most on record by an Australian in the space of a year, and he made another 2000-odd in minor games. His tour average of 98.66 was unheard-of in England and his average of 139.14 was also a record for a Test series. He was generally rated the best fieldsman in the Australian side, shading even the tremendously athletic Vic

Clarrie Grimmett, who broke all previous tour records in 1930 by taking 144 wickets.

Richardson, who kept pressure on England's batsmen throughout the tour with his work at silly mid-off.

The London *News Chronicle* commented that "As long as Australia has Bradman she will be invincible . . . in order to keep alive the competitive spirit, the authorities might take a hint from billiards. It is almost time to request a legal limit on the number of runs Bradman should be allowed to make." The rules of billiards had just been changed to outlaw the rocker cannon, with which Australian Walter Lindrum had made massive scores.

The profit from county and Test matches of the Australian tour was £20,483 sterling, to which £1789 was added because of the favourable rate of exchange when the payment was sent to Australia. Australia's share from all gate receipts when the proceeds from matches in Launceston, Hobart, Perth and Colombo were added was £38,180 sterling. Arthur

Mailey, in his financial analysis of the tour, gave these figures (in pounds sterling) for the Tests:

	Australia	England
Nottingham	£2723	£12,352
Lord's	£6065	£23,518
Leeds	£2602	£ 8,600
Manchester	£3365	£13,821
The Oval	£5864	£18,977
Total	£20,619	£77,268

Like everything else about this remarkable tour, Australia's financial results were a record, although they were clearly inequitable when compared to England's share. In 1921 Australia received £11,175 as her share of the Test profits, and in 1926, £15,727.

Bradman was inundated with offers as the result of his unprecedented run-scoring. Naturally reserved, he did not enjoy standing at the bar or quaffing a few beers in the dressing-room at the end of a hard day in the field. He celebrated his 334 in the Leeds Test playing records in his hotel room. At his age he could not have been aware of any gap between himself and the rest of the team, some of whom were undoubtedly put out about the manner in which he dominated the tour and just could not believe his casual acceptance of success.

Before the team left England vice-captain Vic Richardson asked for a few weeks leave to accept an invitation to gain experience with the London headquarters of the company he represented in Adelaide. Manager Bill Kelly realised this would mean a lot to Richardson, but said he could not grant the request because of the Board of Control's strict instructions that all players must return as a team in the same ship to their home ports. The team sailed to Australia aboard the *Oronsay* and before it berthed at Fremantle Bradman's employers, Mick Simmons, received approval from Board of Control chairman Aubrey Oxlade for Bradman to leave the ship in Adelaide and travel independently the rest of the way home. Manager Kelly knew nothing of the Board's action and was understandably upset when told about it.

The *Oronsay* berthed at Fremantle to a tumultuous reception. Every boat in port saluted the team, while on the wharf police struggled to contain thousands of well-wishers. Bradman avoided all efforts by the crowd to carry him shoulder-high. "If you carry me, you have to carry the whole team," he said. At a civic reception in Fremantle Town Hall Woodfull thanked all Australians for the wonderful messages they had sent the team throughout the tour. Bradman refused to travel in a single-seater car from the wharf to the Town Hall, and insisted on travelling with team-mates when they drove to Perth for a lunch given by the Western Australian Cricket Association.

None of the well-documented reports of the Australians' arrival show any attempt by Bradman to grab the limelight, but he undoubtedly erred in leaving the team at Adelaide and flying to Melbourne and Goulburn in the *Southern Cloud*, a monoplane piloted by T. S. Shortridge, which became lost when the controls iced up on the way to Melbourne, arriving two hours late. When they eventually got to Essendon airport more than 10,000 people were waiting to see Bradman, who arrived frozen in the unheated *Southern Cloud*. From Goulburn he careered to Sydney in a car driven by champion racing driver "Wizard" Smith at the then wild speed of 70 miles (112 kilometres) per hour. The rest of the team travelled more slowly aboard the *Oronsay* and by the time they arrived in Melbourne and then Sydney, Bradman had finished the biggest promotional tour seen in Australia.

He was mobbed in theatres and major stores, with women jostling each other to get close enough to kiss him. A wide range of products, including bats, gloves, pads, shirts

After flying across Australia in the ill-fated Southern Cloud, Bradman completed the trip to Sydney in this car driven by racing driver "Wizard" Smith.

and slacks, which he endorsed, were swooped on by his fans. This had seldom been done before in Australia and there were no rules in the Control Board's guidelines to cover it. England's cricketers, on the other hand, endorsed gear and "Jack Hobbs" bats were best-sellers there.

To the others in the team it seemed that Bradman was usurping the accolades that belonged to Woodfull. Jack Fingleton, Dick Whitington and other critics who conducted long campaigns against Bradman, all started their condemnation from the moment he took that flight. At the time, though, it was an adventurous undertaking. Less than five months later *Southern Cloud* disappeared on a journey from Sydney to Melbourne.

For Bradman the plane trip, at times very bumpy, meant an opportunity to make money in grim economic times, and an earlier re-union with his mother, whose health was always a concern. But when the bulk of the team arrived at Adelaide in *Oronsay* manager Kelly did not mention Bradman, and in a speech at the welcoming reception put on by the South Australian Cricket Association, named Grimmett as the key man on the tour. On an Adelaide radio station a few days later vice-captain Vic Richardson said, "We could have played any team without Bradman, but we could not have played the blind school without Grimmett."

After a hectic reception in Bowral, where the band played a new tune called "Our Don Bradman", Bradman arrived at Mick Simmons' Sydney store to find police trying to control the 2000 people who wanted to get in to meet him. At Sydney Town Hall, after another tremendous ovation he was presented with a two-seater car, a gift from General Motors. Mark Gosling, Chief Secretary in the newly elected Jack Lang government, made a speech in which he compared Bradman to the great racehorse Phar Lap. Phar Lap had won the Melbourne Cup the day before, in the midst of a sequence in which he won 31 races from 33 starts.

Bradman's success was so complete, accomplished as it was in the land of our forebears, that it gave Australians a new sense of pride and proof that they were no longer second-rate. From the time they tottered ashore from prison ships, bodies stinking, skins whipped and burnt, white Australians had been a people willing to be led, a race sadly convinced of its inferiority, but now there was hope that in some fields at least they could take on the world.

Crowds struggle to get a look at Bradman on his first day back at work after his triumphant 1930 tour. He worked at Mick Simmons' Sydney sports store.

Bradman was a problem for the Board of Control long before he left the 1930 team in Adelaide, however. He had sold a series of articles to the London *Star*, against the wishes of manager Kelly. The articles, labelled "My Life Story by Don Bradman", appeared in the *Star* from 4 August 1930, between the fourth and fifth Tests. Kelly considered that they breached the players' tour contract, but Bradman claimed that as none of the articles referred to the 1930 tour he was within his right to publish.

After listening to Bradman defend his actions, the Board fined him £50 on the basis of Kelly's tour report. All the tourists received £600 for the tour, £50 before leaving Australia, £400 during the tour, and £150 on their return. The final payment was subject to a satisfactory report from the manager on the player's behaviour and the Board simply deducted £50 from Bradman's cheque. In his book *Cricket Crisis*, Jack Fingleton said that some Board members wanted to fine Bradman the full £150 due as the final tour

payment. Bradman bitterly resented paying the £50 penalty but was compelled to accept it. Grimmett was also brought before the Board for writing a book on cricket but was let off with a caution because none of it was serialised during the tour.

The Board of Control had banned players writing for newspapers during tours to protect the reputation of Australian cricket. Bradman considered there was nothing in the articles that offended. In fact, the pieces were so innocuous it is doubtful if any newspaper would publish them in the 1980s.

Bradman began the 1930–31 Australian season by scoring 61 and 121 for New South Wales in the Sheffield Shield match against South Australia. This started in Sydney on 7 November, and Bradman was delivering a promise he made to one of the welcoming receptions. He had not picked up a bat since leaving England, but he ran up the 121 in 142 minutes before a crowd of more than 12,000. This was the first season the larger, higher stumps were used in Australia, and the first season in which pitches were covered against rain.

Larger than usual crowds continued wherever Bradman played. Even at grade matches for St George he packed them in and the club became accustomed to record attendances, with spectators cheering Bradman all the way to the crease when it came his turn to bat. When the club hired the Victory Theatre in Kogarah for a welcome-home function for Bradman and Fairfax, every seat was taken, with the overflow standing round the walls. Bradman had to make so many public appearances it was not surprising that he grew to hate them in later life.

At Melbourne in the testimonial match for Jack Ryder between Australia and the Rest, from 14 to 18 November, there was great delight when Bradman fell victim in both innings to the wiles of Arthur Mailey.

The Rest had 224 on the board, thanks to 108 from Port Adelaide right-hand opener Gordon Harris, for the loss of only three wickets. Then Grimmett got to work and they lost their remaining batsmen for only 69. All the Australian side made runs except Jackson, with Bradman scoring 73, Kippax 70 and Woodfull 53 in establishing a lead of 74.

The Rest declared at 3 for 191 in their second innings after Keith Rigg (74) and Ryder (65 not out) scored freely, leaving the Australians to make 118 in 90 minutes. Steady

Victorian Keith Rigg, one of the most accomplished Australian batsmen never to get a trip to England. He broke into Test cricket in 1930–31 when he made one of his 14 first-class centuries for Victoria against the West Indies.

bowling from Ironmonger, Blackie and "Bull" Alexander prevented this and they were 22 short on 5 for 96 when time ran out. Ryder was presented with £3000 from the benefit. There was unrestrained delight when Mailey, who had dismissed Victor Trumper almost three decades earlier, caught and bowled Bradman after clean-bowling him in the first innings. Mailey wrote later that while watching his triumphant English tour in 1930 he had noticed Bradman's discomfort against Peebles' top spinner and so had used his top spinner against Bradman.

The Western Australian proposal for an Australian Second XI competition was formally put to an interstate conference on 11 September 1931. The plan was for Western Australia, South Australia and Victoria to play a round robin in Melbourne and Queensland, New South Wales and Tasmania to do the same in Sydney. The winner of each group would then play off in a final at Melbourne. Tasmania and Western Australia were to field their strongest teams, but the other states were restricted to players who had appeared in a maximum of two Shield matches. The competition would be held every second season, with Tasmania and Western Australia making tours to the other states in the "off" season. Western Australia's persistence forced the Board to appoint a sub-committee to frame conditions of play. Victoria suggested the competition should be for the Donald MacKinnon Shield. MacKinnon was then VCA president and held the job for 26 years.

The whole idea finally was dropped because of the suggestion that all expenses be shared equally by the competing states. Tasmania was very keen on the scheme but had no chance of raising the money to send a team to Sydney. At the time the Tasmanian Cricket Association was impoverished by having to pay for a sewerage service at the TCA ground in Hobart. Tasmania offered to play its matches in Melbourne if Western Australia

would go to Sydney, but Tasmania insisted that it could only pay its own expenses and not share in the heavier expenses of the other states. When the proposal was put to the vote, Tasmania and South Australia opposed it and that killed the scheme, although the other states were ready to go ahead.

Victoria won the Sheffield Shield for the thirteenth time in the 1930–31 season, but New South Wales finished only one point behind. The struggle was keen throughout, with Test places against the West Indies touring team at stake. Victoria and New South Wales were level when the last Shield match between Victoria and South Australia began in Adelaide on 20 February and it ended in a draw. The point Victoria received as the team which trailed on the first innings in a drawn match was enough to win her the Shield.

The Test matches against the West Indies, who were visiting Australia for the first time, kept Woodfull and Ponsford out of some Victorian matches, but young newcomers acquitted themselves well. Victoria beat South Australia in Melbourne and New South Wales in Sydney, both on the first innings. The St Kilda right-hand batsman Hector Oakley and the Richmond left-hander Leo O'Brien impressed, O'Brien scoring 119 against New South Wales in Sydney at the end of January, his first Shield century. The bowling of Ironmonger, who took 29 wickets for 15 runs each and Blackie, 26 wickets at 15, largely contributed to Victoria's success.

After starting with a century Bradman scored 695 in six innings for New South Wales at an average of 115. In the match against South Australia in Adelaide from 18 to

OVER PAGE: The 1930–31 New South Wales team at Brisbane: (L to R) (back) C. Andrews, H. Chilvers, G. Stewart, S. McCabe, A. Allsopp, A. Jackson; (front) W. Hunt, W. Bill, A. Kippax (captain), S. Storey (manager), H. Love, H. Hooker, A. Fairfax.

Australia's oldest Test player Don Blackie going out to bat for Victoria in 1930 at the age of 48.

22 December, Bradman made 258, putting on 334, a record for Shield cricket, with Jackson (166) for the second wicket. Kippax and McCabe were dependable run-getters and of the less known players Wendell Bill scored 404 runs at 50, including two centuries. An outspoken left-hand, slow-medium bowler from Balmain who had grown up with Archie

Jackson, Bill Hunt, took 28 wickets at 18 runs each.

The long argument between players and officials about the administration of the game in Queensland continued and Leo O'Connor dropped out of the game after a long, successful career. Cec Thompson, whose 275 not out against New South Wales in Brisbane, from 28 November to 2 December, was the highest score made for the State to that time, all-rounder Ron Oxenham, and the controversial pace bowler Eddie Gilbert all helped Queensland give a good account of herself. Some prominent southern players claimed Gilbert's delivery was illegal and slow motion films taken by the QCA—but kept secret—supported this view.

Gilbert emerged at a time the public supported the White Australia policy, a concept designed to protect jobs for white men and developed after the employment of cheap Kanaka and Chinese labour. He was born in 1908 at Woodford, not far north of Brisbane. The Protector of Aborigines would not agree to Gilbert's transfer from the Barambah Aboriginal settlement to Brisbane unless he had a job and a suitable place to live. It was arranged that during first-class matches he would sleep in a tent in the QCA secretary's back-yard. Between matches he returned to Barambah.

Gilbert bowled at a sizzling pace from an approach run of five or six paces and his arm swung in a blur which made it impossible for umpires to tell if he was throwing. It is likely that only his faster balls, let go twice an over, were throws. His arms were extremely long, hanging below his knees, and his action was similar to that used in launching a spear from a woomera or spear-thrower. The amazing aspect of his bowling was that he achieved such speed with a small, wiry frame. He weighed only 57 kilograms and was 173 centimetres tall. He should have done a lot better than 15 wickets for 502 runs in his first season, but Queensland slips fieldsmen could

The controversial Queensland pace bowler Eddie Gilbert. Many said he would have played for Australia had he not been an Aboriginal.

not hold some of the catches that Gilbert made fly from the bat.

Gilbert was luckier than Aboriginal batsman Sam Anderson, who scored more runs and more centuries than any player in the history of cricket on the New South Wales north coast. Anderson broke into the headlines with 1038 runs, including five centuries, for Casino in 1913–14. In 1919–20 he made 1458 runs, with nine centuries, for Lismore at an average of 121.50. He continued in this form throughout the 1920s, at one stage winning the inter-district average five years out of six. Anderson was estimated to have made around 100 centuries, with a top score of 261 not out in 1919–20. Although he was a capable

bowler and wicket-keeper, he was never invited to practise with a state team.

The discontent among Queensland players over the competence of their officials finally resulted in members of the state team flouting the authority of the Queensland Cricket Association and setting up their own selection committee. The QCA responded by suspending five players, Frank Gough, Vic Goodwin, Charles Bensted, Gordon Amos and "Pud" Thurlow. Two others, Cec Thompson and "Mo" Biggs, were asked to show cause why they should not be similarly dealt with. The suspensions prevented the players appearing for their clubs as well as for Queensland.

The dispute ended with the vindication of the players and the appointment of a special committee to review the whole constitution of the QCA, with a firm instruction to selectors not to betray confidential opinions on players.

The West Indies, who first played Test cricket in 1928 when they lost all three Tests in England, sent 16 players for their first tour of Australia between November 1930 and February 1931. By then the visits of 10 English teams, starting with the 1894–95 tour by the side organised by Lord Stamford and captained by the Middlesex amateur Robert Lucas, had steadily improved playing standards in the Caribbean.

The West Indian team comprised G. C. Grant (Trinidad, captain), L. S. Birkett (Trinidad), C. A. Roach (Trinidad), E. R. Hunte (Trinidad), L. H. Constantine (Trinidad), E. St Hill (Trinidad), G. Headley (Jamaica), F. R. Martin (Jamaica), I. Barrow (Jamaica), O. C. Scott (Jamaica), E. L. Bartlett (Barbados), J. E. D. Sealy (Barbados), H. C. Griffith (Barbados), G. Francis (Barbados), F. E. de Caires (British Guiana), O. S. Wright (British Guiana), R. H. Mallett (manager) and J. E. Seheult (assistant manager).

The team was badly chosen for Australian conditions, with the attack dependent on fast bowling. Sturdy Barbadian Herman Griffith, the acrobatic son of a plantation owner, Learie Constantine, and poker-faced George Francis all bowled fast and accurately but there was little support bowling of quality. Frank Martin bowled left-arm slows which kept the runs down and O. C. ("Tommy") Scott's leg breaks worried some Australians, but there was really not enough depth and variety in the West Indian attack to concern such an outstanding array of batting talent as Australia boasted.

Many of the West Indian players met for the first time on the ship travelling to Australia and their captain, "Jackie" Grant, though enthusiastic, lacked international experience. Grant, who later became a missionary, had won Blues at Cambridge for both cricket and soccer, and insisted that his players treat the Australian tour in a sportsmanlike manner.

The West Indians won only 5 of their 16 matches and their 8 losses included the first four Tests. Grant's deputy, Lionel Birkett, had won international acclaim for his 253 for Trinidad against British Guiana at Georgetown in 1929–30, but failed to reproduce that form in Australia, apart from a sound 64 in the first Test.

The side included two of cricket's most dramatic entertainers, George Headley, who arrived bearing the tag the "Black Bradman", and Learie Constantine. Constantine's presence on the field guaranteed exciting events, for he took some amazing catches, leaping metres to drag in apparently safe strokes. His big hitting with the bat produced long sixes at almost every ground on which he played and his fast bowling was brimful of pace and energy. Headley took several matches to settle down but finished the tour with four delightful centuries, two of them in the Tests.

The tour began at Sydney with a loss to New South Wales in a match running from 21 to 25 November. The West Indian batsmen struggled against the subtle leg spin of Hughie Chilvers, who had 4 for 84 and 5 for 73. At Melbourne from 28 November to 1 December, Headley made the first tour century (131) and Constantine helped him add 76 in the West Indies' first innings, but after Ponsford (187) and Rigg (126) thrashed the West Indian attack Victoria reached 594. This was enough to give the Victorian players a win by an innings and 284 runs. Ironmonger took 5 for 87 and 8 for 31.

South Australia inflicted the third straight defeat on the West Indians at Adelaide between 5 and 8 December. This time Grimmett (4 for 71 and 5 for 43) was the destroyer in South Australia's ten-wicket victory.

Grimmett sustained his ascendancy over the West Indian batsmen for the rest of the tour, finishing the five-Test series with 33 wickets at an average cost of 17.96. Ironmonger gave him good support with 22 wickets at 14.68. On wickets unsuitable for fast bowlers, the West Indies struggled to get Australia out.

Australia won the first Test at Adelaide, from 12 to 16 December, by 10 wickets. Kippax made 146 in Australia's first innings of 376, but it was Grimmett's 7 for 87 and 4 for 96 that paved the way to the Australian win. Australia needed 170 in the final innings and Ponsford and Jackson got them without being separated, Ponsford scoring 92 not out, Jackson 70 not out.

The West Indies' first win of the tour came at Launceston between 20 and 23 December. They defeated Tasmania by an innings and 50 runs. Tasmania made 184 and 119, the West Indies 353. Constantine put on a crowd-pleasing display and hit a six, a five and 10 fours in his 100. On the last day the sad news came from England that former England captain Johnny Douglas had drowned trying to save his father when the ship in which they were travelling, the *Oberon*, was

Clarrie Grimmett, most subtle and gifted of all leg spinners in Australian cricket. His 7 for 87 and 4 for 96 against the West Indies in the first Test at Adelaide in 1931 paved the way to an Australian victory.

Australia scored 4 for 323 on the first day, New Year's Day 1931, with Ponsford scoring 183. Wickets fell quickly for the rest of the match, which ended on 5 January. Australia were all out for 369, but the West Indies managed only 107 and 90 in trying conditions, batting a man short in both innings after Bartlett crushed a finger catching Kippax.

Constantine revived West Indian spirits with innings of 75 and 97 against Queensland from 10 to 14 January at the Gabba. He also dismissed seven batsmen for 56 and took three great catches to set up a victory by 219 runs. Gilbert took 5 for 65 in the West Indies' first innings, but apart from Vic Goodwin, who made 60 and 54, none of the Queensland batsmen were impressive. Gilbert was hit for six for the first time in this match. He watched the ball soar over the square leg fence from Constantine's bat and then rushed down the pitch and shook Constantine's hand.

Australia took the rubber by winning the third Test in Brisbane by an innings and 217 runs. Play started on 16 January and Queenslander Ron Oxenham came into the Australian side. Once again it was Grimmett, with 9 for 144 in the match, who was mainly responsible for the West Indian batting failure. Australia gained an early advantage on the first day when Ponsford made 109 and Bradman ran up 223. This helped Australia to 588, to which the West Indies team replied with 193 and 148. Headley's 102 not out in the first innings was a great effort but eight of his team-mates failed to reach double figures.

The West Indies played a draw against a weakened Victorian side at Melbourne from 31 January to 4 February; all the senior Victorian players were in Brisbane for a Shield match. Roach made 104 in the West Indies' first innings and time ran out with the last Victorian batsmen at the crease and 129 needed for a win. Headley's two innings in this match yielded 77 and 113.

South Australia defeated the West Indies

involved in a collision off Finland. Tasmanian and West Indian players donned black armbands as a tribute to Douglas.

Rain upset the second match with Tasmania, which was played at Hobart from 24 to 26 December. It was left drawn, with the West Indies only 39 behind Tasmania's first innings total of 289, with eight wickets in hand. Birkett was on 128 not out, Martin 79 not out.

Australia won the second Test at Sydney by an innings and 172. Rain completely changed the character of the match after

George Headley, star of the first West Indian team to tour Australia in 1930–31. He scored the West Indies' first Test century against Australia.

two days, 13 and 14 January, to win by an innings and 122 runs. Ironmonger had exceptional figures, dismissing seven batsmen for 23 runs in the West Indies' first innings of 99, and four for 56 in the second innings of 107. Bradman top-scored with 152 in Australia's innings of 8 for 328, with Woodfull once again wearing down the attack with a stubborn 183.

With their tour in tatters and experts doubting that they were up to first-class standard the West Indies staged a stunning revival, beating New South Wales and Australia in the last matches on their schedule. In both matches their batting showed the consistency lacking in all the earlier displays.

Good sustained batting by the top order gave the West Indians a first innings lead of 149 against New South Wales. Then Derek Sealy, at 18 the youngest of the tourists, steadied their second innings after the fall of three cheap wickets by scoring 92. Constantine supported this with 93 in 100 minutes, including some huge hits for six, and further rapid scoring enabled Grant to declare at 9 for 403 and set New South Wales 553 to win. Bradman made 73 before Kippax (141) and McCabe (100) took the score to 4 for 373, but then New South Wales collapsed and the West Indies won by 86 runs. Constantine scored 43 and 93 with the bat, and took seven for 84 in the match.

In the fifth Test at Sydney from 27 February to 4 March, the West Indies won a notable victory by 30 runs after declaring in both innings. Australia were caught on a sticky wicket in each innings after 123 not out from Freddie Martin and a lovely 105 by George Headley allowed the West Indies to declare in their first innings at 6 for 350. With a lead of 126 in the first innings, the West Indians struggled to 4 for 124 in difficult conditions in their second. The pitch was bathed in sun after continuous rain when Grant's declaration set Australia 247 to win on

by one wicket in an exciting finish at Adelaide Oval. Grant, who had been run out for 84 in the previous match, this time made 102. South Australia trailed by 105 in the first innings, despite 106 from "Perka" Lee, who then took 5 for 57 in the West Indies' second innings. Left to score 314 to win, South Australia got them rapidly, handing out heavy punishment to all the West Indian batsmen. Richardson made a fast 52, Lonergan and Merv Waite put on 96, but the last pair still had to get 22 to win the match.

Dismal batting in both innings brought heavy defeat for the West Indies in the fourth Test at Melbourne, where Australia took only a perfect "sticky".

Half Australia's wickets fell for 74 runs, Bradman playing over a yorker from Griffith for his first Test match duck, which made almost as many headlines as some of his centuries. McCabe and Fairfax appeared likely to get the runs in a fine partnership, with McCabe hitting out while Fairfax defended, but a magnificent catch by Grant ended the stand. Fairfax was left on 60 not out when the innings folded up at 220. Bradman was very impressed with Constantine, Sealy and Headley but said his own concentration was affected by the Board's action in fining him, and the allegations that he had stolen Woodfull's rightful acclaim on their return home.

At the end of the season, in March and April, Bradman went on a tour of northern Queensland with a team captained by Alan Kippax. By the time the side reached Rockhampton he had scored 651 runs and taken 33 wickets but in the first few minutes of play there he sprained an ankle so badly he spent 18 days in hospital. The injury weakened his ankle and may have contributed to his breakdown at The Oval in 1938. At the time his main regret was missing Stan McCabe's innings of 173, including 18 sixes, at Gympie.

The Australian Women's Cricket Council was formed during the 1930–31 season, with New South Wales, Victoria and Queensland foundation members. South Australia and Western Australia joined in 1935–36. The Council emerged just 57 years after the first women's matches in Australia were played at Bendigo, and 45 years after the first women's match on the Sydney Cricket Ground between Fernleas and Siroccos. First task of the Council was to organise regular competition between the states and to produce a team that would not be disgraced when they brought a women's team out from England.

The perfect baggage master

South Africa and Australia on tour 1931–32

The Depression years of the early 1930s produced an exodus of New South Wales players to Queensland. Cricketers frustrated by their failure to find jobs or regular places in the New South Wales side went north hoping for both work and recognition as first-class cricketers, a path first followed by Gordon Amos in 1927–28.

Amos was followed by Roy Levy in 1928–29, "Cassie" Andrews in 1931–32 and, as the Sydney dole queues lengthened, Ernie Laidler and Frank Ward from the St George club in Sydney. Laidler was a talented wicketkeeper batsman, Ward a leg spinner who eventually won a place in an Australian team to England. Laidler and Ward joined Queensland representatives Eric Bensted and Frank Gough in the Brisbane Northern Suburbs

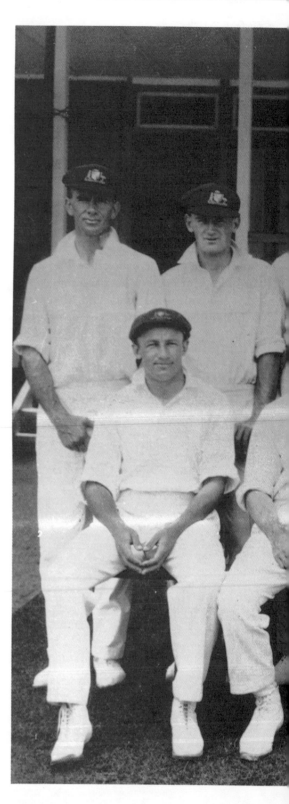

The Australian team that met South Africa in 1931–32 at Brisbane: (L to R) (back) R. Oxenham, S. McCabe, K. Rigg, T. Wall, H. Ironmonger, H. Nitschke, W. Oldfield; (front) D. Bradman, C. Grimmett, W. Woodfull, A. Kippax, W. Ponsford. They won by an innings and 163 runs.

Bill O'Reilly, an unlucky omission from the 1930 England tour, soon proved the selectors wrong. By the 1931–32 season he had become the talk of Sydney grade cricket with his fine leg spins and googlies.

side, but quickly discovered that work was just as hard to get in the north.

The former Australian wicket-keeper Hanson Carter, whose family funeral parlour business prospered, was a compassionate behind-the-scenes supporter of old cricketers down on their luck. He kept the NSWCA informed of the difficulties of former state bowler Andrew McBeath and others unable to support their families, and joined in the collections for Herbie Collins. When Charles Bannerman, hero of the first of all Tests, died of old age in 1930, he left his widow Mary so short of funds that the NSWCA had to make a gift of £50 to her within a few months of his death.

The share market had crashed and thousands of people were bankrupted. Some com-mitted suicide and in Brisbane the lines of unemployed were as long, and the pathetic hessian shacks that housed the homeless were just as ugly as in Sydney. At his own sug-gestion the NSWCA secretary, Harold Hey-don, had his salary reduced by 10 per cent to match the general decline in wages. Heydon's pay was not restored to £600 a year until 1934.

Laidler and Ward went back to the St George club still desperate for work, hoping some of Don Bradman's magic would rub off on them. They were joined by Bradman's Australian team-mate Alan Fairfax, who at the time was considering an offer to go and live in London and set up a cricket school. On their return they found that the talk of Sydney grade cricket was not Bradman, but William Joseph O'Reilly, the leg-spin and googly bowler. O'Reilly had come to Sydney from his teaching job at Kandos, on the central western slopes of New South Wales, and joined the North Sydney club. He took 54 wickets at a cost of only 7.88 in the 1931–32 season and bowled North Sydney to the premiership, ably assisted by a fellow school teacher named Clem Hill, who bowled left-arm at medium pace. North Sydney did not score 200 runs in an innings in the entire season, but the combination of O'Reilly and Hill took them to the premiership, with the star-studded St George side runners-up. O'Reilly also took 25 Shield wickets at 21.00 each.

Crowds of 5000 were not uncommon for first grade matches at a time when cars were a luxury and almost everyone went to the cricket by tram or train. There was intense rivalry among leading clubs. O'Reilly was in the unusual position of working in the St George district—at Kogarah High School—and playing for North Sydney and he col-lected plenty of flak from his pupils in the playground. Each afternoon when he returned by ferry to his home at McMahons Point he saw the arches of the Sydney Harbour Bridge coming closer together until the bridge was finally opened by the Premier, Jack Lang, in March 1932.

North Sydney's triumph was all the more remarkable because of the high scoring by Bradman who ran up 785 runs for St George at an average of 112.14. His innings included 246 in 205 minutes against Randwick and 201 in 171 minutes against Gordon. Playing a Gordon side which included Charles Kelleway, Charlie Macartney, Bert Oldfield and the state leg spinner Norval Campbell, Bradman scored his second century in only 45 minutes. A spectator claimed one Bradman hit for six was a mis-hit, so Bradman repeated the shot for the man's benefit and lobbed the ball out of Chatswood Oval to almost the identical spot.

Before the major matches of the 1931–32 season began, Alan Kippax took a team on tour around New South Wales country towns Lithgow, Parkes, Forbes, Grenfell, Young, Murrumburrah, Wagga Wagga, Tumut, Gundagai and Yass. The once commonly sighted "swaggies", those itinerants with bedrolls on their backs, were rarely seen this time on the country roads the team travelled. At Parkes the players were to open a new turf wicket complex but rain forced officials to switch to the mat, and Kippax had his nose broken by a ball that lifted suddenly. As Kippax was helped to the sidelines a large spike was found under the mat.

On 6 November the New South Wales team appeared in Brisbane for the first Shield match of the season against Queensland, but before play began Archie Jackson, coughing blood, was rushed to hospital. Gilbert's opening over on a green top pitch will always be remembered by Queensland cricket-lovers, for it was widely rated the fastest ever bowled in Australia, Gilbert moving in off that three- or four-pace run to produce an arm swing that defied the human eye.

His first ball to Wendell Bill took off at a speed that forced the red-haired right-hander to top-edge a catch to wicket-keeper Len Waterman. Bradman swayed backwards to dodge the second ball, which clipped the peak of his cap and took it back to the keeper's feet. With his cap back on his head, Bradman then fell avoiding more head-high bouncers. One ball knocked the bat right out of his hands. Another sailed over the wicket-keeper's head, bounced once and struck the sightscreen halfway up. Bradman tried to hook the sixth ball and edged it into the gloves of Waterman, who was standing halfway to the fence.

Gilbert was on 2 for 0 off seven balls, while New South Wales manager Arthur Rose jumped up and down in the stand claiming Gilbert threw every ball and had tried to make an Aunt Sally of Bradman. When teammates commiserated with him about his dismissal, Bradman said, "Luckiest duck I ever made". Unquestionably the pace Gilbert produced from a short, shuffling approach surprised his victims, who would have been more prepared for it had he bowled off a long run. Bradman said in *Farewell To Cricket*, "I unhesitatingly class this short burst as faster than anything seen from Larwood or anyone else. The players all thought his action decidedly suspect. On that green wicket the ball came through at bewildering speed."

Going in at 3 for 21, with Kippax retired hurt, McCabe batted through the rest of the innings for 229 not out, repeatedly hooking Gilbert off his eyebrows. Fingleton helped wear Gilbert down by staying for more than four hours and scoring 93, and New South Wales reached 432. It was a strange match, with nine batsmen failing to score, Thurlow in both innings, and New South Wales winning by an innings and 238 runs.

On 18 December in Melbourne, umpire Andy Barlow no-balled Gilbert 8 times in two overs for throwing, in the Victoria versus Queensland match. One of Gilbert's victims was Jack Ryder. Gilbert took no further part

Eddie Gilbert shows he can handle a bat by hitting this delivery for four during the 1931–32 season.

in the game after bowling 16 balls. But when Queensland played South Australia at Adelaide from 25 December umpire George Hele did not no-ball Gilbert. His fiery bowling brought 26 wickets that summer.

Kippax's outstanding skill in hooking always provided the answer to such bowling. Only the year before in Manchester he had tamed Ted McDonald with the hook shot when McDonald looked likely to burst right through the Australian batting. In Brisbane Kippax seemed set to do it again when he hooked Gilbert for two fours, playing the shot in classic style, head behind the ball. At the other end "Pud" Thurlow bowled fast for Queensland, but appreciably slower than Gilbert, and in attempting another hook Kippax played the shot before the ball reached him. He took the full force of the bouncer on the right temple. Six stitches were needed to close the gash and Kippax spent three days in hospi-

tal with an injury that kept him out of cricket for a spell and hastened his retirement.

Kippax played some attractive knocks after that but the blows he took at Parkes and Brisbane left him in no shape to face the onslaught that was coming from England's pace men, and he never again hooked with the same confidence.

Archie Jackson returned to Sydney with the New South Wales team, believing he was an influenza victim, but within a week he was diagnosed as having tuberculosis. He was sent to Bodington Sanatorium at Wentworth Falls, in New South Wales' Blue Mountains district, his future in doubt.

Learie Constantine went back to England after the West Indies tour and reported favourably on Bradman's suitability for the Lancashire League. Constantine had played in the League for Nelson since 1929 and he considered Bradman had the ideal make-up for success in afternoon matches. Although the Lancashire County Cricket Club was not involved, the prospect of Bradman qualifying for county cricket excited English cricket-lovers. There was a widely held belief that once Bradman had played out the two-year qualifying period with Accrington he would be invited to play for Lancashire.

The difficulty was that Bradman was still bound by his 1930 tour contract with the Board of Control, which specifically said he could not return to England to play cricket within two years of the tour ending. To avoid publicity, Bradman asked his friend Claude Spencer, a well-known sportswriter, to handle the negotiations with Accrington, whose former professionals included Hedley Verity and the South African "Buck" Llewellyn.

The South Africans arrived for their

Gilbert joins in the fun during a mock trial in the Sydney dressing-room when rain stopped play. Gilbert was charged with signing autographs and found guilty.

second tour of Australia in 1931–32—the first had been in 1910–11—to find Australian newspapers full of speculation about whether Bradman would go to Lancashire. The reports said he had been guaranteed £1000 a year, with a bonus of £5 for each innings over 50, £5 every time he took five wickets, and a collection for all centuries. Bradman was not left to make his own decisions any more, and he had no lack of advice on what was a very handsome offer. Bradman's biographer, Irving Rosenwater, dug up this gem from the London *Observer* of 6 September 1931:

No sporting interest would be served by bringing Bradman to Lancashire. He is an ornament to his own country, and in that capacity will always be welcome here, but as a salaried run-getter for an English club he would be only a reminder of how money deranged the order of things. Lancashire did not begin this business of

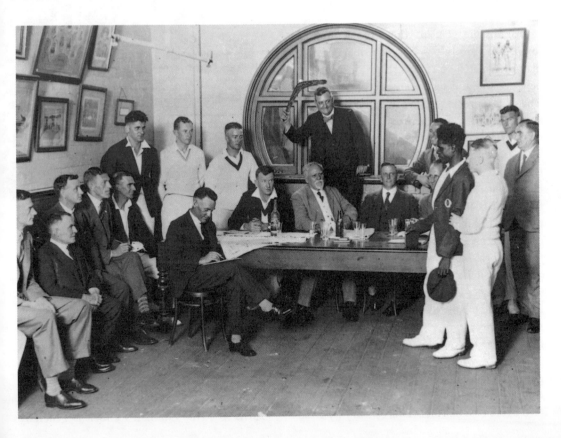

importing players, let her have the distinction of ending it.

Bradman was very tempted but finally cabled his refusal of Accrington's offer. Within hours Alan Fairfax postponed his plans to open a cricket school in London and agreed to join Accrington for a fee of £480 for 20 weeks in Bradman's place. The day after Bradman turned down the Accrington job hordes of people blocked the footpath outside Mick Simmons' store to congratulate him. The Lancashire League speculation then swung to reports that Grimmett and Ponsford were to be signed by League clubs.

Lord Hawke, who in 1927 had criticised efforts to coax Ponsford to play in the Lancashire League, warmly applauded Bradman's refusal to join Accrington and said he was delighted to have Lancashire's assurance that they had had nothing to do with the Bradman offer.

Bradman went to the Blue Mountains town, Blackheath, on 3 November 1931, to play in a match to celebrate the opening of a new ground and test a new malthoid wicket. This was a process that eliminated the need to cover concrete with matting. He enjoyed the new surface, hitting 14 sixes and 29 fours in an innings of 256. In the space of three overs in this innings he scored a century. Bradman began with 6, 6, 4, 2, 4, 4, 6, 1, in an over from Bill Black, who was trying to bowl off breaks. The single from the last ball of Black's over gave him the strike against the next over from Horrie Baker, later Town Clerk of Lithgow, which Bradman dispatched for 6, 4, 4, 6, 6, 4, 6, 4. Wendell Bill hit a single off the first and fifth balls of Black's next over which was hit for 1, 6, 6, 1, 1, 4, 4, 6. Bradman had thus scored 100 out of 102 in only three overs.

Black, who had been boasting about getting Bradman out a few weeks earlier in Lithgow for only 52, was taken off after his two overs cost 62 runs. This century by Brad-

No matter where he played Bradman had the ability to draw capacity crowds, as demonstrated by this photograph taken during the 1930s.

man in three overs has aroused the interest of cricket statisticians ever since. Unfortunately no time was taken. Bradman believed it must have been faster than the 18 minutes taken by Laurie Quinlan to score 100 for Trinity Cricket Club against Mercantile Cricket Club in Cairns in 1910. Quinlan's knock is generally

Oldfield and a better batsman. Christopher Martin-Jenkins recorded in his *Who's Who of Test Cricketers* that a "Jock Cameron stumping was a nonchalant gesture of a smoker flicking cigarette ash". To take around Australia Cameron was given a team which seldom fielded well and had an attack based almost entirely on pace bowling. They found the state sides a handful and in the Tests encountered both Grimmett and Bradman in devastating form. Most of the South Africans played cricket on the mat and were continually puzzled by Australia's turf pitches.

The members of the South African team were: H. B. Cameron (Western Province, captain), D. P. D. Morkel (Western Province), X. Balaskas (Griqualand West), A. J. Bell (Western Province), L. S. Brown (Transvaal), J. A. J. Christy (Transvaal), S. H. Curnow (Transvaal), E. L. Dalton (Natal), Q. McMillan (Transvaal), B. Mitchell (Transvaal), N. A. Quinn (Griqualand West), S. S. L. Steyn (Transvaal), H. W. Taylor (Transvaal), E. A. Van Der Merwe (Transvaal), K. F. Viljoen (Griqualand West), C. L. Vincent (Transvaal) and J. H. Tandy (Cape Town, manager).

South Africa began with a drawn match against Western Australia in Perth from 22 to 24 October 1931. Jim Christy made 102, Syd Curnow 58 and Eric Dalton 53 in a total of 7 for 362 declared. Western Australia replied with 205, and then South Africa closed at 3 for 151, with Dalton 53 not out. In the two hours left for play, Western Australia reached 7 for 159, Ernie Bromley, the Fremantle left-hander, scoring a fast 78.

At Adelaide between 30 October and 3 November South Africa defeated South Australia by 192 runs, after leading by five runs on the first innings, despite Grimmett's 6 for 50. South Africa set South Australia 299 to score for a win by making 293 in their second innings but on a worn pitch the googlies and leg breaks of Quintin McMillan, 9 for 53, hum-

regarded as the fastest century scored in Australia at any level of cricket. Wendell Bill's two singles during Bradman's splurge won him more applause than any of his six first-class centuries.

The South Africans' tour was in jeopardy for a time when it was discovered that exchange rates greatly reduced the value of their money, but the players decided to go ahead for very little reward. They were captained by Horace Brakendridge Cameron, a wicket-keeper who was said to be the equal of Bert bled the South Australians.

Victoria beat the South Africans by 87 runs between 6 and 9 November, largely because of "Dainty" Ironmonger, who took 5 for 87 and 5 for 21. Victoria established a first innings lead of 49 runs, with Woodfull scoring 121 out of a total of 284. Only Christy, who made 119, and Curnow, with whom he put on 181 for the first wicket, impressed in South Africa's first effort of 235. The pace of gangling Richmond opening bowler Ernie McCormick and the 192 centimetre Lisle Nagel shocked the South Africans and they gave Ironmonger little resistance. Chasing 150 to win, the South African team were out for only 53.

At Sydney in the match against New South Wales from 13 to 17 November Herbie Taylor played a fine innings for 124 in South Africa's first innings of 425. South Africa then gained a big advantage by dismissing New South Wales for 168, with fast bowler Sandy Bell and spinner McMillan each taking four wickets. South Africa had enjoyed all the best of the match when they declared at 3 for 190. New South Wales needed 458 to win.

Here the might of New South Wales' batting emerged. Fingleton made 117 before Bradman and McCabe scored with complete

freedom. After McCabe was dismissed Bradman continued on to 135 and when time elapsed New South Wales were only 18 runs away from a stunning victory on 3 for 430.

Rain prevented any play on the first day of South Africa's match with Queensland, from 20 to 24 November. Queensland introduced two outstanding youngsters, Geoff Cook, an all-rounder from the Western Suburbs club, whose father Barney had played for the state in 1909–10, and the South Brisbane left-handed batsman Des Hansen. South Africa made 195 and 6 for 135, Gilbert taking 4 for 42 in the second innings. Queensland headed South Africa by seven runs on the first innings but disappointed with a second innings of 156, Hansen top-scoring with 65, and a draw was a just result.

South Africa paid a heavy price for dropping Bradman at 11 and again at 15 in the first Test on 27 November to 3 December. Bradman went on to 226, at that time the highest score in a Test by an Australian at home, in the introduction of Test cricket to the Gabba. Chasing Australia's first innings total of 450, South Africa were 3 for 126 at stumps on Saturday after Bruce Mitchell had batted for 70 minutes without scoring. They had to wait until 4 p.m. on Wednesday before they resumed on a rain-soaked pitch.

Mitchell carried on to a pugnacious 58 but South Africa could not master the machine-like accuracy of Ironmonger. They were dismissed for 170, which compelled them to

The Gabba ground photographed in 1931 when Test cricket was first played there. Bradman marked the event by scoring 226.

follow on. This time Tim Wall did most damage, taking 5 for 14. Ironmonger's 4 for 44 gave him a match aggregate of 9 for 86. None of the South Africans made 50 and they collapsed for 117, to be beaten by an innings and 163 runs.

Both teams agreed the Gabba pitch and outfield were of first-class standard and there were no complaints from the players about the facilities. But accommodation and catering for the public were primitive and the Queensland Cricket Association admitted that after spending all their available funds on the pitch a similar effort was needed to provide seating and food for spectators. Before the season ended construction began on a Members' Stand and on extensions to "the hill". For Gabba regulars the major disappointment of their initial Test was that Ron Oxenham did not get a bowl in South Africa's second innings.

South Africa's return match against New South Wales, on 5 to 9 December, was upset by rain, but Bradman had time to play another masterly knock. He made 219 in even time and the first mistake he made caused his dismissal. The Balmain all-rounder Sid Hird found himself completely overshadowed after scoring 101; he later played first-class cricket in South Africa. The South Africans batted for a while in the rain, which eventually washed out the match with Curnow 81 not out and Morkel 70 not out.

With Kippax injured, Australia brought in Keith Rigg for the second Test in Sydney from 18 to 21 December and replaced Oxenham with "Perka" Lee, the South Australian off-break bowler. Batting first, South Africa succumbed for 153 to the spin of Grimmett (4 for 28) and the tidy swing bowling of McCabe (4 for 13), an appalling effort on a splendid pitch.

Australia lost Ponsford, clean-bowled by Quinn for 5, but took the score to 1 for 78 by stumps and next day treated spectators to a

Sid Hird, from Sydney's Balmain club, who made a century against South Africa in 1931–32 in only his third first-class match. He spent most of his early career playing league cricket in England.

feast of delightful shot-making. Woodfull scored 58, Keith Rigg 127, Bradman 112, his fourth century in a row, McCabe 79, and "Slinger" Nitschke a blazing 47 as the Australians sped to 469. On the third day Australia completed the rout by rushing the South African players out for 161 to win by an innings and 155. Grimmett's 4 for 44 gave him 8 for 72 for the match against batsmen who were reported to have been accustomed to classy leg spin.

At Melbourne Australia clinched the rubber by defeating South Africa by 169 runs on 31 December 1931 to 6 January 1932. Australia lost Woodfull, Ponsford and Bradman for 25 runs and were 4 for 74 when McCabe was out for 22. Kippax (52) and Rigg (68) staged a minor recovery but none of the other batsmen stayed long in an innings of 198. Sandy Bell bowled tirelessly for 5 for 69.

South Africa's first innings yielded 358. Ken Viljoen made his first Test century, 111, but his team-mates all failed after getting good starts. Australia lost Ponsford at 54 in their second innings. Bradman joined Woodfull with Australia in real trouble—106 runs behind.

The left-arm medium-pacer Neville Quinn who had taken 4 for 42 in the first innings including Bradman for 2, was bowling magnificently when Bradman went in and spectators wondered if at last Bradman had met a bowler who was his master. Bradman answered the challenge with immediate and thrilling aggression. Admirably though Quinn bowled, Bradman absolutely flailed him. Off drives rattled against the iron fence, cover drives sent Viljoen and McMillan racing round the boundary, as four after four flashed from his bat. By stumps Australia had the match won but Bradman was not out. On Monday morning, first day of the working year, thousands deserted their offices to see Bradman continue the slaughter. When he was out with 167 against his name, half the crowd left, content to go back to work.

Woodfull's solid defence produced 161; Kippax (67) and McCabe (71) kept the scorer busy but then the innings petered out. The last six wickets added only 35 but with 554 Australia set South Africa 395 to win.

Grimmett bowled 46 overs for his 6 for 92 and Ironmonger 42 overs for 4 for 54, Australia winning by 169 runs on the sixth morning. Jim Christy top-scored for South Africa with a sound 63. From 1 for 120, South African wickets fell regularly to steady, accurate bowling that gave them little to hit. Grimmett sent down 14 maidens, Ironmonger 18.

After a draw against Tasmania in Launceston and victories over Tasmania in Hobart and South Australia in Adelaide, the South Africans went into the fourth Test determined to make an improved showing. Australia brought in three newcomers for this match at Adelaide Oval between 29 January and 2 February, the loquacious Balmain left-arm spinner Bill Hunt, "Tiger" O'Reilly, and the unlucky Queenslander "Pud" Thurlow. None of them had a big influence on Australia winning by 10 wickets, although O'Reilly's bowling was surprisingly economical for a leg-spin and googly bowler.

South Africa batted soundly to score 308 in the first innings, Bruce Mitchell (75), Herbie Taylor (78) and Jock Cameron (52) defying a varied and shrewdly managed attack. Grimmett had 7 for 116. Hunt, who had replaced Ironmonger as Australia's left-arm spinner, failed to take a wicket in 16 overs.

Bradman played one of the most faultless innings of his career when Australia batted, finishing on 299 not out. Woodfull (82) was the only other Australian batsman to pass 50 and he added 176 with Bradman for the second wicket. Bradman gave only one chance, a difficult one at 185, in 270 minutes' batting. Umpire George Hele rated this Bradman knock one of the most flawless he ever saw and was struck by the way Bradman enjoyed his own mastery.

With Ponsford out for 5, Kippax for a duck and McCabe for 2, Bradman's partners were from the Australian tail. Last man Thurlow was run out as he tried to bring up Bradman's 300. Bradman's 299 not out remained the highest innings by an Australian in a home Test until Bob Cowper made 311 at Melbourne in 1965–66.

South Africa required 205 to avert an innings defeat. After losing Curnow at 22, Mitchell and Christy added 81 at a run a minute for the second wicket. Mitchell made 95, Taylor 84. When Mitchell left, O'Reilly disposed of Taylor and Cameron with deliveries that completely fooled them. Although O'Reilly took only 2 for 81, he bowled 42 overs for those figures, with his loping gait, cocked wrist and flailing arms, and was the ideal foil for Grimmett.

South Africa slumped from 2 for 224 to be all out for 274. Grimmett's 7 for 83 gave him a match analysis of 14 for 199. Ponsford and Woodfull got the 70 runs needed for victory without being separated.

This proved to be Bill Hunt's only Test. He said he had a row on the field with Woodfull about field placements for his bowling and that Woodfull had reported his disobedience to the Board of Control. Players who appeared in the match could not recall any dispute between Hunt and Woodfull and it was not in Woodfull's nature to report players. Anyway Hunt felt he had no future in Australian cricket with Woodfull opposed to his selection—"I was a fair cow to get on with," Hunt said—and he went off to play his prime years in the Lancashire League. Hunt took three hat-tricks for Rishton in his first season and claimed 11 hat-tricks in his career.

Yet another talented spinner, Leslie ("Chuck") O'Brien Fleetwood-Smith, made his first-class debut in the match between the South Africans and Victoria from 6 to 10 February 1932. Fleetwood-Smith remains one of cricket's most beguiling personalities, the son of a family who published a newspaper at Stawell, in the Victorian Wimmera district. He was sent to Xavier College, Melbourne, to be educated and initially bowled right-handed but broke his right hand in a playground accident. While he was recovering he found he could bewilder batsmen with left-arm "corkscrew" deliveries.

Victoria made 231, the South Africans 239, with Fleetwood-Smith taking 6 for 80. Woodfull and Ponsford took Victoria's second innings score to 158. Woodfull was on 73, Ponsford 84, when rain washed out play.

The fifth Test at Melbourne on 12 to 15 February produced sensations galore, most of

Archie Jackson's old schoolmate Bill Hunt, who made his sole Test appearance in 1930 against South Africa. He claimed an argument with Woodfull ruined his Test career but team-mates said there was no such clash.

the play being under conditions provided only by Australian sticky wickets. Hot sun following rain found both teams ill-equipped, lacking the know-how of a Hobbs or a north-of-England craftsman.

South Africa won the toss and batted for only 90 minutes to score 36 runs, Nash lifting the ball awkwardly to take 4 for 18, Ironmonger bowling five maidens in his 7.2 overs to finish with 5 for 6. Cameron top-scored with 11. But by the end of the first day Australia were all out for 153. Woodfull opened with newcomer Fingleton and was out first ball. Bradman could not bat after being injured while fielding, and apart from Fingleton (40), Kippax (42) and Rigg (22), none of the Australians could cope with the conditions.

L. Fleetwood-Smith, who made his first-class debut in the match between South Africa and Victoria in February 1932.

Rain washed out the second day and fell for most of the Sunday rest day. On Monday morning the batsmen were helpless once the sun came out and South Africa collapsed for 45. Ironmonger bowled 15.3 overs for his 6 for 18. O'Reilly, likened by the Adelaide *News* to a windmill in full sail, gave a strong hint of what was to come by taking 3 for 19, and Australia won the match by an innings and 72 runs for a five–nil coup in the series.

Bradman scored 1190 runs against the South Africans, 806 of them at 201.50 in five Test innings, although he did not bat in the fifth Test. In all first-class matches he averaged 116.91, and hit seven centuries. In grade cricket he headed the Sydney competition with 785 runs at 112.14 despite limited appearances due to his first-class commitments.

Ironmonger topped the Australian bowling averages against South Africa with 31 wickets at 9.67. Grimmett, who did not get a bowl in the fifth Test, took 33 wickets at 16.87. Christy headed the South African first-class averages with 909 runs at 39.52, but in Tests Mitchell did best with 322 runs at 32.20. Bell proved a whole-hearted trier throughout the tour—in one Bradman innings he lost 2.7 kilograms in weight—and deservedly topped South Africa's Test bowling with 23 wickets at 27.26. On the entire tour he took 51 first-class wickets.

New South Wales won the Sheffield Shield for the nineteenth time in 1931–32, taking it on averages by finishing level with South Australia. New South Wales had the strongest batting line-up with McCabe having an average of 438, after scoring 229 not out, 106 and 103 not out. South Australia had superior bowling strength—P. K. Lee's 25 wickets cost less than 20 runs each and Grimmett's 44 wickets 22 apiece.

Don Bradman married a former schoolmate, Jessie Menzies, who was the daughter of a Mittagong farmer, on 30 April 1932, at St Paul's Church, Burwood, New South Wales. They had been engaged for five months. The ceremony was performed by Canon Ernest Selwyn Hughes, later president of the Victorian Cricket Association, who flew to Sydney for the service and while there took possession of the Sheffield Shield, which his state had just won. One of the guests, who sang during the ceremony, was baritone Bob Nicholson, later a member of the New York Metropolitan Opera Company. Nicholson had been one of the bowlers who suffered from Bradman's bat at Blackheath.

Robert Coleman in researching his history of the Victorian Cricket Association discovered that after their wedding the Bradmans drove to Melbourne to honeymoon in a house offered by a friend. A few days later

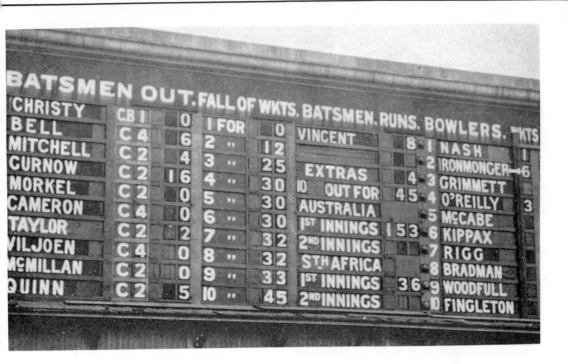

The sad story for South Africa shown on the scoreboard after the fifth Test in 1931–32. The South Africans made only 36 and 45.

Canon Hughes turned up and announced: "Jessie, if you want to get out of this you can right now. Canons don't handle many weddings and I was out of practice. There are documents you must sign in New South Wales which I neglected." He then produced the papers for signature.

While the Bradmans were being united in Sydney, the Marylebone Cricket Club had made significant moves in England. Douglas Jardine had been appointed England captain, and had impressed authorities at Lord's with his handling of the team in the 1931 three-Test series against New Zealand, which England won one–nil. Larwood did not play in any of these matches, which were a warm-up for the 1932–33 series in Australia between England and Australia.

The Australian Board of Control had had a rule since 1927 that no team comprising

players under the jurisdiction of state associations could make an overseas tour without Board approval. Mindful of this, Arthur Mailey sought, and received, Board sanction to take a side to North America in 1932. He had organised the trip with the assistance of the Canadian Pacific Railway, American government offices, the Canadian Cricket Board, and various shipping lines.

The Board agreed to the tour on condition that it had the right to approve of the team chosen and that Mailey submit detailed and complete accounts of all match receipts and travel and accommodation expenses. The Board further laid down that none of the players should receive more than £100 from the tour profits, and all profits after that should be distributed by the Board at its discretion.

Mailey agreed to all these conditions, to the Board's satisfaction, and his team, comprising 12 players, plus Dr Rowley Pope, who could manage their health and their baggage, went off, in May 1932, to play 51 matches in 100 days. The Board lifted its ban on wives

*Bradman with Canon E. S. Hughes, who
solemnised Bradman's marriage to Jessie Menzies.*

*Jessie Menzies, daughter of a Mittagong farmer, who
became Lady Bradman. This photograph was taken
around the time Bradman first played cricket.*

travelling with touring teams to allow Jessie
Bradman to accompany her husband for 26
days on what amounted to a honeymoon
tour. Mailey's team members were V. Y.
Richardson (captain), D. G. Bradman, P. H.
Carney, H. Carter, L. O'B. Fleetwood-Smith,
W. F. Ives, A. F. Kippax, S. J. McCabe,
R. N. Nutt, E. F. Rofe, E. K. Tolhurst, with
A. A. Mailey as player–manager, and Dr R. J.
Pope as baggage-master, scorer, and medical
officer.

Mailey did not consider his Balmain
clubmate Archie Jackson, who in late 1931
returned to Bodington Sanatorium on the recommendation of the trustees of the NSWCA
Cricketers' Fund. Bodington's fee, three
guineas a week, was paid by the fund. Jackson
became restless at Bodington and after a
period in a cottage in Leura, rent for which
was also paid by the fund, he moved to

Brisbane, hoping the warmer climate would
improve his health.

Grimmett's work as a signwriter in Adelaide forced him to drop out of the American
tour. Fleetwood-Smith took his place, with
Mailey hoping Fleetwood-Smith could dismiss plenty of the hordes of batsmen they
were to face. Some of the team paid their own
fares for a tour which was only confirmed by
several of the American sponsors when it
became certain that Bradman would be in the
line-up.

The tourists suffered from one frequent
handicap—the predilection of manager Mailey to go missing when he was needed to produce passports, rail tickets, or health cards.
"Throughout his long life, Arthur has been
noted for hatching the most original ideas and
leaving them for others to implement," wrote
Vic Richardson in *The Vic Richardson Story*.

Mailey's main prop on the tour was the
astonishing supporter of Australian cricket
teams, Dr Rowley Pope. Pope had, at his own
expense, accompanied Armstrong's 1921

The team Arthur Mailey assembled for the 1932 North American tour: (L to R) Dr R. Pope, H. Carter, D. Bradman, E. Tolhurst, Mrs D. Bradman, L. Fleetwood-Smith, R. Nutt, V. Richardson (captain), A. Mailey (manager), A. Kippax, S. McCabe, W. Ives, E. Rofe, P. Carney.

team, Collins' 1926 team, and many other teams to England. On all of these trips he took 40 pieces of luggage.

Tourists in need went straight to Dr Pope's cabin. There in his suitcases he had everything from sleeping pills to button hooks, for those who wore buttoned boots. On the ship returning from England in 1921 Edgar Mayne stumped him by asking for a bicycle pump, a seemingly unreasonable request in mid-ocean. Thereafter Dr Pope always had a bike pump in his luggage.

Mailey told Dr Pope he thought 40 bags were too many and under pressure Pope reduced them to 36. In every town they visited he carefully unpacked every bag and on the day they left repacked the lot. When Vic Richardson realised on the way to America that he would have to make at least 30

speeches he hastened to the good doctor and came away with three books on the history of America and Canada, and one on the history of cricket in Philadelphia.

While on the *Niagara* Richardson learned that cricket had been played in Georgia, the Carolinas, New York and Connecticut in the first half of the eighteenth century, and that in 1751 eleven cricketers of New York had defeated eleven from London by scoring 80 and 86 to 43 and 47.

Jessie Bradman acted as the Australian team's hostess when it entertained, attending all the team functions, and helping Richardson with his speeches. All the players except Rofe, a first-grader from the Manly club, and Carney, a Melbourne district player, had appeared in Sheffield Shield matches, and 54-year-old Hanson Carter was the most senior player. None of their matches were first-class and half of them were against odds. The pitches on which they had to bat, the paddocks on which they fielded, were frequently outrageous, but they had a wonderful tour.

Bradman played in 49 of the 51 games, scored 3779 runs, took more than 100 wickets, and made 18 centuries, which teammates agreed was reasonable for a man on his

LEFT: The former England captain C. Aubrey Smith, whom the Australians encountered in Hollywood in 1932. The team, organised by Arthur Mailey, found Boris Karloff in the slips when they played Smith's team of film stars.

BELOW: Don Bradman and his wife Jessie after returning from their honeymoon trip to America.

honeymoon. Statisticians say that his 260 against Eighteen of Western Ontario is still the highest score ever made in Canada. The unexpected hero of the tour was Fleetwood-Smith, however, whose left-arm spinners accounted for 249 wickets, including two hat-tricks, at nine runs apiece. Fleetwood-Smith was a popular tourist, whose on-the-field imitations of bird calls matched his enthusiastic community singing.

Mailey, of course, could not resist playing at places called Moose Jaw, Medicine Hat and Kicking Horse Falls, as well as Saskatoon and Calgary, and he took 240 wickets at 6.50. According to Dr Pope, whose records were painstakingly kept, the Australians scored more than 10,000 runs in their 51 matches and dismissed more than 10,000 batsmen. One of their main problems was to keep hospitable opposing batsmen at the crease: "Better call no ball," Mailey would tell the umpires. "This chap hasn't scored."

One of the high spots of the trip was a match in Hollywood, against a team which included famous actor C. Aubrey Smith, the former England captain who was then in his seventieth year. Smith played only one Test, but he captained an English team on a tour of Australia in 1887–88. Boris Karloff had to be hidden in the slips. Jean Harlow was among the spectators to whom Douglas Fairbanks Junior, explained the game. At Yankee Stadium, New York, photographers organised a picture of Don Bradman shaking hands with the great baseballer Babe Ruth, captions for which later referred to Bradman as "the Babe Ruth of Australian cricket, who regularly returns to the plate 100 or more times".

Irving Rosenwater calculated that be-

tween September 1931 and August 1932 Bradman scored "the staggering number of 7000 runs at an average of over 100 in all forms of cricket". Most of these innings were not in first-class matches but there was no doubt that he was a better batsman than ever. Bradman returned to Australia with Mailey's team in the *Monowai* to prepare for the 1932–33 visit by the England team captained by Jardine. His repertoire of strokes was wider and he had more experience and more confidence than when he last faced English bowling.

According to Jardine's cousin, Douglas changed his mind about accepting the captaincy for the Australian tour after his appointment was announced. When Jardine told "Plum" Warner he would not be available after all, Warner went to Jardine's father, a fellow Oxonian Blue then living at Walton-on-Thames, for assistance. M. R. Jardine, former Advocate-General of Bombay, told Warner he would do what he could and after he had a talk with his son, Jardine agreed to go to Australia. He then devoted himself single-mindedly to the task, knowing as he read Chaucer in a corner of the *Orontes* on the way to Australia that all depended on dismissing Bradman cheaply.

This is not cricket

The Bodyline series 1932–33

Before he left home to lead the twenty-second England team to Australia Douglas Jardine invited Harold Larwood, his Nottinghamshire fast bowling partner Bill Voce, and their county captain Arthur Carr to dine with him at the Piccadilly Hotel, London. Jardine said he had been struck by reports of Don Bradman flinching when Larwood bounced the ball into his body during the Oval Test in 1930; Larwood agreed that Bradman had ducked awkwardly away from the bouncers.

Jardine asked if Larwood could persistently bounce the ball up into Bradman's chest and head with deliveries pitched on the leg stump. Larwood knew that among county cricketers there was a belief that Bradman could prove vulnerable to such deliveries and he believed that he could provide a sustained barrage of them. What he was *not* told at that dinner was that Jardine planned to increase the threat to Bradman with the most controversial field placings ever known in first-class cricket.

Bodyline only became a threat to the batsman's safety when up to six men were

Bodyline depended on field placement, as this view of Woodfull ducking a Larwood bouncer clearly demonstrates. Woodfull often elected to take blows on his body rather than present a catch to close-in fielders.

positioned on the leg side, close enough to the bat to catch any deflections the batsman might make in defending himself. Many English cricket-lovers have never understood that it was the field settings, as much as Larwood's pace, which caused the unprecedented protests against Bodyline.

Jardine, born in Bombay of Scottish parents, was a stern, iron-willed product of Winchester and Oxford, with a strong admiration for his Surrey captain Percy Fender, whom he considered unrivalled as a cricket tactician. Fender denied that he was responsible for Jardine adopting a concentrated form of leg-theory against Bradman, but agreed that he and Jardine spent many hours discussing the tactics before the tour began.

Carr was enthusiastic about the idea and became a keen supporter of Bodyline. He was an amateur like Jardine and had been briefly at Eton until expelled in 1907 after only three terms, and then at Sherborne. He shared Jardine's dislike for Australians. Carr, in his book *Cricket With The Lid Off*, published in 1935, wrote:

> *My own experience of Australians is that if they cannot win they will not stand to be beaten if they can avoid it. They will go to almost any length to dodge defeat . . . To Australians, cricket is a business pure and simple—a matter of money—and success is all that matters to them.*

Carr added that the only Australian cricketers he knew whom he would give twopence for were Charlie Macartney and Arthur Mailey.

Following the dinner at the Piccadilly Hotel, Jardine visited F. R. Foster at his flat in St James, where he discussed the field settings Foster had used to subdue Victor Trumper in Australia in 1911–12. On that occasion the England team captained by Pelham Warner had directed their attack against Trumper's leg stump, trying to make *occasional* deliveries kick up into the torso. Foster and his team-

mate Sydney Barnes battered Trumper's ribs but at no time was their attack a physical danger to Trumper.

Foster and Barnes had always remained on the friendliest of terms with Trumper, who regarded their tactics as fair. When the Bodyline furore developed Foster said he deeply regretted giving the field placements to Jardine. He said Jardine had "intensified" them to intimidate the batsmen and had instructed Larwood and Voce to aim *every ball* at the body.

The tactics that became known as Bodyline were evolved solely to prevent Bradman sustaining his exceptional scoring. Jardine realised that a repetition of Bradman's 1930 run-getting would end England's chances of regaining the Ashes, and he set himself the task of reducing Bradman to a batsman whose scores his own batsmen could surpass.

Bradman's success in the midst of the Depression had made him a symbol of hope for all who were struggling under the shadow of unemployment queues, harrowing debts and even hunger. He was one of the few encouraging things to come out of a gloomy period in which one-third of Australia's work-force was out of a job, a bold, exuberant country lad who could outplay the English and show them what to do with their theories about wage cuts and the repayment of British loans. His rise to fame came at a time when the Bank of England sent financier Sir Otto Niemeyer to Australia to allay their fears that Australia might default on those huge loans. New South Wales premier Jack Lang had advocated postponement of loan repayments

Douglas Jardine, the strategist, whose one aim was to regain the Ashes in 1932–33. His tactics ultimately threatened the future of international cricket. This photograph was taken several years after the infamous Bodyline series, in Perthshire, Scotland.

until normal times returned, but Niemeyer's solution was for Australians to accept large cuts in pay so that they could meet their debts. A great proportion of Australians bracketed Jardine with Niemeyer: haughty representatives of a privileged class who cared little for the hardship their theories inflicted.

The fact that Bodyline came about at all was a fluke, because the over which spawned it should not have been bowled. The umpires at The Oval in 1930 annoyed players and officials by resuming for just five minutes' play, while Bradman was on his way to scoring 232. If the pitch had been true and if Larwood had not pitched the ball short, wicket-keeper George Duckworth would not have noticed Bradman drawing away, showing a weakness most batsmen share, the instinctive fear of being hit.

Jardine was encouraged by the way that leg theory paid off for Voce and Larwood under Carr's direction in 1931. Bill Bowes followed their example bowling for Yorkshire against Surrey in August 1932 by bouncing the ball repeatedly at Jack Hobbs' head. Pelham Warner condemned Bowes in next day's *Morning Post*. "This is not cricket," Warner wrote, a sentiment he discarded later when his players bowled persistent bouncers at batsmen in Australia.

Plans for the tour began in 1931. The Marylebone Cricket Club announced a selection committee of three, Warner, P. A. Perrin and T. A. Higson, to act for two years instead of the customary one season, with the idea of developing a side which could win back prestige so badly dented in 1930. The Tests in England in 1931 against New Zealand, the one Test in 1932 against India and the Gentlemen *v*. Players fixtures were used to experiment with promising players. Just before the side for Australia was picked Lord Hawke was added as chairman of selectors. Lord Hawke had become the most powerful man in English cricket with the death in March, 1932, of

Bill Voce, a central figure in the Bodyline affair, in action. He partnered Harold Larwood in both the Nottinghamshire and England attacks with controversial results.

his great friend Lord Harris, who had helped stamp out the throwing epidemic of the 1880s.

The selection panel named Jardine as captain for the Australian tour and London newspapers agreed that the only other candidate, Percy Chapman, was a liability as a batsman. A few days later Warner and R. C. N. Palairet were appointed joint managers. On 15 July 1932, the three leading batsmen and the wicket-keepers were named: Hammond, Sutcliffe, Duleepsinhji, Ames and Duckworth. At the beginning of August the selection of Allen, Robins, Brown, Wyatt, Larwood, Voce, and the Nawab of Pataudi was announced. Robins did not accept the invitation and his place went to Tommy Mitchell. Duleepsinhji withdrew just before departure and his place went to Paynter; illness sent Duleep back to a Swiss sanatorium and threatened his career. Bowes was added to the side only five days before they sailed, making 17 players in all, including four fast bowlers. Sixteen of the team sailed from Tilbury on 17 September 1932, in the *Orontes*.

The full team was D. R. Jardine (Surrey, captain), R. E. S. Wyatt (Warwickshire), G. O. B. Allen (Middlesex), F. R. Brown (Surrey), Nawab of Pataudi (Worcestershire), all amateurs, and the professionals W. R. Hammond (Gloucestershire), H. Verity (Yorkshire), H. Sutcliffe (Yorkshire), W. E. Bowes (Yorkshire), M. Leyland (Yorkshire), E. Paynter (Lancashire), G. Duckworth (Lancashire), L. E. G. Ames (Kent), T. B. Mitchell (Derbyshire), H. Larwood (Nottingham-

The 1932–33 England team on board the Orantes, *which brought them to Australia for the infamous Bodyline tour: (L to R) (back) W. Voce, H. Verity, W. Bowes (partly obscured), G. Duckworth, T. Mitchell, L. Ames, P. Warner (manager), Nawab of Pataudi, R. Palairet (manager), E. Paynter, G. Allen, H. Larwood, M. Leyland; (front) H. Sutcliffe, F. Brown, unknown (ship's captain), D. Jardine, R. Wyatt, W. Hammond.*

shire), M. W. Tate (Sussex) and W. Voce (Nottinghamshire). The team had no official vice-captain, though Wyatt took over whenever Jardine was absent.

The only player not well known to Australians was the leg-break and googly bowler Tommy Mitchell, a former coalminer who turned out to be always ready with a quip to make team-mates and opponents laugh. He took more than 100 wickets in ten of his 12 seasons with Derbyshire but at the age of 30 this was his first tour.

Bowes was added to the touring party only after the MCC discovered that Tate was suffering from a nervous disorder. Tate was declared unfit and did not sail with the team, but three weeks later the MCC announced that he was fully recovered and would join the side in Melbourne in plenty of time to practise before the first Test. To Australians Tate's bowling on previous tours had been so formidable it was unthinkable that he would not find a place in the Test team. But by the time Tate arrived Jardine's plans had fallen into place and there was no room in the Test team for such a great bowler.

On the voyage to Australia Jardine carefully nurtured team spirit through nightly performances of his players' choir, conducted by Voce, through deck games and regular callisthenics. He studied diagrams of the leading Australian batsmen's Test innings, supplied by scorer Bill Ferguson, but he still kept his plans to himself. Larwood wrote that he outlined his method of attack to the fast bowlers during the voyage, but Bob Wyatt, Allen and Bowes claimed Jardine did not say a word to them about it on the ship.

This seems to suggest that even as the England team neared Australia Bodyline was only a concept on which Jardine might expand if the chance arrived. Larwood in fact believed that Voce would bowl leg theory better than he, since Voce was 190 centimetres tall, with the stamina of a lumberjack, whereas Larwood was only 173 centimetres and had to pace himself carefully to get through hot days.

After the traditional match in Colombo the tour started in earnest in Perth, where England played Western Australia from 21 to 24 October 1932. Pataudi distinguished himself by scoring 166, the first tour century, in England's first innings, but England were unable to force a victory. England took the honours in the next match at Perth, a draw against a Combined XI which included Bradman. Pataudi and Sutcliffe shared a second-wicket stand of 283, Sutcliffe going on to 169, Pataudi 129, with Jardine contributing 98 and Hammond 77 in an England total of 7 for 583 declared. The Combined XI followed on after scoring 159, Fingleton and Hill-Smith saving them from defeat. Bradman made only 3 and 10, and was clearly puzzled by Verity, who had 7 for 37 in the first innings.

England gained their first victory by beating South Australia by an innings and 128 runs in Adelaide from 4 to 8 November. Sutcliffe (154) and Leyland (127) made England secure on the first day with a stand of 223. Next day Wyatt (61) and Jardine (108) put on

Jardine takes England onto the field in the first Test at Sydney in 1932–33. Bob Wyatt is on his right, big Bill Voce behind him at left.

135 for the seventh wicket and England's total reached 9 for 634 declared. South Australia made 290 and 216, Vic Richardson scoring 134 in the first innings.

Jardine's attention to detail irritated even his own players. Some of them considered that his insistence on every ball being returned to the keeper was absurd, but Jardine persisted. Popularity meant nothing to him.

Jardine suggested to Bowes during this match that he bowl to a leg-side field but refused to elaborate on the reason why. Bowes said he demanded an explanation, and after a heated discussion in the dressing-room Jardine confided in him that he wanted to try fast leg

lian XI scored 218, with Larwood trapping Bradman lbw for 36.

England suffered their first real setback of the trip when Lisle Nagel, bowling into a stiff northerly breeze, took 8 for 32 and had them out for 60. Nagel, who was 198 centimetres tall, swung the ball sharply both ways at a fastish medium pace and nipped the ball quickly from the pitch, something he was never able to accomplish again. The Australian XI needed only 106 to win but after Larwood sent Woodfull and Bradman (13) back cheaply, rain ended the match.

When Jardine came back from his fishing outing Wyatt told him that Bradman had been distinctly uncomfortable against the leg-side attack. Jardine laughed and said: "That's interesting. We'll have to give him more of it." Wyatt said the tour selectors discussed Bradman's showing and believed that out of this conference Bodyline evolved, but this takes no account of Jardine's previous talks with Fender, Carr, Larwood, Voce and Bowes.

England's batting recovered in the next match against New South Wales from 25 to 29 November in Sydney. Fingleton and McCabe scored all but 87 of the New South Wales total of 273. A collapse followed their partnership of 118, with six wickets falling for 65. Wyatt (72), Pataudi (61), Ames (90) and Voce (46) all batted splendidly but Sutcliffe's 182 overshadowed everything in the match. Allen took 5 for 69 in the home side's first innings and Voce 5 for 85 in the second innings of 213, which was 44 short of the total needed to make England bat again.

Larwood was rested for this game but Voce gave as vigorous an exhibition of Bodyline as any seen all summer. Fingleton, in his book *Cricket Crisis*, wrote:

Voce bowled with studied intent at the body, the ball pitching at the halfway mark and sometimes shorter. He had five short legs and for all the purpose they served the stumps could have been

theory against Bradman and other leading Australian batsmen.

England moved on to Melbourne and played Victoria from 11 to 14 November. England won by an innings and 83 runs thanks to a handsome 203 from Hammond, whose cover drive was seen to perfection, and efficient bowling by Allen, Voce and Hammond. Victoria made 231 and 94, England 9 for 408 declared. The English recognised the threat Fleetwood-Smith's sharp left-arm spin represented. Even on a hard MCG pitch that did not suit him he looked dangerous, although his two wickets cost 62 runs each as Hammond went after him.

Wyatt captained England in Melbourne in the fifth match of the tour against an Australian XI on 18 to 22 November while Jardine went fishing. England made 282 and, on what he insisted was his own initiative, Wyatt then set a leg-side field for Bradman. The Austra-

Lisle Nagel, who first played for Australia in 1932.
Opponents joked that Lisle did the bowling but let
his identical twin, Vern Nagel, do his batting.

in the pavilion. Most of Voce's deliveries which
did not hit the rib cleared the stumps by feet.
This was Bodyline in deadly earnest.

Bradman dropped out of the first Test at Sydney, from 2 to 7 December, through illness; Jardine was telling his players the Australians were yellow, or cowardly. By then Jardine had discovered that Larwood was much faster on hard Australian pitches than he was at home, the ball skidding through with the effect of a stone skimming over water. Although the Board of Control was satisfied with the doctors' report that Bradman was in a "seriously rundown" condition, Jardine believed he had a nervous breakdown.

Australia's organisation for this series saw the Board of Control at its worst. The sides Australia sent into each Test never had a manager and the captain Bill Woodfull had no say in selections. Only one of the three Test selectors, Dr Charles Dolling, had ever played in the Sheffield Shield, and neither Dolling nor his colleagues, E. A. ("Chappie") Dwyer and Bill Johnson had any Test experience. The controversy over whether Bradman could write on the Tests in defiance of the Board lasted for months and was only solved when his employers, Associated Newspapers, freed him from his contracted commitments. The Board remained a haven for successful businessmen with Test cricketers notably absent from its ranks, when the advice of experienced players was needed more than ever before.

Barracking against the English tactics began from the first innings of the series when Larwood and Voce bowled to the later familiar Bodyline field. Spectators on the Hill abused Voce for bowling bouncers and when he hit Alan Kippax and Stan McCabe roars of

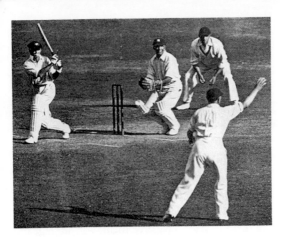

One of the few bright spots of the Bodyline series for Australia was McCabe's innings of 187 not out in Sydney. Ames is keeper and Hammond is at slip.

disapproval swept the ground, and this was repeated when Larwood hit Vic Richardson a stunning blow. Ponsford, who was bowled by Larwood for 32, estimated that he was hit 50 times during the series.

Fingleton and Kippax also fell to Larwood, while Voce got rid of Woodfull before McCabe and Richardson put on 129. The entire McCabe family, including Stan's mother, father and brothers Bill, Les and Bert, had arrived by train from Grenfell for the match. When his turn came to bat Stan rose from his seat between his mother and father and said, "Dad, if I get hit out there, keep Mum from jumping the fence". McCabe was hit, but after Richardson left for 49 he kept on playing his wonderful hooks and pulls and drives, splitting the field with the sheer force of his strokes, every boundary stirring the crowd to raucous applause. His hitting on the on side was so powerful that he eluded fieldsmen with shots which passed only two or three paces from them.

McCabe made 187 not out in 242 minutes, putting on 59 runs with Grimmett in the last 45 minutes of the first day, and adding 60 of the 70 runs scored by the last four Australian wickets. On the second morning McCabe put on 55 runs in 30 minutes, Wall contributing only four. Bill O'Reilly told me many times that if Bradman had been at the other end with McCabe in this form Bodyline would never have been heard of again. The sheer boldness of McCabe's approach against

McCabe hits Larwood through mid-off for four during his memorable knock of 187.

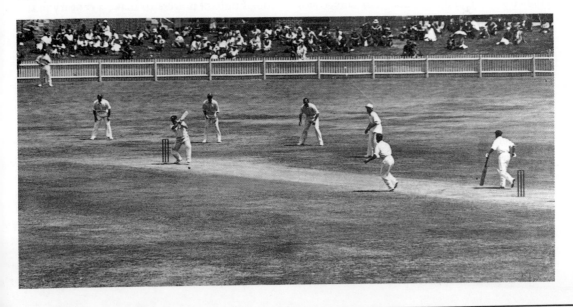

an attack which the crowd considered blatantly unsporting made the Sydney Cricket Ground a thrilling place to be. When it was over, with the Australian total on 360, everyone watching felt emotionally spent. It remains one of the greatest innings ever played, the first of three masterpieces McCabe was destined to play in his career.

By stumps on the second day England were 1 for 252. Wyatt and Sutcliffe put on 112 together and then Hammond stayed with Sutcliffe for the rest of the afternoon, both men batting gloriously. England added a further 227 runs on Monday. Hammond was second out at 300, after helping to add 188, his 112 again showing the mastery of his driving. Sutcliffe and Pataudi put on 123 before Sutcliffe left at 423. Sutcliffe was intent on consolidating a good lead and hit only 13 fours in his 194. Pataudi became the third English century-maker, with 102 in his Test debut, but he too was very slow, hitting only 6 fours.

England's innings ended on the fourth day at 524, 164 ahead. Larwood's speed was awesome in Australia's second innings and he and Voce continued to bruise the batsmen's rib cages as Australia collapsed for 164. Only Fingleton (40) and McCabe (32) stayed for long and England had to score only one run in the final innings to win by ten wickets. Larwood had taken 5 for 96 and 5 for 28 in a display of blistering pace. It was a pity he marred it by directing his attack so regularly at the batsmen.

For a time Englishmen fielding in the leg trap offered solace or apologies to batsmen who were hit, moving up to rub the area hit, but the barrage was so persistent this became hypocritical and as meaningless to the batsmen as it was to the fieldsmen. There was no suggestion of an accidental loss of control by the bowlers; the attack was malicious and intentional.

Watching it, the press-box members struggled at first to find a word that adequately described such a calculated attempt to maim. They tried expressions like "shock attack", and "explosive leg theory", but they seemed inappropriate. The former Australian captain Joe Darling called it "Bradman theory". Finally the world Bodyline was universally adopted because it seemed to fit best. Some say it was the work of Jack Worrall, the ex-Test player who wrote in the *Australasian* of an attack "in line with the body". Others claim Hugh Buggy originated the term in trying to save money in a telegram to the *Melbourne Herald*, whose sub-editor, Ray Robinson, liked it and made it his headline. Larwood claimed the term was invented to damn him and that it did so with great success.

England played a draw with Southern Districts at Wagga Wagga on 10 and 12 December with Tommy Mitchell's spinners returning 7 for 77 for 5 for 26. Ames batted at number three for a punishing 91, proving again that he deserved a Test place ahead of Duckworth, whose advice based on his observations from behind the stumps helped produce Bodyline. At Launceston from 16 to 19 December Ames made 107 and was one of four England players to make a century in the 502 total. Sutcliffe made 101, Pataudi 109, Paynter 102. Tasmania were overwhelmed, scoring only 229 and 147, to go down by an innings and 126 runs. Tasmania's sole consolation was the batting of Clayvell Lindsay Badcock, who scored 100 runs for once out. Badcock had made his debut for Tasmania the summer before at the age of 15. Rain forced a draw in the return match between England and Tasmania at Hobart on 23 to 26 December.

Bradman rejoined the Australian team for the second Test from 30 December 1932 to 3 January 1933 in Melbourne. Lisle Nagel failed to pass a fitness test in the nets before the Test for an injury to his elbow sustained while

Sutcliffe escapes dismissal in the first Test at Sydney in 1932 after playing a ball onto his stumps without dislodging the bail. McCabe throws his arms up in disbelief. Richardson is the close-in fieldsman.

cranking his car, bowing out of big cricket despite his magnificent physical attributes after only one Test in which he took 2 for 110 from 43.4 overs. A crowd of 63,993 attended on the first day to watch Bradman deal with the England bowling. This followed his return to form a few days earlier when he scored 157 for New South Wales against Victoria, the last 50 in 30 minutes. Australia replaced Nagel with Ironmonger and brought in left-hander Leo O'Brien for his first Test. Ponsford was on the field occasionally, but only as Australia's drink waiter.

Sutcliffe later alleged the pitch was deliberately rigged against England's pace bowling to suit Australia's spinners, but the English pace bowlers still managed to inflict some nasty blows on the Australians. Woodfull took a stunning blow over the heart before he was out for 10 but Fingleton struggled bravely on, his body studded with bruises by the time he was fifth out for 83 in a total of 156. Fingleton batted for four hours, taking some sickening knocks, but he kept his body unflinchingly behind the ball.

After Woodfull reeled back in pain from one blow, Pataudi ignored Jardine's call to move from the off to the leg-side cordon. Jardine said: "I see that his Highness is a conscientious objector. You go across then, Hedley." Pataudi did not play another Test in the series.

Spectators around the ground called, "Wait till Don comes in", and when Bradman came into view he received an ovation that lasted all the way out to the crease. He moved slightly towards the off for the first ball from Bowes, swung hard at it to put it away on the leg side and touched it onto his stumps. The

Australian captain Bill Woodfull reels from the pitch after taking a severe blow from Larwood in the Bodyline series. "Gubby" Allen is moving in to assist him.

audience hushed in disbelief as Bradman began the long walk off the Melbourne Cricket Ground. Jardine, for the only time in the series, lost control as he yelled in delight, his arms raised above his Harlequin cap. Bradman had been deceived by a delivery that came off the pitch far slower than he expected and had almost completed his stroke when he edged it.

Australia's innings finished early on the second day for 228. By then the ill-feeling between the teams, which continued throughout the Tests, had players snapping at each other. There was no dressing-room camaraderie, no socialising, and a complete absence of enjoyment. Dr H. V. Evatt, the noted lawyer who later became president of the United Nations, said he was revolted by what

he saw on the field and that it made him feel he never wanted to watch another day's play.

The English batsmen were all puzzled by the slowness of the MCG pitch, failing to recall that it had been saturated just a few days earlier. O'Reilly bowled superbly to take full advantage of their concern and with the help of Tim Wall had England 9 for 161 at stumps. Only eight runs were added for the last wicket next morning and England's total of 169 gave Australia a lead of 59 runs. O'Reilly's 5 for 63 and Wall's 4 for 52 came after they hit the stumps five times.

Almost 70,000 people were present when Bradman went to the crease for his second innings after seven successive failures against England. He did not disappoint them, playing every ball with his body behind the ball, and he reached his century with the last man, Ironmonger, at the other end. England's bowling reached a very high standard but he resisted for more than three and a half hours to finish on 103 not out, with Australia on 191.

The next-best Australian score was Vic Richardson's 32.

On the last day England, all wickets intact, needed 208 to win but the pitch spun awkwardly and they were all out for 139. O'Reilly took 5 for 66 to finish with 10 wickets in the match and earn the place in international cricket that had been too long denied him. Ironmonger provided ideal support, taking 4 for 26. England never appeared likely to get the runs after O'Reilly broke the opening stand at 53 by clean-bowling Sutcliffe.

A nightwatchman caught two men trying to scale the wall of the MCG in the early hours of the morning during this Test. He fired two shots from his revolver over the men's heads and they quickly gave themselves up, explaining that they only wanted to make certain of a seat to watch Bradman bat in Australia's second innings.

With the teams level on a win each, England played a draw at Bendigo against a Victorian Country XIII on 7 and 9 January, before going to Adelaide for the third Test, which started on 13 January. Vic Richardson intensified the public's wrath over England's methods of play by telling Adelaide newspapers that even when he took guard a foot

Public interest in the Bodyline debate was so intense that 50,962 people crowded into Adelaide Oval for the third Test. This remains the ground record.

outside leg stump Larwood's deliveries still came straight at him.

So hostile was the local feeling towards Jardine's strategy that he had to request that the public be locked out of the Adelaide Oval when his team were warming-up there in the few days before the Test. On the morning play began 400 mounted police were marshalled on the adjacent No. 2 ground ready for any emergency and inside the oval 400 more foot police ringed the field.

Wisden described the Test that followed as the most unpleasant ever played, and said the atmosphere it created was a disgrace to cricket. England batted first and scored 341 after four wickets had fallen for 30 runs. This was due to some dogged middle-order batting by Leyland (83), Wyatt (78) and Paynter (77), all of whom could have been forgiven had they succumbed to the tension. On his home pitch Wall gave batsmen little opportunity to hit across the line and he finished with 5 for 72.

Australia began badly by losing 4 for 51 and in this period Woodfull, ducking to avoid an expected bouncer, was hit a tremendous blow over the heart. The crowd went wild and police had to restrain them from jumping the fence as Woodfull reeled back, clutching his chest. From then on Jardine became the target of sustained abuse, some of it extremely vulgar, but he took it all without emotion, even fielding out near the boundary where he

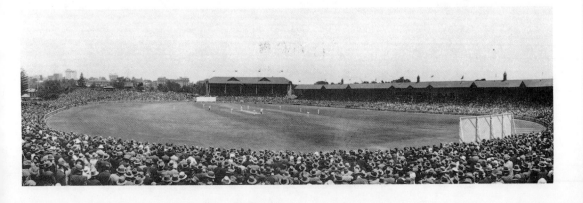

was easy prey for hecklers.

Bradman had apparently decided to make himself a moving target for England's bouncers and he flitted about the crease from the moment he came in, swishing at a ball from Verity to get six, but generally moving towards the off before Larwood released the ball. The harder he swung at deliveries which sailed over his head, the more delirious with delight were the spectators, but he only made 8 before Larwood had him caught by Allen.

On an Adelaide radio station that night the former Australian captain Monty Noble said Bradman had let Australia down and strongly castigated Woodfull for not ensuring that Bradman played a more disciplined

---

The packed leg-side field Jardine set for Larwood and Voce gave Australian batsmen little chance of successfully defending themselves against deliveries aimed at their bodies. Here, however, Oldfield glanced a ball from Voce over the head of Hammond, who is seen leaping in an attempt to take the catch, in the third Test at Adelaide.

innings. Noble said, "Bradman suddenly developed a sensational desire to score off everything, regardless of the safety of his wicket. His opposition revelled in his indiscretion and laughed up their sleeves because they knew he was doing just what they wanted."

Australia finished the second day with Ponsford and Richardson in the midst of a fighting stand. Ponsford pulled off his shirt in the dressing-room to reveal ten nasty bruises. "It will take another ten to get a hundred," he said.

When Richardson was out, Oldfield joined Ponsford and they continued until Oldfield tried to pull a ball, got his feet mixed up and edged it onto his face. Oldfield always blamed himself for this. When he was carried off doctors found he had a fractured frontal linear bone in his skull. An inch lower and the blow could have been fatal, they said.

Right to the end of the innings, at 222, Jardine still kept the Bodyline field with six men close in on the leg side. Once after Larwood started his approach run Jardine

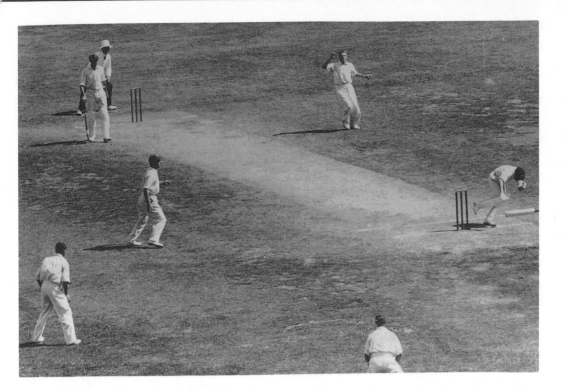

Later, facing Larwood, Oldfield was struck on the head by a fast delivery. He sustained a fractured skull, and the incident almost ended England v. Australia cricket.

clapped his hands to stop him and sent another man to the leg side in the Bodyline trap.

Woodfull was in the dressing-room receiving treatment for his bruises when "Plum" Warner entered. Woodfull had just showered, and with the towel wrapped round him the livid mark over the heart stood out.

"I have come to say how sorry I am and to offer my sympathy," said Warner.

"I don't want to see you, Mr Warner," said Woodfull. "There are two sides out there. One is trying to play cricket, the other is not. The game is too good to be spoilt. It is time some people got out of it."

This interlude and the implications of Woodfull's words did not leak out immediately and when they did Woodfull was very up-set that what had been a private encounter had become public. Jack Fingleton was blamed for the revelation as the only journalist in the Australian side, but Fingleton always denied he was responsible and accused Bradman of telling the story to Sydney journalist Claude Corbett, who in turn told colleagues in the press box.

The Australian Board of Control met at the Adelaide Oval and drafted a cable to be sent to the MCC at Lord's, protesting about the Bodyline attack. Warner and Palairet were informed and when they asked if they could see a copy of the cable were told it had already been sent. There were only four English reporters at the match, including Bruce Harris of the London *Evening Standard*, who was known more for his tennis expertise than for his knowledge of cricket. E. W. ("Jim") Swanton was to have made the tour, but he was late telephoning in some copy and his sporting editor gave the trip to Harris. All the reporters at the Test were summoned to the conference room and told that the following cable had been dispatched to the MCC:

Bodyline bowling has assumed such proportions as to menace the best interests of the game, making protection of the body by the batsman the main consideration. This is causing intensely bitter feeling between the players, as well as injury. In our opinion it is unsportsmanlike. Unless stopped at once it is likely to upset the friendly relations existing between Australia and England.

The sportswriters were shocked that such a cable had been allowed to go. Current *Sydney Morning Herald* reporter Philip Derriman discovered in his research that the cable had been drafted by the four members of the Australian Board of Control who were at Adelaide Oval watching the match, B. V. Scrymgour, H. W. Hodgetts and R. F. Middleton of South Australia, and W. L. Kelly of Victoria. They were particularly annoyed at Jardine's action in moving his fieldsmen into the Bodyline trap immediately after Woodfull, ashen and groggy, resumed after taking the blow over the heart. Derriman believes the cable may have been composed by the Board chairman, Dr Allan Robertson, who was in Melbourne, but was consulted by phone. Eight members of the Board, the delegates from Victoria, South Australia, Tasmania and Western Australia, voted in favour of sending the cable. The five opposed were from New South Wales and Queensland, who took the view that the Board should not have acted until it received a specific complaint in writing from Woodfull.

The clumsy wording of the message undoubtedly worsened the situation Bodyline had created, but it did sway Australian newspapers. From defending Bodyline, they switched to strong condemnation of it. In Sydney the district court judge John Sheridan warned that Bodyline bowling could contravene the *Crimes Act* under which it was an

offence to maliciously wound a man or inflict grievous bodily harm upon him.

Jardine was not worried about the abuse of the crowd but he became very concerned that the hierarchy of the MCC at Lord's would not support him, and he called a meeting of the England team to make certain they remained loyal to him. Allen consoled him with the opinion that the word "unsportsmanlike" would arouse the wrath of the MCC. "Nobody calls an Englishman unsporting and gets away with it—the MCC will back you to the hilt," Allen told Jardine.

Allen's judgement proved correct. The Board's cable brought politicians and diplomats from Australia and England into the controversy and while the Test was played out both the British and Australian governments became involved. In Australian hotels fights broke out following arguments over Bodyline and in Fleet Street newspaper editorials branded Australians as squealers.

England's second innings became a struggle of attrition with batsmen wearing down bowlers while the pitch deteriorated. Jardine batted for four and a quarter hours to score 56 before Hammond and Leyland hit out freely. Bradman brought roars of glee from the crowd by clean-bowling Hammond for 85, but then Ames and Verity put on 98 runs in two hours so that England in the end put together 412 and left Australia to score 532 for a win.

Fingleton and Ponsford were out for only 12 runs but they were followed by Woodfull and Bradman who put on 88 in 75 minutes. Bradman was in dashing form and just when a big innings seemed probable Verity held a difficult return catch. Woodfull finally ran out of partners, but with 73 not out batted through a Test innings for the second time in his career. England won by 338 runs.

On 24 January 1933, the Marylebone Cricket Club replied to the Australian Board of Control cable.

Woodfull takes a blow in the ribs. Incidents like this made the Bodyline series the most acrimonious on record.

We, Marylebone Cricket Club, deplore your cable. We deprecate your opinion that there has been unsportsmanlike play. We have the fullest confidence in captain, team and managers, and are convinced they would do nothing either to infringe the Laws of Cricket, or the spirit of the game. We have no evidence that our confidence has been misplaced. Much as we regret accidents to Woodfull and Oldfield, we understand that in neither case was the bowler to blame.

If the Australian Board of Control wishes to propose a new law or rule it shall receive our careful consideration in due course. We hope the situation is now not as serious as your cable would seem to indicate, but if it is such as to jeopardise the good relations between English and Australian cricketers, and you consider it desirable to cancel the remainder of the programme, we would consent but with great reluctance.

While England played a draw in Ballarat against a Victorian Country XIII on 21 to 23 January, and defeated the powerful New South Wales team by four wickets in a low-scoring match in Sydney between 26 and 28 January (Hammond taking 9 for 65), behind-the-scenes activity intensified. On 31 January the Board of Control sent a second cable to Lord's in which it reasserted that Bodyline was "opposed to the spirit of cricket and unnecessarily dangerous to the players", but did not retract the word "unsportsmanlike".

Jardine, aware now that he had the MCC's full support, announced that he would not play in the fourth Test unless the Board of Control made a complete retraction. Warner realised that the completion of the tour was in

Three Australian batting hopes who were subdued by Bodyline: (L to R) Len Darling, Leo O'Brien and Don Bradman.

jeopardy and in an effort to bring pressure that would force the Board to back down, he turned to the British Government's representative in Australia, Ernest Crutchley, for help. On 1 February Warner and Palairet sent a telegram to Crutchley.

Have under consideration cancellation of remaining matches of tour including Tests owing to failure of Board to withdraw stigma of word "unsportsmanlike" in their first cable. Beg you

to use your influence to get the word withdrawn. Matter very urgent.

Crutchley telephoned the Australian Prime Minister, Joe Lyons, in Melbourne at the time, who in turn called in the Board chairman, Dr Robertson. Dr Robertson, on the same day, 1 February, sent a cable to the Board of Control secretary, Bill Jeanes, saying he had been interviewed by the Prime Minister who had asked him to have the word "unsportsmanlike" withdrawn. He added that Lyons had no doubt that if the word was retracted, the English method of attack would be modified and ended with the words, "Government afraid successful conversion endangered".

Philip Derriman, who unearthed this information for his book *Bodyline*, published in 1984, said:

> *Dr Robertson's cable to Jeanes contains the startling disclosure that the Australian government feared its "conversions", meaning conversion loans from Britain, had been placed at risk by the Bodyline row. These conversion loans—actually old loans re-negotiated or re-converted, to allow easier repayment—were of crucial importance to the capital-starved Australian economy during the Depression. Any interference with them could have had disastrous consequences.*

Derriman found that the official Australian government file on the matter had disappeared without trace and without explanation.

Both Lyons and Crutchley tried to conceal their part in the affair. In Adelaide, the acting governor, Sir George Murray, invited "Plum" Warner and several prominent citizens to Government House to discuss the ramifications of Bodyline. Warner was adamant at this meeting that he condemned what was being done, but insisted that on the field Jardine had complete control.

A special report on the Adelaide get-together went from Sir George to the governor of South Australia, Sir Alexander Hore-Ruthven, who was on leave in England; he thought it so important he consulted the Cabinet minister responsible for the Dominions, Jimmy Thomas. All of this activity bore fruit and on 8 February, two days before the fourth Test was due to start, the Board of Control sent another cable to Lord's which began, "We do not regard your sportsmanship as being in question...."

This was enough to satisfy Jardine, who rang Lord's to confirm the contents of the cable. It saved Australia's loans and allowed the tour to proceed, but did nothing to lessen the animosity among the players. The Australians knew that Sutcliffe and Hammond and the other professionals in the England team supported Jardine's strategy. Often Hammond and Sutcliffe walked straight to their positions in the Bodyline leg-trap, leaving Jardine little option but to persist with it. To have ordered them out of those positions in full view of thousands would have caused loss of face.

Vic Richardson said that the feeling in the Australian side against Jardine was so strong that when he knocked on the dressing-room door during the fourth Test, the door opened, and when he asked, "Is Bill Woodfull there?" the door closed in his face. Woodfull had to go out into the passage to discover what Jardine wanted. The Australian selectors also sought to embarrass Jardine by including left-handers Leo O'Brien, Ernie Bromley and Len Darling, which meant Jardine would have to keep swinging eight leg-side fieldsmen from one side to the other when any of these three partnered right-handers. Like slamming the door in his face, it did not worry Jardine, whose adherence to Bodyline was unwavering.

England drew the match with Queensland Country in Toowoomba from 1 to 2 February and then defeated Queensland by an innings and 61 runs in an ideal preparation for the fourth Test. Australia prepared for this crucial Test in Brisbane with a telephone hook-up between selectors, one (Dolling) in Adelaide, one (Johnson) in Melbourne and the other (Dwyer) in Sydney, but without any on-the-spot knowledge of conditions. They named Bert Tobin the South Australian all-rounder in the twelve. Tobin, who never scored a century or took five wickets in a match in his life, told reporters he could not believe it. Australia took the field with only three regular bowlers, Wall, O'Reilly and Ironmonger, who had to rely on McCabe, Bromley, Darling and Bradman for support in temperatures well over 100 degrees Fahrenheit. O'Reilly in his book *Tiger* described the

*Left-hander Ernie Bromley, who was the first West
Australian to play Test cricket. He played for
Australia in the fourth Test of the Bodyline tour.*

scene in the dressing-room as "Dainty" Ironmonger, about to celebrate his 51st birthday,
got ready:

> He was a heavily-built man, fifteen and a half
> stone and six foot high, and those of us who
> looked closely as he prepared for the fray saw
> that he wore long pieces of rubber band about six
> inches wide wrapped firmly around each thigh.
> Beside this he pulled an elastic knee guard over
> each knee. On his feet he had two pairs of
> woollen socks and he thrust his feet into boots
> with leather soles an inch thick. On that day in

> *Brisbane I honestly believe he deserved the
> Victoria Cross. When he had bowled about ten
> overs I met him as we were changing ends and I
> can recall the tortured look in his eyes as he
> enquired what my reaction was to the pitch.*

On a lifeless pitch England had toiled in
the Brisbane heat throughout the first day, 10
February, and by stumps the barracking that
had accompanied Bodyline field settings in the
morning had subsided. From 3 for 251, Australia slumped to be out for 340, Richardson
scoring 83, Woodfull 67 and Bradman 76.
England ground out her reply at the rate of 35
runs an hour, Jardine at one stage batting 82
minutes without scoring. At 6 for 216, with
England facing a first-innings deficit, Jardine
ordered Eddie Paynter out of his hospital bed
where he had been taken with influenza and a
temperature of 103 degrees. Paynter came
forward to drive one of the first balls he
received from O'Reilly, missed his wrong-un,
but was reprieved when keeper Hammy
Love, substituting for the injured Oldfield,
moved the wrong way.

After this let-off Paynter made 26 by
stumps, when he was driven back to hospital.
Next day his captain insisted he continue his
innings and he defied the bowlers for another
two and a half hours to score 83 in four hours
and help take England's score to 356.

At the end of the innings, Stan McCabe
suggested to Woodfull that a glass of champagne might revive his bowlers. Woodfull, a
teetotaller, agreed and sent dressing-room
attendant Sid Redgrave out for a bottle with
instructions to charge it to the Board of
Control. Queensland president Jack Hutcheon
refused permission for the drink to be served.
Woodfull was furious and went out and got
the bottle for his bowlers himself.

Australia made a promising start, but
Jardine brilliantly caught Richardson at mid-
off, Woodfull guided a Tommy Mitchell leg
break into the slips, Bradman stepped away to

The Australian team for the fourth Test at Brisbane in 1932–33 included one of the strangest selections of all time — B. Tobin, an obscure Adelaide all-rounder. The team: (L to R) (back) B. Tobin, T. Wall, W. O'Reilly, H. Ironmonger, E. Bromley; (front) H. Love, W. Ponsford, V. Richardson, W. Woodfull, S. McCabe, D. Bradman, L. Darling. Tobin was 12th man.

crack Larwood through the off side and was caught at deep point, and Ponsford was out to a spectacular diving slips catch by Larwood for a duck. This took Australia to 4 for 100 at stumps. McCabe next morning ducked six successive balls without offering a stroke, but he could not reproduce his first Test fireworks and when Darling was run out in a mix-up with Love, Australia were all out for 175. Needing only 160 to win, Jardine sent Leyland in when Sutcliffe was out at five. This proved a winning move. Leyland made 86, leaving Paynter, the first innings hero, to win the match and the Ashes with a six. The Australian public showed appreciation of Paynter's pluck by subscribing to a testi-

monial. The bashful Paynter brought Maurice Leyland and George Duckworth along for support when the cheque was presented. In England, cheering greeted the mention of Paynter's name in the House of Commons.

On the last day of the Test, 16 February 1933, Archie Jackson died of tuberculosis at Ingarfield Private Hospital, Brisbane, aged 23. He had become engaged to the dancer Phyllis Thomas on his death-bed, a few days after collapsing while playing club cricket for Northern Suburbs. Dr Evatt paid for his parents and his lifelong friend Bill Hunt to travel from Sydney to Brisbane in a special plane piloted by noted aviator P. G. Taylor. Hunt took his body back to Sydney on the same train that carried the England and Australian cricketers. He was given one of Sydney's biggest funerals, a mile-long cortege moving from the Jacksons' Balmain home to the Field of Mars cemetery in Ryde. Bradman, Woodfull, Richardson, Oldfield, McCabe and Ponsford were chosen as pall-bearers, but McCabe became ill and was replaced by Kippax.

With the Ashes won, Larwood did not

want to play in the fifth Test in Sydney from 23 to 28 February. Jardine, however, insisted he forget his weariness and shin soreness and use the Bodyline formula again even though the series had been decided. Australia dropped Ponsford, reasoning that he had been demoralised by Larwood. Darling top-scored with 85 in Australia's first innings of 435, Larwood bowling Bradman this time for 48. Jardine was fielding on the fence in boiling heat. Flies kept worrying him and he made some irritated swipes at them. A voice from the crowd called, "Hey, Jardine, you leave our flies alone".

When England batted, fast bowler Harry ("Bull") Alexander, who replaced the injured Wall, wanted to retaliate by bowling bouncers at the Englishmen but Woodfull refused to allow it. Australia twice dropped Hammond, who put on 122 with Sutcliffe. With stumps near, Jardine sent Larwood in as nightwatchman, much to Larwood's annoyance. Next morning Larwood batted in such admirable style that he appeared certain to score his first Test century, but at 98 Ironmonger held an amazing shin-high catch, one of the few in his long career that stuck. The crowd cheered Larwood all the way to the dressing-room in a reception that delighted him.

When Australia batted again Richardson was caught off his glove in the first over, trying to hook. Bradman began with an astounding tennis shot, which struck Larwood's bouncer on the first bounce into the sightboard. He went on batting with quick-footed abandon.

Larwood broke down in this innings with the fracture of two small bones in between his toes and it became so painful he could barely walk. Jardine was adamant that he bowl the five balls remaining although Larwood was in agony. Larwood swung his arm over without an approach run and Woodfull politely patted the five balls straight back to him.

Even then Jardine refused to allow Lar-

The Bodyline series umpires George Hele and George Barwick. Many believed they should have intervened against England's intimidatory bowling.

wood to leave the field, demanding he remain until Bradman was out. When Verity yorked Bradman for 71, Jardine clapped his hands. "Rightoh, Harold, you can go now," he called. Bradman and Larwood left the field together, Larwood limping, neither speaking a word, both realising Bradman had been tamed by placing the safety of his body ahead of the security of his wicket. Larwood never played Test cricket again.

That afternoon, when England set out after the 164 they needed to win, Jardine drew attention to footmarks made by Alexander, and asked if he could bowl in sandshoes. All the animosity of the preceding weeks surfaced again as the crowd hooted Jardine. When Alexander hit Jardine a painful blow in the ribs 35,000 spectators rose and cheered as one. Hammond (75 not out) and Wyatt (61 not out) finished off the victory by eight wickets,

Hammond hitting sixes off O'Reilly and "Perka" Lee.

England wound up their 22-match tour of Australia with a tie against Victoria and a draw against South Australia, but their visit had generated such feelings of bitterness and hostility that not even the tied match attracted any pleasure. Victoria had to score 178 in two hours to win and wanted seven to win off the last over, but only made six of them, finishing on 3 for 177. When the English team left for the New Zealand part of their programme nobody regretted their departure, and no Australian player went to see them off. Before they arrived for their first match at Wellington a special committee, appointed by the Australian Board of Control, comprising Roger Hartigan, Monty Noble, Bill Woodfull and Vic Richardson, was studying how to prevent a repetition of what had occurred.

"My constant dread," said George Hele, who umpired in all five Bodyline Tests, "was that a batsman would be killed."

After the Bodyline series ended the NSWCA organised a match between Past and Present New South Wales players for the Archie Jackson memorial fund. Bradman caused a lot of mirth when he positioned five men in close on the leg side for a ball to state coach George Garnsey just as Jardine had done for Larwood. Garnsey failed to hit it. He was too busy laughing. The memorial fund raised £453 and after paying for Jackson's headstone and grave, the NSWCA gave the remaining £357 to Jackson's mother.

Bodyline ended many lifelong friendships, permanently scarred cricket's good name, and took it to diplomatic conference tables. In the Sydney Domain a junior match ended in a brawl after only three overs when one team began with a Bodyline attack. In Adelaide, a match was abandoned after two overs following a similar brawl. The Sydney Centennial Park competition had an alarming rise in head injuries to teenagers.

The Bradman and Ponsford show

Australia in England 1934

Australia emerged from the Bodyline series without the Ashes but with a superb three-pronged spin attack comprising Clarence Victor Grimmett, William Joseph O'Reilly, both exponents of leg spin, googlies and top spin, and Leslie O'Brien Fleetwood-Smith, who concealed his changes of spin better than any left-arm googly bowler. All of them were such masters of deception that even their wicket-keepers often went the wrong way in taking them. All three were ready to bowl their fingers raw.

Fleetwood-Smith was so difficult to detect master keeper Bert Oldfield had special practice taking him without a batsman present. He bowled with a trigger action, cocking his arm back before bringing it over, using a stock ball aimed at the right-handed batsman's leg stump. On Australia's rolled-and-baked pitches he was the only one who could unfailingly secure turn on the first day. Of Australian bowlers who have taken 200 wick-

Policemen escort Bradman and Ponsford through the crowd as they resume their record partnership in the fifth Test at The Oval in 1934. Bradman made 244, Ponsford 266.

ets in Shield matches, Fleetwood-Smith achieved it quickest (26 matches). All of the 597 wickets he was to take in 123 first-class matches were secured before he turned 30.

Grimmett's renown as a spinner of the highest class did not always impress selectors who gave him a rough, almost shabby time throughout his career. Only in 1928–29 did he play a full Test series in Australia, and he had to wait until he was 34 to start on a Test career that made him the first bowler to take 200 Test wickets. He was dropped from the Australian side in 1932–33 before he found himself in the team for England in 1934.

Watching O'Reilly bowl gave no hint of his companionable, good-humoured off-the-field disposition. He bowled with his first and second fingers wrapped round the ball and the others folded onto the palm of his vast right fist, barely able to contain his rage. Hit for four, he took it as a personal affront. When the ball bounced a few inches off its intended mark he cursed his own incompetence.

Spectators often had trouble deciding how O'Reilly took his wickets. It was not always apparent to his victims either. Batsmen who popped up a catch from his bowling frequently looked to the wrong fieldsman for the ball and they were not always certain whether it was the leg break or wrong-un that brought their downfall. More than any other bowler of his time O'Reilly made the ball bounce high from a persistently good length, as if he were using a tennis ball. His mixture took a lot of working out and very few recipients recognised the components often enough to give him a hiding.

He took 11 more Test wickets than any of his team-mates in the Bodyline series, 27 at 26.81, 10 of them in the only Test Australia won, and headed the New South Wales bowling averages in Shield matches, with 31 wickets at 14.19. He also managed to top the Sydney grade cricket averages with 31 wickets at 8.38. Tim Wall had a slightly better Test average, his 16 wickets costing 25.56 apiece, but O'Reilly bowled 138 more overs than any Australian and it was clear that he had become the mainstay of the Australian attack.

England lost only 1 of their 22 tour matches in 1932–33, with 1 tie and 10 draws. Larwood headed England's Test bowling averages with 33 wickets at 19.51 and in the first-class matches on the tour he took 49 wickets at 16.67. Allen took 21 Test wickets at 28.23, Voce 15 at 27.13, Verity 11 at 24.63. The big advantage England enjoyed was that her batsmen scored 19 tour centuries, while her bowlers allowed only seven to be scored against them. Paynter headed the Test batting averages with 61.33, with Hammond and Sutcliffe both 55.00. Sutcliffe scored most runs on the tour—1318 at 73.22, which topped the first-class averages.

Bradman led Australia's Test batting averages with 56.57. He played in only three Shield matches but scored 600 runs at an average of 150, with a highest score of 238 in the match against Victoria played in Sydney between 4 and 8 November 1932. Ponsford also scored 200 in this match, and New South Wales won by nine wickets. O'Reilly took 5 for 81 in Victoria's first innings but Syd Hird's 6 for 56 in Victoria's second innings of 150— with Ponsford absent injured—was the match-winning display.

New South Wales won the Sheffield Shield for the twentieth time, winning five of their six matches in a season in which England's tour drama overshadowed all else. Victoria and South Australia both won three matches but Queensland, defeated in all six games, had their worst year. At Brisbane, from 28 to 31 October, Len Darling and Leo O'Brien had an Australian record stand of 301 for the fourth wicket to set up a Victorian triumph by 329 runs. O'Brien made 145 not out, Darling 185.

The sensation of the Shield came in the match between South Australia and New

The furore over Bodyline probably meant Tim Wall did not get the publicity he deserved when he took all ten wickets for South Australia v. New South Wales in 1932–33.

J. H. Fingleton *b.* Wall		43
W. A. Brown *c.* Whitington *b.* Wall		0
D. G. Bradman *c.* Ryan *b.* Wall		56
S. J. McCabe *c.* Walker *b.* Wall		0
R. C. Rowe *b.* Wall		0
F. S. Cummins *c.* Walker *b.* Wall		0
H. S. Love *b.* Wall		1
C. J. Hill *b.* Wall		0
W. H. Howell *b.* Wall		0
W. J. O'Reilly *b.* Wall		4
G. L. Stewart *not out*		2
Sundries		7
		113

Wall was the seventh Australian to take all ten wickets in first-class cricket but the first to accomplish it in a Shield match. He bowled steadily, well short of express speed, a great favourite with spectators at all Australia's major grounds because of the leisurely manner in which he went back to his bowling mark. He enjoyed the heckling for what was the slowest walk-back seen in Australia. He could bowl for hours off a 27-pace approach in which he made a scissors movement of his legs. He always looked exhausted as he walked back, even in his opening overs.

Wall and off spinner P. K. Lee each took 25 wickets in the season, giving Grimmett considerable assistance. Apart from Bradman, who played in only three Shield matches but still scored 600 runs at an average of 150, including 238 against Victoria, Darling scored consistently this season for Victoria. At Brisbane from 28 to 31 October 1932, Darling put on 301 for the fourth wicket against Queensland, a Victorian record, Darling finishing on 184, O'Brien 145. At Adelaide between 25 and 29 November 1932, Darling (150) put on 281 for the third wicket with Keith Rigg (166), another Victorian record. In the very next match against Queensland at Melbourne from 16 to 20 December 1932, Darling made 128. Ironmonger took 7 for 13 in this match, Victoria winning by an innings and 139 runs.

South Wales at Sydney, from 3 to 6 February 1933, when Tim Wall took all 10 wickets in New South Wales' first innings, only to see his team lose the game. New South Wales had 87 on the board for the loss of two wickets, but after lunch Wall was unplayable and took the wickets of Fingleton, McCabe, Ray Rowe and Frank Cummins without conceding a run. Six of Wall's ten victims were clean-bowled on a pitch which offered little assistance. A stiff breeze enabled Wall to swing the ball a long way. The New South Wales score-card read:

Cook batted right through the Queensland second innings of 74 to 36 not out. The other outstanding feat in an historic season was Grimmett's 13 for 135 (6 for 49 and 7 for 86) against Queensland at Brisbane between 21 and 31 January, 1933.

Bradman, who had surrendered his qualification to play for St George when he married and moved to the North Sydney district in 1932, joined the North Sydney club at the start of the 1933–34 season. North Sydney wanted him as captain, a role he had undertaken successfully towards the end of his stint with St George. But Albert Vincent, the North Sydney first grade captain and the club's delegate to the NSWCA, objected to being passed over and dropped himself to second grade rather than play under Bradman. In 1949–50, Bradman and Vincent served as selectors of the Australian side that toured New Zealand. Largely because of injury, Bradman played only three innings for North Sydney. Apart from his representative commitments, he was in the midst of a contract shared between sporting goods firm F. J. Palmer and Associated Newspapers, who used him for writing and broadcasting and for coaching schoolboys on holiday camps and tours.

Victoria's younger players were responsible in 1933–34 for winning the Shield for the first time in five seasons. Darling, casting aside his reputation as a dasher, batted with control and consistency to score 604 runs at 54.90, and the other left-handers O'Brien and Bromley played valuable knocks. Rigg and wicket-keeper Ben Barnett supported them splendidly. Fleetwood-Smith bowled too fast at the start of the summer but when he slowed his pace he troubled every batsman in Australia, finishing with 39 wickets at 22.41, including 12 for 158 in the Melbourne match from 29 December to 2 January 1934, in which Roy Lonergan made 115 and 100 for South Australia and still saw his side lose by five wickets.

A promotional photograph distributed by Don Bradman's bat company after he became an international celebrity.

Nitschke made 82, 44 not out, 130 not out and 6 in the two matches between South Australia and New South Wales. Arthur Allsopp scored 146 and 123 not out for his new state, Victoria, against Western Australia and Tasmania respectively. Badcock hit 274 and 71 not out for Tasmania against Victoria, but the highlight of the three matches between these states was the stand of 424 for the fourth wicket by Victorians I. S. Lee (268) and S. O. Quin (210) which saved the match for Victoria after they had been dismissed for 68 in the first innings.

But Australia's two greatest cricketers topped the Shield averages. O'Reilly, with 33 wickets at 18.30, was the only regular Shield bowler whose wickets cost under 20 runs. Bradman again proved the finest batsman in Australia by scoring 922 runs at an average of 184.40, including two double centuries (200 and 253) against Queensland, two centuries (187 not out and 128) against Victoria. Bradman and Kippax set a Shield record for the third wicket by scoring 363 against Queensland in Sydney. Bradman exceeded 1000 runs in all first-class matches for the sixth successive season, a performance without equal in Australia.

The interstate conference adopted an "anti-Bodyline" law proposed by South Australia for the Shield competition before the 1933–34 series began. The law empowered umpires to call "no ball" when a bowler deliberately tried to intimidate or injure a batsman. Bowlers who repeated the offence were barred from bowling for the rest of the innings.

Only New South Wales, who regarded it as a "mind-reader's" law, opposed introduction of this law. New South Wales officials were incensed when it was passed because they said it meant the smaller States could muster enough votes to frustrate New South Wales or Victoria. New South Wales' distrust of the manner in which the Board conducted its affairs led, in September 1935, to an attempt to remove voting rights from Tasmania and Western Australia and relegate them to associate membership. When this proposal was defeated by ten votes to three, there were rumours that New South Wales would withdraw from the Board, but they proved unfounded.

The Board has always been open to this kind of rumour-mongering and to wild, unsubstantiated criticism because it has always preferred to hold its meetings in private, handing out statements on what has been decided when their discussions ended. The Board members claim that they like most pressmen and enjoy their company but their

West Australian Dick Bryant, who came under the spotlight in 1933–34 after an innings of 103 against Victoria. He was the brother of Frank Bryant who toured with Frank Tarrant's team to India.

presence during Board meetings would inhibit candid discussion. The fact that some of the official statements issued after Board meetings have proved to be hopelessly inaccurate and have even been challenged by Board delegates has further eroded the Board's public image.

The Board of Control instructed its London representative, Dr Robert Macdonald, to obtain a promise from the MCC that Bodyline bowling would be outlawed for Australia's 1934 tour of England. The MCC declined, although an MCC sub-committee comprising Lord Hawke, Lord Lewisham, Sir Stanley Jackson and MCC secretary William Findlay, agreed that bowling which made a direct attack on a batsman was undesirable. Macdonald pointed out that Australia was

Dr Robert MacDonald, a Queenslander who represented the Board of Control in London, failed to get assurances from the MCC at Lord's that there would be no repetition of the Bodyline tactics on Australia's 1934 tour.

several Board members who said the reply was not an expression of the majority's sentiments. Queensland delegate J. S. Hutcheon told Board chairman Aubrey Oxlade, "The responsibility for letting Australian players down is on your shoulders." For all the good they did, the deliberations of the Board's anti-Bodyline committee were a waste of time.

The MCC were by now aware that they had erred in prematurely defending Jardine when it was not fully understood in London that his bowlers deliberately aimed at the batsmen. But the men at the helm at Lord's were aristocrats whose backgrounds prevented them admitting their error to Colonials or even accepting the word Bodyline into cricket's vocabulary. They were helped in their cover-up by the election of solicitor Aubrey Oxlade as Australian Board of Control chairman in place of Allen Robertson, and the shift of power from Melbourne to Sydney. Oxlade advocated appeasement and acceptance of the MCC's promise that there would be no repetition of Bodyline tactics. Oxlade was rewarded in the 1934 New Year's Honours list with a CBE, while in London letters in the Dominions Office file on Bodyline were destroyed.

Bradman's three-way contract with men's clothing store owner, F. J. Palmer, the *Sydney Sun* newspaper and radio station 2UE ended on 1 February 1934, and in the weeks leading up to this he and his wife talked over a number of offers. Bradman had been concerned at his lack of energy during the Bodyline Tests and attributed it partly to a lifestyle which had him concerned with cricket day and night. While Don was on the field, Jessie kept notes on his matches on which he based his nightly radio broadcasts. He decided to look for a job outside the game which would leave him free to tackle his batting refreshed and enthusiastic.

After Bradman had moved out of the St George district to McMahons Point when he

entitled to know if England's tactics would justify the inclusion of four fast bowlers in the Australian side.

Lord Hawke: "Reprisals, by God!"

Dr Macdonald: "No, I would call it reciprocity, merely neutral action and reaction."

In Australia some delegates to the Board spoke of abandoning the 1934 tour but Board secretary Syd Smith strongly supported the tour. "Our team must go," he said. "We cannot afford, from an Empire point of view, for the Tests to disappear. They mean more than cricket." The majority of the states wanted a firm guarantee before the tour proceeded but, without waiting for a vote, the Board meekly cabled Australia's acceptance of the tour invitation. This aroused the ire of

The Secretary,
N.S.W.C.A.
254a George Street,
SYDNEY.

Dear Sir,

A report has appeared in the Sydney press to the effect that I have accepted an offer to enter the business of H.W.Hodgetts & Co. Adelaide. I wish to confirm this statement and to advise your association that I shall be taking up permanent residence in South Australia before sailing for England with the 1934 Australian XI.

For some years past it has been my pleasure and privilege to play for N.S.Wales under the auspices of your association. During that period we have linked together very harmoniously and I can assure you it is with extreme regret I have to advise you of my decision to leave N.S.Wales, which means of course that I shall in future be a friendly enemy of this state on the cricket field.

Apart from this official notification of my intentions I have advised the President of the Association and the Chairman of your Executive Committee of my movements and the reasons therefor. It is sufficient to say here that I am making the change for private business and health reasons.

May I take this opportunity of expressing my appreciation of the treatment meted out to me by your Association in the past and I do hope the members will realise that though lost to N.S.Wales I am still essentially Australian.

Yours faithfully,

Don Bradman

The letter in which Bradman confirmed that he was lost to New South Wales cricket and would play instead in South Australia — a costly move for New South Wales.

married, an old back injury put him out of action. The injury dated back to his long partnership with Kippax against Queensland, and it recurred just after he had scored 127 in 90 minutes for North Sydney against Western Suburbs.

There had been plans late in 1933 of a sporting goods business being opened in his name with the backing of a group of local businessmen but the venture could not be financed. Another offer Bradman considered while he recuperated was to play for Rochdale in the Lancashire League. Meanwhile the New South Wales Cricket Association announced that it was taking action to ensure that Bradman remained in New South Wales, but whatever this action was it never came to fruition.

On 12 February 1934, Sydney newspapers announced that Bradman intended to move to Adelaide to join the stockbroking firm conducted by Henry "Harry" Warburton Hodgetts, a prominent South Australian official and delegate to the Board of Control. Two days later Bradman wrote to NSWCA secretary Harold Heydon from Mittagong confirming the news. The letter said Bradman intended to set up house in Adelaide before sailing to England with the 1934 Australian team so that he would qualify to play for South Australia on his return in 1934–35. New South Wales had lost the greatest drawcard in cricket history. Part of the six-year contract Bradman negotiated with Hodgetts was that Bradman would captain South Australia.

Bradman became alarmed at his indifferent health after they had moved to Adelaide and although he was passed fit by the Board's doctors he consulted two Adelaide specialists at his own expense before the team left for overseas. They found only that he was rundown and advised complete rest, indicating that he should be fully fit after the long voyage to England. Cricket-watchers were surprised when the Board of Control named Bradman vice-captain of the touring team in preference to the more experienced New South Wales captain Alan Kippax, a clear indication the Board considered Bradman a future Australian captain.

The 1934 team, the eighteenth to tour England, was W. M. Woodfull (captain), D. G. Bradman (vice-captain), A. F. Kippax, W. H. Ponsford, W. A. Brown, A. G. Chipperfield, B. A. Barnett, S. J. McCabe, L. S. Darling, W. J. O'Reilly, W. A. Oldfield, E. H. Bromley, C. V. Grimmett, H. I. Ebeling, T. W. Wall, L. O'B. Fleetwood-Smith, W. C. Bull (treasurer) and H. F. Bushby (manager). Bushby was the Tasmanian delegate to the Board of Control, noted for the help he had given cricketers struggling to survive during the Depression.

Chipperfield had been picked for the England tour after only three first-class matches for New South Wales, largely on the recommendation of former Australian captain Warren Bardsley, who rated Chipperfield the best slips fieldsman he had ever seen. Chipperfield had won a place in the New South Wales team in 1932–33 by scoring 152 for Northern Districts (Newcastle) against Jardine's MCC team. He was well known in Sydney grade cricket for centuries studded with crisp, front-foot driving but was far from a seasoned cricketer at the first class level. Before the end of the England tour he had become a permanent member of the Test team, a renowned slips fieldsman, and according to Neville Cardus the best wet-wicket player in the Australian side. He also bowled useful leg breaks when it was necessary to rest Grimmett or O'Reilly.

The selection of Fleetwood-Smith, Grimmett and O'Reilly denied Sydney leg spinner Hughie Chilvers of a trip many less talented bowlers have had. From the time he came into the New South Wales side in 1929–30 Chilvers was a recognised world-class spinner, with a top spinner that fooled even the finest batsmen. He was destined to take 151 first-class wickets, 11 times taking five wickets in an innings and three times capturing 10 wickets in a match for New South Wales, but the masterly skill of O'Reilly, Grimmett and Fleetwood-Smith denied him a Test berth and he never made an overseas trip. O'Reilly said Chilvers, an English-born (at Sawbridgeworth, Hertfordshire) analytical chemist, was the best leg spinner never to play for Australia.

The tour was seen as a peace-making exercise after the bitterness of the Bodyline series, but took place on terms staunchly rejected by five members of the Board of Control. Allen Robertson, no longer chairman following the appointment of Oxlade, wrote to other members of the Board with the support of Victorian delegates Mailey and Kelly and the Queenslanders Hartigan and Hutcheon, insisting that the time for conciliation had passed. Robertson said an assurance should be extracted from the MCC that direct attacks on batsmen would be outlawed in the 1934 tour. By eight votes to five, the Board accepted the MCC invitation to tour, but on terms that disgusted Australia's leading players.

Two factors eased the tension. First, cricket had the good fortune to receive Jardine's retirement as captain of England, after leading his country against Australia, the West Indies and India. He retired while still at the peak of his playing powers after leading England in 15 Tests, for only one loss. Jardine quit in an exclusive telegram to the London *Evening Standard*, for whom he covered the 1934 series. Cricket's second stroke of good fortune came in the appointment of Woodfull as Australia's captain. He was such an essentially

honest and virtuous man, instinctively tactful, that he quickly won over English critics who claimed Australia had squealed without justification during the Bodyline Tests.

Larwood was made the scapegoat for the Bodyline series when he refused to apologise for the published interviews he gave his county captain Arthur Carr on the way home to England. He continued in first-class cricket until 1938, but refused to play Test cricket. The leg injury he blamed on hard Australian wickets troubled him for the rest of his life. His Bodyline colleague, big Bill Voce, was available for the 1934 series but was not picked, although still an outstanding bowler. Voce's refusal to abide by the spirit of the game and eliminate direct attacks on batsmen made him a highly controversial figure and finally led to the sacking of his captain, Arthur Carr, before the 1935 season began.

The Australians were assured at all the pre-tour functions that they would not be subjected to persistent bouncers aimed at the body. The 17 county captains had agreed to outlaw this form of attack at a meeting of the County Cricket Advisory Committee in November 1933.

The 1934 Australian team to England: (L to R)
(back) W. Ferguson (scorer), C. Grimmett,
W. Brown, H. Ebeling, H. Bushby, W. O'Reilly,
T. Wall, L. Fleetwood-Smith, W. Bull (treasurer);
(centre) E. Bromley, A. Chipperfield,
D. Bradman, W. Woodfull (captain), A. Kippax,
L. Darling, W. Ponsford; (front) B. Barnett,
S. McCabe, W. Oldfield.

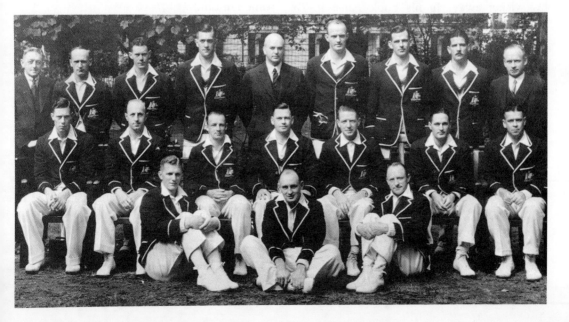

Woodfull said, before a ball was bowled, that he would have to pin his faith on Grimmett and O'Reilly to get opponents out, but he had no doubt about the batting, which was very strong. His main fear was that the team would not field well. His views on Australia's bowling and batting proved accurate but he was wrong to worry about the fielding. From the time they were first on view, Billy Brown, Arthur Chipperfield, Ernie Bromley and Len Darling fielded like champions, and Bromley's throwing was one of the delights of the summer. With Oldfield as competent as ever behind the stumps, Australia's cricket reached a standard no England team could match.

Bradman was unwell before the first match against Worcestershire from 2 May at Worcester but Woodfull persuaded him to play for fear his withdrawal would give England a psychological advantage. Grimmett bundled Worcestershire out for 112 by taking 5 for 53 and Australia were 1 for 29 in reply when Bradman went in 20 minutes before tea. He had an uncomfortable 20 minutes, but after tea batted with his old confidence and was 112 not out at stumps. Next day he took his score to 206, before he deliberately gave his wicket away. In his book *Farewell To Cricket* Bradman wrote:

> *I played under considerable strain but steeled myself to see through my innings of 206. It was made in quick time (208 minutes) but I was only too well aware of the drain on my resources. Indeed it was largely as a result of this initial exertion that my cricket fell away, and I only once more exceeded 50 before the end of May. In that time I registered two unimpressive ducks.*

Bradman's double century enabled Australia to reach 504. When Grimmett whipped through the Worcestershire batting to have them out in the second innings for 95, Australia chalked up a solid first-up win by an in-

nings and 297 runs. Grimmett took 10 for 80 in the match.

McCabe made a grand 108 not out in the drawn match against Leicestershire from 5 to 8 May at Leicester, where rain on the last day prevented the Australian bowlers forcing home the advantage of a 216-run first innings lead. O'Reilly took 7 for 39 on his first appearance in England, in Leicestershire's first innings, and finished the match with 11 for 79. An easy win followed at Cambridge against Cambridge University, between 9 and 11 May. Ponsford contributed 229 not out, Darling 98 and Brown 105. Grimmett had 9 for 74 in Cambridge's first innings, Australia winning by an innings and 163 runs.

The strength of the Australian batting was again evident at Lord's in the match against Marylebone Cricket Club from 12 to 15 May. Hendren made 135 in MCC's first innings of 362 before Australia rushed to 6 for 559 declared. Ponsford made his highest score in England, 281 not out, and put on 389 for the third wicket with McCabe, whose share was 192. Wyatt saved MCC from defeat by scoring 102 not out while eight wickets fell at the other end. MCC were still 15 behind when time ran out.

Facing genuine fast bowling for the first time on their schedule against Essex, the Australians acquitted themselves well enough to win by an innings and 93 runs. This game was played at Chelmsford from 16 to 18 May. Chasing Essex's 220, Australia were 5 for 170 when Brown and Chipperfield put on 141. Chipperfield made 175 in his first innings in England and his last-wicket stand with O'Reilly put on 62 and lifted Australia's lead to 218. On a crumbling pitch O'Reilly (9 for 132 in the match) and Grimmett (8 for 134) put Essex out for 125.

The Essex bowlers Ken Farnes and H. T. O. Smith bowled extremely fast, but did not worry the Australians because they kept the ball below chest height. Farnes, who was 195 centimetres tall and had a well-coordinated right-arm action which brought the ball down from almost 2.5 metres, bowled with plenty of nip and lift, but finished with 3 for 111, disappointing figures for such a good athlete.

Fleetwood-Smith took 5 for 30 off 9.3 overs and Grimmett 7 for 109 from 36.3 overs to spearhead an innings and 33 runs win over Oxford University. Darling made 100 in this match at Oxford between 19 and 21 May. At Southampton Phil Mead made 139, W. G. Lowndes 140 and they were partners in a 247-run stand that ended any hope of Australia forcing a win. Darling again batted well for 96 and Chipperfield hit another century (116 not out).

Middlesex fought hard on the first day of their match with Australia at Lord's on 26 May. The Middlesex batting broke down badly in the second innings and Australia won by ten wickets. Grimmett's five second-innings wickets cost slightly more than five runs each, but a hat-trick by Tommy Enthoven, following a dazzling 160 by Bradman in only 120 minutes—one of the finest innings he ever played—earned more attention.

At The Oval between 30 May and 1 June Andy Sandham made a double century (219) and Robert Gregory 116 in Surrey's 7 for 475 declared. With little likelihood of a result, the Australians gained valuable batting practice, Ponsford scoring 125, McCabe 240, Bradman 77 and Bromley 56 in Australia's 629 total. The match petered out in a draw with Gregory 59 not out in Surrey's second innings of 2 for 162. The match against Lancashire at Old Trafford from 2 to 5 June was also drawn, despite centuries from McCabe (142), Woodfull (172 not out) and Brown (119).

Australia introduced batsmen Billy Brown and all-rounder Arthur Chipperfield for the first Test at Nottingham from 8 to 12 June. Farnes made his debut for England, who had difficulty finding a captain when Bob Wyatt,

Grimmett and Bradman take some time off to match wits across the tennis court.

Jardine's heir apparent, broke a thumb. The selectors finally settled on Worcestershire captain Cyril Walters, a stylish right-hand opening batsman. They hoped Walters would also fill the gap left by Hobbs as an opening partner for Sutcliffe. Without Larwood and Voce, England's attack looked innocuous.

Woodfull and Ponsford put on 77 before Farnes, in his second spell, had Ponsford caught by Ames, who had now proved his superiority to Duckworth behind the stumps. Woodfull, Brown, Bradman and Darling soon followed Ponsford and at 5 for 153 Chipperfield joined McCabe. Bad light restricted play but when he was out next morning for 65 McCabe had dominated a stand of 81. Supported by Oldfield and Grimmett, Chipperfield added 82 to his overnight 17 and went along to 99 not out at lunch, mindful that at the age of 42 Grimmett could not be asked to run brisk singles. Third ball after the break Chipperfield tried to drive Farnes and edged the ball to Ames to become the only player to make 99 on debut in Test cricket. About fifty years earlier Harry Graham made 99 for Australia *v.* England, but not in his first Test, which Graham had adorned with a century.

When England set out after Australia's 374, only Sutcliffe of the early batsmen looked at ease against a varied and hostile Australian attack. His 62 accounted for a lot of the total as England struggled to 6 for 165, with 60 still needed to avoid the follow-on. Close mates Grimmett and O'Reilly bowled for long periods together, each spinning the ball either way from a good length, rejoicing in their rivalry and the tense struggle to decide who would take most tour wickets. Hendren saved the follow-on with 79 to go with the two centuries he had already taken from the Australians on the tour, but with a total of 268 England were 106 behind.

In the second innings, Woodfull, Ponsford and Bradman went cheaply but Brown steadied the innings with 73 while McCabe attacked superbly for 88. When Woodfull declared on the fourth morning England wanted 380 to win in 285 minutes.

England were 5 for 115 at tea and when Leyland and Ames batted for 70 minutes a draw appeared likely. But with O'Reilly bowling at the crumbling end and Grimmett full of tricks at the other, Australia won in a thrilling finish by 238 runs only ten minutes from time. O'Reilly took the last three wickets for four runs to finish with 7 for 54 and 11 for 129 in the match. Sprinting from the ground in an attempt to elude well-wishers Bradman caught his foot in the boundary rope and seriously injured his thigh.

Arthur Chipperfield, who made 99 in his first Test against England. He was not out on that score at lunch but was dismissed by the third ball after the interval. He remains the only batsman to score 99 on his Test debut.

Farnes bowled with exceptional fire to take five wickets in each innings—5 for 102 off 40.2 overs and 5 for 77 off 25 overs—but for economy Geary, then in his forty-first year, took the honours. His 43 overs in the first innings yielded 3 for 101 and his 23 overs in the second innings brought 1 for 46. The difference between the teams was most marked in fielding, where Australia was far more efficient.

Australia had the best of a drawn game against Northamptonshire at Northampton from 13 to 15 June. Brown scored 113 and Fleetwood-Smith followed his first innings 5 for 63 with 5 for 29. Bradman batted with a runner and made 65 and 25. At Lord's from 16

The great Yorkshire left-arm spin bowler Hedley Verity in action against Australia in 1934. Oldfield is the batsman at the non-striker's end.

to 19 June against the Gentlemen Australia led by only 53 on the first innings but a great second innings of 105 not out by McCabe led to a comfortable win by eight wickets. In the Long Room, Lord's members spoke of the wonderful timing that enabled McCabe to score fours from even his defensive strokes.

Brown scored his second successive century at Lord's in the second Test from 22 to 25 June, but his team-mates failed in what became known as "Verity's match". After Leyland made 109, Ames 120 and England 440, Australia had to bat on a rain-affected pitch and Verity made the most of the conditions to take 15 wickets, 14 of them for 80 runs on the third day. Australia followed on 156 behind after a first innings of 284, and with the pitch deteriorating, managed only 118 at the second attempt. Verity had 7 for 61 and 8 for 43, including the last seven in an hour.

O'Reilly, who won so many matches for Australia, believed he made the fatal contribution to Australia's heavy defeat at Lord's with a silly swipe that attempted to land a six into the Long Room. O'Reilly joined Chipperfield at 8 for 273 in Australia's first innings with 17 needed to prevent the follow-on. With only six runs needed he lost control, swung wildly and was bowled. This gave Verity a chance to bowl again on a rain-sodden pitch where O'Reilly would have been devastating.

The high calibre of the Australian spin-

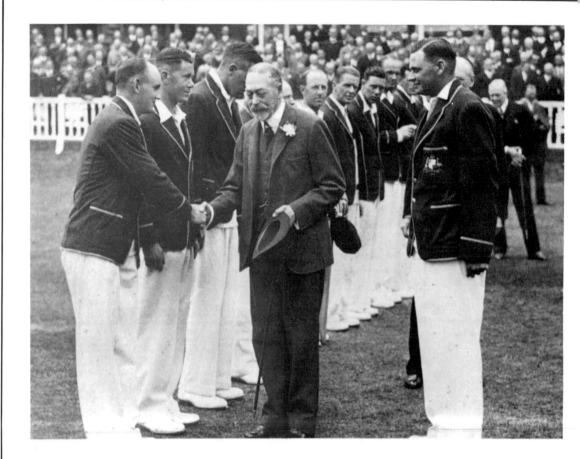

Woodfull, introducing his players to King George V, comes to Stan McCabe at the end of the line during the Lord's Test, 1934.

ners was shown again when they defeated Somerset by an innings and 77 runs at Taunton on 27 and 28 June—O'Reilly 9 for 38, Fleetwood-Smith 6 for 56—and in the six-wicket win over Surrey at The Oval from 30 June to 3 July where Grimmett took 4 for 64 and 5 for 33.

The Australians were intrigued to read the following advertisement in a local paper when they played Somerset:

Australians v. Somerset
If Don Bradman comes to Jones' Garage he can have a second-hand Austin 7 for a present.
(1 dozen still in stock)

Bradman did not take advantage of the offer, but Arthur Chipperfield collected a second-hand car as his prize for winning a golf match. Bradman did accept an old cheque endorsed by W. G. Grace, however, the only autograph he ever kept except for those that came on team photographs. Grace's cheque, dated 1907, the year before Bradman was born, was sent by a Bradman admirer.

The third Test at Manchester began on Friday 6 July but was left drawn after 1307 runs were scored in four days and only 20 wickets fell. The Australians played through the match severely handicapped when throat infections struck Bradman and Chipperfield and others to a lesser degree. Chipperfield defied his doctors by leaving Monsall Fever Hospital to play despite a rasping, painful larynx.

England made 68 in an hour in near tropical heat. A stop for drinks was extended by a complaint about the ball losing its shape, which the umpires Hardstaff and Walden accepted. O'Reilly then took three wickets in four deliveries with the replacement ball. He had Walters caught off his first ball after the break and Wyatt was bowled by the second. Hammond glanced the third for four and was bowled by the fourth. Despite losing three wickets in four balls England took lunch on 3 for 128.

Sutcliffe went for 63 when England were 149 and Hendren, then 45 years old, continued his supremacy over the Australian spinners by scoring 132. After a stand of 191 with Hendren, Leyland (153) had a partnership of 142 with Ames and by lunch on the second day England were 8 for 533. Instead of declaring Wyatt continued batting to tire the Australians and wear the wicket, eventually closing at 9 for 627.

Allen began the Australian first innings with a sensational over which lasted for 13 balls, four of them no-balls, three of them wides and two which Brown hit for four. Australia were 1 for 136 at stumps and on the third morning Brown defended while McCabe cut, hooked and pulled, together adding 196. Woodfull came in and was dropped first ball by Hendren and Ames missed a chance to stump him when he was 31. Woodfull helped McCabe take the score to 242 before McCabe was out for 137.

England missed catches and a run-out chance against Darling, whose stand with Woodfull brought 78 and then Woodfull and Bradman put on 58 before Bradman (30) gave Ames a sharp catch off Hammond. Woodfull was run out for 73 after resisting for just short of four hours, and at stumps Australia, with only two wickets left, were still 55 runs short of preventing the follow-on. On the last morning O'Reilly lashed out and this time his innings (30 not out) did save the follow-on,

Young Stan McCabe, who scored a total of 2078 runs at 69.27 on the 1934 tour.

adding 35 runs for the ninth wicket with Chipperfield and 37 for the tenth with Wall. Chipperfield tottered about for 26 and went straight back to hospital when he was dismissed, leaving the tour for a week. As most of their batsmen were unwell the Australians considered that keeping England in the field for more than 10 hours, while they scored 491, was almost as satisfying as a victory.

England closed their second innings at 123 without loss, but there was no hope of Australia scoring the 260 runs needed to win in the time left. *Wisden* could scarcely believe the weather: "Seldom can an international engagement in this country have been played through the whole four days in such wonderful conditions. From the first to the last the sun blazed down, the heat being at times almost unbearable."

Australia then defeated Derbyshire by nine wickets between 11 and 13 July at Chesterfield. The combination of sound batting, Hans Ebeling's first innings 5 for 28 and the fast-improving Fleetwood-Smith's 5 for 38 in the second innings proved too much for their adversaries. Gutsy Brian Sellers made 104 for Yorkshire in the drawn match at Sheffield from 14 to 17 July, to which Bradman responded with 140.

England replaced the injured Sutcliffe with the Notts professional William Keeton for the fourth Test at Leeds, although Keeton had no experience of O'Reilly and Grimmett. Allen, Clark, James Langridge and Nichols went to the ground but were left out, Nichols acting as twelfth man for the third time. Bowes replaced Allen and Tommy Mitchell took Clark's spot.

Australia looked good on the first day, 20 July, when they dismissed England for 200 and were left with only 45 minutes' batting. They were 37 without loss when Bowes changed ends and immediately bowled Brown and then had nightwatchman Oldfield caught behind. Woodfull came in instead of using a second nightwatchman and with two minutes left, played on. Australia had collapsed to 3 for 39 in 10 balls and Bowes had 3 for 0 since changing ends.

Bowes had two deliveries left in his unfinished over next morning. Both were short, and Bradman clubbed both straight back past the bowler to the boundary. For the rest of the day Bradman returned to his best form of the 1930 tour, playing copybook cricket without hint of risk, accelerating only in the final session when England's bowlers were weary. His stand with Ponsford was Australian batsmanship at its best, with neither man dominant, as they added 388 for the fourth wicket, a Test record.

Ponsford was out for 181 when he struck his own wicket only 39 minutes before stumps. They had batted for 5 hours 41 minutes. McCabe joined Bradman and they took the score to 4 for 494 at stumps, when Bradman was 271 not out. Bowes bowled both of them next morning, Bradman for 304, his second triple century in a Leeds Test. He hit 2 sixes and 43 fours in an innings of 7 hours 10 minutes and while he was at the crease 511 runs were added of the Australian total of 584.

Keeton was bowled by Grimmett, Hammond was run out, O'Reilly bowled Walters, and England were 3 for 87 when Hendren and Wyatt put on 65, before Grimmett bowled Wyatt. Heavy rain that night upset all predictions. On the next morning, 24 July, England lost two more wickets, those of Leyland and Ames, and another storm ended the match. England were still 155 behind with four wickets left, and all the honours went to Australia.

Matches against Durham and Scotland ended in draws, followed by more rain-affected draws against Gloucestershire at Bristol, Glamorgan at Swansea, and Warwickshire at Edgbaston. Woodfull made a fine 131 at Bristol and 228 not out at Swansea. Fleetwood-Smith took 7 for 40 at Bristol, O'Reilly 7 for 37 at Swansea and Grimmett 5 for 76 at Edgbaston, but in all three matches there was not enough time to force a result.

Bradman was in a nursing home recovering from a torn thigh muscle, sustained while fielding in the fourth Test, when the Australians went to Nottingham for what turned out to be the most unpleasant match of their tour. The Nottinghamshire crowd heckled

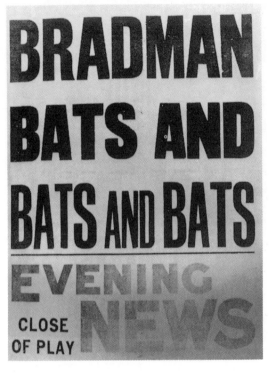

Billboards for London newspapers in July 1934, after another marathon Bradman innings.

the Australians from the time Woodfull and Brown went out on 11 August to start the match, apparently believing the complaints about Bodyline were inspired by Australia alone. The barracking worsened when Voce bowled and he reacted by firing in numerous short-pitched deliveries, with five men on the leg side, four of them in the leg-trap where they could catch deflections.

Fielding a side of 11 professionals, Notts were without Carr and Larwood, but had Australia out for 237. Voce took 8 for 66, all of them caught. Notts replied with 183. At the end of the first day Woodfull sent for the Notts secretary and told him the agreement under which Australia were touring England had been broken. Woodfull said the county committee must make the final decision, but if Voce took the field when Australia batted a

second time, the Australians would return to London without finishing the match.

Before the second Australian innings began the county announced that Voce had shin soreness, which did not impress spectators who had seen him score 22 runs in Notts' first innings. The crowd realised there was more to Voce's absence than shin troubles, and when the Australian batsmen came out they were greeted with loud boos. There was great joy in the stands when Butler bowled Woodfull for one, but Brown, McCabe and Kippax batted so well Australia was able to declare at 2 for 230, with Brown on 100 not out. Nottinghamshire, needing 285 to win, were 6 for 128 when time expired.

The Notts committee subsequently called for the umpires in the match to report on the fairness of Voce's bowling and they found that the charge of direct attack on the batsmen was proven. The committee than expressed its regret and sent a report to the MCC, saying it deprecated Voce's bowling and would take the necessary measures to prevent its recurrence. At the end of August Middlesex also complained about Voce's bowling in the match at Lord's and again the Notts committee apologised, after acknowledging that Middlesex had a genuine grievance.

In December 1934, the Nottinghamshire committee announced that Carr had been sacked and that S. D. Rhodes and G. F. H. Heane would be joint captains in 1935. "It is obvious from Carr's statements that his view of fair bowling is so far different from that of first-class umpires and many leading cricketers that a recurrence of trouble under his captaincy would be practically certain to arise," said the committee, who then all resigned, a move *Wisden* agreed was their only honourable course.

The Notts committee were forced to resign at a packed meeting attended by 2500 people. When Carr rose to speak, the meeting sang "For he's a jolly good fellow". Eventually, with the backing of Lord's, the committee was reinstated, the anti-Carr faction prevailed, and Rhodes and Heane shared the captaincy in an unsuccessful 1935 season.

The Australians were relieved by Woodfull's sequence of 131, 228 and 81 in his last three innings before the decisive fifth Test. Woodfull had been so unhappy with his form that he had advocated his own omission from the Test team. The only changes to the Australian squad were Kippax and Ebeling, for their first Test of the series, in place of Darling and Wall. Sutcliffe returned to the England side after injury and the 47-year-old Woolley took the place of the unfit Hendren. Spectators were shocked when they realised

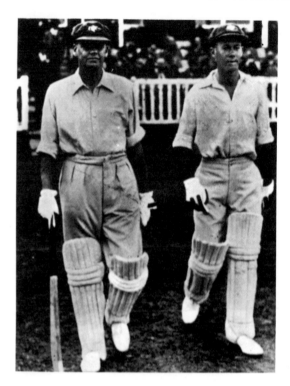

Billy Brown (right), opening the batting for Australia with Woodfull during the 1934 tour.

England's players did not know where captain Wyatt wanted them to field.

The Test at The Oval started on 18 August and was to be played out until a result was obtained, but Australia practically won the match on the first day when another record stand by Bradman and Ponsford lifted the score to 2 for 472. Brown was out with the score on 21 and the Bradman–Ponsford partnership did not end until a few minutes before stumps, when Bradman was out for 244. Ponsford continued the next day until he was out for 266, hit wicket for the second time in the rubber.

Bradman became more daring as his innings wore on, driving and cutting with rare freedom and certainty and when bowlers dropped the ball short he simply stepped back and pulled it to the fence. Ponsford was not as assured as Bradman and several times turned his backside to the ball, an action the Englishmen wrongly interpreted as a show of pique when facing rising balls, but he drove with great power and placed the ball away from fieldsmen with consummate ease. They kept up a run-rate of around 80 an hour for the entire day and their 451 in 316 minutes remains the highest stand for any wicket anywhere in the world. England's attack lacked variety on a dead pitch and the fielding was often appalling, but in the face of such magnificent batting errors were certain.

Australia made 701, to which England replied with 90 without loss at the end of the second day. But in 75 minutes next morning England lost 5 for 52. Ames and Leyland then put on 85 in less than an hour and after Ames retired with a strained back Leyland dominated the innings, scoring 110 before he was bowled by Grimmett. Bowes could not bat because of an injury and England's innings ended (with eight men out) for 321.

Australia began their second innings 380 ahead and after Brown went for one, all the leading batsmen except Woodfull made useful contributions. McCabe and Bradman were the most entertaining, adding 144 together in 90 minutes. Woolley, who allowed 37 byes, kept wicket in place of Ames, and this remains the most byes in a Test involving Australia. Bowes recovered to bowl and dismissed Bradman and Woodfull and helped run through the tail to finish with the outstanding figures of 5 for 55.

England had to score 708 to win after Australia's innings ended on 327, and after losing two wickets for three runs they were always in trouble. Grimmett and O'Reilly bowled skilfully on a pitch which helped their spin and took Australia to a 562-run win.

One of the reasons Australia recovered the Ashes in 1934 was the batting of Bill Ponsford.

Australian captain Bill Woodfull chatting with King George V during the 1934 tour of England. His team upset forecasts by winning the rubber.

Grimmett's 5 for 64 in the final innings gave him 25 wickets at 26.72 for the series, whereas O'Reilly took 28 wickets at 24.92. They had completely subdued Hammond. The only England bowler to match them was Verity, with 24 wickets at 24.00. No batsman on either side came near Bradman's total of 758 Test runs, though Ponsford edged him out in the averages with 569 runs at 94.83, compared with Bradman's average of 94.75. Leyland was the best English batsman with 478 runs at 68.28.

Newcomer Chipperfield's prevailing memory of the series was the courtesy players on both sides extended to each other. At first slip next to keeper Oldfield he watched Sutcliffe come in to bat in the morning, clothing well-pressed and immaculately tailored, hair gleaming and neatly parted. "Good morning," Sutcliffe said before he took guard and Chipperfield spread his legs and cradled both hands across his knees, fingers inches from the turf.

Grimmett's inability to perform after the fifth Test caused concern after his successful early displays. He bowled only one over in first-class matches after the fifth Test and during this period Fleetwood-Smith, 19 years Grimmett's junior, shouldered the spin bowling burden by taking 33 wickets. On the whole tour Fleetwood-Smith's 106 wickets cost 19.20 runs each, Grimmett's 109 wickets 19.80.

After the fifth Test most of the dressing-room discussion centred on Alan Kippax's brilliant batting to score the 250 that meant victory by an innings and 35 runs over the strong Sussex team. At Hove between 25 and 28 August, Kippax batted for 285 minutes and hit 4 sixes and 28 fours in an innings that was vintage Kippax, his late cuts plucking the ball from the keeper's gloves, his drives travelling like bullets to the boundary. The fast-

maturing Fleetwood-Smith took 10 wickets in the game. His imitation of a hoot owl became well known to team-mates but often startled opponents, uttered as it was during boring partnerships.

Three drawn matches followed after rain curtailed play. McCabe made 108 in the first of these against Kent at Canterbury from 29 to 31 August, a sick Bradman scored 149 not out against an England XI in the second at Folkestone from 1 to 4 September, and Ben Barnett, in his best display of the tour, scored 80 in the third against Minor Counties at The Oval on 5 and 6 September. Almost 25 years later Barnett was to play for Minor Counties.

The Australians wound up their tour with wins over H. D. G. Leveson-Gower's XI, between 8 and 11 September at Scarborough, where Bradman made 132, McCabe 124, Ponsford 92, and Fleetwood-Smith took 10

Bradman at the piano entertaining team-mates Arthur Chipperfield (left) and "Chuck" Fleetwood-Smith during the 1934 England tour, only a few days before his near-fatal illness.

for 201, and the North of Scotland in a one-day match at Forres on 14 September. Bradman completed the tour with 2020 runs in first-class matches at 84.16, the best of the six batsmen who scored more than 1000 runs. O'Reilly headed the bowling averages with 109 first-class wickets at 17.04, and Fleetwood-Smith took 106 at 19.20, Grimmett 109 at 19.80, in a spinners' triumph. The best of the medium-pacers was Hans Ebeling with 62 wickets at 20.80.

The brilliance of Bradman's batting in his 304 at Leeds and his 244 at The Oval has been frequently praised. But the magnificence or the motivation of his 132 in the match against Leveson-Gower's team in the Scarborough Festival match has been strangely neglected. Bradman rates it among his best innings and admits that it was the one knock he played in his life when anger was part of his approach. "Shrimp" Leveson-Gower broke his promise that the game would be a light-hearted picnic match and treated it as an extra Test by including four of the finest bowlers in England (Farnes, Bowes, Nichols and Verity) and an England batting line-up. After a stormy meeting with Leveson-Gower, Bradman went to the crease in a fury and made novices of the attack, hitting one six and 24 fours in 90 minutes of sustained mayhem. His 132 remains the highest score by any Australian or touring batsman before lunch on the first day of a first-class match in England. Bradman reached 100 in 82 minutes and added 32 more in eight minutes; scoring 102 in boundaries.

The eighteenth Australian Test team won 15 of their 34 matches, lost one, and drew 18. They had to overcome constant setbacks through illness and accident. Before the first Test they had to contend with a flu epidemic which affected every player, Chipperfield, Kippax and treasurer Bull being the worst victims. Bradman had periods of listlessness and prolonged·problems with his thigh injury. Ponsford missed the second Test through illness. A throat complaint the doctors suspected might be diphtheria swept through the side during the Manchester Test and forced Chipperfield and Kippax to be detained in an isolation hospital. Ernie Bromley developed appendicitis on the eve of the fifth Test and underwent emergency surgery.

The worst was yet to come, however. At the end of the tour Bradman collapsed with a gangrenous appendix. The distinguished Melbourne surgeon Sir Douglas Shields performed an emergency operation within an hour of Bradman's arrival at the London Clinic. For several days Bradman was near death, with all visitors barred apart from team manager Harold Bushby. Blood transfusions were given and as word of his danger spread the hospital foyer filled with reporters and the switchboard jammed.

Jessie Bradman rushed from Australia to her husband's bedside but by the time she arrived he had survived the critical post-surgery days and the threat of peritonitis. Slowly Bradman recovered and after a time in Switzerland and the Riviera with his wife he went to his father-in-law's farm at Mittagong for several months more recuperation. Doctors stopped him playing any cricket in the 1934–35 Australian season and he had to resign as an Australian selector as he was unable to watch players. Vic Richardson took over as selector and following the retirement of Bill Woodfull captained the Australian team on its 1935–36 tour of South Africa.

The first women's international matches were held in Australia in 1934–35 when an English team captained by Betty Archdale was unbeaten in 21 matches, winning 15, with six unfinished. All 16 members of the English team bought their own equipment and paid their own fares—the boat passages cost £80 each—for a tour that lasted six months. The English wicket-keepers, Betty Snowball and Grace Morgan, were outstanding, and the all-rounders Myrtle Maclagan and Molly Hide far superior to the Australians. Maclagan averaged 63.25 in nine tour innings, including 119 in the second Test at Sydney, the first-ever century in women's international cricket. The players wore dresses, long white stockings, and caps, and used the light 5 oz ball that had been adopted in England. Australia drew one and lost two of the three Tests.

The happiest tour

Australia in South Africa and India 1935–36

The two Bills, Woodfull and Ponsford, were close friends as well as an outstanding opening pair of batsmen and when Woodfull decided to retire after the 1934 tour of England, at the age of 37, Ponsford, three years Woodfull's junior, decided to quit with him. They had been in 23 century partnerships and five that scored more than 200 and their Test records were remarkably similar.

The friendliness between the Australian and South African teams was such that they agreed to pose on a hill overlooking the Durban ground before the first Test at Durban.

1. S. McCabe
2. V. Richardson
3. E. McCormick
4. L. Darling
5. J. Fingleton
6. W. O'Reilly
7. W. Oldfield
8. W. Ferguson (scorer)
9. W. Brown
10. A. Chipperfield
11. L. O'Brien
12. B. Barnett
13. C. Grimmett
14. M. Sievers

The Australian Board of Control gave them a joint testimonial match at Melbourne, scene of so many of their triumphs, from 16 to 20 November 1934. Woodfull's retirement was known before play began and Ponsford followed him during the match. They delighted the crowd by batting together in a stand of 132 for Woodfull's XI after Vic Richardson's XI scored 196. Woodfull was at the crease for three hours for 111, Ponsford two and a half hours for 83.

This stand paved the way to victory for Woodfull's XI by seven wickets, despite some exhilarating batting from Vic Richardson (107) and "Jack" Badcock, who had come over from Tasmania to play. Badcock, a strutting gamecock of a batsman with flair and a full range of shots, made 64 and 87. Woodfull took his only first-class wicket when he had Fleetwood-Smith caught. Ponsford did not take a wicket. Woodfull and Ponsford each received £1042 from the match.

During the match it became known that Ponsford was reluctant to continue in Tests with Bradman, eight years his junior. Ponsford, always over-sensitive to criticism, resented the constant comparisons of their skill and worth to the Australian side. Since Bradman and Ponsford first started setting cricket records, Australian cricket fans had looked forward to the day when they would bat together in a long stand. Larwood and Bodyline deprived Australian spectators of this, but English fans had seen it twice on Australia's 1934 tour. Ponsford's retirement at 34 surprised team-mates because he had given no hint of his intentions after his masterly performance in the Fifth Test or in any of the six matches that followed. He had scored a century in both his first and last Tests, a feat later to be emulated by Greg Chappell.

Although Ponsford set more records, Woodfull's consistency allowed him to finish with almost as many runs after 13 first-class seasons as Ponsford in 14 seasons. Woodfull made 13,388 runs at an average of 64.99, with 49 centuries, highest score 284. Ponsford scored 13,819 runs at 65.18, highest score 437, with 47 centuries. In Tests, Woodfull made 2300 runs at 46.00, with seven centuries, Ponsford 2122 runs at 48.22, with seven centuries.

Woodfull was known variously as "The Unbowlable", "The Rock", and "The Worm Killer", because he batted with such a slight back lift. Ponsford was known simply as "Puddin'". Bill O'Reilly always said he found Ponsford harder to bowl to than Bradman. "With Bradman you always felt you had a small chance, but with Ponsford you had no hope," O'Reilly said. Hans Ebeling agreed, saying he never tackled Bradman with the same hopeless feeling he had when bowling to Ponsford.

The great Yorkshire left-hander Hedley Verity dismissed Bradman eight times in Tests, but the only time he got Ponsford's wicket was a fluke. On 181, Ponsford stepped back and hooked Verity to the boundary and as the ball was returned to Verity he saw Ponsford walking out. He had dislodged a bail with his left foot and was given out hit wicket.

With Bradman out of action because of illness, Victoria won the 1934–35 Sheffield Shield competition with a team composed largely of young players, following the retirement of Woodfull, Ponsford, and the 51-year-olds Ironmonger and Blackie. Ironmonger had taken 464 first-class wickets at 21.50, 74 of them in 14 Tests at 17.97. Blackie took 211 first-class wickets at 24.10, 14 of them in three Tests at 31.71. Neither ever toured England, which deprived spectators there of enjoying two of the game's most colourful figures.

The Victorians won their first five matches outright because of productive batting by Darling, O'Brien and Rigg, but they owed most to Fleetwood-Smith, who took 60 wickets at 18.95 runs each, a record for the com-

Victoria largely owed its 1934–35 Shield win to Fleetwood-Smith who also formed a magnificent spin bowling trio in South Africa with O'Reilly and Grimmett.

petition. The quick bowlers McCormick and Ebeling supported him well. Victoria farewelled their chance of establishing a Shield record by winning every match outright when they lost the last to South Australia.

Badcock, after considering offers from New South Wales and Victoria, left Tasmania for South Australia and his presence partly compensated for the absence of Bradman. When South Australia made their highest-ever Shield score in Adelaide between 22 and 26 December against Queensland, Badcock was one of four batsmen to score a century. Richardson made 185, Nitschke 116, Lonergan 137 and Badcock 137 to take the South Australian total to 7 for 644 declared. After scoring 430 in their first innings, Queensland lost by eight wickets. Grimmett, who captured 16 wickets in this game, headed the South Australian bowling averages for the eleventh summer in a row. His 49 wickets surpassed his previous best for a Shield season by six wickets.

Queensland continued to rely heavily on the imports from New South Wales, "Cassie" Andrews and Roy Levy, but took some encouragement from the form of South Brisbane left-hand batsman Des Hansen, who made 415 runs at an average of 51.87, and the rapid development of Bundaberg wicketkeeper–batsman Don Tallon. South African Jim Christy, Queensland's new captain, failed to lift the state out of last place but provided valuable coaching for Brisbane and country young cricketers.

Andrews, a wide-shouldered figure below medium height, gave a thrilling exhibition of driving, pulling and cutting in scoring 253 for Queensland against New South Wales at Sydney from 31 December to 3 January 1935. He hit 26 fours and shared in a seventh-wicket stand of 335 with Charles Bensted (155), which failed by only ten runs to beat the world record. The seventh-wicket world record was set by K. S. Ranjitsinhji and W. Newham, of Sussex, in 1902.

Bert Oldfield, in his fifteenth first-class season, took over the New South Wales captaincy from Alan Kippax, who was unavailable for some matches for business reasons. New South Wales also lacked the services of McCabe in all but one match through injury. O'Reilly could not play regularly because of his teaching duties, and this allowed Hughie Chilvers to establish himself as a top-class leg spinner. Chilvers took 46 wickets in the season at only 18 runs each, including 11 for 125 *v.* South Australia in Sydney, 10 for 109 against the same state in Adelaide, and 10 for 192 at Brisbane *v.* Queensland.

In addition to competing in the Sheffield Shield, New South Wales visited Perth for two matches against Western Australia, who were still struggling for a Shield place. Both matches were drawn. In the first game, from 9 to 12 March, Douglas McKenzie scored a spirited 59 in Western Australia's first innings of 233, and 53 in the second innings of 6 for 220. This double helped hold up a New South Wales attack in which big St George fast bowler Harry Theak shone. New South Wales made 416, with Fingleton top-scoring on 124.

Fingleton also made a century (100) in the second match. New South Wales' batting strength took their first innings score to 5 for 427 declared. Apart from Fingleton's century, Brown made 116, Les Fallowfield 101 not out, and Ray Little 53. Western Australia replied with 272 in the first innings (Fred Taaffe 79) and 7 for 119 in the second innings.

Brown and Fingleton put on 249 for the first wicket for New South Wales against South Australia in Sydney. Fingleton made 134, Brown 111. Gulgong-born Clement John Hill, no relation to the South Australian clan, took 2 for 8 and 4 for 33 to help Chilvers wrap-up this match by an innings and 158 runs. In a triumphant summer for spinners, Grimmett took 11 for 232 for South Australia

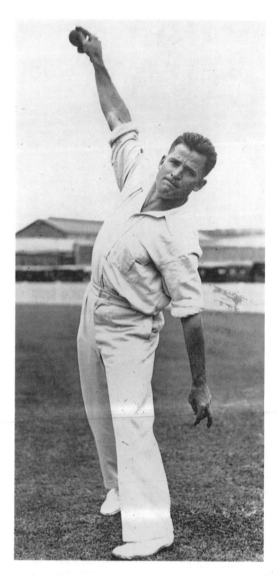

Hughie Chilvers, the Sydney leg spinner, who despite his fine performances in Sheild cricket, was prevented from touring India with Tarrant's team by the Australian Cricket Board, thus missing the one overseas trip his talents deserved.

v. Queensland, 11 for 230 *v.* New South Wales and 16 for 289 in the return match against Queensland to bag 38 wickets in three matches. Fleetwood-Smith joined in with 11 for 129 for Victoria *v.* Queensland, 11 for 228 *v.* New South Wales, and 15 for 226 in the return match. Victoria's status as the No. 1 state was emphasised when four batsmen made centuries against long-time rivals New South Wales, O'Brien (126), Rigg (111), Darling (106), and Bromley (102).

Victoria continued her long-running contest against Tasmania in Melbourne from 5 to 7 February. Des Fitzmaurice, the South Melbourne right-hander, made 102 in Victoria's first innings of 370, but the star turn was the South Hobart leg spinner Syd Putnam, who took 7 for 102. Tasmania made 255, badly missing Badcock's brilliance to lift the innings. Victoria's second innings brought an attractive century (122) from hard-driving Arthur Allsopp and ended at 8 for 285 declared. Tasmania had reached 47 without loss when time ran out.

The 1935–36 Shield competition lost many of its top performers because of Australia's first full tour of South Africa and the visit to India of an Australian side captained by Jack Ryder, organised by Frank Tarrant and sponsored by the Maharajah of Patiala. On his doctor's advice Bradman did not join the South African tour which began on 23 November 1935. He took long walks and played a lot of golf and finally felt fit enough to test himself in South Australia's first match of the season against New South Wales. This was played in Adelaide from 18 to 21 December. He took over as captain in Richardson's absence and led his adopted state to their first Shield win since 1926–27, their fifth since the competition began in 1892–93.

The Glenelg right-hand batsman Ron Parker helped Badcock put on 139 for the first wicket and then Bradman and Badcock put on 202 for the second. Badcock made 150, Bradman 117. Nomadic Frank Ward, after failing to find work in Queensland and unable to beat O'Reilly or Chilvers for a place as a leg spinner in the New South Wales side, had played his way into the South Australian team with solid figures for the Adelaide club. Now

Frank Tarrant, who took an unofficial Australian side to India in 1935–36 while the No. 1 team was in South Africa. All expenses were met by the Maharajah of Patiala.

Ward had his chance at first-class level. He took 6 for 127 and had New South Wales out 224 runs short of South Australia's total of 575, despite a faultless 102 by Ray Robinson, a clever right-hander playing in his first Shield match. New South Wales followed on and lost by an innings and five runs.

Bradman followed the century against his old state with 233 to set up another innings win over Queensland in Adelaide between 24 and 28 December. Next he made 357 against Victoria in Melbourne where South Australia, from 1 to 4 January, won on the first innings.

He scored 739 runs at 123.16 in Shield matches and 1173 runs at 130.33 in the full Australian season, confirming his complete recovery. Badcock also made a triple century, 325 against Victoria in Adelaide between 21 and 25 February.

Once again Bradman received almost as much publicity for a duck—made against New South Wales in Sydney on 17 January 1935—as he did for his big scores. Alan McGilvray captained New South Wales in this match and when Bradman went in positioned Ray Little at short fine leg. Big Gordon left-arm pace bowler Lincoln ("Bob") Hynes let go the famous delivery which Bradman tried to glide down the leg side, only to see Little take the catch, an event on which McGilvray, Hynes and Little dined out for half a century.

Ray Robinson looked a coming champion in this season. Only a handful of Australians have ever wielded a cricket bat with such style. He had an elegance in his stroke-play reminiscent of Trumper, Jackson and Kippax, timing the ball intuitively and producing several shots he made his specialty. The Gordon club had shown good judgement in bringing him to Sydney from Newcastle and installing him in a caretaker's job. He made 613 Shield runs at 61.30 as well as a lot of runs in grade matches.

Alex Marks played an innings of 201 for New South Wales against Queensland from 1 to 4 January. Les Fallowfield and Harold Mudge proved reliable opening batsmen and Frank Easton kept wicket with style as well as scoring runs while Oldfield was playing in South Africa.

Eddie Gilbert took 19 wickets in the season for Queensland. His wickets were costly at 36.84, but he still topped the Queensland averages. In the match against New South Wales in Sydney he was no-balled under the Board of Control's new intimidation rule, the first instance of the rule being invoked. Just before he was called for bowling at the batsman he made the ball lift awkwardly and split the fingers of both Mudge and Robinson. Queensland's consolation in a season which did not see a win was the continual progress of Don Tallon, who scored 503 runs, including a knock of 193 against Victoria in Brisbane, at an average of 55.88. He looked to be a class above all the other Shield keepers.

Tasmania, still trying to lift their playing standards, surprisingly won two matches at home against Victoria. At Launceston, from 31 December to 2 January, Tasmania scored 330 and 4 for 123 to win by six wickets after Victoria made 240 and 212. At Hobart, on 3 to 6 January, Tasmania made 300 and 9 for 163 to win by one wicket. Victoria scored 363 and a rather generous 2 for 96 declared. Jack Ledward, the Richmond club's right-hand bat, provided the highlight in these matches with 154 in Victoria's first innings at Hobart.

Tasmania were not so lucky when they sent a team to the mainland a month later. Victoria declared at 9 for 531 at Melbourne between 24 and 26 February, six batsmen scoring half centuries. Horace Grangel from the Carlton club top-scored with 108 but was never chosen again. Tasmania could manage only 188 and 209 in reply, giving Victoria victory by an innings and 134 runs. Fitzroy leg spinner John Frederick took nine wickets in the match at around nine runs each, as well as scoring a fast 69.

At Adelaide on 2 and 3 March South Australia defeated Tasmania by an innings and 349 runs. Ron Thomas batted extremely well in Tasmania's innings of 158 and 181, but lacked support from team-mates who could not handle spin. Frank Ward took 6 for 47 in Tasmania's second innings. South Australia's batsmen crushed the Tasmanian attack, scoring 688 in fast time. Bradman had a useful workout in scoring 369 and Hamence contributed 121.

Bradman's score was the highest ever made on Adelaide Oval and took only 253 minutes. Bradman made his first 100 in 70 minutes and added 356 with Hamence in 181 minutes. His last 168 came in 80 minutes. He hit 4 sixes and 46 fours. One of the first telegrams of congratulation came from Clem Hill, whose 365 not out for South Australia in 1900 Bradman had edged past. His telegram read: "Congratulations you little devil for breaking my record."

Meanwhile Fleetwood-Smith took 11 for 44 against Western Australia for the Australian team on the way to South Africa. The Australians were among the first to hear the news of the early death of another great wicket-keeper, H. B. "Jock" Cameron. Vic Richardson's players learned as their ship approached Cape Town that Cameron had died suddenly of enteric fever. He had just come back to South Africa from England and a tour on which he scored three blazing centuries and made 48 dismissals. He was the batsman who took 30 in an over from Hedley Verity against Yorkshire at Sheffield.

The South African tour presented Victor York Richardson with his biggest challenge. He had captained the Sturt club since 1920, South Australia since 1921, and had led Australian teams to New Zealand in 1927–28 and to America in 1932, but this was the first time he had been entrusted with a full-strength Australian side. He brought an imposing background to the job. Apart from his cricket he had represented South Australia at golf, tennis, baseball, and as an Australian Rules centre man, and played first grade hockey. He was also noted for his prowess as a gymnast, and at swimming, basketball and lacrosse.

Richardson was a product of Kyre College (later Scotch College) in Adelaide's Unley Park, where he excelled as an athlete and tennis player. His family ran a home–decorating business. Every night he indulged in one of his sports and at weekends he played foot-

Vic Richardson, who led the Australians to South Africa in 1935–36 in what the players regarded as the happiest ever tour. He was a tough but fair disciplinarian.

ball or cricket on Saturdays and baseball or lacrosse on Sundays. He matured into a straight-backed, neatly groomed man with an Errol Flynn moustache, who by his very bearing seemed born to lead.

The team Richardson took to South Africa comprised B. A. Barnett (Victoria), W. A. Brown (NSW), A. G. Chipperfield (NSW), L. S. Darling (Victoria), J. H. Fingleton (NSW), L. O'B. Fleetwood-Smith (Victoria), C. V. Grimmett (South Australia), S. J. McCabe (NSW), E. L. McCormick (Victoria), L. P. O'Brien (Victoria), W. A. Oldfield (NSW), W. J. O'Reilly (NSW), M. W.

Sievers (Victoria) and S. H. D. Rowe (WA, manager).

Nine of the team including the three great spin bowlers, O'Reilly, Grimmett and Fleetwood-Smith, had toured England in 1934. The retirement of Woodfull and Ponsford and the unavailability of Bradman provided rare opportunities for Fingleton and O'Brien and gave Brown and Fingleton the possibility of establishing themselves as a Test opening pair. McCormick, who replaced Wall as the main fast bowler, was a noted comedian as well as a bowler of frightening pace who moved in to bowl with his arms still. He bowled right-handed and batted left-handed, like Jack Gregory, and in five seasons with the Victorian side had endured frequent problems with his run-up. Sievers, who was 193 contimetres tall, was a fast-medium bowler with the Fitzroy club and had shown exciting promise in his one season in the Victorian team. He was able to get exceptional lift as well as being a very useful right-hand batsman.

The tour began smoothly for Australia with Brown and Fingleton putting on 215 for the first wicket in the first match, which was played against Natal at Durban from 23 to 26 November, 1935. Brown made 148, Fingleton 121. McCabe (65), Richardson (75) and Chipperfield (60 not out) continued the punishment of the bowlers and Richardson was able to declare at 5 for 522.

Only Dudley Nourse showed any assurance against Grimmett in Natal's first innings of 242, Nourse reaching 124 before he was a victim of McCormick's pace. In the follow-on, Ivan ("Jack") Siedle and Robert Harvey put on 129 for Natal's second wicket and when Siedle was caught and bowled by Chipperfield for 68, Harvey went on to 104. Natal's remaining batsmen struggled hard but were all out for 254, giving Australia an innings and 26-run win.

Fleetwood-Smith was largely responsible for Australia's defeat of Western Pro-

Clarrie Grimmett's performance in South Africa in 1935–36 established him as the finest bowler in the world according to team-mates, but the Australian selectors did not agree once he returned home.

vince by an innings and 44 runs between 30 November and 3 December at Cape Town. He took 7 for 71 in Western Province's first innings of 170 and after all the Australian batsmen had made runs in an innings of 318, Fleetwood-Smith took 5 for 32 in Western Province's second knock of 104.

At Johannesburg from 7 to 10 December against Transvaal, it was Grimmett's turn. He started with 6 for 57 in Transvaal's first innings of 201. Australia responded with 9 for 411 declared with Fingleton out for 99, Darling 106 and Chipperfield 105 not out. Transvaal avoided an innings defeat by scoring 247 in their second innings, but Australia made the 38 needed to win without loss.

McCormick took 4 for 61 in Transvaal's

second innings. "I just bowl the shine off the ball for those vultures who feed off the bones of fast bowlers, the spinners," said McCormick, commonly known as "Goldie" because of his work with the most precious metal as a jeweller.

The first Test at the Old Kingsmead Ground at Durban from 14 to 18 December began with a near gale-force wind whipping across the field from the Indian Ocean. South Africa struggled to 248, with Eric Rowan making a dour 66. Bad light prevented Australia starting their first innings until the second day when the wind was still strong enough to repeatedly blow off the bails. Richardson suggested the umpires use chewing gum to stick them on but after a time they ran out of gum and put the bails in their pockets. The stream of spectators' hats blowing onto the field became so huge that a collection point was set up by the boundary fence where they could be picked up by their owners.

South African fast bowler Bob Crisp bowled with every fieldsman behind the stumps. Strokes played towards mid-off and mid-on simply blew back towards point and square leg. Running between wickets was a major concern, the striker struggling desperately to make headway into the wind, the non-striker streaking down the pitch in a few strides. After losing Fingleton at 12, Brown and McCabe put on 161 before Brown was out for 66. Darling and McCabe then added 96 before McCabe was out to a wonderful catch at forward short leg for 149. After Darling went for 60, Chipperfield put together his second tour century, 109, for Australia to finish in front on 429.

Richardson placed a "suicide fieldsman" close in on the leg side to add menace to O'Reilly's bowling, a field placement that became famous but had not been used until then. Fingleton took a fine catch in this position to dismiss Nourse for 91 in South Africa's second innings and clinched an Australian victory. South Africa were out for 282, with O'Reilly dismissing the last four batsmen. His 5 for 49 gave him 8 for 104 in the match. Australia made the 102 needed to win for the loss of Brown's wicket.

When it was all over the Australians' most vivid memory was the sight of the Western Province spinner John Robinson floating the ball towards the square-leg umpire. He delivered 55 overs this way in Australia's first innings, landing enough deliveries on a respectable length to take 3 for 143. As they left the ground the Australian players had to pick their way past trees uprooted in the storm.

The second Test from 24 to 28 December at Johannesburg was full of incidents, some of them historic. From the beginning most batsmen struggled on the newly laid turf of the Wanderers ground and Australia had South Africa out in three hours for 157. Australia played three spinners, with only McCormick and McCabe for relief, and the ball spun so freely on the new pitch that Richardson had difficulty getting the ball away from O'Reilly, Grimmett and Fleetwood-Smith, accustomed as they were to bowling on over-prepared, unresponsive pitches.

Brown and Fingleton appeared to have set up a big score when they put on 105 for the first wicket as Australia batted, but with a lead of 11 runs and only three men out, Arthur Langton and the versatile Bruce Mitchell bowled so skilfully only 82 more runs were scored. Mitchell took the last four wickets, three of them for only three runs, to polish off the innings at 250.

Wade and Siedle put on 50 for the first wicket when South Africa batted a second time before Mitchell and Nourse began a partnership which produced 129. From 4 for 254 at the close of the second day, Nourse went on to the highest score ever hit for South Africa in a Test match. It was also the first century for South Africa against Australia on this ground since Nourse's father made 111 in

1921. Nourse made 231 and hit 36 fours in just short of five hours, repeatedly jumping down the pitch to drive Grimmett, who was never so harshly treated in his entire career.

All out for 491, South Africa left Australia to score 399 to win. Brown was out at 17, but McCabe then joined Fingleton in a memorable stand of 177, McCabe batting magnificently. Worried about his breathing at the altitude of 1800 metres above sea level, he concentrated on hitting boundaries so that he would not have to run. He was 38 not out overnight and on the fourth morning took his score to 138 not out at lunch. His pre-lunch century included 20 fours.

After Fingleton went for 40, Darling supported McCabe who carried on in masterly fashion. Huge storm clouds gathered above the ground but Richardson sent a message to his batsmen not to appeal against the light, fearing the approaching storm would wash the game out. When McCabe had reached 189 and Australia, with eight men left, required 124, the South African captain Herbie Wade appealed against the light, arguing that his fieldsmen were in danger from McCabe's back cuts and drives.

The umpires, J. C. Collings and R. G. Ashman, allowed Wade's appeal and the players left the field. Ten minutes later a thunderstorm ended the match. This remains the only Test in which play was halted on the grounds that the fielding side was in danger.

Earlier in the tour Richardson had been far from satisfied with the state of the Newlands ground at Cape Town for the match against Western Province, because the covers used were primitive and offered no protection against rain. When he raised this with local officials they told him not to worry about the Test as it never rained in Cape Town in January. When the Australians arrived for the start of the third Test at Newlands on New Year's Day, however, the covers were afloat. Richardson described the ensuing events in his

Stan McCabe in the form that thrilled South Africans. His 189 not out in the second Test at Johannesburg caused Springbok captain Herb Wade to appeal against the light, claiming it was unsafe for his fieldsmen to face such hitting in fading light.

autobiography, *The Vic Richardson Story.*

> *Herbie Wade and I inspected the pitch and agreed to look at it again after lunch. A general protest came from the 5000 spectators admitted to the ground when they learnt of this decision. For the second inspection, most of the 5000 accompanied us to the wicket. They felt play was possible and were most unhappy when we agreed to have a third look at tea. We inspected again, with the help and advice of the 5000 but kept our decision secret until we returned to the pavilion. This was that no play was possible that day. Pandemonium followed. The paying customers invaded the stands to heap coals of fire, mainly on my head. One fervent spectator*

jumped the fence, collected an ancient wood stove, and started a fire in it on the pitch. He and his contraption were bundled from the ground.

Next day the pitch rolled out splendidly and Brown and Fingleton scored 233 for the first wicket. Wade held a difficult catch at short leg to have Fingleton out for 112. The thickset Greek-born Xenophon ("Bally") Constantine Balaskas bowled his leg spinners and googlies at a brisk pace to worry all the remaining batsmen and after Brown was out for 121 wickets fell regularly until stumps. Australia were 8 for 362.

Torrential rain fell overnight and Richardson declared, knowing the poor quality of the covers. Wade objected, but this time officials did not allow spectators into the ground until play resumed. No play was possible before lunch and after the interval Wade and Richardson disagreed about the fitness of the ground. Richardson now wanted to play. The umpires were brought into the argument and it was decided to start at 3 p.m.

Richardson gave McCormick and McCabe four overs and then brought on his master spinners. South Africa made only 102, Grimmett taking 5 for 32. South Africa followed on and after the pitch had been rolled the Australians got little response from it.

Sensing that O'Reilly was simply rolling his arm over, Richardson took him off and sent him to the outfield. Players who were in on Richardson's plot kept needling O'Reilly. "Aren't you playing today, Tiger?" they called. His answers were vulgar but pointed. At lunch Richardson distanced himself from his team so that O'Reilly could not speak to him. By the resumption of play Richardson knew that O'Reilly's "Irish" would be up, and threw him the ball. O'Reilly finished off the match in a few overs, taking three of the last four wickets and ending with 4 for 35.

Grimmett, however, was the bowler who triumphed in this Test. His 10 for 88 took him past Englishman Sydney Barnes' all-time Test record of 189 wickets. South Africa's second innings of 182 gave Australia the match by an innings and 78 runs, and a two–nil lead, with two Tests to go.

McCormick had a steady, controlled bowling spell in the second innings against Eastern Province at Port Elizabeth on 8 January. His 5 for 29, coupled with his 2 for 5 in the first innings, gave him seven wickets at less than five each and provided Australia with a win by an innings and 144 runs in less than two days. Eastern Province scored 92 and 89, Australia 325.

O'Reilly overwhelmed Border at East London between 11 and 14 January after Richardson had again won the toss and put the home side in to bat. Border made 209 and 128, Australia 351. This time Australia won by an innings and 14 runs. O'Reilly took 8 for 73 and 5 for 32. McCabe was in dazzling form again with the bat, scoring 115, and Chipperfield made 105, both in just on two hours.

The next match was at Bloemfontein, against a Combined Orange Free State and Basutoland XI on 18 and 20 January. Australia's victory by an innings and 146 runs was won by O'Reilly's 4 for 38 and 5 for 34, and Grimmett's 5 for 35 and 5 for 67. The Combined side made 88 and 127, with Australia declaring at 4 for 361, O'Brien scoring 109, McCabe 112.

The tougher opposition that was expected from Transvaal at Johannesburg did not eventuate and Australia won by an innings and 31 runs on January 25 and 27. O'Reilly took 7 for 54 and 2 for 54 in Transvaal's innings of 160 and 155.

Fingleton, who amused the crowd by lighting a succession of matches over the last Transvaal batsman as he walked to the crease, clearly indicating what he thought of the prevailing light, top-scored with 110 in Australia's innings of 346.

O'Reilly in full flight during the South African tour. He could turn leg breaks and googlies at a brisk medium-pace.

The Australians won their sixth victory in a row without having to bat twice at Kimberley from 31 January to 3 February against Griqualand West. This time O'Reilly had 7 for 88 and 6 for 54, Griqualand West scoring 198 and 120. Australia declared at 6 for 423, O'Brien (113) and Oldfield (132) scoring the centuries which helped achieve a win by an innings and 105 runs. The match with Rhodesia at Bulawayo from 8 to 11 February was washed out after Australia scored 357 (Darling 108, Brown 97) and Rhodesia had reached 4 for 157 in reply.

Australia won their third Test of the series and the rubber by taking the fourth Test at Johannesburg, from 15 to 17 February 1936, by an innings and 184 runs. South Africa began well when Siedle and Wade put on 81 for the first wicket in their first innings, but after McCormick and McCabe had taken the shine from the ball O'Reilly took 5 for 20, Grimmett 3 for 70, to wrap up the innings for

157. There was not a failure in Australia's reply of 439, Fingleton scoring the only century, 108. Grimmett took the honours in South Africa's second innings of 98 with 7 for 40, which made him the first bowler to take 200 Test wickets.

The match at Durban against Natal between 22 and 25 February was drawn after the Australians were led on the first innings for the only time on the tour. Australia began with an innings of 256, all the team struggling against the bowling of A. P. Murray, who finished with 5 for 91. Natal replied with 272, with Robert Harvey scoring freely. Harvey was out for 138, his second century of the tour, Wade for 75. After their departure Natal collapsed to lead by only 16. Fingleton's 167 overshadowed everything in Australia's second innings, which was declared at 9 for 326 with only 35 minutes' play remaining.

South Africa started the fifth Test at Durban from 28 February to 3 March with steady, efficient batting, but gradually the Australian spinners took command. From 5 for 183, South Africa collapsed to be out for 222, the last five wickets adding only 39 runs. Fingleton and Brown put on 162 for the first wicket and Fingleton was not dismissed until the third morning. His 118 was his third century in as many matches. Leading by 233, Australia put South Africa out for 227 to win by an innings and six runs. Grimmett's 13 for 173 gave him 44 wickets in the Tests for 642 runs at an average of 14.59.

The tour ended with a win over Western Province at Cape Town from 14 to 17 March. O'Reilly took 6 for 35 and 6 for 64. Western Province made 198 and 262, Australia 398 thanks to 107 in two hours by Chipperfield. Left to score 63 runs in 38 minutes to win the Australians got them in the last over of the match with the loss of two wickets.

Australia won 13 of their 16 matches, including four Tests, with 3 draws, one of them a Test, and in the process scored 21 individual centuries and allowed only four to be scored against them. Fingleton, who made six centuries, topped the first-class batting averages with 1192 runs at 79.16. His opening partner Brown was the only other Australian to exceed 1000 runs, with 1065 at 62.64. O'Reilly took most first-class wickets and headed the bowling averages with his 95 victims costing only 13.56. Grimmett's 92 wickets cost an average of 14.80 each. The success of the spinners gave Morris Sievers few opportunities for his medium-pacers and he bowled only 136 overs for seven wickets at 42.71 each, whereas O'Reilly bowled 662.5 overs, and Grimmett 663.1 overs. O'Reilly called it the most enjoyable tour he ever made.

South African critics agreed the Australians were one of the finest fielding sides ever to tour. Oldfield kept wicket superbly and Richardson captained the team with rare flair, especially in placing his field for the spinners. The spirit Richardson aroused in his players was largely responsible for each member's good showing and the solid defeat of a South African side which had beaten England only three months earlier in Britain.

The Australians agreed to play an extra match against Transvaal for the benefit of the family of the late "Jock" Cameron, but when planning began the Transvaal officials suggested that they play baseball instead of cricket. The Australian team had already dominated their opponents in four appearances on the Wanderers ground and it was felt that the switch to baseball would attract a larger crowd. The Australians agreed, manager Rowe got Board of Control approval, and preparations began.

Len Darling had represented Australia as a third baseman, Ben Barnett played second base for Victoria and Ernie McCormick had a big reputation as a first base. Leo O'Brien pitched regularly in Victorian first-grade baseball and Vic Richardson had represented South Australia 14 years earlier at baseball.

They formed the nucleus of the Australian side. Of the others Jack Fingleton seemed a natural for short stop, while Bill Brown, Stan McCabe and Clarrie Grimmett seemed right for outfieldsmen. O'Reilly practised with the team but then said he would not play after all his attempted hits spooned off his bat for catches.

The Wanderers Baseball Club supplied gear for the entire Australian team, including manager Harold Rowe, and all 15 took their places on the bench wearing the Wanderers' uniforms and cricket boots. With Australia leading by 11 runs to 5 in the last innings, McCabe made a good catch in the outfield, but in his excitement forgot the game was baseball and tossed the ball in the air, and kept tossing it. Two runners got home before he heard the screams of team-mates to throw the ball to the catcher.

Trailing 7–11, Transvaal had two men out when one of their batters made a long soaring hit into right field. Grimmett staggered back into the path of the ball, raised one hand, then the other, and eventually thrust his bare right hand up again and caught the ball, a sensational catch that ended the match in Australia's favour. Next day the Johannesburg papers said the Australian baseballers had out-played and out-talked the home side. None of the Australians disagreed.

While the Australian team was in South Africa and Don Bradman was demonstrating in Shield cricket that he had recovered his fitness, an Australian side played in Ceylon and India. This tour was sponsored by the Maharajah of Patiala, an ardent cricket-lover, who after a number of setbacks invited Frank Tarrant to select the team and organise their matches. This side has always been known as Tarrant's team, although former Australian captain Jack Ryder was the on-the-field leader. The team was a colourful blend of famous veterans, some of whom came out of

The 1935–36 Australian cricket team turned baseballers to play a benefit game in Johannesburg for the widow of former South African captain Jock Cameron.

retirement for the trip, and promising youngsters. The players were J. Ryder (Victoria, captain), C. G. Macartney (NSW, vice-captain), H. H. Alexander (Victoria), A. H. Allsopp (Victoria), O. W. Bill (NSW), F. J. Bryant (Western Australia), J. L. Ellis (Victoria), H. L. Hendry (Victoria), H. Ironmonger (Victoria), T. W. Leather (Victoria), H. S. Love (NSW), F. Mair (NSW), R. O. Morrisby (Tasmania), L. E. Nagel (Victoria) and R. K. Oxenham (Queensland).

The Maharajah of Patiala originally asked the Indian Cricket Board to invite a team from Australia organised by the Australian Board of Control. Although all expenses were guaranteed the Board of Control rejected this invitation because of the South African tour. When Tarrant took over arrangements the

Board would not let him include Woodfull, Ponsford and Kippax, who were still bound by contracts they signed when they toured England in 1934. The Board also denied Keith Rigg, "Jack" Nitschke and Hugh Chilvers places on the grounds that they might be required as substitutes if players were injured on the South African tour.

The Board's action in refusing to send even a second-string team and preventing deserving players from making the tour aroused widespread criticism. The Melbourne *Truth* considered that "The Board's decision to decline the magnificent offer of the Maharajah of Patiala without a penny cost to Australia has disgusted all followers of the game. The decision has made a laughing stock of Australian cricket." A more respected view came from author Ray Robinson, who chastised the Board for refusing Chilvers the one chance he had to make an overseas trip. "In my opinion, officialdom has shown no poorer spirit," he wrote in *Sporting Life*.

Apart from the troubles with the Austra-

The 1935–36 Australian team in India: (L to R) (back) umpire (not named), H. Alexander, H. Hendry, J. Ellis, L. Tarrant, L. Nagel, F. Tarrant, R. Morrisby, F. Warne, umpire (not named); (front) F. Bryant, R. Oxenham, T. Leather, C. Macartney, the Maharajah of Patiala, J. Ryder (captain), H. Love, F. Mair, W. Bill.

lian Board, the Indian tour ran into difficulties when the Maharajah became seriously ill in Paris in June 1935, five months before the tour was due to begin. In India thousands of his subjects prayed in relays for his survival; in Australia the selected players were equally concerned for his recovery. The Maharajah, an ostentatious figure who was reported to have 500 concubines, recovered, and with financial backing for the trip secure the Australians sailed for India in the *Mongolia*.

The tour started with a match against All Ceylon at Colombo from 25 to 27 October 1935. All Ceylon scored 96, with Oxenham taking 9 for 18, and 111 in the second innings, when five Australians shared the wickets. Wendell Bill scored the first tour century, 101, in the Australian innings of 334, enough to ensure victory by an innings and 127 runs.

The visitors had been warned to take precautions against typhoid, smallpox and dysentery but within a few days of their arrival Lisle Nagel contracted cholera and was admitted to Bombay Hospital. He recovered, but throughout the 23-match tour illness kept affecting the team. Manager Tarrant was still able to bowl accurate left-arm medium-paced off breaks and as he had been playing cricket in India since 1911, exploited the conditions well. Tarrant also brought in Frank Warne, the former Victorian player who had just qualified for Worcestershire, to help in a few matches, along with an Australian then coaching in India named Joe Davies.

In view of the difficulties the Australians did well to win 11 matches, leave 9 drawn and lose only 3. The Maharajah took them into his billiard room and showed them two tables covered with his personal jewellery; he always wore diamond earrings worth £30,000 and emerald bracelets worth £60,000. Each player was assigned a servant while they were at his palace. The Australians were open-mouthed at the sight of the Maharajah's own cricket ground, a magnificent arena with a perfect pitch and beautifully grassed outfield.

The four main matches of the tour were against fully representative Indian teams at Bombay, Calcutta, Lahore and Madras. The Australian team won the first by nine wickets, with the aid of a century by Ryder (104) and a fine spell by Ironmonger (5 for 70). They won the second by eight wickets after great bowling by Oxenham (5 for 7), Macartney (5 for 17), and 5 for 29 by St Kilda Club's fast-medium-pacer Tom Leather, dismissed India for 48 and 127. The third representative match brought their first defeat, All India winning by 68 runs after punishing the Australian bowling in a second innings of 301. All India won again in the fourth big game in a thrilling finish by 33 runs, despite Charlie Macartney's 6 for 41 in All India's first innings, so that the series ended all square.

The only other Australian defeat was at Secunderabad between 29 and 31 January 1936. Moin-ud-Dowlah scored 5 for 413 declared, with Lala Amarnath, then 24 years old, scoring 144, S. M. Hussain 73, and P. E. Palia 61 not out. Australia replied with 144 and 154, Ladha Amar Singh taking 7 for 36 to go with his first innings bag of 4 for 51. In winning by an innings and 115 runs, Moin-ud-Dowlah achieved the most decisive victory made by an Indian team over a visiting side to that time, and also reached the highest-ever total (413) by an Indian team.

Ryder was the top batsman on the tour. He scored 1121 runs at 48.74, at the age of 46. Wendell Bill made 740 at 43.53, the 20-year-old Tasmanian Ron Morrisby 958 at 36.85, and the 24-year-old West Australian Frank Bryant 754 runs at 27.93. Of the Australian bowlers, the hardworking Ron Oxenham

Tasmanian Ron Morrisby at 20 years of age, a consistent scorer on the 1935–36 tour of India by Tarrant's team.

took 101 wickets at 8.19 apiece, Fred Mair 71 at 20.46 and Tom Leather 56 at 16.79.

The Indians were delighted with the coaching so freely given by the famous players like Macartney, Ryder and Hendry.

The Australians in turn were delighted to see a world in which the whole top deck of a grandstand was reserved for wives, who arrived in purdah cars, and where entire harems watched the cricket from tents draped in mosquito nets.

The major disappointment was that Arthur Allsopp, after missing two (1930 and 1934) tours of England for which some critics claimed he was a certainty, contracted enteric fever, spent 11 weeks in hospital during which he was critically ill, and was left with damaged eyesight and stomach ulcers. It was the end of competitive sport for a gifted, immensely strong man who his family believed would have worn a Test cap had he received a normal upbringing. Allsopp made five centuries in 21 first-class matches, scoring 1469 runs at 45.90 and amid a long list of Australians who blame their lack of social graces for missing tours to England he and Dainty Ironmonger appear the most likely to have been justified in their belief.

The tour ended the career of Frank Tarrant, one of the finest cricketers produced in Australia, regarded by many as the greatest all-rounder of his generation. In the middle of the order Tarrant's cautious batting enabled him to score 1000 runs nine times in an English season and once took him on to 2000 runs (2030 at 46.13 in 1911). He achieved the double in eight of these seasons by taking more than 100 wickets with his slow-medium left-arm spinners and was an outstanding slips field. He played 13 matches for Victoria, 206 for Middlesex and his 17,857 runs included 33 centuries. He made four double centuries. He took 1489 first-class wickets at 17.66 and included a best analysis of 10 for 90. He took nine wickets in an innings seven times. He took five wickets in an innings an amazing 129 times and ten wickets in a match 36 times. He also held 296 catches. But as an Australian living in London he was never chosen for Test matches.

The biggest drawcard

England tours Australia 1936–37

Australian cricket survived the Depression years with a surfeit of talent. Public interest in the sport had never been higher, exciting new players abounded in every state, and competition for places in the Test team was intense. Long before "Gubby" Allen's players arrived for the twenty-third tour of Australia by an English team in 1936–37 advance bookings for the main matches had broken all records. The major discussion point was whether Bradman could captain Australia without any loss of his amazing run-getting powers.

There was no doubt that although he was only 28 the Board of Control, dominated by businessmen who were motivated by profit, wanted Bradman as Test captain. He had not led New South Wales and had only brief experience of the job with St George and North Sydney before he settled in Adelaide. His main grounding in cricket's toughest job was in six matches in England in 1934 when Woodfull was absent and as vice-captain he took over.

Australia's team for the second Test at Sydney against England in 1936–37, when Bradman took over the captaincy: (L to R) (back) A. Chipperfield, E. McCormick, M. Sievers, W. O'Reilly, F. Ward; (front) R. Robinson, L. O'Brien, S. McCabe, D. Bradman, J. Fingleton, W. Oldfield.

Bradman was appointed state captain by a South Australian Cricket Association aware of the terms of Bradman's contract guaranteeing him the job. The SACA knew the Board of Control was unlikely to look beyond the state captains in appointing a successor to Woodfull and gave Bradman the job while Vic Richardson was leading Australia through an unbeaten tour of South Africa.

Bradman ended any doubts about his captaincy by leading South Australia to win the 1935–36 Sheffield Shield in his first season with the team, blending a side that had lost Richardson and Grimmett to South Africa, and was without Lonergan and Nitschke, into a splendid combination. South Australia's spin bowling came mainly from Frank Ward, who took 33 wickets at 23.51 in inter-state matches. In the match between South Australia and the visiting MCC team captained by Errol Holmes, Bradman gave Ward 49 overs, which yielded 8 for 189.

The MCC side played six matches in Australia between October and December 1935, on their way to New Zealand. They drew with Western Australia in Perth, defeated South Australia by 36 runs in Adelaide, drew with Victoria in Melbourne, but lost to the strong New South Wales line-up in Sydney because of weak batting. After defeating Queensland by an innings and 106 runs in Brisbane, the MCC had the best win of their Australian visit against an Australian XI in Sydney.

Keith Rigg's 112 for Victoria was the only century scored against the MCC team, whose 14 players included eight amateurs. Joe Hardstaff jnr, an elegant stroke player, made 230 not out and 63 for MCC in the match against the Australian XI and two further centuries in New Zealand, finishing the tour with 1400 runs at 53.76. Jim Sims was the leading MCC bowler with 109 wickets in all matches, including 7 for 95 against Western Australia. The best Australian bowling display came from Hans Ebeling, who took 5 for 101 and 6 for 58 for the Australian XI.

South Australia's appointment of Bradman in preference to the long-serving Richardson, who was 41, was immediately rewarding. Bradman's presence brought big crowds to Adelaide Oval, and with a century likely at an average better than every third time he batted, large profits accumulated wherever he played. As his biographer Irving Rosenwater observed, "He was so far above all others that comparisons quickly became unreal. He was virtually a complete batting side in himself, and in theory if all his colleagues did not score a run, the side's total would still be good enough simply from Bradman's contribution." Jack Fingleton wrote that cricket was subservient to Bradman, his team-mates merely lay actors, but Bradman told me he considered that comment preposterous. He prided himself always on being a team member.

In Sydney, Bradman's absence from the state team was disastrous for the New South Wales Cricket Association, whose revenue plummeted in the first season after he left; only a £6000 bonus from the 1934 Australian tour of England rescued them from crippling losses. When the NSWCA treasurer presented a budget predicting a loss of £3500 for 1936–37, the association delegates went into committee, emerging with the recommendation that umpires' pay for grade matches be reduced from 10 shillings to eight. Their hopes of balancing the budget hung on Bradman travelling to Sydney to play for South Australia against New South Wales. They could only pray the weather would remain fine for that match.

Bradman and his wife picked out a block of land in Holden Street, in the Adelaide suburb of Kensington Park, and lived in a house down the road while their home was being built. Bradman played grade cricket for Kensington for the rest of his career. In his first year in Adelaide he won the Mount Osmond Country Club's golf championship.

By day he busied himself learning the ins and outs of stock and share broking and found it was just what he wanted—a vocation which took his mind off cricket. He was never a partner of Hodgett's, which was only a registered trade name, but carried out the same duties as the rest of the staff, attending to the needs of clients and learning the details of the investment business, experience which gave him invaluable training.

The MCC were aware when it appointed England's captain for the 1936–37 tour of Australia that a player of tact was required for what had become a peace-making trip. On this score Allen's appointment was unanimously acclaimed, for in the seemingly endless post-mortems on the Bodyline tour it became clear that Allen had refused to bowl Bodyline, at the risk of clashing with his captain. Allen gave Philip Derriman this account of the confrontation:

> *Douglas [Jardine] came to me in the dressing-room and told me he wanted me to bowl a few more bouncers and have a stronger leg-side field. I said, "No, Douglas, I never bowl like that and I don't think it's the way the game should be played." When he insisted, I said he would have to make up his mind if he wanted me to play or not.*

"Gubby" Allen was a careful choice as England captain for the 1936–37 tour of Australia. He had refused to bowl Bodyline during the 1932–33 tour and was unanimously considered the best choice for what was considered a peace-making trip.

For the rest of the tour Jardine respected Allen's point of view and they remained the best of friends, although Allen took no part in discussing tactics. "As a matter of fact, I was probably Jardine's best friend in Australia," said Allen. "He didn't have many."

Thus the one fast bowler who had refused to use Bodyline was in charge of the very next Australian tour, which pleased Australians as much as the fact that Allen had been born in Sydney. Errol Holmes was originally included in the English team but had to drop out. His place was taken by the deposed captain

Bob Wyatt, from whom Allen had taken over for the 1936 series in England against India. The English team was G. O. B. Allen (Middlesex, captain), R. W. V. Robins (Middlesex), R. E. S. Wyatt (Warwickshire), K. Farnes (Essex), and the professionals W. R. Hammond (Gloucestershire), H. Verity (Yorkshire), M. Leyland (Yorkshire), L. E. G. Ames (Kent), W. Voce (Nottinghamshire), C. J. Barnett (Gloucestershire), J. Hardstaff (Nottinghamshire), T. S. Worthington (Derbyshire), W. H. Copson (Derbyshire), J. M.

Sims (Middlesex), A. E. Fagg (Kent), L. B. Fishlock (Surrey), G. Duckworth (Lancashire) and Captain R. Howard (manager).

The major surprises were the omission of Eddie Paynter, who had performed heroically on the last Australian tour, and the inclusion of Bill Voce, who Australians believed had disqualified himself by bowling Bodyline at Woodfull's team in England in 1934. It transpired that although the umpires had found Voce guilty, the MCC had later accepted his apology. Australians received him politely, without a single boo, and his bowling proved superior to his earlier displays, swinging the ball away sharply and not wasting his efforts banging it into his own end of the pitch. His Notts pace bowling partner, Harold Larwood, was not considered as he had declared himself unavailable.

When Allen's team arrived at Fremantle on board the *Orion*, they were greeted with the customary joshing, with wharfies and tugboatmen teasing them to bet on the Tests. "Have you heard Bradman's latest score?" the hecklers shouted. "It was 212!"

From 9 to 13 October 1936 Bradman had captained the Rest of Australia against a team made up of the tourists just back from South Africa, led by Vic Richardson, in a testimonial for Jack Gregory and Warren Bardsley. (Six candidates were nominated for a joint testimonial, but Mailey, Taylor, Oldfield and Kippax were eliminated in a NSWCA ballot for the honour.) This match provided the long-awaited clash between Bradman and O'Reilly and brought Bradman back to the Sydney Cricket Ground. It also gave Bradman the chance to answer the snipers who claimed his high scoring of the previous summer had only been possible while the best bowlers were out of Australia. The result underlined how weak Australia's opposition had been in South Africa.

Vic Richardson's side scored 363 in the first innings, Brown reaching 111 before he

South African tourists Jack Fingleton (left) and Vic Richardson going out to bat against a team captained by Bradman in 1936. Defeat for Richardson's team virtually ended his claims to the Australian captaincy against England.

was out hit wicket to Ward. McCabe made 76, Oldfield 78. Ward puzzled all the batsmen with his mixture of leg breaks, top spinners and googlies to take 7 for 127 from 32.3 overs, a display which startled his detractors.

Bradman quickly forced Richardson to remove the close-in leg-side fieldsmen when he batted to O'Reilly and completely mastered the O'Reilly–Grimmett combination in an innings of 212. His second century took only 61 minutes. This knock meant that in his last six first-class innings Bradman had scored 233, 357, 31, 0, 369 and 212. The so-called burdens of captaincy had apparently improved his concentration and certainly confirmed Bradman's view that a top-class batsman and not bowlers or wicket-keepers make the best captains.

When Ward repeated his first innings coup by taking 5 for 100 in Richardson's XI's second innings, Bradman's side won the match by six wickets. Ward took 12 wickets at 18.90 each in the match, Grimmett 7 at 32.50. Despite the success of O'Reilly and Grimmett in South Africa, Ward's display set up an intense struggle for spin bowling places in the Australian team. The struggle was all the more piquant because of Grimmett's antipathy to Bradman, who became fixed in the view that he could expect no loyalty from Grimmett. O'Reilly's view was that Grimmett had proved the best bowler in the world in South Africa.

Gregory and Bardsley received only £762 each from their testimonial match. Bradman's double century provided marvellous entertainment and boosted Australia's Ashes hopes in 1936–37, but the returns demonstrated yet again how poorly Australians were rewarded for testimonials compared with players' benefits in England.

The Board of Control appointed Bradman Australian captain a few days after his twenty-eighth birthday. He joined E. A. Dwyer (New South Wales) and W. J. Johnson (Victoria) in choosing Australian Test teams. Bradman was the youngest selector on record. He held the job for 34 years.

England began their twenty-third tour with an easy win over Western Australia in Perth from 16 to 19 October. The Western Australian batsmen found the pace of bowlers Farnes and Allen too much for them. After the batsmen had been softened up, the Middlesex leg spinner Jim Sims took care of what was left. Sims, a lanky, droll humorist who spoke out of the side of his mouth, took seven wickets in the match at slightly more than eight runs each, including 5 for 37 in Western Australia's second innings.

Western Australia were out for 142 and 147 and the English innings of 4 for 469 was enough to win the match by an innings and 180 runs. Wyatt made 106 as an opening batsman but was beaten for the honour of scoring the first tour century by Hammond, who went in first wicket down and hit out lustily for 141, including 2 sixes and 14 fours. The Wyatt–Hammond partnership put on 221 for the second wicket. England suffered the first of a long sequence of injuries when Duckworth fractured a finger stopping a ball from Farnes, and Robins broke a finger when fielding. Before the second match, from 22 to 24 October, against a Combined Australian XI in Perth, Ames had back trouble.

Without a regular keeper after one first-class match, England had to use Fagg, who had a bruised thumb, behind the stumps. Hammond drove with power to reach 107, Worthington made 89, Fishlock 91 and Allen 65 in England's first innings of 497. The Combined Australian XI, who reached 436, were equally severe on the bowling, Badcock (167) hooking short balls from Copson, Allen and Voce in stunning style. Horrocks made 140, benefiting from dropped catches. Time ran out with England 4 for 120 in their second innings.

At Clare, in a one-day match, a ball from fast bowler Lindsay McKay broke a bone in Wyatt's left wrist, which left England unable to make up a team. They solved this dilemma by co-opting Tom Wade, an Essex professional visiting Australia, for two matches, and he took over the gloves. The Englishmen arrived in Adelaide expecting Bradman to be among the opposition for their match against South Australia from 30 October to 3 November. The night before the match the Bradmans' first child, a son only a day old, died in an Adelaide hospital and Bradman stood down.

Hammond saved England with centuries in each innings. Under Vic Richardson's captaincy, Ward's 43 overs cost 177 runs and brought 10 wickets; Grimmett's 30 overs yielded 2 for 88. England's first innings

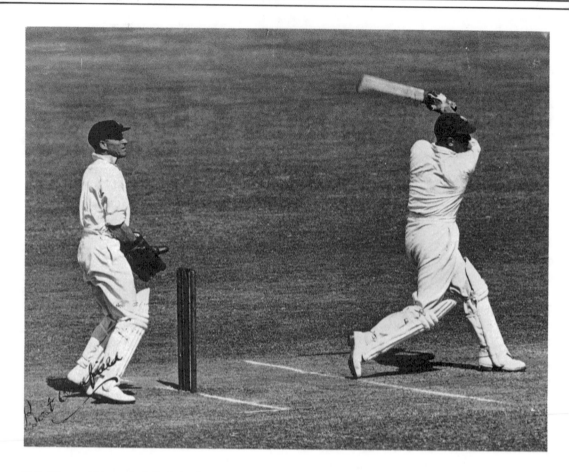

*Wally Hammond drives majestically during the
1936–37 rubber between Australia and England,
with wicket-keeper Oldfield following the ball.*

reached 233, after Hammond scored 104, and
the second innings reached 236, Hammond
this time making 136. Ward took 5 for 79 and
5 for 98 and worried all the English players.
Allen bowled at exceptional pace to give his
side a 71-run first innings lead. He and Verity
then ended the match by dismissing South
Australia for 202 and England won by 105
runs.

The match with Victoria in Melbourne
from 6 to 10 November was drawn after two
more England players were injured; neither
Barnett, bruised jaw, nor Voce, strained chest
muscle, could field on the last day. With
keepers Ames and Duckworth still out of
action, England went into the match with
stop-gap wicket-keeper Wade again behind
the stumps. Robins and Wyatt were still
nursing broken fingers.

Barnett hit a brilliant century (131) and
after England had taken their total to 344,
Victoria lost 3 for 27. Ian Lee, a 21-year-old
left-hander from South Melbourne, and Ross
Gregory, a 19-year-old right-hander from St
Kilda, then became associated in a fourth-
wicket stand of 262. Lee made 160, Gregory
128. Victoria managed 384, a lead of 40.
England were 3 for 36 when time ran out.
Round-faced John Frederick exposed England's weakness to leg breaks. He took 6 for
75 and 2 for 10 for Victoria. A week later
Frederick took a hammering from Bradman
(192) in the Victoria *v.* South Australia match

in Melbourne, finishing with 1 for 90, which ended his first-class career.

England met with their first defeat at Sydney from 13 to 17 November when New South Wales beat them by 135 runs in an exciting finish. New South Wales began with 273, a total which should have been far higher after Ray Robinson and Stan McCabe put on 145 with classic batting. Hammond's clever bowling earned him 5 for 39 and caused the late-order New South Wales collapse.

Harold Mudge, a right-arm leg spinner, took 6 for 42 in England's first innings of 153, which gave New South Wales an advantage they never lost. Leading by 120 on the first

NSWCA coach George Garnsey (left) chatting with Stan McCabe during a session at the nets in 1936–37, a season which saw unprecedented crowds attend the Tests.

innings, they batted steadily to reach 326 in their second innings, Chipperfield finishing with 97 not out. With 447 needed to win England were worn down by the accuracy of the spin attack, although Hammond batted grimly for five hours and Leyland showed spirit. O'Reilly took four wickets for four runs, all of them lbw, to finish with 5 for 67 and bowl New South Wales to a win. Oldfield made three fine stumpings in the match.

England narrowly averted defeat by an Australian XI from 20 to 24 November in Sydney. Chipperfield, denied the regular bowling that might have made him a great spin bowler, grabbed the chance to have an extended bowl and his 8 for 66 had England out for 288 in the first innings. The Australian XI then made 8 for 544 declared, Badcock scoring 182 to celebrate his twentieth birthday. Leyland batted gallantly to save England

and when time elapsed he was still at the crease on 118 not out, with England two wickets and 11 runs away from an innings defeat.

Another thriller followed when England met Queensland from 27 November to 1 December at the Gabba, this time with the home side fighting to prevent a loss with their last pair at the crease. England made 215 and 8 for 528, Fagg (112) and Barnett (259) putting on 295 for the first wicket in the second innings. Queensland scored 243 and were 9 for 227, chasing 501, when time ran out.

For his first Test as captain Bradman was given a new-look side that introduced four players to international cricket, Badcock, Robinson, Sievers and Ward. Fleetwood-Smith was unavailable because of an injured tendon and Grimmett was omitted. England had major problems finding opening batsmen or players as accustomed to spin as Sutcliffe, Hendren or Walters, but all of the team England picked for the first Test at the Gabba between 4 and 9 December had appeared in Tests.

Queensland's dictatorial chairman Jack Hutcheon caused a fuss when he barred C. B. Fry, a distinguished member of the MCC, from the Gabba members' pavilion because he was commentating on the match for English newspapers. Journalists had to remain behind a barbed wire fence separating them from the players.

The match began sensationally. McCormick got his approach run under control for once and bowled at terrifying pace. His first ball dismissed Worthington, he then had Fagg and Hammond out, Hammond off the first ball he faced. From 3 for 20, Barnett and Leyland hung on until lunch. Leyland took 140 minutes to reach 50 but he went on to 126 despite frequent problems with O'Reilly. England, 6 for 263 overnight, did well to add 95 next morning and take the first innings total to 358.

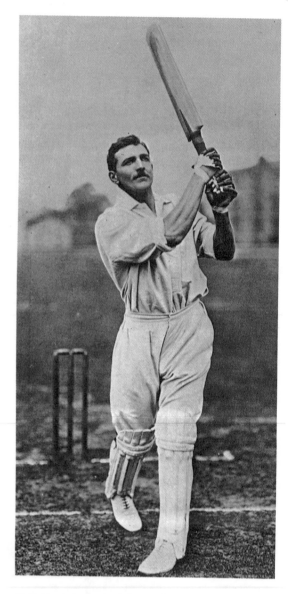

C. B. Fry, in his heyday before World War I. The famous English amateur and gentleman cricketer was barred from the Brisbane members' stand during the England v. Australia series in 1935–36.

Badcock, who had replaced the injured Brown as Fingleton's opening partner, was out when Australia had scored only 13, Bradman for 38 with the total 89, but McCabe and Fingleton went along comfortably until stumps when Australia were 2 for 151. Under the tour conditions of play only the ends of the pitch were covered, to prevent the bowlers slipping, and after overnight rain Voce was able to get alarming lift and move the ball away from the bat with late swing. He got McCabe, Robinson and Chipperfield while Fingleton completed a watchful century, his fourth in a row. Voce then finished off the innings for 234 with the new ball.

McCormick dropped out of the match after bowling eight overs in the first innings because of chronic lumbago, badly handicapping Australia's attack. Sievers could not match McCormick's penetration, though he tried hard, but all the English batsmen struggled against the spin of Ward, who, operating throughout on a firm pitch, took eight wickets (2 for 138 and 6 for 102), compared with O'Reilly's 5 for 161. With the total on 6 for 144, Allen and Hardstaff put on a crucial 61 runs and Australia were set 381 to win.

After Fingleton went for a duck, five appeals against the light were rejected. More rain fell that night and a heavy shower at 6 a.m. next morning turning the pitch into a real sticky wicket. Batting a man short in the absence of McCormick, Bradman changed the order, sending in tail-enders in the hope that the strip would dry before the best batsmen went in, but on such a pitch, with Allen and Voce able to bowl fast without slipping, nobody could have held out for long. Australia's total of 58, the lowest at home in this century, gave England a win by 322 runs. Voce took 6 for 41 and 4 for 16, Allen 3 for 71 and 5 for 36. Ward had his nose broken on the sticky wicket in Australia's second innings.

In hindsight Australia erred in playing Ward and McCormick in the second Test at Sydney on 18 to 22 December, although both had passed medical tests. McCormick's back was still bothering him and Ward still could not breathe freely through his broken nose. Their woes increased when Badcock fell ill on

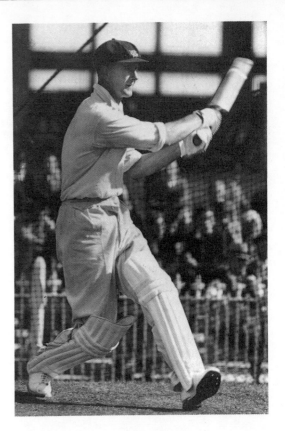

One of the surprises of the 1936–37 series was Victorian medium-pace bowler Morris Sievers, who was dropped despite his 5 for 21 in the third Test.

the opening day and could not bat in the first innings.

England batted first in ideal conditions and another hostile opening spell by McCormick should have done more than dismiss Fagg cheaply. Hammond narrowly missed playing him on when he first came in and Barnett was dropped in the slips by Chipperfield off Ward. At stumps England were 3 for 279 and they continued next day until Hammond reached 231 not out and the total 6 for 426 by stumps. McCormick bowled a few bouncers which created comment but they were easily dealt with as he had lost all his speed. Leyland was out lbw to McCabe under the new rule; this allowed appeals on balls pitched outside the off stump, but these were rarely successful.

Heavy rain fell over the weekend and Allen declared immediately. The pitch was a nasty sticky and the Australian batsmen were completely unnerved by it. O'Brien, Bradman and McCabe were out without scoring in the first quarter of an hour to Voce's seventh, eighth and tenth balls. Seven wickets were down for 31 when, with lunchtime near, O'Reilly decided on desperate measures and hit three huge sixes, one off Verity and two off Sims. The blow with which he lobbed the ball into the upper section of the old Sheridan Stand drew prolonged cheering from every corner of the ground. O'Reilly was still there on 37 not out when the innings ended at 80.

Facing the tricky decision of forcing the follow-on or batting again on a pitch which was recovering, Allen decided to send Australia straight in again. With the wicket drying out, Australia did much better, Fingleton and Bradman adding 124 for the second wicket,

England's captain "Gubby" Allen captured midair as he delivers a speedy ball to McCabe in the Brisbane Test.

Fingleton being bowled then by Sims for 73. England made sure of the match, however, soon after Bradman passed Clem Hill's 2600 runs in Tests between England and Australia, when Verity bowled Bradman for 82. McCabe carried on bravely for 93 but there was not enough class in the rest of the Australian batting and the innings folded up at 324. England had won by an innings and 22 runs and taken a completely unexpected two–nil lead in the rubber.

Australia's shock defeats touched off snide rumours in every pub and club in the country as the man in the street sought reasons for these disasters. The tour playing conditions had seen Australia twice caught on sticky wickets and aroused debate over the strange business of the bowler's take-off area being covered while the pitches remained open to the elements. Some of the Australian cricketers were said to have been too fond of the bottle and late-night parties. The headmaster of Sydney Grammar School, where Bill O'Reilly taught, was told that O'Reilly and McCabe were drunk on the train taking them to the third Test in Melbourne. He knew this was not true as they had called in to see him

Bradman moves in from silly mid-off to gather the ball from Hammond, batting on a sticky wicket, in the third Test of the 1936–37 series.

before they left Sydney by car.

While Australia's gossip-mongers had their field day, England went to Newcastle for a match against a New South Wales Country XI on 26 and 28 December. This fixture was enlivened by a sparkling innings by the Newcastle right-hand batsman Reg Beattie, then 23 years old. Beattie made 124 not out in a total of 4 for 188 declared, holding up an attack which included Allen, Voce, Hammond, Robins and Sims for three hours. England made 4 for 178 in reply before time ran out, rain having cost a day and a half's play.

Australia made four changes for the third Test at the Melbourne Cricket Ground from 1 to 7 January 1937. Brown, Darling, Rigg and Fleetwood-Smith, now recovered from injury, replaced Chipperfield, McCormick, O'Brien and Badcock. Crowds which broke every known record for attendances and receipts at a cricket match turned up in the hope of seeing Australia atone for their two earlier losses. They saw a magnificent match in which the strategies of the captains decided the outcome.

Bradman won the toss and batted on a lifeless wicket. Brown and Fingleton took half an hour to score seven before Brown edged an attempted hook off a Voce bouncer to wicket-keeper Ames. Bradman was caught by Robins at short leg for 13, a dismissal which understandably annoyed Bradman, who knew Robins had moved as the bowler approached the crease. Rigg was caught in the same place for 16, Fingleton was caught in the covers off a long hop, and at tea Australia were 5 for 129,

One of Len Darling's three spectacular catches that helped win the Melbourne Test for Australia in 1936. This one dismissed Maurice Leyland.

the rubber and the Ashes seemingly lost. McCabe and Oldfield took the score to 6 for 181 when rain ended play for the day.

Heavy overnight rain flooded the pitch and held up the start of play next day until 2.15 p.m. McCabe was out for a plucky 63 and at 9 for 200 Bradman declared. Hammond and Leyland were the only English batsmen not dismayed by the gluepot wicket and they added 42 in the only stand of the innings, Leyland assured and Hammond eager to try daring strokes. Both were out to incredible catches at short leg by Darling, diving full length to drag down the ball in one hand.

After the English batting stars were out Bradman told his bowlers to keep the lower-order batsmen in. He did not want Australia to bat again on such a wicket. England were 9 for 76 before Allen woke up to Bradman's stalling ploy and declared, Sievers having taken 5 for 21. This gave Australia 35 minutes to bat before stumps, but this was subsequently reduced by poor light. Allen was strongly criticised later for delaying by those who believed he should have forced Australia to bat a second time while the pitch was at its worst.

Bradman sent his tail-enders in first to play out time and when an appeal against the light ended play for the day Australia were 1 for 3. Shocked that he and O'Reilly should be told to go in first Fleetwood-Smith asked Bradman for the reason. Bradman answered: "Chuck, the only way you can get out on this wicket is to hit the ball. You can't hit it on a good pitch so you've got no chance on this strip."

Fleetwood-Smith survived that afternoon and although the pitch improved during the Sunday rest day, he was out the first time he touched the ball on Monday morning. Four others batted while the pitch dried some more before Bradman went in seventh to join Fingleton, with Australia 221 ahead. They put on 346, a record for the sixth wicket, taking the score from 97 to 443. Fingleton made 136 and Bradman, in his longest Test innings, batted 7 hours 38 minutes for 270, the highest score by a Test captain in Australia.

Bradman had batted with a severe chill and when England set out after the 689 needed to win McCabe took over the Australian captaincy. He achieved an early breakthrough when Ward got rid of Worthington and O'Reilly had Barnett lbw. Hammond batted as if England were in charge of the match but after a delightful 51 was out to a careless stroke.

On the sixth morning Leyland and Robins batted with great responsibility but when Robins went for 61 Leyland ran out of partners. He was still there on 111 not out when the innings ended at 323, Australia winning by 365 runs. Fleetwood-Smith took a hammering from Hammond but ended with flattering figures, 5 for 124, when he dismissed Voce and Sims with the last two balls of the match.

The aggregate attendance for the match was 350,534, a record that still stands for any match in the world. Takings were £30,124, £7405 of which came from the third-day crowd of 87,798 who watched Fleetwood-Smith get his duck.

Immediately play ended some of the players were told to go to the Victorian Cricket Association rooms nearby. They found that only five of them were wanted— McCabe, Fingleton, O'Reilly, O'Brien, and Fleetwood-Smith, who was one of Bradman's closest friends and had just finished his first Test in Australia. They were welcomed with handshakes by the Board of Control chairman Dr Allen Robertson, and three other Board members, R. A. Oxlade (NSW), Roger Hartigan (Queensland) and H. W. Hodgetts (South Australia), Bradman's employer.

Dr Robertson read from two sheets of foolscap paper a turgid epistle about players who drank too much liquor, kept late hours, neglected their physical fitness and did not give their captain their full support. The players were mystified, having just brought off a notable victory, and one of them asked:

"Doctor Robertson, does this mean that we are accused of these things?"

"I can assure you there are no charges whatsoever," replied Dr Robertson.

"In that case, sir," said O'Reilly, "this is just tiggy-touchwood and we all might as well go."

As the meeting broke up the players were offered cigarettes and the Board members invited them to a club for drinks, which they declined. The players were then instructed not to talk to the press about the meeting and when one of them explained that the press had followed them to the VCA rooms a committee member went to the window to see if he could sight any reporters. In the street, as the cricketers emerged, they saw newspaper posters which read "Board Carpets Five Test Men", which meant the reporters had known of the confrontation in advance.

The purpose of this strange interview has never been disclosed, nor has the name of the instigator. McCabe said that he asked Bradman if he had reported the five and he assured McCabe he knew nothing about it. Later Bradman was told that the Board did not consult him because they did not want to embarrass him, so it seems likely the Board listened to the prevailing rumours. Bradman, a Mason, realised immediately that by carpeting his team's Catholics the Board had created divisions in the side.

The Masons *v.* Catholics argument was

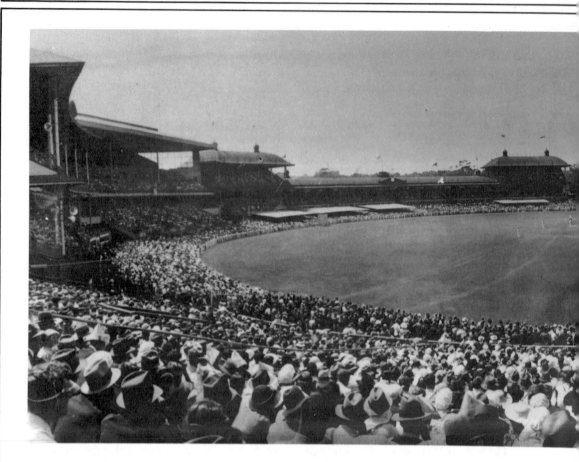

The Melbourne Cricket Ground photographed on 4 January 1937, the third day of the third Test. For the day there was a world record attendance of 87,798 and gate takings were £7405.

very topical in all cricket clubs at the time. Philip Derriman in his official history of the NSWCA, *True To the Blue*, says: "There is no doubt Masons dominated the Association's officialdom until the 1960s at least, and possibly advanced their own interests from time to time. Although the Catholics *v.* Masons differences were well enough known in the cricket world, they were rarely, if ever brought into the open." Derriman points out that long-time NSWCA president Sydney Smith was a Mason, continuing a Masonic influence that had begun with Richard Driver

and been carried on by John Portus. Catholics felt they were deprived of the big jobs on the NSWCA and given secondary roles such as "Chappie" Dwyer's selection committees. Dwyer was the boss of a chain of Catholic bookshops and to many would have made a better NSWCA president than Syd Smith, splendid in the 1920s but hopelessly out of touch in the late 1930s. According to Derriman the NSWCA did not employ a Catholic until the 1970s.

A trip to Tasmania by England and a match against South Australia were sandwiched in between the third and fourth Tests. At Launceston between 9 and 11 January Tasmania's batsmen were bewildered by Sims, whose match figures were 9 for 59. Les Ames made a good century (109) and England won by an innings and four runs. At Hobart,

between 15 and 18 January, England did not enforce the follow-on against a Combined Tasmanian XI, to ensure the match went into the third day and they could get some practice. Barnett made 129 before Grimmett had him lbw, and Hardstaff 110 before Ward had him caught, in an English total of 418. Old-field made 60 not out in the Combined XI's innings of 134. England were 1 for 111 in their second innings when torrential rain cut the match short.

England scored 301 in their first innings against South Australia in Adelaide from 22 to 26 January, Barnett scoring 78, Allen 60. Fishlock had a bone in his hand broken by fast bowler Harold Cotton. South Australia were 4 for 194 when rain again washed out the last two days.

The fourth Test, on the Adelaide Oval between 29 January and 4 February 1937, turned on one wonderful delivery from Fleet-wood-Smith after Bradman had set up Australia's chance to win with yet another double century. The young Victorian stylist Ross Gregory made an impressive debut, replacing Darling, whose catching had helped swing the third Test.

Australia were disappointing on a perfect wicket, scoring only 288 in the first innings after all the top-order batsmen had got splen-did starts. At 3 for 73 Bradman and McCabe staged a 63-run partnership before Bradman swung lustily at an Allen delivery and edged it onto his stumps.

McCabe played a great innings in adding 70 with Gregory to make 88 but when he was out trying to hook a ball out of the ground, Australia's innings ended fairly quickly. Eng-

Stan McCabe survives an lbw appeal by 'keeper Les Ames, as Wally Hammond fields the ball at first slip during the 1936–37 series.

land fared only marginally better, despite a stubborn 129 from Barnett, who batted for 5 hours 45 minutes and hit 1 six and 13 fours. Ames (52) was the only other impressive batsman, England forfeiting a grand opportunity to establish a commanding position.

With England's fieldsmen positioned in the deep to prevent boundaries, Bradman played one of his most controlled innings to build up Australia's second innings. After two wickets had fallen for 88, he had stands of 109 with McCabe, 135 with Gregory, and by the fifth morning took Australia to a good lead. When Bradman was out for 212 the Australian innings folded up and the total of 433 meant that England had to get 392 to win. It was the slowest double century of Bradman's career, 7 hours 21 minutes, and included only 14 fours. At stumps England were 3 for 148 after Hardstaff batted well against the spinners.

All depended on the not-out batsmen,

Hammond and Leyland, and as Australia took the field for the sixth day Bradman handed the ball to Fleetwood-Smith and "tried to inspire that erratic genius by telling him the result of the match was in his hands". Fleetwood-Smith responded by bowling Hammond in his first over with a wonderful ball that curled away from the bat and spun back viciously between bat and pad as it drew Hammond forward. A prediction that Fleetwood-Smith would one day win a Test for Australia, which Bradman said "Sammy" Carter had made years before, had come true. A few minutes later Fleetwood-Smith induced Leyland to edge a catch to Chipperfield in the slips.

Wyatt offered stout resistance in scoring 50, but the variety and skill of the Australian spinners confounded England, who were all out for 243. Fleetwood-Smith took 6 for 110 in the second innings and 10 for 239 in the match and the teams went to Melbourne for the fifth Test all square with two wins each.

Two country matches followed before England met New South Wales in mid-February in Sydney, where a 182-centimetre-tall tearaway fast bowler and aggressive middle-order batsman named John Grantley ("Ginty") Lush had been given his chance in big cricket after several outstanding seasons with the Mosman club. After New South Wales scored 231 New South Wales captain Alan McGilvray threw Lush the ball to open the bowling. Lush responded by bowling with exceptional pace and stamina to take 6 for 43. Leg spinner Hughie Chilvers took 4 for 2 and England were out for 73.

Ken Farnes matched Lush's fire when New South Wales batted a second time, bruising most of the batsmen and Lush went to the crease as Chipperfield left it with his jaw smashed by Farnes. Lush batted with skill and enterprise to top-score with 49 and New South Wales' second innings of 246 left England to score 405 to win. Lush bowled New South Wales to a shock victory by taking 7 for 72 in England's second innings of 299. His 13 for 121 was the best by a New South Wales bowler against England and took Lush to the forefront of pace bowling candidates for the fifth Test and the Australian tour of England in 1938. Gentleman Ken Farnes sent Chipperfield a telegram regretting breaking his jaw and wishing him a speedy recovery.

Most critics thought the selectors erred in preferring Laurie Nash to Lush for the fifth Test. The selectors, E. A. Dwyer (NSW), W. J. Johnson (Victoria) and Bradman (South Australia) named a squad of 13 for the Test. Nash, a brilliant Australian Rules footballer, had played almost all his cricket for Tasmania. His selection caused grumbles among the English players who objected to the number of bouncers Nash bowled for Victoria against them in the drawn match at Melbourne from 19 to 23 February. Victoria had the better of this match, scoring 292 against England's 187 and 3 for 132.

The Board of Control asked the selectors to reduce their list for the Test to 12, in the belief that Nash would be squeezed out. Nash had not played Test cricket since 1931–32 when he took 4 for 18 against South Africa, striking batsmen nasty blows on a Melbourne sticky. Although he really made the ball fizz through from a furious, charging approach run, he had never appeared in a Shield match because he lived in Tasmania.

The selectors told the Board it would be unfair to reduce the Test squad before the morning of the match when prevailing conditions could be assessed, and threatened to resign if the squad was altered. The Board retreated with a heavy loss of dignity, some of them shocked that a selection committee which included Bradman in his first season as Australian captain should take such a strong stand.

Allen was apprehensive that too many bouncers would revive the animosity of the Bodyline series. Bradman told him that despite the presence of Voce and Farnes in the English team and McCormick and Nash in the Australian side it was simply up to the captains to ensure their tactics were not detrimental to the game. Warwick Armstrong heard of the Bradman–Allen discussion and wrote a newspaper article claiming that the legitimate use of fast bowlers had "been restricted by a ridiculous agreement that prevented pace bowlers using the bumping ball". There was no such agreement as Allen and Bradman had agreed bouncers could be bowled within reason.

The fifth Test from 26 February to 3 March was watched by the sole survivor of the first Test played 60 years earlier, 78-year-old Tom Garrett. Australia strengthened her bowling by playing Nash instead of Brown and Badcock replaced the injured Chipperfield for the first Test to begin with the teams on two wins apiece since 1894–95. England preferred Worthington to Robins, leaving the spin bowling entirely to Verity, which proved a mistake.

Bradman won the toss and after fiery fast

bowling from Farnes, in the fastest display since Larwood, had dismissed Rigg and Fingleton for 54, McCabe and Bradman batted brilliantly. McCabe was missed by Allen at short leg early in his innings and again at 86, before he was out for 112. Bradman did not give the semblance of a chance until he was out early on the second morning for 169. Badcock and Ross Gregory (no relation to the celebrated Sydney Gregorys) then confirmed Australia's supremacy with a fifth-wicket stand of 161. Badcock, short and stocky, reminded spectators of Hendren and he hit 15 fours on his way to 118, his first Test century. Gregory, frail and artistic, made 80, falling to a Verity catch off Farnes when a century looked assured.

In an English attack that took heavy punishment Farnes finished with the wonderful figures of 6 for 96 in an innings of 604, the highest total Australia had ever made against England in Australia. Verity was the costliest of the seven England bowlers, with 1 for 127.

Barnett and Worthington gave England a dazzling start, scoring 33 in 17 minutes. Barnett nicked a bouncer from Nash into Oldfield's gloves and then, after an entertaining innings of 44 Worthington dislodged a bail with his heel before he completed a hook off Fleetwood-Smith and was out hit wicket. From then on English wickets fell regularly and although Hardstaff's 83 was his best contribution of the tour England were all out for 239.

Forced to follow on 365 runs behind, England lacked spirit in their second innings, which featured another tense duel between Hammond and O'Reilly. When O'Reilly had Hammond caught for the second time in the match for 56, England slumped to 8 for 165 by the end of the fourth day. Two balls from Fleetwood-Smith accounted for Voce and Farnes on the fifth morning, and Australia had won by an innings and 200 runs to become the first side to win the Ashes from two–nil

Laurie Nash, whose recall for the fifth Test in 1936–37 after four years in the wilderness shocked cricket experts.

down. The five Tests proved the biggest drawcard in the entire history of international cricket; 960,794 people paid £90,909 to watch 25 days and two balls, figures which in 1986–87 had still not been approached.

With their captain "Gubby" Allen crestfallen over the loss of the Ashes after winning the first two Tests, England completed their tour with draws against a Victorian Country XII between 5 and 6 March at Benalla, and against Combined Universities at Sydney from 8 to 9 March 1937. Laurie Fishlock, whose form had been bad throughout the summer compared with his outstanding batting in England during the previous Australian tour, made 104 at Benalla, his sole tour century. The England team then spent a fortnight in New Zealand, where they drew two and won one of their three matches.

Hammond headed both the tour first-class and Test batting averages, scoring 468 runs at 58.50 in the Tests and 1242 runs in all first-class matches at 59.14. He was also the leading century-maker, with seven to his credit, compared to five centuries by Barnett and three each by Wyatt and Leyland. Altogether England made 22 centuries and had 14 scored against them, Bradman and Badcock heading the list with three each. Bradman topped Australia's Test batting averages with 810 runs at 90.00. O'Reilly was Australia's leading Test wicket-taker with 25 at 22.20, but Morris Sievers had the best average with 9 wickets at 17.88.

The worst defeat

The nineteenth Australian team
to England 1938;
domestic cricket 1939–40

Although they did not win Test selection, the Australian cricketers who made the biggest advances in 1936–37 were Sid Barnes and Lindsay Hassett. They were both remarkably versatile games players, dextrous, quick-footed and nimble-witted, and both in their own way were to win an important place in Australia's cricket history.

Barnes was born into a family who farmed sheep in the Charters Towers region of northwestern Queensland. His father died just before he was born in 1916 and, unable to continue the unequal struggle in the outback, his mother brought her brood to Sydney. Young Sid became an urchin accustomed to tilting at those about him among the dead-end kids of Stanmore, a smart aleck who never lost the habit of saying something outrageous.

His tough apprenticeship in a slum suburb developed a strong body and throughout his

The Australian team chosen for the 1938 tour of England: (L to R) (back) W. Jeanes (manager), S. Barnes, W. Brown, E. McCormick, E. White, W. O'Reilly, L. Fleetwood-Smith, F. Ward, W. Ferguson (scorer); (middle) J. Fingleton, M. Waite, S. McCabe, D. Bradman (captain), B. Barnett, A. Chipperfield, C. Badcock; (front) A. Hassett, C. Walker.

life there was seldom a surplus ounce on his 173 centimetre, 79 kilogram frame. He began as a schoolboy cricketer with the Marrickville club before switching to Petersham, and his first coach was Marrickville's Algy Wright, who once gave his class of schoolboys a talk on the fundamentals of cricket and its ethics and then asked for questions. Barnes' was "What's the weight of a bail, Mr Wright?"

Hassett had an altogether different background. He was born in 1913, one of six sons of a Geelong real estate agent. The games which Barnes learned in the street, Hassett learned in the playground of the exclusive Geelong College, where he was captain of cricket and football. Lindsay was the Victorian Public Schools tennis champion in 1931, and in five years at the college scored a record 2191 runs in 41 innings, including six centuries. One brother, Harry, was an interstate tennis player, and another, Dick, five years Lindsay's senior, took 21 wickets as a googly bowler, and averaged 56.71 with the bat in eight matches for Victoria between 1929 and 1931. Dick scored two centuries, 114 not out and 102, both against Tasmania, and highly impressed Jack Hobbs with his spin bowling for Victoria against England in 1929.

Barnes played his initial first-class match at the age of 20 in the New South Wales v. South Australia match in Sydney from 19 to 23 February 1937. He was twice out padding up to Frank Ward's top spinner, scoring 31 and 44, one of the few times he did not hoodwink the umpire into giving him the benefit of the doubt. Hassett, who made his debut for Victoria at the age of 19 in 1932–33, headed the Sheffield Shield batting averages in the 1936–37 season with 449 runs in eight innings at an average of 74.83, highest score 93. This effort won him a permanent place in the Victorian team, although he scored only one century in his first 20 matches.

Victoria won the Shield in 1936–37, largely because of classy youngsters like Hassett filling in for the leading players who were away at the Tests. The Shield was decided in the last match when South Australia, needing an outright win to retain it, lost to Victoria by nine wickets. Hassett, Ross Gregory, Ian Lee, Keith Rigg and Len Darling, who appeared in only one Test, all made more than 300 runs.

The Victorian bowling was equally strong. Fleetwood-Smith and McCormick both had sensational match figures. Fleetwood-Smith took 7 for 17 and 8 for 79 against Queensland at Melbourne from 18 to 22 December, and in the decisive final match took 6 for 66 in South Australia's first innings. McCormick was almost unplayable in taking 9 for 40 in South Australia's second innings of 79.

South Australia suffered from the slump in form of Bradman and Badcock, after phenomenal performances the previous summer. Bradman scored 323 fewer runs in the same number of innings as in 1935–36, Badcock 373 fewer. Whitington and Hamence were very consistent, both scoring centuries in the match against Queensland on Adelaide Oval from 25 to 29 December. Grimmett was again the mainstay of the South Australian attack, adding 30 wickets to his already amazing first-class total.

New South Wales, unlike Victoria and South Australia, could not find adequate replacements for their Test players, McCabe, Chipperfield, Fingleton, Oldfield and O'Reilly. Ray Robinson—no relation to the author—was the only batsman to average more than 50, scoring 407 runs at 58.14, which included two centuries. Bob Hynes took most wickets for New South Wales, 23 at 28.56, but O'Reilly's 13 wickets in two appearances cost only 19.53.

Queensland were again without a win. Tallon headed the batting averages again with 434 runs at 36.16 and threw out strong

A shock omission from the 1938 touring side, Queenslander Don Tallon. All three selectors said they had him on their lists but he missed out to Ben Barnett and Charlie Walker.

best keeper behind Oldfield. Rex Rogers, a left-handed batsman from the Cairns district, with arms like hams, made an impressive debut at the age of 20, his 113 against South Australia, between 25 and 29 December in Adelaide, providing some dramatic hitting. Les Dixon, a right-arm fast-medium bowler from Brisbane University, helped give the Queensland attack its strongest look in years by taking 22 wickets at 24.04.

The first Australian women's team visited England in 1937 under the captaincy of Margaret Peden, who had been largely responsible for England's Australian tour in 1934–35. The team lost only one of their 19 matches, the second Test. Australia won the first Test and the third was drawn. Peden captained Australia and Archdale led England in both these international series, which firmly established the future of women's international cricket. Peden opened for Australia in four of the first six Tests, scoring 87 runs in 12 innings, top score 34.

New South Wales regained the Shield in 1937–38 after a five-year break, due to the bowling of O'Reilly who took 33 wickets at 14.06 runs each. He received splendid support from Fingleton, with 494 runs at 54.88, McCabe, who hit two centuries, and Barnes, whose 492 runs at 44.72 were made in entertaining style. At this stage in his career Barnes played every shot in the coaching book including a variety of cuts, occasional lofted drives, and hooks that went skywards, shots he was later to drop from his repertoire.

In July 1937 news arrived from Bolton in Lancashire that Ted McDonald, the great Australian fast bowler, had been killed in a car accident. He had stopped to assist a motorist who had crashed, and was hit by a passing car. He was 45.

The 1937–38 Australian season opened in Adelaide with a testimonial match for Vic Richardson and Clarrie Grimmett at the end

challenges to the southern State wicket-keepers Barnett (Victoria) and Walker (South Australia) for ranking as Australia's second of November. The teams were captained by Richardson and Bradman. Before play began umpire Jack Scott called in fast bowlers Bob Hynes, "Ginty" Lush and Ernie McCormick and informed them they were not to bowl bouncers—a warning they felt was ironic to come from a man who in 1930 had been barred from Sydney grade cricket for his bad-tempered bowling of short balls.

Rain restricted the match to two days and Grimmett and Richardson received only £1028 each from it. But in the time available Grimmett had the last word with Bradman in their long-standing argument about the use of Grimmett's "flipper", the wrong-'un, or bosey with top spin. Bradman, from the time he took over the South Australian captaincy from Richardson, had urged Grimmett to concentrate on his leg break and only bowl the wrong-'un or flipper as a surprise delivery. Grimmett was so delighted with his invention that he kept bowling it and Bradman suggested he had forgotten how to bowl a leg break.

There was promise of a huge crowd when Bradman took block in the pre-lunch over before spectators who had come just to see him bat. But Grimmett, with his fourth ball, produced a perfectly pitched leg break which turned sufficiently to remove Bradman's off bail.

"There y'are, I told you I could still bowl the leg break," said Grimmett with pleasure. Richardson, his hopes of an after-lunch crowd of 40,000 gone, said, "Maybe, Grum, but you've cost us a couple of thousand quid each with that leggie."

Grimmett looked sorry for Richardson's sake, but for himself the reward of bowling Bradman with a beautiful leg break was worth it.

Richardson knew that at 43 his Test days were over, although he still continued to play for South Australia. His international career had been surprisingly brief for such a wonder-

Although over 45 years old in the 1939–40 season, Clarrie Grimmett could still move in to bowl like a dancer.

ful all-round athlete, covering only 19 Tests which had yielded only 706 runs at 23.53. His first-class career apart from Tests was far more impressive, producing 10,727 runs at 37.63. None of his 27 first-class centuries were scored in a Test, but his service to South Australian cricket was so valuable the SACA later named the Adelaide Oval gates, near where his hook shot so often cleared the fence, after him.

Richardson, later a popular radio cricket commentator, was married twice, first to Vida Knapman and then Peggy Chandler. One of his and Vida's daughters, Jeanne, became the mother of the Chappell clan. Vic often played cricket with the three boys, Ian, Greg and Trevor, in the backyard of Martin and Jeanne Chappell's Glenelg home when the boys were small, but when they left school he preferred to let them go their own way.

Unlike Richardson, Grimmett refused to concede that his international career was over at the age of 46. He was a model of physical fitness, practising daily in his back garden, and never missed a net in the state side. While he could still produce balls like the one that defeated Bradman in the testimonial match he reasoned he was worth a place in the Australian side.

In 1937–38 Grimmett had skin like a grape left too long in the sun, but he still moved in to bowl like a dancer. Few bowlers have ever dropped so quickly into a perfect length or bowled so consistently to their field. He bowled so few bad balls that he was seldom expensive and it was common for him to start a spell with three or four maiden overs. O'Reilly considered him the finest partner he ever had because Grimmett never gave up when punished, whereas he cited examples of Ward folding up when hit about.

Leading candidates for the 1938 tour of England made their bids amid growing excitement. Newspaper and radio commenta-tors dwelt on who might make the tour, with the media in four states pressing for the inclusion of local heroes without thought for the balance of the team. O'Reilly and Fleetwood-Smith were established as Australia's leading spinners and if a third were to be chosen it was obvious he would be a reserve to these bowlers. Grimmett, in his 47th year, had not been chosen for a Test in Australia since being dropped in 1932–33. He faced a strong challenge from Ward, who was 29, with Chilvers, aged 36, the outsider.

New Zealand played three matches in Australia in 1937–38 on their way home from England. South Australia defeated them by 10 wickets, thanks to a sparkling 114 from Badcock. Victoria beat them by five wickets, Hassett taking the opportunity to impress selectors with an exhilarating 127 not out in Victoria's second innings. At Sydney Barnes made 97 and O'Reilly took 9 for 119, with New South Wales the winners by eight wickets.

O'Reilly had a captivating duel with Bradman in the New South Wales *v.* South Australia match at Adelaide, taking 9 for 41 and 5 for 57, dismissing five batsmen for one run at one stage in the first innings. This effort set New South Wales on the way to winning the Sheffield Shield for the first time since Bradman was in the side in 1933–34. Fleetwood-Smith had 9 for 135 and 3 for 137 for Victoria *v.* South Australia, while Ward took 11 for 111 for South Australia against New Zealand. Keith Miller, a lean 19-year-old from Sunshine, Victoria, made 181 for Victoria *v.* Tasmania in his first-class debut.

Bradman scored 983 runs in Shield matches, with four centuries, and in all first-class matches exceeded 1000 runs for the ninth time in ten seasons. He made 246 and 39 not out against Queensland and 107 and 113 in the return match. At Sydney against New South Wales he took over as wicket-keeper when

A youthful Keith Miller when he first came into big cricket just before World War II.

Charlie Walker broke a finger and was responsible for three of the four dismissals made while he had the gloves.

Selectors Bradman, Bill Johnson and "Chappie" Dwyer deliberated at length on their team for England, knowing they would cause more than the usual mixture of joy and disappointment. In the end they preferred Ward to Grimmett. To Bill O'Reilly this was unpardonable. "Grimmett's omission was the most biased, ill-considered piece of selection known to Australian cricket," O'Reilly wrote in 1986. "His absence made my own tour in 1938 a litany of frustrated endeavour."

Ward had taken 25 wickets from 180 overs, Grimmett 30 wickets from 207 overs in 1937–38 Shield matches, but the selectors considered that at 46 he was too old for the reserve spin bowler's role, a poor batsman, and a liability in the field. Ward in contrast appeared to have far more cricket ahead of him in which he could use his English experience and was fiercely loyal to Bradman. The selection turned, however, on Ward's strike rate. Bradman had calculated that he took a wicket every 5.6 overs, better than O'Reilly (6.6), Fleetwood-Smith (6.3) and Grimmett, who sent down 9 overs for each wicket in 1934. On these figures it seemed likely that Ward would provide the team on a long tour with more rest periods than Grimmett.

My researches strongly suggest that Grimmett talked himself out of the 1938 tour of England. He was openly critical of selectors who omitted him from the 1936–37 Tests against England, when he would have done better to let his bowling genius speak for him. There was, too, the unexplained mystery of why he had bowled only one sustained spell in the six matches after the fifth Test on the 1934 English tour, virtually disappearing from the Australian attack although physically fit.

The 1938 team was D. G. Bradman

(captain), W. A. Brown, A. L. Hassett, S. G. Barnes, C. L. Badcock, J. H. Fingleton, S. J. McCabe, B. A. Barnett, A. G. Chipperfield, M. G. Waite, C. W. Walker, E. C. S. White, F. A. Ward, W. J. O'Reilly, L. O'B. Fleetwood-Smith, E. L. McCormick, with W. H. Jeanes, secretary of the Australian Board of Control, as manager.

One of the major decisions the selectors made was the omission of Bert Oldfield as wicket-keeper, after 56 Tests, four tours of England and one tour of South Africa. Oldfield believed that at 44 he was still worth a place but he retired gracefully, upset only that one of the two wicket-keeping places had not gone to Don Tallon, whom he rated far and away the finest keeper in Australia. Oldfield's 20-year career had included 245 first-class matches and he had dismissed 661 batsmen, 399 of them caught and 262 stumped. In Tests he had 130 victims, 78 caught and 52 stumped. He also scored 6135 first-class runs at 23.77, with six centuries.

Tallon's failure to win a place in the nineteenth Australian team to England has never been satisfactorily explained. All three selectors were reported to have included him in their wicket-keeper pairings, Bradman picking Walker and Tallon, Dwyer Oldfield and Tallon, and Johnson Barnett and Tallon, but somehow he was squeezed out. My enquiries leave me convinced none of the selectors realised how good he was.

One argument was that in a team so heavily dependent on spinners Tallon's lack of experience against spin counted against him. Another theory was that he had not improved his chances by standing back to Geoff Cook, one of Queensland's medium-pace opening bowlers. The truth there was that Tallon and Cook had agreed the best chance of wickets from Cook's pronounced swing would come with Tallon standing back to his opening overs, a procedure which allowed Tallon to

One of Queensland's finest all-rounders in the 1930s was Geoff Cook. Strong competition, however, ended his Test hopes.

move up to the stumps and make stumpings off Cook later on when the ball had lost its shine.

New South Wales pace bowler J. G. "Ginty" Lush was so disappointed about missing one of the pace bowling places that he eagerly accepted when former Australian Test all-rounder Alan Fairfax offered him £600 a year to join Sir Julien Cahn's team, for whom Fairfax was an agent. At the time Lush earned £5 a week as a cadet journalist in Sydney and £1 a day for each Shield match in which he played. Harold Mudge, Jack Walsh and Vic Jackson all felt similarly frustrated after sterling displays for the New South Wales side and also joined Lush in Cahn's side.

The four Australians lived a life of luxury at the Nottingham headquarters of Sir Julien

Sir Julien Cahn's privately run team in England included Australians "Ginty" Lush and Jack Walsh (third and second from right at back), Vic Jackson (second from right at front) and Harold Mudge (second from left at front).

Cahn's XI, playing midweek and weekend matches on Sir Julien's private ground. The players were drawn from all the cricket nations and were entertained regularly at Sir Julien's stately home, Stanford Hall, where their host, a member of the "Magic Circle" of magicians, performed all sorts of tricks for their amusement. All the cricketers' expenses were paid by Sir Julien, a self-made millionaire whose fortune came from furniture retailing. He occasionally captained his side, batting in pneumatic pads, pumped up for him by his chauffeur before he went onto the ground. Sir Julien always had his mascot, a wooden fox with a movable tail, fastened into the ground in front of the pavilion. When things went badly for his team, which was not often, he would lower the fox's tail.

The Australian team assembled in Melbourne on 25 February 1938, and after the customary matches against Tasmania and Western Australia sailed across the Indian Ocean and through the Suez Canal to Naples. On the wharf Italian marines were being drilled. Bradman counted 36 destroyers, 72 submarines and 8 cruisers in the harbour and wrote to a friend in Adelaide: "I guess they were not built to rust. It's obvious that Europe is contemplating a grim future."

At Gibraltar Sid Barnes had a nasty fall on the wet deck. For a time it was thought that he had simply sprained his wrist but when the team arrived in England X-rays showed that it was broken. With Barnes unable to play for more than three months, Bradman and manager Jeanes decided to cable the Board of Control and ask for a replacement to be flown over. They expected either Keith Rigg or Ross Gregory to join them, but the Board refused to send an extra player. This decision was to put unnecessary strain on key members of a side that had more than the usual share of injuries and sickness.

Before the tour began the chairman of the Australian Board of Control, Dr Robertson, was asked his opinion of the team. He replied: "I doubt whether England will ever produce a team to make an even go with Australian cricketers. In my lifetime they are not going to produce a team to equal ours." It was a view which anyone with an understanding of the wonderful uncertainty of cricket would never express: it did not take long for Dr Robertson to bitterly regret his words.

McCormick arrived in England with the reputation of being the fastest bowler Australia had ever sent on tour, and there was almost as much interest in his appearance in the first tour match as there was in Bradman's attempt to start with a double century for the third time. Playing against Worcestershire at Worcester, between 30 April and 3 May, Bradman was asked to bat after the Honourable Charles Lyttelton won the toss. Bradman fulfilled all expectations with a chanceless innings of 258, which included 33 fours.

Tasmanian prodigy Cyril Badcock attracts a smile from Bradman as he films the team's arrival in England.

McCormick was not so lucky. He marked out his run with his customary series of skips, followed by 20 running strides, setting down his marker like a surveyor without a theodolite. Then he moved in, arms rigid at his sides, legs going at a tearaway speed, and let the ball go at tremendous pace. Unfortunately he was well past the crease when he released the ball and the corpulent umpire Herbert Baldwin, the former Surrey middle-order batsman and leg-break bowler, no-balled him so often that his first over comprised 14 balls and his second 15 balls. After three overs, in which McCormick had been no-balled 16 times, Bradman went to Baldwin and asked if McCormick was "dragging". Baldwin replied, "Is he dragging over the line? He's jumping at least a yard over it."

In the midst of this sensation, opener Charles Bull tried to hook one of McCormick's no-balls and turned it onto his face, going down in a heap. Bull retired, his right eye almost completely closed from the swelling. Meanwhile McCormick shortened his run, lengthened his initial skips, slowed down his pace, and did everything he could to rectify the problem. At one stage he tried sprinting 18 metres from the bowling crease to his marker; as he burst towards the crowd a voice cried, "Shut the gate or he'll be out on the road!"

Despite McCormick's contribution of 35 no-balls, Worcestershire lost by an innings and 77 runs. Following on 273 runs behind Australia's 541, Worcestershire managed only 196 in their second innings, Fleetwood-Smith taking 8 for 98 and 3 for 38. Bull batted with one eye almost closed and a finger broken at practice to score 37 not out and 69.

McCormick spent most of the remainder of the tour experimenting with changes to his run-up, but with little success. *Wisden* concluded that "McCormick was the most overrated bowler ever to come here". By the tenth match McCormick had achieved a century of no-balls, including 50 in his first 48 overs, and batsmen, with plenty of time to swing the bat under the back foot rule, scored off 49 of those 100 no-balls.

He took his ordeal in sporting spirit and even apologised to umpires for giving them so much work. "I'll be right after lunch," he told team-mates at one match, "the umpire's hoarse." Bradman got films to help McCormick solve his problem and team-mates set down caps and handkerchiefs to mark key spots in his run-up, but during the 18 matches in which he appeared on tour—half the team's itinerary—the dreaded "no-ball" call was invariably heard.

Three further wins by an innings followed, with Australia's batting and spin bowling too strong for Oxford University at Oxford from 4 to 6 May, Leicestershire at Leicester from 7 to 10 May, and Cambridge University at Cambridge from 11 to 13 May. Fingleton (124), McCabe (110) and Hassett (146) made centuries against Oxford University, Fleetwood-Smith taking 5 for 28 and 4 for 31. Badcock (198), Hassett (148) and Chipperfield (104) made centuries against Leicestershire, Ward taking 5 for 69 and 4 for 73. Fingleton (111), Bradman (137), Badcock (186) and Hassett (220 not out) hit centuries against Cambridge in a total of 5 for 708, while O'Reilly took 5 for 55, Ward 6 for 64 and Waite 5 for 23.

A superb innings of 278 by Bradman overshadowed everything in the match between Australia and the MCC at Lord's on 14 to 17 May. MCC followed on after scoring 214 in reply to Australia's 502 but rain prevented further play with MCC still 201 runs behind with nine wickets in hand. The gates had to be closed with 32,000 present on the first day.

At Northampton, from 18 to 20 May, Australia defeated Northants by an innings and 77 runs. Brown scored 194 not out in Australia's innings of 6 for 406 declared and Northants were dismissed for 194 and 135. Ward took 6 for 75 in Northants' first innings, McCabe 4 for 28 in the second.

Brown made 96, Bradman 143 and Hassett 98 against Surrey at The Oval from 21 to 24 May, when Australia reached 528 in the first innings. Splendid bowling by O'Reilly gave him 8 for 104 in Surrey's first innings of 271 but Bradman refused to enforce the follow-on, reasoning that some of his players badly needed rest. Bradman's decision caused a mild demonstration among the crowd and detracted from Ben Barnett's performance in scoring his maiden first-class century. Sent in to open with Badcock (95), Barnett hit 18 fours to score 120 not out, the opening stand

Australia's No. 1 'keeper on the 1938 tour, Victorian Ben Barnett.

producing 206. Bradman declared the second innings closed at 2 for 232 and the match was left drawn with Surrey on 1 for 104 (Fishlock 93).

The match against Hampshire at Southampton, from 25 to 27 May, was made memorable by Bradman completing 1000 runs in May for the second time on his three tours of England. O'Reilly took 6 for 65 to help dismiss Hampshire for 157 after rain prevented play on the first day. Brown was out for 47 when Australia batted and Bradman then joined Fingleton in a stand which yielded 242 runs in 210 minutes, Bradman finishing on 145 not out and Fingleton 123 not out.

The Australians faltered on a rain-sodden pitch against Middlesex at Lord's, between 28 and 31 May, and Jim Sims took 4 for 25 from 7.3 overs in Australia's innings of 132. McCormick was no-balled six times when Middlesex batted but in his best display of the tour took 6 for 58 to restrict Middlesex's lead to 56. Bradman was again heckled when he closed Australia's second innings at 2 for 114, the crowd believing he had terminated the match early. The boos changed to cheers when Edrich appeared with Compton to start Middlesex's second innings: Bradman had closed the innings to give Edrich a chance of scoring 1000 runs in May. Every run Edrich scored was now greeted with enthusiastic applause. Bradman was cheered just as noisily as Edrich when Edrich passed the 1000-run mark, the match ending in a draw with Middlesex 0 for 21.

The matches against Gloucestershire at Bristol, from 1 to 3 June, and Essex at Southend, on 4 and 6 June, were played without Bradman, who was acting on doctors' advice. He had injured his back and was told to rest it for a week before the first Test. Australia beat Gloucestershire by 10 wickets thanks to O'Reilly's 6 for 22 and 5 for 45. The tourists then defeated Essex by 97 runs. Ward's match

One of Bradman's fan letters that reached him safely during the 1938 tour.

figures were 11 for 77, Fleetwood-Smith's 7 for 45. Australia's batsmen were not impressive on the damp pitches but their spinners were unplayable.

The first Test at Nottingham, from 10 to 14 June, produced a sprinkling of records, as well as seven individual centuries. On a pitch that heavily favoured batsmen Hassett and Barnett made their debuts for Australia, Bill Edrich, Reg Sinfield, the Gloucestershire all-rounder, and Doug Wright, the Kent googly bowler, theirs for England. Hutton and Compton, who made their first Test appearances the year before against New Zealand, played against Australia for the first time. Hammond, who had played all his previous cricket against Australia as a professional, captained England throughout the series—and for 20 Tests in all—as an amateur, though nobody explained how such a status could be acquired once he had been paid to play.

The pitch was so perfect that even Fleetwood-Smith could not get a ball to turn until lunch on the second day and when he did so he gave a loud joyful hoot, and did a little dance. Charlie Barnett gave a thrilling display of stroke-making to reach 99 not out by lunch on the first day. As the boundaries flashed from Barnett's bat the Australians realised that he might steal a record of which they were proud, and thwarted him of that single run by some inspired fielding. Only Australians—Trumper, Macartney and Bradman—had scored Test centuries before lunch on the first day.

Barnett put on 219 for the first wicket with Hutton, beating the previous best opening stand against Australia in England by F. S. Jackson and Tom Hayward with 185 in 1899. Hutton made an even 100 before Fleetwood-Smith had him lbw. Barnett reached his century off the first ball after lunch and finished with 126 in 175 minutes. After Barnett left, O'Reilly raised Australian hopes by bowling Edrich and Hammond, but then Compton and Paynter became associated in a stand which produced 206 runs. Compton batted with remarkable assurance and Paynter mastered the spin bowling with quick foot-work. Paynter escaped being stumped at 88 when the ball lodged in wicket-keeper Ben Barnett's pads.

When Compton was out for 102, Ames helped Paynter put on a further 90, and then with Wright batting steadily after the fall of the eighth wicket, Paynter passed 200. Hammond declared England's innings closed at 8 for 658. As Paynter left the field for an unbeaten 216 the Australian players joined with the 30,000 spectators in applauding him all the way to the dressing-room. Paynter hit a six, a five, and 26 fours in 5 hours 20 minutes' batting. This was the first time that four batsmen scored centuries in the same innings of a Test, and Compton, at 20 years 19 days, was the youngest Englishman to make a century against Australia.

Australia started badly when Fingleton played a long hop from Wright—Wright's fourth ball in Tests—onto his stumps. Brad-

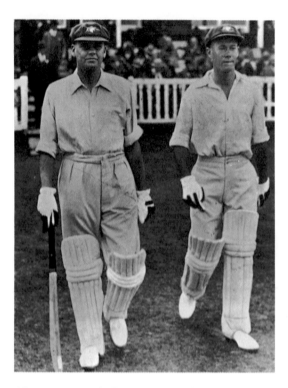

After a poor start in the first Test at Nottingham, Fingleton (left) and Brown became one of Australia's best opening pairs in 1938.

man and Brown batted quietly until at 111 Bradman hit a ball into his pads, from which it glanced up into the wicket-keeper's hands. Two appeals against the light were denied before Australia lost Brown. Ward, going in as nightwatchman, played out the last two overs despite a ring of close-in fieldsmen.

When the third day began, Australia were 3 for 138, with McCabe 19 not out. Three more wickets fell—including Hassett, who was caught when a leg break jumped from a worn patch—for Australia to be 6 for 194 before McCabe unleashed one of the most memorable displays of aggressive stroke play cricket has known. Assisted in turn by three left-handers—Barnett, O'Reilly and McCormick—he cleverly dominated the strike, driving with tremendous force, hooking with power and certainty.

McCabe reached his first hundred in 140 minutes and then fours came from his bat with a rush. Three overs from Wright produced 44 runs, and in an hour McCabe decimated the field and demoralised the English bowling. In the Australian dressing-room Bradman called to his players not to miss a ball of it as McCabe cut, glanced and drove, upright and lissom, his touch flawless.

Wisden recorded that in the last ten overs bowled to him McCabe took the strike in eight and hit 16 of his 34 fours. Partnered by Fleetwood-Smith, he scored 72 out of the 77 added for the last wicket in 28 minutes with almost all of the English fieldsmen close to the fence. Noted cricket author Neville Cardus called it one of the greatest innings ever seen anywhere in any period of the game's history, "moving cricket which swelled the heart". Bradman called it the greatest innings he ever saw or hoped to see. When it was over, with McCabe caught in the covers by Compton, attempting a big hit off Verity, McCabe had scored 232 out of the 300 added while he was at the crease. Bradman wrote in *Farewell To Cricket*:

> When McCabe returned to our dressing-room at the end of this epic performance, I was so moved by the majesty of his innings I could scarcely speak. However, I gripped his hand, wet with perspiration. He was trembling like a thoroughbred racehorse. I recall saying to him after expressing my congratulations, "I would give a great deal to be able to play an innings like that".

Despite McCabe's masterly batting, Australia's 411 was not enough to avoid the follow-on and Australia was compelled to defend grimly the whole of the last day on a pitch showing distinct signs of wear. The crowd wanted more of the pyrotechnics McCabe had given them and when Brown and Fingleton stonewalled they started to barrack them noisily.

Fingleton objected to this demonstration, took off his gloves and sat on the turf beside the pitch. This caused the crowd to hoot more loudly. Fingleton remained where he was until finally the spectators quietened enough for him to resume batting. There were raucous cheers when he was out for 40 with the score on 89.

Brown and Bradman then batted for most of the day, Brown going for 133 after five and a half hours at the crease. Bradman, troubled by leg strain, batted for six hours for 144 not out and hit only 6 fours, realising that victory was impossible and Australia had to play for a draw. Bradman took the English bowler Sinfield aside and asked him to stop finishing his run by planting his right foot in front of the stumps and worsening a worn patch. Further catcalls followed and Bradman stood clear of his wicket until the noise subsided. Australia were 6 for 427 when the match ended in a draw.

Australia defeated the Gentlemen of England by 282 runs at Lord's between 15 and 17 June, thanks to further brilliant batting and an outstanding effort from the spinners Ward and Fleetwood-Smith. Australia began with 397, Bradman scoring 104, McCabe a dazzling 79. Ward took 5 for 108 in the Gentlemen's first innings of 301. Then Fingleton (121) and Badcock (112 not out) scored centuries to allow Australia to declare at 4 for 335, a lead of 431. Fleetwood-Smith stopped a sustained attempt to hit him out of the attack and his 7 for 44 had the Gentlemen out for 149.

Right-arm fast-medium bowler William Phillipson, one-time star of Sir Julien Cahn's XI, was brought into the Lancashire side for the match against Australia at Old Trafford, between 18 and 21 June, and he gave the

tourists plenty to think about. Running the ball away to the slips Phillipson took 5 for 93 in Australia's first innings of 303, and only a sound 118 from Hassett prevented an Australian collapse. Phillipson then made a fine 52 in Lancashire's reply of 289.

With little hope of a result Bradman gave the last day crowd wonderful entertainment by scoring a century in 73 minutes. His first 50 took 38 minutes and he hit 15 fours, stroking the ball all round the wicket on a ground which had often been his downfall. Australia declared at 2 for 284, with Bradman 101 not out, and in the 70 minutes remaining Chipperfield twice hit the stumps with leg breaks. Lancashire finished on 3 for 80.

Chipperfield's effort won him a place in the second Test at Lord's instead of Ward. The match was played from 24 to 28 June. Hammond won the toss for England and after McCormick had dismissed Barnett, Hutton and Edrich for 31 runs, Hammond and Paynter took the score to 253 before Paynter was out for 99. Hammond continued in imperious style despite a painful blow on the elbow from a McCormick delivery that swung and lifted, and at stumps on the first day England were 5 for 409. One of Hammond's drives carried so much power it split Chipperfield's finger.

The next day Hammond and Ames took their sixth wicket stand to 186 with superlative batting in front of 33,800 spectators. The stands were so crowded the audience spread out onto the grass. Hammond went for 240, Ames for 83 and the English batsmen who followed hit out with little result. Despite the high English total of 494 Australia's fielding was always efficient. Hammond's 240 took

King George VI shaking hands with Arthur Chipperfield when he met the 1938 team at Lord's.

367 minutes and was the highest score by an English captain until Peter May made 285 not out in 1957 against the West Indies.

Bill Brown held Australia's innings together and in the process scored the one-hundredth century for Australia against England. Wright had Fingleton caught by Hammond, Bradman played on to Verity, and then Verity took a wonderful gully catch to dismiss McCabe from a shot struck right in the centre of the bat. Hassett helped Brown add 124 but with the shine gone from the ball Wellard dismissed Hassett and Badcock in one over. At stumps Australia were 5 for 299, Brown 140 not out.

On the third morning Verity disposed of Barnett and Chipperfield in eight deliveries and when O'Reilly went in at the fall of the seventh wicket Australia still needed 37 to avoid the follow-on. Swinging vigorously, O'Reilly was dropped by Paynter at long-on, a misjudgement that proved costly with Australia still 17 runs short of saving the follow-on. O'Reilly immediately pulled two successive deliveries from Verity for six and with 16 off the over forced England to bat again.

Meanwhile Brown continued to score steadily with well-timed hits to leg and stylish drives and cuts, supporting O'Reilly's onslaught so well that 85 runs were added in 42 minutes. Then Farnes was brought back into the attack and had O'Reilly and McCormick out with successive balls. Compton deprived Farnes of a hat-trick by dropping a slips catch from Fleetwood-Smith and after three hours had been lost because of rain Australia finished on 422, only 72 behind. Brown ended on 206 not out, one of a select group to bat right through an Australian innings.

McCormick made the ball lift alarmingly on the damp pitch and England slumped to 5 for 76, only 148 ahead, before Compton prevented any danger of defeat in partnerships

The great Hedley Verity is a study in concentration as he reaches his delivery stride. He died of war wounds three years later in Italy.

with Paynter and Wellard. Australia were left with only 170 minutes' batting to save the match. Bradman accomplished this with consummate ease, scoring his fourteenth century against England. His 102 not out included 15 fours and left Australia 111 short of victory with four wickets in hand.

After the Lord's Test Bradman called his team together to discuss a clause in their contracts that banned their wives from joining them during the tour. Bradman wanted his wife Jessie to join him *after* the last match, but the Board of Control refused his request. Bradman was so angry he drafted a letter of resignation from all Test cricket, but he was talked out of delivering it by the team doctor,

Rowley Pope. All Bradman would say was that he was very disappointed. The Board eventually relented under pressure of a joint cable from all the other players, both married and single.

Brown followed his double century at Lord's with another against Derbyshire at Chesterfield in the match played on 29 and 30 June. This helped Australia to a win by an innings and 234 runs. Waite and Ward showed their best bowling form of the tour in this game which also saw the return of Sid Barnes. Derbyshire made 151 and 56, Australia 4 for 441, with Brown 265 not out, Badcock 86 and Barnes 42. Ward took 5 for 45 and 3 for 8, Waite 3 for 50 and 5 for 40.

Rain rescued Australia from almost certain defeat by Yorkshire at Sheffield between 2 and 5 July. At lunch on the third day Yorkshire needed 67 to win, with seven wickets left, when showers ended hopes of their first win over Australia since 1902. Smailes, opening up with swingers and later bowling off breaks, took 6 for 92 and 4 for 45 for Yorkshire. Only Hassett (94) and Bradman (59 and 42 not out) offered sustained resistance in Australia's innings of 222 and 132. Yorkshire were restricted to 205 by Waite's 7 for 101, and were 3 for 83 when the weather intervened.

The third Test, scheduled for Old Trafford between 8 and 12 July, was abandoned because of rain without a ball being bowled. The captains did not toss and neither side announced their team. This gave the Australians a week's rest and they resumed the tour with overwhelming wins over Warwickshire and Nottinghamshire. They played Warwickshire at Birmingham on 13 and 14 July and won by an innings and 93 runs. The match with Nottinghamshire was at Nottingham from 16 to 19 July and they won by 412 runs. Brown made 101 and Bradman 135 against Warwickshire; Bradman 144 and Hassett 124 against Notts. The spinners took the majority of the wickets in both matches.

Australia seized the chance to retain the Ashes with brilliant play by Bradman and O'Reilly in the fourth Test from 22 to 25 July at Leeds. This was a match which provided thrills galore. After weeks of bowling on over-prepared pitches, O'Reilly and Fleetwood-Smith were given a soft pitch which took spin and made batting far from easy. England was hampered in the fight against some great spin bowling by the absence through injury of Hutton, Leyland and Ames and their selectors' failure to correctly read the pitch. They left out the spinner Tom Goddard on a pitch which was ideal for him, and relied instead on the pace of Bowes and Farnes.

England's innings began slowly and at

lunch they were 2 for 62. Barnett took 145 minutes for 30 and only Hammond batted freely, although Verity and Wright hit out at the end in a total of 223. O'Reilly struck his first major blow when he clean-bowled Hammond for 76 and he finished the innings with 5 for 66 in a marvellous piece of controlled spin bowling.

On the second day Bradman batted in gloomy light on the moist pitch to put his team ahead with yet another century. His 103 included nine boundaries and took three hours. Australia led by 19 but before stumps Barnett and Edrich put England ahead with a stand of 49.

With six men on the leg side close to the bat, and nobody in the outfield, O'Reilly demoralised all the English batsmen. He was always at his best when he was angry and he was enraged when he was no-balled when bowling to Hardstaff with England 1 for 73. Next ball he bounded up to the crease and

Wally Hammond leading England out in 1938, followed by Ken Farnes (left), Les Ames (right) and Hedley Verity.

produced a vicious fast leg break that removed Hardstaff's bails. Hammond came in and with the very next delivery O'Reilly had him caught at short leg by Brown. These two deliveries all but clinched the Ashes for Australia. From 5 for 95, England collapsed to be all out for 123. O'Reilly took 5 for 56 to give him 10 for 122 in the match. Fleetwood-Smith took 4 for 34 to finish with match figures of 7 for 107.

Set to score 105 to win, Australia began to bat with rain clouds covering the ground. Bradman told his batsmen to force the pace and not to appeal against the light, and when the fourth wicket fell for 61 play became so exciting that for the first time in his life Bradman could not bear to watch. Manager Jeanes also could not stand the strain and went for a walk outside the ground.

Hassett attacked with some glorious lofted drives as the weather closed in. In the Australian dressing-room O'Reilly walked up and down with his pads on hoping he would not be needed. On the other side of the team's massage table Bradman walked up and down eating bread and jam to prevent his teeth chattering, while team members provided a running commentary. Missed at slip off the second ball he received, Hassett skied the ball to point to be fifth man out at 91 for a brave 33. With nine runs needed, rain interrupted play, but Barnett and Badcock guided Australia to a five-wicket win before rain swamped the ground. Wright had looked so dangerous he might have won the match had Australia needed 50 runs more.

The mystery of why Badcock could not score runs in Tests deepened when he scored a dazzling 110 against Somerset at Taunton between 27 and 29 July. Somerset were out for 110 to some fine spin bowling before Bradman and Badcock made a thrilling stand. Bradman's 202, his thirteenth century of the tour, included 32 fours. Fleetwood-Smith

took 5 for 30 in Somerset's second knock of 136, Australia winning by an innings and 218 runs. Only five hours play was possible in the match between Australia and Glamorgan at Swansea scheduled for 30 July to 2 August, because of rain. Three two-day matches followed in Scotland and Sunderland before Australia played a draw against Surrey in a rain-affected match at The Oval between 10 and 12 August.

Sid Barnes had been steadily playing himself into form and he followed his 63 against Surrey with a brilliant 94 against Kent at Canterbury between 13 and 16 August. Australia scored 479, Kent 108 and 377, Australia scoring the seven runs needed to secure a ten-wicket win without loss. Waite confirmed his Test place with 4 for 43 and 5 for 85.

For the fifth Test at The Oval between 20 and 24 August England stacked their team with batsmen, playing with only Farnes, Bowes and Verity as front-line bowlers. Australia had to leave out McCormick who had been suffering from neuritis in the shoulder, and Barnes made his Test debut. The Australians were amazed when the English selectors dropped Barnett, whom they considered second only to Hammond among England's batsmen. Edrich was promoted to open with Hutton and Leyland brought in as the fifth Yorkshireman in the team.

Australia gambled on winning the toss and were in trouble because of the lack of bowlers in their side from the moment Hammond won his fourth successive toss. When Hutton and Edrich took strike, they had no-one more hostile than Waite and McCabe to face. O'Reilly took the first wicket at 29 when he had Edrich for 12 but the next wicket did not fall until England had scored 411. Hutton gave an astonishing display of concentration and stamina in batting for two and a half days but he should never have got past 40 runs. At that point he jumped out to hit an off break from Fleetwood-Smith, missed, and while Hutton was well out of his ground wicket-keeper Ben Barnett failed to gather. Hutton went on to score steadily, batting from the crease with deflections, cuts and drives, on a pitch that was over-prepared. He was so laborious that when he drove a ball past O'Reilly at the bowler's end, Bill said: "Congratulations—I didn't know you had the strength." Leyland was more adventurous, dancing out to the spinners.

With the spinners unable to turn the ball it was a brilliant piece of fielding which ended the stand after they had added 382, the highest for any wicket by England against Australia. Hassett fumbled a drive from Hutton but managed to pick up the ball and throw a fast return to the bowler's end. Bradman sprinted from mid-on to intercept the throw and break the stumps before Leyland completed his second run. Leyland's 187, the highest of his seven three-figure scores against Australia, took nearly six hours and included 17 fours.

Hammond watched as Hutton sped past his England home Test record score of 240 and went on to surpass all individual achievements in Test cricket. Bradman was the first to congratulate Hutton when he passed his England *v*. Australia record of 334. He had brought several fieldsmen in close as Hutton neared the record and made him fight for every run. Hutton showed the strain when he completely missed the ball on 331, but he went past Bradman's record with a perfect cut off Fleetwood-Smith. Every Australian, as well as his partner, Hardstaff, congratulated Hutton as 30,000 people rose to applaud him. He had taken twice as long as Bradman had eight years earlier since time did not matter in this Test.

At 364 Hutton lifted a stroke towards cover and Hassett held the catch easily low down. Hutton's innings, until then the long-

Len Hutton back cuts a ball from McCabe during his record innings of 364 at The Oval in 1938. Australia sustained her biggest defeat ever.

est ever played in first-class cricket, had lasted 797 minutes (13 hours 17 minutes)—from half past eleven on Saturday morning until half past two on Tuesday afternoon, with the Sunday a rest day. Hutton, then aged 22, hit 35 fours, 15 threes, 18 twos and 143 singles. His dismissal brought a change in tempo but no change in England's desire to build a huge total, with Arthur Wood hitting out boldly for 53 in another three-figure stand with Hardstaff.

Shortly after Wood was caught and bowled by Barnes, Bradman took a turn at bowling to rest his weary bowlers, caught his foot in a hole, and fractured the same ankle that had sent him to hospital years before in Rockhampton. He was carried off on the shoulders of team-mates. Bradman's accident influenced Hammond to declare at 7 for 903 at

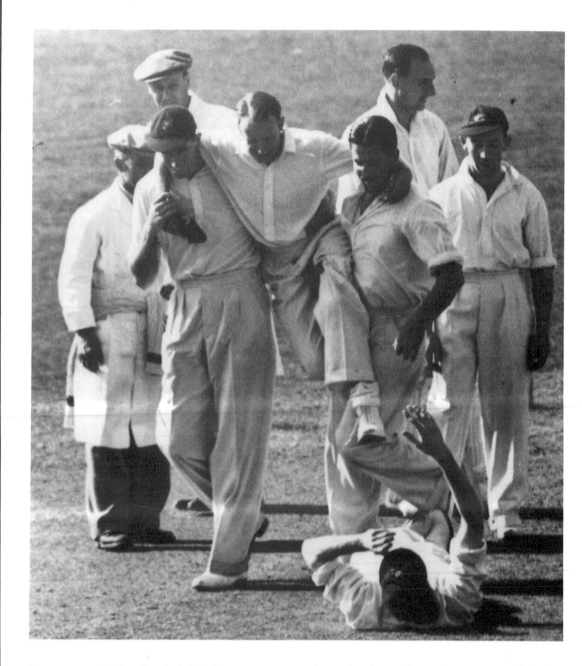

Team-mates carry Bradman from the field after he fractured his ankle while bowling in the fifth Test.

tea on the third day. O'Reilly had worn the skin from his finger trying to spin the ball, Fingleton was incapable of continuing because of a strained muscle, and X-rays revealed that Bradman had fractured a small bone in his ankle. Among all the records that fell in this innings Fleetwood-Smith achieved one no bowler would enjoy by conceding more runs than any bowler in Test history, finishing with 1 for 298. Years later he explained how it felt: "You woke in the night and your arm was still going round."

In the dressing-room O'Reilly raged about the doping and over-preparation of Test pitches: "Where's the groundsman's hut? If I had a rifle I'd shoot him now." His 85 overs had yielded 3 for 178 and had included 26 maidens. The Australians were instructed before they began batting that they must not ask their bowlers to bowl again, with only a skeleton team left to get through the remaining six matches of the tour. They lost their first wicket without scoring a run, and despite some splendid stroke play by Hassett and Barnes were all out for 201. Brown just missed batting right through Australia's innings for the second time in the rubber when he was last man out.

There was a minor sensation when Brown cut a ball for a single and Hutton kicked the ball to the boundary, trying to give the strike to a less capable batsman, Fleetwood-Smith. The umpire awarded Brown five for the stroke and let him retain the strike. Only a stand of 74 between Barnes and Barnett delayed England's move to victory in Australia's second innings of 123. Two batsmen short in both innings, Australia had been beaten by an innings and 579 runs, the biggest margin in Test history. Board of Control chairman Dr Robertson had been made to look extremely foolish.

The Australians completed their tour with a draw against Sussex at Hove from 27 to 30 August; a 10-wicket win over an England XI on 31 August and 1 September at Blackpool (where O'Reilly had match figures of 9 for 74, Ward 10 for 64); a draw against an England XI at Folkestone from 3 to 6 September; a 10-wicket defeat by H. D. G. Leveson-Gower's XI at Scarborough from 10 to 13 September; and two comfortable wins over the Gentlemen of Ireland in Belfast and Dublin. Barnes had scores of 91 and 90 in these matches to end

what had been an unlucky tour.

The nineteenth Australian team to England won 20 of their 36 matches, drew 13, lost 2 and had one abandoned. They scored 35 individual centuries, Bradman heading the list with 13, and had 12 scored against them. Bradman also made most runs on the tour, 2429 in all first-class matches at 115.66, and five other batsmen scored more than 1,000 runs. Brown made 1854 at 57.93, Hassett 1589 at 54.79, Badcock 1604 at 45.82, Fingleton 1141 at 38.03 and McCabe 1124 at 36.25. Bradman also headed the Test batting averages with 434 runs at 108.50. Badcock made only 32 runs in eight Test knocks.

O'Reilly was the only bowler to exceed one hundred wickets on tour, his 104 first-class victims costing 16.59 each. He also topped the Test bowling averages with 22 wickets at 27.72. Ward took 92 tour wickets at 19.27 but he went wicketless in his only Test. Fleetwood-Smith was the third most successful bowler, with 88 victims at 19.53 apiece, but his 14 Test wickets were very costly at 51.92 each.

The team fielded brilliantly throughout, although Barnett was well below Oldfield's standard behind the stumps. The failure of McCormick to reproduce his best Australian form underlined the lack of a second virile opening bowler such as Lush. Each player in the Australian team was paid £600 for the eight-month tour, compared with the £30 for Test matches and £1-a-day for Shield games they received for domestic cricket.

As the Australians left London air-raid trenches were being dug and several team members ignored the advice of their travel agents to travel across Europe. Most of them returned to Australia in time to appear in the match at Melbourne to celebrate the Melbourne Cricket Club's centenary. Played between 9 and 13 December 1938, the sides captained by Bradman and Keith Rigg, the match ended in a draw. Bradman showed he had completely recovered from his injury by scoring 118, sharing in a stand of 163 with McCabe, who made 105. O'Reilly was the most successful bowler with 5 for 75 in Rigg's XI's first innings.

Bradman continued in great form until he had equalled C. B. Fry's world record of scoring six successive first-class centuries, set in 1901. Following the 118 in the Melbourne Club's Centenary match, he made 143 for South Australia *v.* New South Wales at Adelaide on 16 December, 225 for South Australia *v.* Queensland at Adelaide on 24 and 26 December, 107 for South Australia *v.* Victoria at Melbourne on 31 December, 186 for South Australia *v.* Queensland at Brisbane on 9 and 10 January, and 135 not out for South Australia in a rain-affected match *v.* New South Wales at Sydney between 14 and 18 January. He gave only one chance in those six successive innings—when he was six in his 107. He was out for five in his next innings for South Australia *v.* Victoria in Adelaide when he attempted to surpass Fry's record. South African Mike Procter joined Fry and Bradman with centuries in six successive innings for Rhodesia in 1970–71.

Bradman's 107 at Melbourne against Victoria was his 22nd first-class century for the year and easily beat the previous record of 19 centuries in a calendar year by Herbert Sutcliffe in 1932. Bradman's average for the 12 months of 1938 was 112.88. Denis Compton equalled the 22 centuries in a calendar year record in 1947.

On the day Bradman completed his sixth successive century, the Melbourne Cricket Club committee deliberated for almost four hours on an issue that affected Bradman's future. He had been one of 150 applicants for the job as secretary of the Melbourne club, following the death in August that year of Hugh Trumble. Bradman, then 30 years old, had been assured when he returned from the English tour that he only had to apply to get the £1000-a-year post, which would have ended his work in stock broking, forced a move from Adelaide to Melbourne, and almost certainly prevented him from making any further overseas tours. The leading candidates went to ballot at the Melbourne club's committee meeting and when votes were counted Bradman and the former Victorian Test left-hander Vernon Ransford finished level on top. On the casting vote of the chairman, Ransford—a Melbourne resident and Melbourne club committeeman for 25 years—got the job, which he held until 1958. It was one of the few times Bradman's plans had been thwarted but a blessing for Australian cricket.

South Australia won the Sheffield Shield for the 1938–39 season by one point from Victoria. In the six state matches Bradman scored 801 runs at an average of 160.20. Badcock scored 489 runs at 97.80, including innings of 271 not out and 100, completely confounding critics of his English form. At Perth, Victorian-born Alec Barras made 113 against his home state in an innings of such vigour it was still talked about 40 years later.

Victoria's Lindsay Hassett enhanced the reputation he had earned in England by scoring 830 runs at an average of 92.22 and hitting four centuries. Victoria produced one of the discoveries of the season in Robert Barrington ("Barry") Scott, who made headlines with displays of 7 for 33 and 5 for 46 against New South Wales in Sydney.

The dominating performances of both the 1938–39 and 1939–40 seasons in Australia came in the bowling of Clarrie Grimmett, whose successor Frank Ward had been dropped after bowling 30 overs for 142 runs without taking a wicket in his one Test on the 1938 England tour. Grimmett took a record 72 wickets in 1938–39, including 11 for 175

One of the enigmas of the 1938 English tour, Cyril Badcock. He made huge scores in minor matches but could not reproduce them in Tests.

against New South Wales and 10 for 195 for The Rest *v.* Australia. In 1939–40, his figures included 9 for 244 in the first match against New South Wales and 11 for 229 in the second. He also took 10 for 195 against Victoria. Bowling as always in his cap, he kept going in first-class cricket until 1941, and in 1987 his 668 wicket total for South Australia was almost 350 wickets more than any other bowler.

Outstanding batting in those two summers before the Second World War came from Billy Brown, who in 1938–39 made 95 and 168 for Queensland *v.* New South Wales and scored 87 and 137 against the same opponents the following year; from Bradman, who made 251 not out and 99 not out, followed by 42 and 209 not out in the two 1939–40 matches for South Australia *v.* New South Wales; from Badcock, who made 236 for South Australia *v.* Queensland in 1939–40; and from Hassett, who played two superlative knocks of 122 each for Victoria against New South Wales in Sydney, when he repeatedly jumped down the pitch to lift O'Reilly straight back over his head for four. After one such stroke O'Reilly bellowed: "You little bastard—you wouldn't know the difference between a wrong-'un and a leg break." Hassett replied: "With you, Bill, I don't have to."

NSWCA secretary Harold Heydon found himself in court after an SCG match in 1939–40. Police reported to him that two turnstile operators were permitting people in a side gate and pocketing the entrance money. Heydon had the two men arrested. One was convicted in court, the other acquitted. The freed man, whose name was Miles, won £500 damages for false imprisonment in a court action against Heydon and later the NSWCA paid him a further £650.

Tallon demonstrated the folly of his exclusion from the tour of England by equal-

Bill Brown, who provided some outstanding batting in the two seasons before World War II. Here he back cuts during his wonderful double century at Lord's in 1938.

each innings (nine caught, three stumped). His other record was the dismissal of seven batsmen in Queensland's match against Victoria in Brisbane, while against South Australia from 7 to 11 January, he scored 115. O'Reilly, Fingleton, Chipperfield and Mc-Cabe rested, leaving New South Wales to finish last in their worst Shield season since the 1914–18 war.

Alan Kippax and Bert Oldfield were to have shared a testimonial match in the 1939–40 season between teams led by Bradman and McCabe, but war broke out just as the season began and it was agreed that the testimonial should be postponed until after the war. After Prime Minister Robert Menzies announced the outbreak of war on 3 September 1939, the states agreed, on government advice, to complete the Sheffield Shield competition, with most of the players involved on leave from the services.

New South Wales regained the Shield in 1939–40 when O'Reilly returned refreshed after a long rest to bowl superbly, taking 52 Shield wickets at 13.50 and dominating the Sydney grade competition with 86 wickets at only 7.74 each. He had agreed to help his friend Stan McCabe when McCabe opened a sports store in the NSWCA's new building at 254 George Street, Sydney. The Association offered McCabe the premises for £5 a week, but McCabe said he could not afford even that amount so they cut it to £2 10s for the first two months. The market rate in 1940 was £10.

The construction of Cricket House enabled the NSWCA to push ahead with the formation of a Cricketers' Club inside the building. Solicitor Syd Webb, a NSWCA committeeman, drew up the articles for the club in August 1938, and it was opened as a registered company on 11 September 1939. It began in business on 1 July 1940, and by 1942 was doing well enough to lend the NSWCA

ling two world records. At Sydney in the match against New South Wales, from 31 December to 4 January, he disposed of 12 batsmen, a feat only once before achieved—by Pooley, of Surrey, in 1868 against Sussex at The Oval. Tallon sent back six batsmen in

£1000 to help it through the war years.

Apart from the Shield competition all the state control bodies supported patriotic matches aimed at raising funds for the services. In one of these in Melbourne the young airman Keith Miller, who had made his debut for Victoria in 1937–38 from the South Melbourne club, filled in as an opening bowler when McCabe and Sievers dropped out. He made one delivery lift sharply from a full length, and Ken Ridings, one of South Australia's rising stars, edged it into the slips to give Miller his first wicket in big cricket. Miller had scored a century the previous season against South Australia in Adelaide, where Clarrie Grimmett first aroused his interest in bowling, reasoning that it was a far more satisfying occupation than batting.

Miller in fact was a frustrated would-be jockey, who in a family of four children was the only one who grew too big to become an apprentice. He went off to the war under the Empire Air Training Scheme for the RAAF. Bradman also enlisted in the RAAF after a summer in which he scored 1062 runs for eight times out, including a knock of 267 against Victoria. Bradman's age was close to the air crew limit so the army sought his help on special work in order that he could become involved without the prolonged training necessary for flying. After three spells of fibrositis, the army medical board invalided him out as rest was the only cure. He went back to Bowral again in excruciating pain, incapable of lifting his right arm so that his wife had to shave his face each day for him.

Ross Gregory, Lindsay Hassett, Ben Barnett, Ian Johnson, Frank Sides and Barry Scott joined up from Victoria; Arthur Morris, Cec Pepper, Stan Sismey, Colin McCool, Bob Cristofani, Ken Gulliver, Stan McCabe, Albert Cheetham, Bill Hird, Keith Carmody, Jim Minter, Ray Lindwall, Charles Price and Jack Pettiford from New South Wales; Ross

Ross Gregory, whose batting against England in 1936–37 delighted Neville Cardus, was killed in action with the RAAF in World War II.

Stanford, Dick Whitington, Ken Ridings, Charlie Walker, Graham Williams, Jim Workman, Roger Kimpton and Merv Waite from South Australia; Glen Baker, Frank Sides and Bill Brown from Queensland. When Bill Ponsford was being examined by the services doctors they found he was colour blind, a fault they found hard to reconcile with his cricket success.

"Well," said Ponsford, "I never worried about what colour the ball was— only how big it was."

The Melbourne Cricket Ground was taken over by US forces and later by the RAAF, and most of Australia's major grounds were at one time or another used to billet service units. Sid Barnes was exempted from war service as he and golfer Norman von Nida produced chemicals vital to the war effort. Barnes managed to score several centuries in charity matches during the war years.

Charlie Walker, killed at Sultau in Russia while on active service with the RAAF, and Ross Gregory, killed at Ghafargon in Assam while on an RAAF raid, were the only Australian Test cricketers to die in the Second World War but at least 12 other first-class players, some of them close to Test selection, were lost. They included Ken Ridings, one of the noted South Australian family whom some tipped as a future Test captain, Queenslanders Glen ("George") Baker and Frank Sides, Victorians Stuart King and Frank Thorn, South Australians Gilbert Jose and Edward Moyle, Western Australians Dudley Everett, Alan Jeffreys, William Roach and Barney Wood, and the brilliant St Kilda Victoria Cross winner Bill Newton who, after 90 bombing raids, was beheaded by the Japanese.

Another fatality was leading north coast cricketer, John Brewer, who was struck by lightning on the Saturday before Christmas, 1941, while fielding at first slip on the aerodrome pitch at South Casino. A ball had just been delivered when a thunderclap hit the ground. When the players recovered from the shock, they found Brewer lying on his back, his trousers torn to shreds from the knees down, his sandshoes full of large holes. A two shilling piece in his tobacco tin had melted. Doctors said he was dead before he hit the ground.

The years between the First and Second World Wars had seen Australian cricket build up support unprecedented in any other sport, with most of the money it attracted going back into the development of the game. Most of the crowd records set in the period can never be surpassed because ground capacities

Another fatality was Australian wicket-keeper Charlie Walker, killed in action over Europe during war service with the RAAF.

have been reduced. In the years before floodlights, Sydney had a record one day crowd of 58,446 (1928), Adelaide 50,962 (1933), Brisbane 30,598 (1936) and Melbourne a match total of 350,534 for the third Test against England in 1937. Crowds for a day's play in Shield games went past 30,000 six times and for the 1923–24 New South Wales *v.* Victoria match in Melbourne totalled 89,386, remarkable figures considering Australia's population in 1930 was 6.5 million.

Many great players had been produced, many memorable matches had been played, but amid all the controversies, thrilling moments and high drama, Australian cricket had had the good fortune to unearth one person who had dominated it, Don Bradman. His achievements and those of his less publicised colleagues in the Australian team, inspired thousands of Australian schoolboys to emulate them and cricket rose to a high standard in the 1930s in Great Public Schools competitions, in high schools, and in district club premierships. Despite the huge defeat at The Oval in the last Test before the Second World War, Australia's cricket future, interwoven as it was with a burgeoning British Empire, looked rosy. An encouraging sprinkling of the boys in the nation's playgrounds were practising their spin bowling, as well as their Bradman-like strokes.

The Victory Tests

The Australian Services XI
1945–46

Before they could draw their expenses members of the Australian Services XI sometimes had to render two choruses of "Bye Bye Blackbird" for team-mates. On tour in England in 1938 Stan McCabe and Bill O'Reilly woke in the middle of the night in Derbyshire to find a muddied goat breathing heavily around their beds. In a Park Lane hotel when a waiter dropped a Peach Melba down an Australian cricketer's jacket he apologised and took the jacket away to have it cleaned. The cricketer noticed a further stain on his trousers, took them off and handed them to the waiter, continuing his meal in shirt, tie and underpants.

The man at the centre of all these incidents and dozens more pranks around the cricket world was Arthur Lindsay Hassett, who did more than anybody else to revive Australian cricket after the Second World War ended. Hassett was a wonderful mixture of showman, witty after-dinner speaker, subtle cricket strategist, team jester, class batsman,

The Australian team that toured New Zealand in 1946 under the captaincy of Bill Brown (centre front). At the end of this tour Bill O'Reilly (fourth from left, standing) retired, throwing his boots through the dressing-room window.

Donald Bradman in his army uniform. He was invalided out of the service after working as a physical training instructor.

and guardian of the game's highest standards of sportsmanship. To Hassett, cricket was fun to play even at the highest level and he extracted every possible laugh from it without ever over-stepping the mark and becoming ill-mannered or oafish. He had a rare ability to conceal impish thoughts behind a poker face and although he could be brutal in deflating the pompous or pretentious he committed some heart-warming acts of chivalry. Australian cricket never had a better ambassador.

Hassett joined the Australian Imperial Forces (AIF) at 26 and in 1941 went to Egypt and Palestine as a gunner in the 2/2 Anti-Aircraft Regiment. He captained an AIF cricket team against a Palestine Police side captained by a Major Swaine, who insisted

that munitions trucks taking supplies to the front make a long detour so that their noise would not upset his batsmen's concentration. Then he led the AIF XI to victory by six wickets over a strong British Forces XI at Alexandria, scoring 101 not out in 88 minutes and making the winning hit.

The AIF team included four Test players —Hassett; Lieutenant E. C. S. White, who toured England with Bradman's 1938 team; Gunner Alex Hurwood, who went to England with Woodfull's 1930 side; and Private Ray Robinson, who batted against England in 1936 in Australia. Other well-known players in the team included Sergeant R. S. Whitington and Warrant Officer Jack Rymill (South Australia), Lieutenant Horace Hunt (Victoria) and Captain Albert Cheetham (New South Wales). The Alexandria team included three South African Test players, Bob Catterall, H. E. Dalton, and W. W. Wade.

Kenneth Slessor, official war correspondent with the AIF, described how the Australians took the field in spotless whites, with dark green caps and blazers embroidered with golden rising suns. The Alexandria side played mostly in khaki, with Springbok Wade in a white topee. War casualties and nurses studded the capacity crowd. "There was some good humoured barracking to bring back memories of The Hill," wrote Slessor, "but it was all done by Australians at the expense of Australians. The crowd centred most of its interest on Hassett, who was out for seven in the first innings but made up for it with his sparkling century in the second."

Hassett made another century for the AIF against a strong New Zealand Base XI at Maadi Sporting Club and at Cairo helped the AIF finish its Egyptian program unbeaten, by scoring 39 against a Gezira Sporting Club team that included England bowlers Freddy Brown and Bill Bowes. Hassett finished with an average of 89.60 for the three matches and Ted White headed the AIF bowling with 20

*The Australian Services XI during one of the
Victory "Tests" in England, with captain Lindsay
Hassett in the centre of the front row.*

wickets at 11.40.

The success of the AIF team under Hassett delighted the Australian Commander-in-Chief in the Middle East, Field-Marshal Sir Thomas Blamey, who had over-ruled one of his senior commanders, General Sir Leslie Morshead of the Ninth Division, to secure Cheetham's release from the siege of Tobruk to play for the AIF. When Staff Headquarters in Cairo directed Morshead to send Cheetham to the cricket Morshead replied: "Don't you know there's a war on?" Blamey himself answered this message, informing Morshead that he certainly knew about the war but that he still wanted Cheetham released.

While Hassett's players kept cricket alive among the pyramids and palm trees, Royal Australian Air Force teams did a similar job while on leave from their flying duties in Britain. Watching Squadron-Leader Keith Carmody and Flight-Sergeant Keith Miller bat for the RAAF against British Services sides at Lord's, Sir Pelham Warner determined as early as 1943 that there should be a "Test" series involving these brilliant cricketers. Warner knew what a big mistake the MCC had made in not playing "Tests" against Herbie Collins' Australian Services XI immediately after the First World War and did not want it repeated.

Warner's plans for a Victory "Test" series

began to take shape in 1944 when Australian Prime Minister John Curtin and Field-Marshal Blamey visited London. Hearing they were in town, Warner invited them to Lord's to watch a match between the RAAF and a British Services XI captained by Wally Hammond. During the play he stressed how the zest and exuberance of Miller, Carmody and the other RAAF cricketers had captivated English fans. Hammond, Len Hutton, Bill Edrich and Denis Compton would all be available to play against the Australians immediately peace came, said Sir Pelham. Curtin replied: "You Englishmen will always be able to find enough Australians to defend those twenty-two yards of yours out there. Lord's and its traditions belongs just as much to Australia as it does to England."

Warner had heard all about the splendid cricket played by Hassett's team in the Middle East and when he asked where these players were, Blamey said: "Dotted all over the Pacific. We do have a war on out there, you know." But by then the implications of Warner's enquiries were becoming apparent to Blamey, who saw at once that he had to prevent the RAAF dominating victory celebrations on the cricket field. "I dare say we could find some of them for you, however. Only a few million Japanese to stop us."

Blamey left Warner with the promise that he would handle the Japanese without the help of Gunner Hassett, and for such an artful C-in-C the problem of moving cricketers about without incurring the ire of the supreme commander, General Douglas Macarthur, was child's play. Blamey simply seconded them to a unit called the AIF Reception Group, which was given the role of helping to welcome back 6000 prisoners-of-war and organising victory celebrations in Europe.

Gunner Hassett, Captain Albert Cheetham, Sergeant Cecil Pepper and several other promising cricketers all found themselves on board the S. S. *Bloemfontein* when it sailed from Sydney for San Francisco in June 1944, but unfortunately without Arthur Morris, Colin McCool and Ray Lindwall, outstanding players serving in New Guinea. Their first task was a ticker-tape parade down Broadway to thank Americans for their war support. They were also given the job of parachuting into European prisoner-of-war camps to look after the interests of Australian prisoners, but from the time they landed at their headquarters at the Cumberland Hotel, Eastbourne, on England's south coast, the over-riding motive for the unit's formation became apparent: they were to make sure the army was not outdone by the air force in the Victory "Tests".

Carmody had won the admiration of all the RAAF players by the manner in which he conducted their matches. From his beginnings in Bradman's F. J. Palmer classes for promising boys, he had matured into a thoughtful, innovative cricketer whose captaincy matched his daring batting. He was never afraid to loft the ball over the heads of close-in fieldsmen, a trait uncommon in opening batsmen, and in the field he packed the slips in what later became known as the "Carmody field", pressuring batsmen into the belief that their nicks would certainly be caught.

Hassett arrived not long after Carmody was shot down, early in 1945, while attacking four German ships off the Hook of Holland. Carmody was plucked from the water by a German boat and taken to a series of camps for interrogation, before being force-marched 250 kilometres to a concentration camp near Berlin. The RAAF wicket-keeper Stan Sismey had been shot down in the Mediterranean in 1942 and fished from the water full of shrapnel after eight hours in a dinghy. Keith Miller turned up to play for an RAAF XI at Lord's in 1944 only to find the captain Ken Ridings had been shot down and killed during the night on a Sunderland patrol over the Bay of Biscay.

Carmody was freed by the Russians when they entered Berlin but then held for weeks by

Norman Yardley (left) and Hedley Verity photographed during the early part of World War II. Yardley survived the war to captain both Yorkshire and England.

them before he escaped, crossed the Elbe, and joined the Americans. He arrived back in England just as the Australian Services XI was being formed, a hero to his RAAF mates, who felt that as they had done the groundwork through the war an airman should captain the Services side.

Blamey's staff officers had anticipated that such a clash might arise but they had failed in their efforts to persuade Hassett to take a higher rank. He had advanced from gunner to lance-bombardier to sergeant because of his prowess as a soldier and the best he would accept was Warrant Officer II, which his duties with his new unit justified. He refused a commission based on his skills as a cricketer. Field-Marshal Blamey, the GOC of the Australian Army Staff in London, Lieut-General Ken Smart, and Hassett's amiable unit commander Brigadier Eugene Gorman all tried to change Hassett's mind, but he refused.

At a time when Bradman was not expected to resume playing first-class cricket, Has-sett must have seen that a successful stint as Services' captain would have given him an easy ride to the Australian captaincy, but he declined to accept Blamey's offer of a captaincy or a lieutenant's pips. The RAAF hierarchy, including their senior liaison officer to the War Office, Squadron Leader Rex Rentoul, were annoyed when Hassett was appointed team captain for the entire Victory "Test" series in May 1945. They considered Hassett should have been given the job for one "Test" only and the issue put to a team vote for the second Victory "Test" when Carmody would be available.

Hassett's nerve remained steady in the face of this inter-Services friction. He prepared for the forthcoming Victory "Tests" by taking teams of servicemen to villages for one-day games. The teams included John McMahon, a left-arm bowler from Balaklava, South Australia, who served with the AIF in the Middle East before transferring to the RAAF; Sergeant Cec Pepper, big-hitting spin bowler from Forbes, New South Wales, who in November 1939 smashed 7 sixes and 8 fours in an innings of 81 for New South Wales against Queensland and later made a century in 23 minutes for a High Wycombe camp side; Graham Williams, who had played 17 times for South Australia and had just returned from teaching blind POWs Braille; Sergeant Charlie Price, a Sydney grade player; Dick Whitington, the Adelaide lawyer who had played 32 matches for South Australia; and Captain Albert Cheetham, who had 18 matches for New South Wales behind him. McMahon later wrote in *Wisden Cricket Monthly*:

> *At the end of the day Hassett took his players into pubs like Codgers off Fleet Street, the Nag's Head or the Cheshire Cheese, grouped them around a keg, and explained they would not get their travelling allowance until they sang for it.*

McMahon described Hassett, small frame balanced on top of a keg, conducting each player through his chorus of "Down Came A Blackbird", "Champagne Charlie", or the "Desert Song". Some of the verses had to be hummed, others carried off in silence as Hassett followed his imaginary score. The show-stopper was Hassett's own rendition of "There's A Bridle Hanging On The Wall", which ended with Hassett wiping huge tears from his eyes while gazing sadly at a handkerchief strung up on a pot or clock to represent the bridle.

Hassett's steadfastness and refusal to accept officer rank impressed the RAAF cricketers but they remained loyal to their usual captain, Carmody. "There were RAAF members of the Services side who resented Hassett's appointment," Keith Miller said. "But we all realised Hassett had not sought the captaincy and accepted him. We were all servicemen, and just happy to be alive."

The Australians faced formidable odds in the Victory "Test", fielding a side comprising six state players and four who had not got beyond grade cricket. Hassett was their sole international. Their opposition included some of the greatest cricketers to have appeared for England, led by master batsman Wally Hammond, who had Len Hutton, Les Ames, Bill Edrich and Walter Robins as the likely stars of a line-up made up entirely of seasoned county players.

They began the post-war revival of international cricket on 19 May 1945, at Lord's, and after Hutton had been dismissed for one, England recovered. Hammond (29), Washbrook (28), Jack Robertson (53), Les Ames (57), and Edrich (45), took the England score along steadily. With only four wickets down and the score on 200, England seemed set for a big total when Hassett called on Miller, the fifth bowler used. Miller immediately bowled Edrich, a breakthrough on which the Australians capitalised and had England out for 267.

Squadron-leader Stan Sismey, who captained the RAAF side for several matches against England, about to toss with Wally Hammond during a wartime match at Lord's.

On the second day Hassett's lack of practice at the highest level was painfully apparent as Australia struggled to 3 for 136. Miller joined his captain, with Doug Wright and Robins bowling their guileful spinners, aware that he had always had trouble until that time against top-class spin. They took the score to 171 before Hassett was bowled by J. W. A. Stephenson. Ross Stanford, a South Australian club cricketer, came in for his initial first-class innings and when he left for a

courageous 49, the Australians had moved to 5 for 270 and a first innings lead. Miller's driving through the covers and back cuts past point enabled him to go on to 105, at this, his first appearance at Lord's and with the assistance of Cec Pepper to take Australia to 6 for 357, 90 runs ahead. In the pavilion, Charles Fry, Harry Altham and other English experts realised a brilliant new Australian cricketer had arrived.

Graham Williams, whose average for South Australia was 17, then contributed a breezy 53 to go with 40 from Pepper and 35 from Charlie Price, to take the Australians to 455. England's team looked so superior on paper that commentators could scarcely believe it. Trailing by 188 runs on the first

innings, England managed 294 in their second innings, which left the Australians 107 runs to score in less than 70 minutes for victory. Hutton (21), and Hammond (33), again disappointed, but wicket-keeper Stan Sismey had seven victims in the two England innings.

Hassett promoted himself to No. 2 in the batting order and Miller to No. 3, but Miller was run out for a single to make the score 2 for 11. Hassett hit the ball far more fluently than in his first knock and scored 37 before Hammond caught him to leave the score 3 for 63. At 76 Albert Cheetham was run out, bringing Pepper together with Price, with 34 runs needed in 12 minutes. Price left the fireworks to Pepper, who fulfilled his reputation for hitting. Only 11 runs were needed when he hit Stephenson onto the top tier of the grandstand for a glorious six.

Alf Gover, the Surrey fast-medium bowler, had the last over. Price took a single off the first ball to place the Australians within four runs of victory with five balls left. Then Pepper lofted a drive high in the air behind Douglas Wright, who, running back, juggled the catch several times before spilling it, accidentally kicking the ball towards midwicket as it eluded him. They ran two and Australia was within two runs of victory. Pepper blocked the third and fourth balls as the 17,000 spectators hushed, and hit the fifth ball through mid-wicket over the boundary rope. Pandemonium ensued as Australian, South African and Canadian servicemen in the crowd shouted their joy. The *Daily Express* applauded the upset win by the Australians who, it said, "set the tempo of the match all the way through".

Although he had scored an admirable 49 in the first "Test", Flying-Officer Ross Stanford insisted on standing down for Squadron-Leader Keith Carmody for the second "Test" at Bramall Lane, Sheffield, on 23 to 26 June. England replaced Ames, Gover and Robins with George Pope, Maurice Leyland and the

Lancashire seam bowler Dick Pollard. Just before play began Leyland and Stephenson had to withdraw and were replaced by Errol Holmes and the Lancashire spinner W. B. Roberts.

Brammall Lane was still battered from German bombing and the stands fire-scarred, when Hassett won the toss and sent England in. An even century from Hammond, now back to his pre-war best, ended Australia's hopes of dismissing England cheaply. Washbrook made 63, Pope 35 to help England to 286. Pepper worried all the batsmen with a superb display, which Hammond described as the best spin bowling he had ever faced, and the fielding of the Australians reached a very high standard.

The Australian team made only 147 in reply, with Miller run out for the second time in three innings and Hassett out for 5. Carmody's stylish 42 proved Australia's top score against an England attack in which George Pope's 5 for 58, with his late out-swingers, was outstanding. Inadvertently, the temperamental Pope inspired Miller's aspirations as a bowler. When Miller asked how he managed to continue swinging the ball long after the shine had left it, Pope, who bowled in a cap which team-mates thought was to protect his bald head, went to his cap and handed it to Miller. Inside the lining, Miller found heavy daubs of hair cream. Thereafter Miller, noted for his long hairstyle, often found the need to rub his bowling fingers through hair liberally laced with a wellknown hair cream.

England's second innings totalled 190, with Miller taking 2 for 28 from 13 overs and starting to enjoy his new role as a bowler. Set to score 330 to win, Australia were 1 for 108 and 2 for 171 at various stages but failed to reach the target by 41 runs. Pepper produced another spectacular exhibition of hitting, smashing one ball right through Errol Holmes' hands on the boundary, at which

Australian cricket never had a better ambassador than Lindsay Hassett, who was a wonderful mix of showman, strategist, team jester and class batsman. Above all he was guardian of the game's highest standards of sportsmanship.

point a Yorkshireman in the crowd suggested Holmes tighten the scarf he wore round his neck.

With the series balanced at one-all and three to play, Fleet Street covered every ball bowled when the third "Test" began at Lord's on 14 July. England dropped Robertson and Holmes and brought in Repton School star Donald Carr and naval cadet John Dewes for their first-class debut. When Pope pulled out, Cambridge student the Hon. Luke White took his place. The Australians made only one change, preferring the medium-pace right-arm leg-break and googly bowler Bob Cristofani to Price.

When England batted and moved to 2 for 72 through a stubborn partnership between Hutton and Dewes, Hassett called up Miller to bowl. Until then Miller had always bowled off a short run, but now he stepped out a longer run which took him to the crease with a momentum that produced pace bowling unmatched since Larwood was in action.

The ball flew off the pitch at alarming speed as Miller bowled Dewes, Carr and Hutton (104) and took the score to 5 for 169. England were all out for 254. Miller's 18 overs yielded 3 for 44. Cristofani took the honours with 4 for 43 but it was Miller's pace with the old ball that took the eye. Despite his century, Hutton had learned to be wary of Miller.

Only a patient 68 from Hassett, well supported by Carmody (32), and Cristofani (32), enabled the Australians to reach 194 in reply. Pollard bowled two invaluable shooters which skidded under the bat and hit the stumps of Miller and had Pepper lbw. Handed the new ball for the first time in his career, Miller responded by clean bowling Dewes for a duck. With Hammond absent because of fibrositis and unlikely to bat, England were virtually 2 for 1. Hutton and Edrich defied the Australians for the rest of the day to take the score to 3 for 110, with Hutton on 48 not out. It was exciting cricket, both sides straining for an advantage, and rich entertainment for a capacity crowd starved of big cricket for so long.

Next morning Miller bowled Edrich for 58 and then had Pollard for 9, to finish with 3 for 42 and six wickets in the match. England's second innings of 164 (Cristofani 5 for 49) gave Australia the task of scoring 224 in 300 minutes to win. They were on 3 for 104, Sismey 51, when Miller joined Hassett for the crucial period of the match.

They batted without blemish as they wore down the tiring England bowlers, Miller carrying on serenely after Hassett left to finish on 71 not out. At 6 for 225, Australia had won by four wickets and taken a 2–1 lead in a series in which the Australian Board of Control had feared they would be overwhelmed. Charles Fry described Miller's innings as a showpiece in which "superbly stroked and directed cover driving of the pace bowling formed the most telling and majestic feature". Cheetham returned home after this match, leaving a gap that was never satisfactorily filled.

Miller did even better in the fourth "Test" from 6 to 8 August at Lord's, scoring a chanceless 118, his 10 fours all drives. England responded to Australia's score of 388 with some resolute, skilful batting. Laurie Fishlock made 69, Hammond 83, Washbrook 112, and Edrich 73 not out in a splendid team effort which gave England a lead of 80 runs. When the three days ran out, Australia were 60 runs in front in their second innings, with six wickets left and Miller on 35 not out. Stanford made 33 not out, Pettiford 39. This drawn match was watched by more than 93,000 spectators, but above all the high standard of the cricket delighted "Plum" Warner, who told me he had had to use all his influence at Lord's to gain approval for the series.

Warner in his old age was a mesmerising figure, given to skipping around his South Kensington flat as he demonstrated his points, and he had the diverting habit of insisting that those who were interviewing him for the first time show him their stance with the bat. Mine passed muster, though he did think I had too much weight on the front foot. His gratitude to the towering figure of Miller in those Victory "Tests" was as impressive as his imagery in recalling great players. He also made no secret of his annoyance with the Australian Board of Control for failing to grant the Victory "Tests" the full Test status.

The fifth Test at Old Trafford from 20 to

Leading players in the Combined Services side included (L to R) N. Stocks, R. Cristofani, S. Sismey and M. Roper, shown here before a match at Selkirk.

22 August produced wonderful cricket. Miller continued in brilliant form, going in to bat with Australia on 4 for 66 and remaining undefeated on 77 in the total of 173. All this on a difficult green pitch overhung with cloud that enabled fast-medium bowlers Pope, Pollard and Eddie Phillipson to achieve sharp lift and unpredictable movement in the air. Miller's bowling had Fishlock lbw for 9 and England 1 for 14, but Hutton's 64 and Hammond's 57 lifted England to 243 and a lead of 70.

Australia were in desperate trouble at 5 for 46 before Cristofani produced a memorable show of swashbuckling hitting, to back up his 5 for 55 with the ball. Disdaining even to take block, he attacked in spectacular fashion to add 95 with Williams, who defend-

ed stoutly. Cristofani reached his century with a towering six that had every spectator on his feet applauding. His 110 not out at better than a run a minute was still not enough to worry England, who scored the 140 needed to win in the final innings with the loss of only four wickets. The series finished all square on two "Tests" apiece, with one draw.

Miller had the best aggregate in the five "Tests", 443 at an average of 62.80 and took 10 wickets at 27.70 each. He outshone Hammond, 369 at 46.10 and Hutton, 380 at 42.20. Only Cristofani, who took 14 wickets in the last three "Tests" at 15.20, looked more hostile with the ball and only Pepper could match Miller's powerful hitting.

Thrilled by the success of the Victory Tests, "Plum" Warner organised a match between England and the Dominions in August 1945 at Lord's. The New Zealander Martin Donnelly captured the early headlines with a fine innings of 133 out of the Dominions' first innings score of 307. Hammond made 121 in 160 minutes in a spirited reply for England, hitting two straight drives into the Members' Stand and adding 177 in a seventh wicket stand with Bill Edrich, who scored 78. At stumps on the second day the Dominions were 3 for 145 in their second innings, with Miller and Donnelly both not out. When play resumed, Miller took his score to 185 in a superfine display of shot-making, hitting 13 fours and 7 sixes, one of which landed on the roof of the broadcasting box. This was higher than the ball which Albert Trott hit over the pavilion in July 1899. *Wisden* said:

Miller outshone even Hammond and for the latter part of his innings played faultless cricket. The shot experts said was longer than Trott's landed high on the broadcasting box occupied by Howard Marshall. Miller's other six sixers bounced into seats in front of the Long Room, forcing elderly members to seek safety in the bar. Despite another craftsmanlike century from

Hammond, the Dominions defeated England by 45 runs with 10 minutes to spare.

Hassett then took his team to Scarborough for what are mistakenly labelled festival matches, but usually amount to an attempt by English cricket to get square for indignities suffered in the summer. This time Pepper overshadowed everybody with a tremendously powerful innings of 168, which included 6 enormous sixes. Miller was made to look a mere mortal by scoring 71, with 3 sixes, in the Australian score of 506. Pepper took six important wickets as the Australians went on to defeat the England side, carefully chosen by "Shrimp" Leveson-Gower, by an innings and 108 runs.

The achievements of Australia's cricketers in this memorable English summer have always been underestimated in Australia. When they got home the players found their performances counted for nothing. They did not expect heroes' welcomes but for men still elated at emerging with honour from such an exciting series, the lack of recognition among those who should have been their staunchest supporters was deflating and unjust.

Pressure from the Indian government found its way from Canberra to Field-Marshal Blamey, resulting in an instruction for the Services team to stop and play nine matches in India on the way home. The players were all desperate to get home, but after enduring the hardships of war accepted as their duty the task of helping cricket to get started again in a land of 400 million.

They encountered opposition of a standard Hassett and others consider India has never since matched, with players like Vijay Merchant, Lala Amarnath, Vinoo Mankad, Rusi Modi, Gul Mahomed, Madhusudan Rege and Vijay Hazare at the peak of their powers. The Indians were the absolute opposite of Hammond's England players, lacking adventure, failing to take a single risk, which with Merchant's defensive captaincy and the biased umpiring cricketers expect in India, resulted in a hard tour far removed from the joyful celebration of victory in war that was intended.

The first match against North Zone at Lahore from 28 to 30 October 1945, took the Services side on a 4000 kilometre round trip from Bombay in an ancient frontier mail train. Sleep was impossible on a journey that took 44 hours each way, with the Hindu engine driver constantly blowing his whistle to scatter beggars, pedlars and cows from the track. The Australians took four wickets before Cristofani was denied a clear–cut catch from Imtiaz Ahmed. Cristofani stalked from the field in disgust and did not reappear until North Zone were approaching 400. When Cristofani sought instructions on where he

Vijay Merchant, captain of the post-war Indian team, a team which Hassett considered has not been matched since.

should field, Hassett moved him this way and that until he had the open gate behind him, whereupon Hassett waved him straight back and out of the game.

Abdul Hafeez made 173, Imtiaz Ahmed 138 not out, in North Zone's 410, Pepper 77 and Hassett 73 in the Services' 351 in reply. The North Zone were 7 for 103 in their second innings when time ran out. After enduring this gruelling match before 30,000 Punjabis, the Australians moved to New Delhi from 1 to 3 November to play against the Maharajah of Patiala's Prince's XI. Mushtaq Ali (108) and Amarnath (163) made centuries as the Services side, most of them suffering from dysentery, kept a close eye on the whereabouts of toilets. The Maharajah, whose father had left 94 sons and squads of daughters when he died in 1938, did not bat, but he fielded at mid–off accompanied by an aide in a pink turban who intercepted anything below waist height. A fine double from Hassett, 187 and 124 not out, and an even 100 not out from Graham Williams enabled the Services to force another draw.

At Bombay, from 6 to 8 November against the West Zone, the Services bowling was hammered again. Miller scored 106, Price 55 in the Australians' first innings of 362. Modi hit 168 in West Zone's reply of 9 for 500. The Services were 2 for 88 in their second innings when time elapsed.

The first "Test" at Bombay from 10 to 13 November saw some enterprising Australian batting. Carmody began it all with 113 studded with the lofted drives and sweep shots so characteristic of him. Hassett made 53, Pettiford 124, Pepper 95, as the Services moved to 531. India responded with 339, not enough to prevent the follow–on but enough to avoid defeat. After scoring a further 304, Merchant left Australia to make 104 to win in just over half an hour. Hazare opened the bowling with an over of outswingers that passed a metre and a half outside the off stump.

Lala Amarnath, who played in Merchant's 1945 team, later took the captaincy when Merchant was unavailable for the Indian tour of Australia in 1947.

The match ended in a draw with the Services 1 for 31. Dick Whitington in *The Golden Nugget* recorded that as Merchant led the Indians from the field Kumar Shri Duleepsinhji called across several rows of seats: "Merchant, you have brought eternal shame on Indian cricket by the timing of your declaration and the placing of your field."

A further draw followed against a young Combined Universities XI on 15 and 16 November at Poona, where the Services bowlers took another hiding. M. R. Rege made 200 not out, Abdul Hafeez 161 in a score of 1 for 385. At the Services' Poona hotel Mick Roper organised a team meeting to protest against any further train travel. Roper

wanted to sack Hassett as captain unless he demanded that the Indian authorities organise all future travel by air, but before a vote was taken Squadron-Leader Sismey solved the crisis by arranging for an Australian Air Force unit in India to fly the team to places like Calcutta, Madras and Colombo.

At Calcutta, in the curtain-raiser before the second "Test", an East Zone team that included English Test star Denis Compton beat the Services by two wickets from 21 to 23 November. The Services players had just been told the Australian Board of Control had organised them to play each of the six states immediately they arrived home. Depressed at this further absence from their families, the Australians scored 107 and 304 (Hassett 125) against East Zone's 131 and 8 for 284.

When Compton was 88 not out in East Zone's second innings chase for runs, dozens of rioters spilled over from the crowd onto the field. Their leader advanced threateningly on Compton: "You play very fine innings for us, Mister Compton, but you must go. Six of our friends have just been shot by British police." Compton told him to speak to Hassett, who was in charge. The rioters promptly turned and rushed towards Hassett.

"Have any of you fellers got a cigarette?" he said.

All the anger drained from the rioters and their protest ended. Play resumed after an hour's delay while the ground was cleared of debris, Hassett shaking hands with the leading protesters as they left. Compton went on to 101 and Mushtaq Ali made 58 to clinch the Services' defeat.

India began the second "Test" from 25 to 28 November in Calcutta with an innings of 386, to which the Services replied with 472. Miller went out to bat with the score at 3 for 250, brandishing a bat belonging to Dick Whitington, who was unbeaten after passing his century. "Keith, I asked you not to use my bats—why don't you find one of your own?"

asked Whitington. Miller assured him he would take good care of the bat and proceeded to hit four of the five balls remaining in the over right out of the ground into a lily pond. "I thought I told you to be careful with my bat," moaned Whitington. "I am being careful," said Miller, "Look, there's not a mark on the bloody thing!"

Whitington scored 155, his career highest, and Pettiford 101. Miller went on to 82 but aggravated a wartime back injury and was unable to bowl in India's second innings. This ended any chance of a result, with India declaring at 4 for 350. Merchant made an unbeaten 155, but there was no applause for him from the Australians who calculated that he was either caught behind or leg before seven times before he reached 100.

The Services had their first win of the Indian tour against South Zone at Madras from 2 to 4 December, scoring 195 and 4 for 198 against 159 and 233. Ellis set up this six-wicket win by taking 4 for 21 in South Zone's first innings and Carmody helped with a vigorous 87 not out in the Services' second innings.

They were outplayed in the final tour match, the third "Test" at Madras from 7 to 10 December. India won by six wickets. The Services scored 339 in the first innings and 275 in the second, India 525 and 4 for 92. Hassett made 143 in the Services' first innings, Carmody 92 in the second but the outstanding batting of the match came from Rusi Modi, who made 203, and Amarnath, 113. India had shown that they had batsmen of the highest class and bowlers who compared favourably with the best in England and Australia. Only in wicket-keeping were the Indian teams below world standard.

Throughout the tour the wicket-keeping of Sismey was a revelation to the Indian fans, unaccustomed as they were to stylish, mistake-free keeping. But they were puzzled on very hot days when he left the field to have slivers of shrapnel that had worked their way to the skin surface removed from his back.

Hassett headed the Services' batting averages for the Indian tour, with 826 runs at 82.60, top score 187, followed by Carmody, who made 557 runs at 50.64, top score 113. Whitington, Pettiford, Miller and Williams also made centuries, but apart from Hassett and Carmody the batsmen lacked consistency. Ellis had impressive figures with 29 wickets at 28.17 but Pepper took most wickets, 32 at 33.53. On pitches unsuited to pace bowling, Ellis and Pepper did most work, both bowling more than 300 overs.

Although they won only one of their nine matches in India, the Services XI played regularly before capacity crowds and achieved the main purpose of the tour by reviving big cricket in India. They lost three matches, drew five, and would undoubtedly have improved on this record had they been able to include Albert Cheetham in their side.

They defeated an All-Ceylon XI at Colombo by an innings and 44 runs, between 14 and 16 December, in the last match before they returned home. Miller made 132 in this match, Hassett 57, out of the Services' 306. Ellis took 5 for 25 in Ceylon's first innings of 103, Pepper 4 for 46 in the second innings of 159.

Meanwhile in Australia a team captained by Stan McCabe made a tour of northern Air Force stations, playing one match on an air strip from which aircraft took off to fight the Japanese fleet in the Coral Sea battle. In another match enthusiastic airmen sewed tent flies together to produce an improved matting pitch. Around the states the Associations did their best to keep cricket alive. Captaining a Services side against New South Wales in Sydney from 30 December 1944 to New Year's Day 1945, Bill Brown made 100 in two hours before cutting loose to add a further 73 in 36 minutes. Barnes made an exhilarating century for New South Wales, who won

The Australian Services team which helped revive cricket immediately after World War II. Captain Lindsay Hassett, who refused a commission and led a side full of officers as a Warrant Officer II, is the small man standing in the centre.

thanks to Brown's sporting declaration: Services 393 and 5 for 95, New South Wales 8 for 412 declared and 1 for 78.

Hassett's Services side flew home from Colombo, via the Cocos Islands, in a Liberator laid on by the RAAF, sitting on their service packs and cricket bags. They were met by Major Bert Oldfield, one of the heroes of the First AIF side, who had been deputed to take them round Australia in his role as an army amenities officer. Oldfield surprised them with the news that Bradman had recovered from his severe fibrositis but would be tested for the first time in the match against them at Adelaide, where he would lead South Australia.

Miller did not disappoint spectators eager to get their first glimpse of him, with a bril-

liant innings of 80 against Western Australia in Perth from 24 to 26 December 1945. Western Australia made 322, to gain a first innings lead of 21 thanks to a fine 88 by Doug McKenzie, and 2 for 144 in their second innings, in a drawn match. The Services' first innings of 301 included 61 from Williams.

The Services players arrived in Adelaide to find that although Bradman's health had recovered he had suffered a serious setback the previous July through the collapse of his employers, H. W. Hodgetts. An affidavit filed in the Adelaide Bankruptcy Court disclosed that Hodgetts' deficiencies were £82,854. Debts totalled £102,926 and there were 238 unsecured creditors. Bradman was owed £762 in unpaid wages. The failure of Hodgetts' had forced Bradman to set himself up as Don Bradman and Company, with a seat on the Adelaide Stock Exchange. The South Australian Cricket Association had elected him to take Hodgetts' place as one of their delegates to the Australian Board of Control.

Bradman was 37 and apart from a match against Queensland a few days earlier (he made 68 and 52 not out) had played no serious cricket for almost six years when he took the field against the Services, who surprisingly left out Miller. Albert Cheetham rejoined the Services side for this match. The Services began with 314, with Whitington contributing 77 and Pepper 63. A young leg spinner named Bruce Dooland, who was in his initial season of first-class cricket, took 5 for 104. Bradman went out to join Reg Craig at the fall of the first South Australian wicket, with his entire future virtually at stake. Nobody knew if his health could support a return to big cricket.

He began tentatively and before he found his timing a top spinner from Pepper struck him low on his left pad as he played forward. Pepper and wicket-keeper Sismey were in no doubt that it was out but umpire Jack Scott rejected the appeal. Pepper threw his arms in the air despairingly and called to Scott: "What do you have to do?" Bradman took a single and at the end of the over asked Scott: "Do we have to put up with this sort of thing?"

Bradman found touch and went on to a splendid 112. He and Craig, who made 141, contributed all but 66 of South Australia's 319. Ellis took 5 for 88 in an attack sadly missing Miller's pace and fire. The Sydney *Sun* next day featured a story from Whitington—who had decided to forsake law for journalism—which said: "Bradman batted better for his 112 than anyone I have seen bat since I last saw Bradman, and that includes Hammond, Compton, Amarnath and Hutton. Bradman is still in a class of his own."

The match fizzled out in a draw after the Services' second innings of 255, to which Hassett added 92, Cristofani 58 and Stanford 58, but South Australia did not have time to get the 251 Hassett set them to win and were 1 for 130 or 120 behind when time ran out. After the match Jack Scott lodged a report on Pepper's behaviour with the South Australian Cricket Association, which was for-

warded to the Board of Control. Pepper, believing the report ended his hopes of playing Test cricket for Australia, at the end of that summer went off to complete his career in the Lancashire League. The extent of his loss to Australian cricket can never be precisely gauged but his departure deprived Australians of the chance to regularly watch an exciting cricketer, a massive hitter and a top-rank spinner.

The Services team were completely outplayed by Victoria in Melbourne from 4 to 8 January 1946. Ian Johnson's cleverly-flighted off spinners had all the Services batsmen floundering and he finished the match with 10 for 44 (6 for 27 and 4 for 17). Only Miller, who made 37 out of the first innings total of 118 and 59 out of the second innings of 182, handled Johnson comfortably. Des Fothergill, 99, and Gordon Tamblyn, 97, were unlucky to miss centuries in the Victorian innings of 451.

The one-sidedness of this Victorian win caused most Australian critics to under-rate the Services team and their outstanding achievements in the Victory "Tests" against England. This poor opinion was underlined when they lost by an innings and 8 runs to New South Wales in Sydney from 11 to 14 January. But the margin would have been much closer had Hassett accepted a catch from Sid Barnes in the gully off the fifth ball of the match. A vicious Miller bouncer flew off the edge to the normally reliable Hassett, who put it down. Barnes did not make another error until he was out for 102.

Bill Alley, the former prizefighter, boiler-marker and nightclub bouncer, made 119, Ken Grieves 102 not out, Bill Donaldson 99, as New South Wales moved to 7 for 551 declared. Miller, 105 not out, went to the crease after the Services had lost Carmody, Stanford and Hassett for only 25, and treated the crowd to his finest English form, defying a splendid attack which included Lindwall, Grieves,

Prime Minister Ben Chifley (left) and his External Affairs Minister H. V. Evatt watching the Services XI play New South Wales in 1946 at the SCG.

Toshack, and O'Reilly at his best. He was 93 not out when the last Services wicket fell but O'Reilly, impressed by an innings that deserved a century, suggested the Services' twelfth man, Jimmy Workman, be allowed to bat in place of Pettiford, who had retired with appendicitis, until Miller passed 100. This enabled Miller to take his score to 105 not out in a total of 204, although it breached the laws on substitutes, who are not permitted to bat or bowl.

Following on the Services then made 339 in their second innings, Pepper top-scoring with 63. O'Reilly's 4 for 48 gave him 7 for 94 for the match. Lindwall's six wickets cost 95 runs. Although he had been handed 12 extra runs on a platter, the quality of Miller's batting remained vivid in memory long after the match ended.

Too old for war service, O'Reilly had worked through the war years in a reserved occupation as secretary of a brick and tile company. The Sheffield Shield competition had been suspended in 1940–41 but grade cricket continued in all states. Some of O'Reilly's performances for St George in these seasons were phenomenal. He took 108 wickets

at a cost of only 9 runs each in the 1941–42 seasons, for example, and in 1943–44 took 147 wickets at 8.20. The standard of Sydney batting was not at all weak, with Sid Barnes scoring 1333 at 88.36 for Waverley in 1942–43 and Bill Alley making 1413 at 70.65 in 1943–44 for Petersham.

Stan McCabe's bad feet had compelled him to take a desk job during the war at Sydney's Victoria Barracks but he made only occasional appearances in charity matches before his feet forced him to retire permanently. Prematurely bald like his brothers, a curious fate for a barber's sons, Stan had scored 11,951 first-class runs at 49.38 and taken 159 wickets at 33.72. He hit 29 centuries in all, with three of his six Test centuries (average 48.21) ranked as cricket masterpieces. By the time Hassett's team arrived in Sydney, McCabe had built his sports shop in the NSWCA's Cricket House into a flourishing business. When Hassett confessed he had no job to go to when he left the army, McCabe offered to lend him the money to set himself up in a sporting goods business in Melbourne. Hassett accepted the offer and also some very sound advice on pitfalls to avoid in the trade. Within a couple of years Hassett had made a big success of his Melbourne venture and returned McCabe's loan, plus bank interest for the term he had borrowed the money. McCabe sent back a cheque for the interest.

The Services XI encountered some spirited batting from right-hander Bill Morris and excellent leg-spin bowling from Colin McCool when they went to Brisbane for the match against Queensland from 18 to 21 January, 1946. The Services made 296 in their first innings, with Whitington (84), Hassett (67) and Sismey (60) batting soundly. Queensland replied with 8 for 334 declared, Billy Brown delaying the declaration until Morris had reached 104 not out. The Services second innings ended at 8 for 227 declared. Set to score 190 to win, Queensland failed by just four runs in a thrilling finish, with five wickets in hand. Morris was on 66 not out. McCool's match bag was 11 for 176 (4 for 102 and 7 for 74).

The Services XI played their last match against Tasmania at Hobart over the Australia Day holiday weekend of 1946. They won the toss and scored 459, Ross Stanford playing his finest innings of the tour for 153. Ron Morrisby and Malcolm Thomas gave Tasmania a splendid start with an opening partnership of 136, Morrisby striking some glorious strokes in his 82. Thomas played the anchor role in a mainly dour 151 not out, which included 15 fours and one mighty six off Pepper which went right out of the ground. Next day Thomas took his score to 164 before he was run out after six hours at the crease. His score equalled the highest by a Tasmanian in first-class cricket, set by J. H. Savigny back in 1904, and ensured a draw. The Services had failed to win a match in Australia.

Victoria wanted to resume the Sheffield Shield competition in the first season after the war, 1945–46, but mainly because of New South Wales' opposition the Shield matches did not resume until 1946–47. Instead the states played a series of non-competition matches against each other. Aspiring bowlers had the best of these games. McCool formed a deadly partnership with wicket-keeper Tallon for Queensland; Bruce Dooland took the first post-war hat-trick for South Australia against Victoria in Melbourne after returning from army service in Darwin; Ernie Toshack proved a swarthy left-arm medium pacer of immaculate accuracy, and Ray Lindwall, a right-arm pace bowler from O'Reilly's St George club (after three years of war in the jungles of New Guinea and the Solomon Islands) was yet another to make a big impression. Of the batsmen, Barnes was in a class of his own. When McCool took 6 for 36 to set up a Queensland win over New South Wales in Brisbane,

The Australian Services side, before their last match at Hobart against Tasmania, photographed with the Tasmanian players.

Barnes still got a masterly double century. Victorian Ken Meuleman showed great promise and so did Ron Hamence, a cousin of former Test keeper Charlie Walker who was shot down and killed over Germany with the RAAF.

Wisely, Bradman made no forecasts about his future. He was unavailable for the tour of New Zealand by an Australian side captained by Billy Brown, although he picked the team

with Jack Ryder and "Chappie" Dwyer and was party to the omission of Hassett as captain. Despite his splendid captaincy of the Services XI, Hassett got only one vote for the job in a Board of Control poll for the leadership in New Zealand. Brown's side won all their five matches by wide margins. They beat Auckland by an innings and 180 runs at Eden Park from 1 to 5 March 1946, Canterbury at Christchurch by an innings and 35 runs from 8 to 11 March, Otago by eight wickets at Dunedin from 15 to 19 March, and Wellington by an innings and 160 runs at Wellington from 22 to 25 March. Both O'Reilly and Toshack returned sensational bowling figures

and the Australian batsmen made six fast centuries in these matches.

In the first-ever Test between Australia and New Zealand at Basin Reserve, Wellington, from 29 to 30 March 1946, Australia caught New Zealand twice on a wet pitch. New Zealand made 42 and 54; O'Reilly took 5 for 14 and 3 for 19, Toshack 4 for 12 and 2 for 6. Australia's 8 declared for 199 was enough to ensure victory by an innings and 103 runs.

The 12 Australians who made the New Zealand tour received £1 per day from the Australian Board of Control, the same as players received for Shield games. Such big crowds turned up for their matches New

Frustrated by the loss of opportunities during the war, Sid Barnes set out to make amends immediately peace arrived. Here, he is making the first double century by an Australian after the war, for New South Wales v. Queensland in Brisbane, thanks to a lucky snick past 'keeper Don Tallon.

Zealand asked the Board to increase that allowance, but the Board refused. Four of the team were still in uniform, and most were concerned about whether they could find jobs with any prospects. They all got home from the tour out of pocket, with only a blazer to show for their work.

O'Reilly knew when he played in the Test at Wellington that his left knee could no longer withstand the strain of big cricket. He sat in the dressing-room and slowly removed his boots in what he called a gesture of complete surrender which ended as he threw them through an open window. Australian cricket had lost the greatest bowler in its history, a wonderful competitor with 774 wickets at 16.60 in first-class matches, and 144 wickets at 22.59 in 27 Tests. In his very last Test he had humiliated the New Zealanders so comprehensively that their claims for regular Tests against Australia were denied for 27 years.

The departure of O'Reilly, McCabe, McCormick, Grimmett, Waite, Fingleton, and Fleetwood-Smith from Australia's pre-war teams left the field open to challenges from a remarkably talented list of cricketers, ambitions fired by the feeling that war had cheated them of opportunities. Many of them had learned in the services discipline which their cricket had lacked before the war and all of them were fitter and more resolute in achieving their ambitions. The result was that Australian cricket immediately after the Second World War gave promise of great days to come, with every Test place boasting a number of highly skilled challengers.

Post-war revival

England in Australia 1946–47;
the first Indian tour 1947–48

Eight years after sustaining the heaviest defeat
in her history against England at The Oval,
Australia resumed Test cricket in the intense
heat of the Woolloongabba ground in South
Brisbane. Bradman had returned to lead Australia against the advice of his doctors. He was
38 and after a long period of illness his
reputation was once again under challenge.
Some critics even suggested Sid Barnes had
become Australia's No. 1 batsman after
Barnes made a series of brilliant centuries
around the states. Others senselessly blamed
Bradman for the debacle at The Oval in 1938.

Bradman looked pale and unwell as he
went out to toss with Wally Hammond,
captain of the side that had so thoroughly
beaten Australia at The Oval. England had
prepared for the Australian tour with a Test
series at home against India and looked a
balanced, settled team, combining experience
with an array of newcomers. Australia's team
included eight players who, since approval
had not been given for recognition of the
Australia *v.* New Zealand match at Wellington as a Test, were new to Test cricket. Asked

Bradman and Barnes leaving the field to the
applause of English opponents after their 405-run
stand in Sydney in the second Test. Both made 234.

Bradman resumed his Test career to the delight of fans.

to smile as they tossed, Hammond and Bradman obliged: that was the last laugh they had together.

Australia won the toss and batted, and when Morris was out for 2 Bradman joined Barnes, facing Alec Bedser for the first time. Bradman was so out of touch he had to be shielded by Barnes, when several of his snicks and pushes narrowly missed going to hand. Hammond said later that Bradman batted like a schoolboy. When Barnes left at 46, Hassett went in for what became a historic partnership.

Behind him, as he shaped up to old rival Bill Voce on that morning of 29 November 1946, Bradman had a scratchy innings of 76 for South Australia against England, a second innings of 3, a knock of 106 for an Australian XI against England in which he had been

badly missed being stumped by Godfrey Evans at 76, and scores of 43 and 119 in a Shield match against Victoria. In all of these appearances before the first Test his health caused concern and there was already talk that Hassett might take over as Australian captain. Now as Voce moved in to bowl at Bradman the *Yorkshire Post*'s J. M. Kilburn considered his survival had been downright miraculous.

Voce's second ball was a half volley, which Bradman chopped down on. The ball flew waist high to John Ikin at second slip, for what the Englishmen believed was an easy catch. The English cricketers did not immediately appeal but when Bradman did not walk off they broke the momentary silence with their appeal. Umpire George Borwick, who had umpired in the previous England–Australia Tests ten years earlier, ruled not out on the grounds that it was a bump ball. At the non-striker's end, Hassett agreed, but in the press box, where the view of some of the critics was obstructed, there was little doubt that Bradman was out.

In the dressing-room Keith Miller, seeing the Englishmen congratulating Ikin for his catch, reached for his bat and gloves and prepared for what he believed was his first Test innings. At second slip, Hammond was furious with Bradman for not walking. Norman Yardley in the gully and Doug Wright at third man both thought it was a fair catch, and claimed the ball had flown from the top edge of the bat.

Hassett was quite certain the umpire was right in disallowing the appeal but said that during the luncheon interval he noticed agitation among the Englishmen over the affair, which, he feels, resulted in the incident becoming one of the most discussed in Test history.

Bradman survived until lunch and after the interval came out with Hassett to bat with all his old certainty. They added 276 for the third wicket, a record for England *v.* Australia

One of the great players developed in Australia immediately after the war, fast bowler Ray Lindwall, who lets go a fireball against England in 1946–47.

Tests. Bradman's 187 was a record for the 'Gabba ground, easily surpassing Leyland's 126 ten years earlier. Bradman hit 19 fours and was not dismissed until the fourth ball of the second day. Hassett then shared in another long stand with Miller, before the fourth wicket fell at 428. Hassett made 128, Miller 79. McCool (95), and Johnson (47), continued the heavy punishment of the England bowlers until Australia set up their highest total in Australia against England, 645.

When England batted, the fast bowling of Lindwall and Miller quickly produced a spate of false strokes from Hutton and Washbrook. Miller bowled Hutton before rain and thunder ended the third day with England on 1 for 21. A violent storm overnight gave England a treacherous pitch on which to bat on the fourth day and half the side were out for 56 despite a brave and clever innings from Edrich. A further storm then flooded the

ground. Half an hour after it started, the stumps were floating, with hailstones as big as golf balls crashing down.

The ground made a surprising recovery on the fifth day but hot sun converted the pitch into a gluepot on which it was impossible to bat. Fifteen wickets fell in three and a half hours despite the absence of Lindwall with chickenpox. Forced to follow on after scoring 141, England lost Hutton to the first ball of the second innings. Toshack, who had been taken out onto the pitch before play began and shown by Bradman where to pitch the ball, took 6 for 82 in England's second innings to finish the match with 9 for 99. Miller took the honours, however, with 9 for 77 (7 for 60 and 2 for 17).

Australia's win by an innings and 332 runs was her first Test win in Brisbane and her biggest over England in Australia. The overwhelming nature of the win was sweet revenge for the 1938 trouncing at The Oval for Bradman, who, with all the luck in the weather, saw his Test career restored. He grew in strength almost daily after that win, fully exploiting the poor selection of the opposing team. The England team was W. R. Hammond, N. W. D. Yardley, P. A. Gibb, A. V. Bedser, D. C. S. Compton, W. J. Edrich, T. G. Evans, L. B. Fishlock, J. Hardstaff, L. Hutton, J. T. Ikin, James Langridge, R. Pollard, T. P. Smith, W. Voce, C. Washbrook, D. V. P. Wright, with Major R. Howard manager and Bill Ferguson scorer and baggage master yet again. Bedser's twin brother Eric travelled with the side. The team had sailed to Australia in the *Stirling Castle* which made only one stop, overnight at Port Said, and the trip took 24 days.

Criticism that the team was too old proved valid long before the first Test, with Voce, Hardstaff and Langridge clearly past their best and Gibbs a fumbling, awkward keeper who only emphasised England's lack of catching skill and athleticism in the field.

Bill Ferguson, who spent 52 years as scorer and baggage master to touring teams in Australia, England, South Africa, West Indies and New Zealand.

Voce and Pollard had been given special leave from the army to make the trip but neither had enough pace or ball movement to worry batsmen in the leading states. Even before the disaster at Brisbane Hammond had begun to nurse Bedser and Wright, realising they were the major hopes in his weak attack. Hammond never found the wonderful form with the bat of pre-war years and lacked inspiration as a captain.

The tour began on October 2 1946, with an England victory by an innings and 215 runs in a non–first-class match against Northam and Districts at Northam. Hammond started well with 131 retired and he continued in fine form with an innings of 208 against Western Australia from 11 to 14 October in Perth. Missed catches prevented England winning and the locals hammered all the England bowlers except Wright, who had 4 for 55. A

further draw followed against a Combined XI at Perth from 17 to 19 October. Compton (98) and Washbrook (80) batted impressively but all the England batsmen had trouble against leg spinner Dooland, who took 4 for 88. David Watt, the Subiaco right-hander who had made 85 in the previous match for Western Australia was run out for 157 in the Combined XI's innings of 462. Ian Johnson also helped expose England's bowling weakness in scoring 87, putting on 217 with Watt in a stand prolonged by missed catches.

England's victory by an innings and 308 runs over South Australian Country at Port Pirie from 22 to 23 October, gave Hutton (164), Fishlock (98) and Compton (100) good practice. England made 6 for 487, South Australian Country 87 and 92, Peter Smith taking 8 for 43 and Wright 8 for 78 in the match.

Hutton and Washbrook failed to take advantage of an easy pitch at Adelaide, batting all the first day of the match against South Australia from 25 to 29 October for only 237 runs. England declared at 5 for 506 after batting through the second day, Compton and Edrich, who both made 71, providing entertainment lacking in the centuries by Hutton (136) and Washbrook (113). Bradman, looking very frail, batted two and a half hours for his 76 in South Australia's first innings of 266. Opener Bob Craig saved South Australia by batting for four hours and a quarter for 111, with the home side 8 for 276 when time expired.

England gave their Ashes hopes a boost by defeating the strong Victorian team by 244 runs at Melbourne between 31 October and 4 November. England began with 358, Compton scoring 143, Yardley 70, before Wright took 6 for 48 to bundle Victoria out for 189. Hutton then pressed home England's advantage with 151 not out. This allowed England to declare at 7 for 279. Wright then took a further 4 for 73 with Ikin holding some brilliant catches to have Victoria out for 204.

McCool confirmed his place in the first Test by taking the first six England wickets for an Australian XI at Melbourne from 8 to 13 November. McCool finished with 7 for 106 in England's innings of 314. His figures were 5 for 47 at one time. Bradman (106) shared in a long stand with Arthur Morris (115) before rain ended play with the Australian XI on 5 for 327.

At Sydney from 15 to 19 November, England's match against New South Wales was also ruined by rain. Morris was 81 not out when Barnes declared the New South Wales innings closed at 4 for 165. Hutton had made 97 before being run out in England's 2

for 156 when rain washed out play.

Queensland took the honours in a drawn match with England at the 'Gabba from 22 to 26 November, thanks largely to an unbeaten 169 by Geoff Cook. The powerful left-hander Rex Rogers hit 11 fours in his 66 in an opening stand of 111 with Cook, who continued batting for 7 hours 15 minutes. England's attack looked mediocre in Queensland's innings of 400. McCool again showed his mastery over England's batsmen by taking 6 for 105 in 35 overs of clever spin. Queensland's second innings yielded 6 for 230 declared, the declaration made possible by a fast 33 not out by newcomer Ken Mackay. England were 6 for 238 chasing 321 when time ran out, Washbrook having made 124, Edrich 71 to go with his first innings of 64. Six of McCool's nine wickets in the match came from catches or stumpings by Tallon, whose speed and agility made England keeper Paul Gibb looked

Once cricket resumed after the war one of the first to demonstrate his rare talents was wicket-keeper Don Tallon, shown here completing a stumping off spinner Colin McCool.

second-rate, a judgement that proved valid when Gibb missed easy chances in the first Test three days later.

After playing a draw with Queensland Country at Gympie from 7 to 9 December, England went to Sydney for the second Test from 13 to 19 December desperate for bowling talent. Australia on the other hand was blessed with a surfeit of outstanding bowlers. Any one of a dozen could have filled Test places with confidence, with players like Bill Johnston, Bruce Dooland, the gifted Queensland medium-pacer Len Johnson, hard-working Western Australian Charlie Puckett and Victorian leg spinner Doug Ring unable to force their way into the side.

England's difficulties were compounded by the refusal of her leading batsmen to use their feet against the spinners and they were in continual difficulty against the leg spin of McCool and the subtly flighted off spin of Ian Johnson. Edrich was the only player ready to move out and kill the spin and apart from Ikin, who batted coolly as wickets fell at the other end, the English batsmen gave a wretched display to be all out for 255. The Australian spinners were so effective that the big Victorian Fred Freer, who had come into the side for Lindwall (still suffering from chickenpox), had limited opportunities once the shine left the ball.

McCool dismissed Compton and Hammond cheaply, both to Tallon, before Edrich and Ikin staged a grim stand. Johnson here bowled 11 overs in 70 minutes, eight of them maidens, and took one wicket (Ikin) for three runs. Yardley gave Tallon his fourth catch before Johnson mopped up the tail to finish with 6 for 42 from 30.1 overs. Bradman, who had limped badly on the first day, did not field on the second day, Hassett taking over as captain. England's innings lasted half an hour longer and Australia had batted for only nine minutes when rain held up play for three hours.

Morris turned his back on a ball from Edrich and was bowled off his legs with Australia's score on 24. Bradman preferred to rest his injured leg and sent Johnson in to bat out time with Barnes. Immediately Johnson arrived at the crease Barnes began making repeated appeals against the light.

The umpires gave way at the fifth appeal and play ended for the day amid boos from spectators with Australia on 1 for 27. Only 93 minutes play had been possible on the second day. Hot sun all through the Sunday rest day transformed the pitch and it rolled out into a perfect batting strip on Monday when 51,459 people watched Barnes bat all day. When Johnson went for seven Hassett and Miller helped him take the score along to 169. When the fourth wicket fell, Bradman appeared just before tea. At stumps he and Barnes were still together with Australia on 4 for 252. They were not separated until 20 minutes before stumps on the fifth day. Bradman batted for six and a half hours and hit 24 fours. Barnes was out a moment later for the same score, 234. They had established a new fifth-wicket world record of 405, only 46 runs short of the highest partnership for any wicket, 451 by Bradman and Ponsford at The Oval in 1934.

Barnes had played himself in eight times because of interruptions, intervals and overnight stops in an innings that lasted from Saturday morning until Tuesday afternoon. He had so many mid-pitch conferences with his partners that spectators called out for more shots and less talking. The running between wickets of two masters in the art of hogging the strike was fascinating, with neither responding to calls that did not suit them.

Wright had occasionally beaten Bradman with his mixture of high bouncing leg breaks and googlies but he did not get a ball past Barnes, who batted for 10 hours 40 minutes and hit only 17 fours. Wright was in his 42nd over before he got a wicket, holding a hard return catch from Tallon. Freer and Tribe put

With his fitness and confidence improving with every match, Bradman was soon leaping down the pitch to drive in his pre-war style. His off drive here in front of 'keeper Godfrey Evans hit the boundary fence before a fieldsman moved.

on 42 in 30 minutes before Bradman declared at 8 for 659.

Hutton then played a gem of an innings for 37 against Freer and Miller, but he stood on his stumps playing the last ball before lunch. All the leading England batsmen resisted stubbornly, Edrich leading the way with 119, his first century against Australia. McCool paved the way for Australia's victory by an innings and 33 runs by taking 5 for 109 off 32.4 overs, striking crucial blows when he dismissed Hammond for 37 and Yardley for 35. The wicket-keeping on both sides was superb. Evans did not concede a bye in his first Test and Tallon figured in five dismissals, adding menace to every ball the superb Australian spinners bowled.

By now the performances of the Test team and an array of outstanding displays in interstate matches had clearly shown that Australia had recovered from the war faster than England. Sam Loxton and the Harvey brothers were in splendid touch for Victoria, Aub Carrigan, Geoff Cook, Rex Rogers and Bill Morris were showing considerable ability for Queensland, as was Eric Lukeman for New South Wales and Ron James and Ron Hamence for South Australia.

After draws against New South Wales Country at Newcastle on 21 and 23 December and against New South Wales Southern Districts at Canberra on 27 and 28 December,

England defeated a Victorian Country team in a one-day match at Bendigo on 30 December. Fishlock, Hammond, Hutton and Washbrook all made centuries in one or other of these matches but the England bowling remained unimpressive.

England appeared to have Australia in danger at 6 for 192 in the first innings of the third Test at Melbourne from 1 to 7 January. Here the immense all-round strength of the Australian side emerged as McCool and Tallon added 63 in the last 55 minutes of the first day. Next day McCool hooked and drove with supreme confidence as he moved to 104 not out, his first Test century, which included 8 fours and lasted three hours.

When England began the chase for Australia's 365, Hutton snicked a fiery delivery from Lindwall and McCool capped his perfect day by holding a spectacular slips catch. Dooland, who had replaced Tribe in the Australian side, took 4 for 69 in an impressive Test debut to help restrict England to 351. Edrich was given out lbw for 89 when he seemed to hit a ball from Lindwall, Compton did not offer a shot at a ball from Toshack and was also given out lbw, and when Hammond was caught and bowled by Dooland any chance England had of taking a lead ended.

On the fourth day England took only four wickets. Morris batted all day and next morning took his score to 155. The seventh Australian wicket fell at 341 and some English critics felt that England could still win. Tallon and Lindwall quickly dissipated such thoughts with a violent attack on the England bowling, grabbing 154 runs in only 85 minutes. Tallon took 95 minutes for his 92 and hit 10 fours. Lindwall completed a magnificent century by straight-driving Bedser all along the ground to the fence, striking the ball three metres down the pitch. With the fiercely struck drives ricocheting off the fences in front of the wicket, Hammond persisted with three slips.

Left to score 551 in seven hours after

Bradman introducing the Duke and Duchess of Gloucester to the Australian team during the Melbourne Test against England in 1946–47. Colin McCool is shaking hands with the Duchess.

Australia's innings ended at 536, England survived a barrage of bouncers from Lindwall and Miller to end the fifth day on 91 without loss. On the sixth day Washbrook went on to a patient 112, his initial century against Australia. Yardley saved the game for England by staying for 90 minutes, thwarting the Australian bowlers in stands with Bedser and Evans. The England tail's sportsmanship in refusing to appeal despite bad light and rain was much admired in a drawn match watched by 343,675 spectators, who paid a world record of £44,063 for the privilege.

Desperate for a win, England had to be content with draws against a Combined XI at Hobart from 10 to 13 January, against Tasmania at Launceston from 15 to 17 January, and against South Australia at Adelaide from

24 to 28 January. Compton made 124 against the Combined XI, and 163 against Tasmania, during which he and Hardstaff (155) had a stand of 282. Hammond returned to form with a fine 188 against South Australia and was well supported by Langridge (100) and Hutton (88). Any chance England had of beating South Australia was ruined by Ron Hamence's 145.

There was little to choose between the teams after each had completed an innings in the fourth Test at Adelaide between 31 January and 6 February. Despite a temperature of around 100 degrees Fahrenheit throughout the match, Morris and Compton both scored centuries in each innings and Lindwall finished off England's first innings by taking three wickets in four balls. The SACA rewarded these achievements with specially engraved watches. England's openers Hutton and Washbrook put on more than a hundred in both innings but England's bowlers still could not force a win.

England scored 460, with Hutton contributing 94, Compton 147. Superb batting by Morris (122), Hassett (78) and Miller (141 not out) enabled Australia to lead by 27 with a score of 487. Hutton's 76 again demonstrated his mastery of the Australian pace attack in England's second innings of 8 for 340 declared, Compton this time reaching 103 not out. Tallon missed stumping Evans on the second-last afternoon, a mistake that probably cost Australia a win. Evans survived for 95 minutes before he got his first run and was not out on 10 when Hammond closed. Australia had to make 314 in 195 minutes to win but Bradman declined the challenge. Merv Harvey stayed 100 minutes to help Morris produce Australia's first century opening stand of the rubber. The draw ensured Australia held the Ashes.

Three further draws completed the tourists' dismal record before the fifth Test. Hammond left the field before lunch in the

Leg spinner Colin McCool bowling to Hammond in the 1946–47 Melbourne Test.

match at Ballarat against Victorian Country (from 11 to 12 February) and did not play again in Australia. Compton failed by only seven runs in an attempt to score his fifth successive first-class century against Victoria in Melbourne from 14 to 18 February, in a match graced by a delightful 120-run stand for the fourth wicket between 18-year-old Neil Harvey (69) and Hassett, who went on to 126. England scored 355 and 118, Victoria 327, and only rain on the third day prevented Victoria winning following a woeful England display against Tribe, who had 6 for 49 in their second innings. Peter Smith's leg spinners produced 9 for 121 in the drawn match with New South Wales from 21 to 25 February. Smith's second innings bag of 3 for 97 gave him 12 for 218 in the match but rain prevented a result with England batting brilliantly in a chase for 339 runs in 240 minutes.

The fifth Test in Sydney, played from 28 February to 5 March, produced the most ex-

*New South Wales captain Sid Barnes (left),
NSWCA secretary Harold Heydon (centre) and
England captain Wally Hammond go out to toss
before the England v. New South Wales match.*

citing cricket of the tour with rain continually
helping the bowlers, without ever becoming
spiteful. Hutton was again the target of a
barrage of Australian bouncers, a tough as-
signment for a batsman whose wrist had been
badly damaged in a wartime gymnasium
accident. He met the challenge bravely by
compiling his first Test century in Australia
before tonsillitis forced him to retire and seek
hospital treatment. He had made 122, but he
took no further part in the match.

When the first new ball was taken with
England on 3 for 207, the Englishman faced a
further barrage of bouncers in failing light.
Protecting his head, Compton trod on his
stumps and after two unsuccessful appeals
against the light Yardley and Ikin were also
dismissed, leaving England 6 for 237 at
stumps. Rain washed out the second day but
the Sunday rest day gave the pitch plenty of
time to dry out. It rolled out into a splendid
batting pitch after England's innings ended on
280.

Barnes, who had returned after injury,
combined with Morris to give Australia a fine
start, the first wicket falling at 126. Then for
the first time in the rubber Wright got on top,
bounding in off the long run which early in
the tour had spectators laughing at him,
lengthening stride as if avoiding holes in the
ground and bringing the ball down from an
extended arm that made his wrong-uns and
top spinners kick rib-high. After the igno-

miny McCool, Johnson and Dooland had put England's batting stars through earlier in the summer, it was strange to see the best spin bowling in the match come from an Englishman. Wright's 7 for 105 off 29 overs reduced Australia's first innings to 253 and at one stage allowed Yardley to set three slips for him.

McCool struck back at once for Australia, clean-bowling Washbrook and worrying everyone bar Compton. McCool's 5 for 44 included three stumpings by Tallon and reduced the England second innings to 186 after England had held a clear advantage. Left to score 214 to win, Australia looked shaky when Bradman edged Wright to Edrich at slip, but the chance was missed. Bradman and Hassett then became engaged in a tense struggle against some superb bowling by Wright and Bedser, gradually wearing the bowling down in a stand of 98 that saw Australia home by five wickets. Miller hit brilliantly for 34 not out as the pitch deteriorated.

This gave Australia a three–nil margin in the Test series with two Tests drawn. The England team's record was the worst by any since Australian tours began. Of the 25 matches played in Australia, only four were won and three of those wins were against country sides. The only first-class team defeated by England were Victoria. But the tour was an unqualified financial success, with the MCC share of the profits reaching £50,000, and successfully revived big cricket in Australia.

England's major failure was in bowling, with Wright the only bowler to take more than 20 wickets in the five Tests. His 23 wickets were expensive, however, as they cost 43.04 apiece. Alec Bedser's 16 Test wickets cost 54.75 each and leg spinner Peter Smith a horrendous two wickets at 109.00. None of the England batsmen scored 500 runs in the Tests. Hutton headed the Test averages with 417 runs at 52.12. Hammond was the major failure with his eight Test innings producing a top score of only 37.

Australia improved as the series progressed, with Bradman (97.14), Miller (76.80), Barnes (73.83), Morris (71.85) and McCool (54.40) all averaging more than 50 with the bat in the five Tests. The wickets were shared evenly in a well balanced attack. Lindwall headed the averages with 18 wickets at 20.38. Miller took 16 wickets at 20.87, Toshack 17 at 25.70, McCool 18 at 27.27, Johnson 10 at 30.60. The wicket-keeping on both sides reached a very high standard once Evans took over from Gibbs, an unfortunate selection, but Australia's catching and ground fielding was far superior to England's. England won two of their four matches in New Zealand after the Australian tour, with the other two drawn. More than a million people watched the Englishmen, including 846,263 in the Tests in Australia.

The England tour provided a much-needed boost for the finances of the state associations, heavily hit by the war. The NSWCA had stopped supplying free cigars and cigarettes to delegates and was not having team pictures taken. The association, by accepting the loan in 1942 from the Cricketers' Club, was able to continue its programme of sending food parcels to Britain, a practice it did not stop until 1948.

The success of the Australian team in the first post-war series against England saw the best part of a Test team leave Australian cricket to try their luck in England. Bill Alley, Cec Pepper, Jack Pettiford, Ken Grieves and Jock Livingston were in the first wave, but with Test berths and places in state teams very hard to consolidate they were followed by Fred Freer, Wal Walmsley, Ron James, John McMahon, Vic Jackson, and many others who at various times gave promise of winning Test selection. Most of them headed for the Lancashire League, but a group qualified for county teams. In Australia competition for places in the powerful New South Wales and Victorian

Warwick Armstrong wrote bitter Test match commentaries for Frank Packer's newspapers just after World War II. This photograph shows him in one of his last public appearances before his death in 1947.

teams forced highly talented players to change states.

Victoria won the first Sheffield Shield competition after the Second World War when it won five of its six matches and played a draw in the other in 1946–47. The batting of Loxton (average 143), Hassett (141.75) and Miller (133.40) provided the foundation for Victoria's wins, all outright, but the left-arm spin of George Tribe was invaluable. Flighting the ball cleverly and sustaining an immaculate length, Tribe took 33 wickets at 16.54 runs apiece and it was a major blow to Australia's overall cricket strength when he signed for three seasons with Milnrow in the Lancashire League. Tribe had taken 86 wickets for only 19.25 in just 13 games for Victoria, but after playing in three Tests against Hammond's team he felt his Test place was not

secure. Tribe was the only bowler Bradman ever asked keeper Tallon to practise with in the nets—to ensure Tallon could "read" his wrong-un.

Loxton made the highest score of a Shield competition overshadowed by the English tour, 232 not out against Queensland in his first match for his state. Just as impressive was a long-legged left-arm bowler with an action that was all elbows and wide arm-swing named William Johnston, who could deliver both pace and spin. Johnston was so loose-jointed Ray Robinson said his wrists seemed to become uncoupled as he moved in. He began as a spinner but switched to fast-medium swingers on the advice of Frank Tarrant, former Middlesex all-rounder.

The Board of Control admitted Western Australia to the Sheffield Shield competition on a restricted basis in 1947–48 when the Indian team led by Lala Amarnath was in Australia. Western Australia played four matches compared with seven by the other states and the Shield was decided on averages. Western Australia had to pay a subsidy to the other states when they made the trip to Perth, paying them the difference between their normal trip to Adelaide and the trip to Perth. The payment of the subsidy aroused ill-feeling in Perth but was forced on the other states because revenue from Shield games was so poor these matches often sustained losses. New South Wales declined to collect the subsidy from the WACA in the nine seasons it applied.

The Indian tourists were handicapped by the inability of Vijay Merchant and Rusi Modi, who batted so capably against Hassett's Services team two years earlier, to join the first official tour of Australia. The Australian Board of Control offered to cover the pitches against rain but Amarnath declined the offer, apparently reasoning that his bowlers would benefit more than Australia's pace men from bowling on rain-affected strips. Bradman won the toss in four of the five Tests and in two of them India were caught on wet wickets. India also erred in sending 17 players for 14 first-class matches, which compelled Amanarth to provide opportunities for as many players as possible instead of retaining his strongest side.

The Indian team was L. Amarnath, V. S. Hazare, D. G. Phadkar, V. Mankad, G. Kishenchand, H. R. Adhikari, C. T. Sarwate, Gul Mahomed, C. S. Nayudu, M. S. Ranvirsinhji, S. W. Sohoni, J. K. Irani, Amir Elahi, K. M. Rangnekar, P. Sen, Rai Singh, C. R. Rangachari.

Rain interfered with three days of the Indians' first tour match in Perth against Western Australia on 17 to 21 October 1947. Put in to bat, Western Australia struggled against Mankad's left-arm spin. From 6 for 166, Western Australia collapsed and were out for 171. Mankad followed his 5 for 68 by topscoring with 57 in India's innings of 127. Googly bowler Morgan Herbert had 7 for 45 for Western Australia, the match fizzling out in a draw.

India's bowling sustained heavy punishment in the drawn match with South Australia at Adelaide from 24 to 28 October, but India's batsmen acquitted themselves well enough to take the team within 52 runs of victory with five wickets in hand. South Australia made 8 for 518, with left-hander Dick Neihuus scoring 137, Bob Craig 100, Bradman 156. India responded with 451, Amarnath contributing 144, Mankad 57 and Hazare 95. Bradman declared South Australia's second innings closed at 8 for 219, leaving India 287 to win. From 5 for 60, India recovered splendidly thanks to an unbroken stand of 175 by Mankad (116 not out) and Amarnath (94 not out).

Amarnath sustained his brilliant batting form against Victoria from 30 October to 3 November in Melbourne, scoring 228 not out in the first innings of 403. Victoria managed

273 after a stand of 152 by Neil Harvey and Sam Loxton prevented the follow-on. Hazare (83) and Mankad (59) then resisted some fine bowling from Bill Johnston, who had match figures of 6 for 96, to ensure a draw. Johnston had opened the match by taking three wickets before India scored. India's second innings of 203 left Victoria with 333 to get for victory but they had time only to reach 2 for 138. Amarnath used eight bowlers in the match.

At Sydney from 7 to 11 November, New South Wales' all-round strength gave them victory by an innings and 48 runs. India's bowlers suffered heavy punishment from Morris (162), Lukeman (58), Moroney (96), Miller (72) and Pettiford (73), which allowed Morris to declare at 8 for 561. Despite stands of 99 between Hazare and Mankad and 133 between Hazare and Adhikari, India followed on 263 behind. Hazare's 142 against high quality bowling from Miller, Lindwall, Toshack, Pettiford and Randwick leg spinner Fred Johnston impressed experts. Only Adhikari (65) passed 50 in India's second innings of 215.

India staged a stunning revival by defeating a Test-strength Australian XI at Sydney from 14 to 18 November by 47 runs, their first win of the tour. A thrilling last-wicket stand of 97 by Irani (43) and Kishenchand (75 not out) contributed to this upset after nine wickets had fallen for 229, lifting India's first innings score to 326. Bradman completed his 100th first-class century with an innings he took very seriously, going to the crease at 1 for 11 and playing himself in very studiously. He took no risks until he reached 50 but thereafter hit out freely. When he was on 99, Amarnath threw the ball to Kishenchand for the last over before tea. Bradman pushed his second ball to leg for a single to reach his hundred in 2 hours 12 minutes. After tea he added 72 in 45 minutes. His 172 was faultless and included a six and 18 fours.

As the entire audience rose to cheer Brad-

Broadcasts of big cricket won an increasing audience after World War II thanks to these three commentators: (L to R) Arthur Gilligan, Allan McGilvray and Vic Richardson.

man, the first man to congratulate him was Miller, with whom he added 252 for the third wicket. Miller made 86 of them. This was Bradman's 295th first-class innings, compared with the next-fastest to score a hundred centuries, Wally Hammond, who needed 679 innings. Denis Compton later did it in 552 innings. When Bradman and Miller were out, the last six wickets fell for 38 runs and the Australian XI's advantage was lost.

India took their chance and declared at 9 for 304, leaving the Australian XI to score 251 in 150 minutes to win. The Australians accepted the challenge but received an early setback when Brown (30), backing up too far, was run out at the bowler's end by Mankad, who had previously warned him for the same offence. Bradman went in at 1 for 60 and made 26 in half an hour but after he went the score slumped to 5 for 120. Neil Harvey could not find a partner to stay with him and was on 56 not out when the last wicket fell at 203 with 30 minutes remaining.

At Perth, while this match was in progress, Western Australia made a dramatic entry into the Sheffield Shield competition by defeating South Australia by an innings and 124 runs. Keith Carmody, former Services team and RAAF opening batsman, made 198 in brilliant style in his first appearance for Western Australia. Missed in the first over, Carmody, newly appointed captain–coach, helped Western Australia to a first innings total of 444. Dr George Robinson, the Mount Lawley right-hander born at Boulder on the goldfields, made 90 for Western Australia, and David Watt the Scottish-born Subiaco right-hander who had made 85 and 157 the previous summer against England, made a fast, typically unorthodox 43. Left-arm slow bowler Tom O'Dwyer then set up Western Australia's victory by taking 5 for 47 and bundling South Australia out for 109, the mercurial Watt finishing off the innings by taking 2 for 2 off ten balls.

Following on, South Australia, who had Bradman, Hamence and Dooland absent in the Sydney match, managed 211. Niehuus (65) and Ross Stanford (71) resisted stoutly but both were bowled by Wally Langdon, who finished with 4 for 28. O'Dwyer took 3 for 56 in this innings to complete the match with 8 for 103, but much of the hard work was done by postman Charlie Puckett, whose 44 overs were all accurate and aggressive, yielding 5 for 105.

India demonstrated their crowd-pleasing attributes again in a thriller against Queensland at Brisbane from 21 to 25 November. Queensland began with 341, Bill Morris again impressing with the bat in an innings of 115. Mick Raymer made a quick-time 82. Amarnath (172 not out) and Mankad (65) took India to 369 and a lead of 28. McCool then hit an admirable 101 not out which allowed Queensland to declare at 7 for 269. India set out boldly in the bid to score 242 in 90 minutes and did extremely well to reach 217. McCool took 5 for 68.

Australia won the first Test at the Gabba by an innings and 226 runs from 28 November to 4 December, after India had been twice caught on a treacherous pitch. Australia made 8 for 382 in good conditions. Bradman took 2 hours 50 minutes to make 100 and then with the sky darkening hit out to add 60 in 45 minutes, adding 101 in 89 minutes with Hassett (48). Only an hour's play was possible because of rain on the second day, but more than 11,000 people stayed to watch Bradman resume at 5 p.m. A further downpour saturated the pitch on the Sunday rest day. Bradman's 185 included 20 fours, but the big hits of the Australian innings came from Miller (58).

Bradman, who had amazed onlookers by taking Toshack out to show him where to pitch the ball the previous season when Australia had England trapped on a sticky, did not need to give Toshack further instruction this time. Lindwall had Mankad and Gul Mahomed out in the first over, before Johnston and Miller took wickets. Then Toshack took the last five wickets for two runs from 19 balls to finish off the Indian innings in sensational style for 58. India followed on 324 behind and were 4 for 41. Further rain restricted play to an hour on the fourth day but conditions improved for the fifth day when Sarwate batted stubbornly for three hours. Toshack made the most of the still-damp pitch at the other end and none of Sarwate's team-mates stayed long. Toshack finished with 6 for 29 and the amazing match figures of 11 for 31.

Meanwhile Western Australia created another shock in Perth by beating the previous summer's undefeated Shield winners, Victoria, who had Ian Johnson, Bill Johnston and Hassett playing in the Test. Merv Harvey made 141 in Victoria's first innings of 370 and his brother Neil an entertaining 94. Alan Edwards, a stylish left-hander (104), and the reliable medico George Robinson (134), punished the Victorian attack, and Watt produced another knock studded with belligerent blows before he was run out for 76 and Western Australia took a first innings lead of 59 with a score of 429.

Victoria struggled desperately to regain the initiative in their second innings when Ken Meuleman, the Essendon right-hander, made 135 but a sustained display of right-arm fast bowling by Ken Cumming, who took 6 for 62, held the Victorians in check. Victoria declared at 9 for 304. Western Australia lost 5 for 123 chasing 245 to win and were 5 for 205 when time ran out, Alan Edwards adding 67 to his first innings century.

Rain restricted the second Test at Sydney between 12 and 18 December to only ten hours, the first time a six-day match had been completely washed out in Australia. India began with an indifferent batting display in scoring 188. Mankad then provided a historic dismissal that will be discussed as long as cricket endures when he ran out opener Bill Brown at the bowler's end for the second time that summer. Mankad had warned Brown about backing up too far in a previous match but this time he gave Brown no warning and as soon as Brown (18) moved out of his crease Mankad whipped off the bails.

With Australia on 1 for 28, the third and fourth days were washed out and play began on saturated turf on the fifth. Morris, Bradman and Hassett fell cheaply before a brief stand by Miller and Hamence boosted the score by 38 runs. From 5 for 86, Australia lost her last five wickets for 21 runs to be all out for 107, Hazare taking 4 for 29. When India batted again, Johnston and Johnson restricted them to 7 for 61 before rain dispelled hopes of an exciting finish on the last day.

After defeating Western Districts at Bathurst on 20 and 21 December by 104 runs and drawing against Southern Districts at Canberra on 27 and 29 December, India encountered Bradman at his run-hungry best in the third Test at Melbourne on 1 to 5 January, 1948. Bradman added to his long list of records by scoring centuries, 132 and 127 not out, in each innings, the first time he had achieved this in a Test. His first innings included a stand of 169 for the third wicket with Hassett (80) which enabled Australia to score 394. India replied with 9 for 291 declared, Mankad (116) and Sarwate (36) putting on 124 for the first wicket.

With India on 5 for 198 overnight rain changed the match and forced Amarnath to declare 103 behind. Bradman changed his batting order but Australia lost 4 for 32 before Bradman and Morris shared in an unbroken partnership of 223 for the fifth wicket. Bradman was first to his century and Morris followed soon after. Australia were 4 for 255 and 358 ahead at stumps. Heavy overnight rain allowed Bradman to declare and bundle India out for 125. Ian Johnson, with 8 for 94 in the match, was the best Australian bowler, Australia winning by 233 runs.

India won her second first-class match of the tour in Hobart from 10 to 13 January by defeating Tasmania by an innings and 139 runs. Tasmania struggled throughout against the bowling of Amarnath (2 for 27 and 3 for 18) and Rangachari (6 for 45 and 3 for 35), scoring 142 and 125. Centuries by Amarnath (171) and Hazare (115) gave India the winning margin with a first innings of 7 for 406 declared. Tasmania made a much better fight of the second match at Launceston from 15 to 17 January, taking a first innings lead of one run after India declared at 7 for 457. Sarwate contributed 128, Amarnath 135. Tasmania's 458 in reply included 138 from Ron Morrisby and 180 not out by Wal Walmsley. The match was left drawn with India 1 for 12 in the third

Sid Barnes, a remarkable all-rounder, traps Indian captain Lala Amarnath for a duck in the third Test at Melbourne in 1947–48.

innings. Needing a win to save the rubber, India were outplayed in the fourth Test at Adelaide from 23 to 28 January. All the Indian bowlers were savaged as Australia ran up 674 in the first innings, Barnes (112) sharing a second-wicket stand of 236 with Bradman (201) after Morris had gone at 20. Further free scoring came from Hassett (198 not out) and Miller (67) in a fourth-wicket partnership of 142. Australia's total was her highest in a Test in Australia.

India started disastrously, losing two wickets for six runs before centuries from Hazare (116) and Phadkar (123) boosted the total to 381, a deficit of 293. Following on, India managed 277 thanks to 145 by Hazare, his second century in the match. Lindwall had

7 for 38 in India's second innings, in which six batsmen failed to score. The win gave Australia the series.

The fifth Test at Melbourne, from 6 to 10 February, brought a further one-sided win to Australia, this time by an innings and 177 runs. Australia made 8 for 575 declared after Brown scored 99, Harvey 153 in only his second Test appearance, at the age of 19, and Loxton 80. Bradman retired hurt with a torn rib muscle for 57, an injury that troubled him for the rest of his career. India again started badly, losing their first wicket at three, but a fine 111 from Mankad, 74 from Hazare and 56 not out by Phadkar took the total to 331. Following on 244 behind, India collapsed for 67, Len Johnson's 3 for 8 giving him 6 for 74 in the match.

Although overshadowed by the Tests, the Shield competition had thrown up plenty of shocks, the most remarkable being Western Australia's victory at her first appearance in the competition. After wins over South Australia and Victoria in Perth, Western Australia succumbed to New South Wales by 98 runs in Sydney from 30 January to 3 February because of a majestic 170 in three hours by Miller, who hit 3 sixes and 24 fours, supported by 105 from Bill Donaldson. One of Miller's sixes landed on the top deck of the Ladies' Stand.

Western Australia struggled desperately to reach New South Wales' 396, with Alan Edwards (83), and Wally Langdon (70), both batting soundly, the innings closing on 293. New South Wales declared at 4 for 200 in their second innings, leaving Western Australia to score 304 in 240 minutes. Apart from Carmody, who made 81, the Western Australians found the bowling of Miller, Toshack, Fred Johnston and Pettiford too accurate and succumbed to their only defeat of the summer.

At Brisbane from 6 to 10 February, Western Australia clinched the Shield by beating Queensland by 183 runs. Puckett was the hero, bowling unchanged for more than

The West Australian players who startled Australian cricket buffs by winning the Sheffield Shield in 1947–48. Team captain-coach Keith Carmody is in front on the left.

two and a half hours to help dismiss Queensland for 130 in the final innings and finish with 6 for 48. Tom O'Dwyer was the other bowling star, taking 7 for 79 in Queensland's first innings of 325. Western Australia made 446 (Watt 129) and 192. Puckett finished the season with 24 wickets at 24.79, but O'Dwyer topped the Western Australian averages with 20 wickets at 21.60.

A feature of the Shield season was four batsmen who passed 500 runs: Phil Ridings 649 at 59.00, with three centuries, for South Australia; Bill Morris 538 at 44.83, with one century, for Queensland; Ron James 528 at 44.00 with a top score of 210 for South Australia; and Ken Meuleman 501 at 50.10, with two centuries, for Victoria. Colin McDonald, at 19, played for Victoria in his first season of club cricket.

Western Australia wound up a wonderful

season by defeating India by six runs in Perth from 20 to 24 February in the last match of the Indians' tour. Mankad bowled splendidly in Western Australia's first innings, taking 5 for 60, but Carmody's equally impressive 85 allowed the home side to reach 270. Puckett then took 5 for 56 in another courageous display to have India out for 252, 18 behind. Western Australia's second innings of 172 set India 191 to win and this time Puckett had 6 for 78 to seal victory. Puckett's 11 for 134 in the match lifted him to the forefront of contenders for a place in Australia's side to tour England in 1948, and brought India's seventh defeat in a tour of 14 first-class matches. Defeated 4–0 in the Tests, in three of which Australia batted only once, the Indians won just two first-class games.

Only two Indians, Amarnath with 1162 at 58.10, including five centuries, and Hazare, 1056 runs at 48.00 with four centuries, topped 1000 runs, although Mankad scored three centuries. He was easily the outstanding Indian bowler with 61 wickets at 26.14. The next best Indian bowler, Amarnath, took 30 wickets at 28.43. Bradman headed the Australian Test batting with an average of 178.75, including four centuries, whereas the leading Indian batsman in the Tests, Phadkar, averaged 52.33. India were out-classed in the field, with catches frequently dropped. Bill Johnston was Australia's most successful Test bowler with 16 wickets at 11.37, Amarnath the best Indian with 13 wickets at 28.15.

The most brilliant cricket of the summer, however, came from Keith Miller with his 170 against India in his first season with New South Wales. Miller had been offered a dead-end job in Melbourne on discharge from the RAAF. He refused to accept it and instead spent his deferred pay on a trip to America where he married Margaret Wagner, known as Peg, a secretary from Boston, who shared his keen interest in classical music. He returned to Australia with his new wife but without a job and was happy to accept an offer to become assistant to A. G. ("Johnnie") Moyes, editor of *Sporting Life* magazine in Sydney. Early in his employment under Moyes he noticed bits of paper being handed surreptitiously to Moyes on race days. These were special tips for that day's races. Sharing them, Miller found his boyhood interest in racehorses rekindled, just as the realisation that cricket could help provide a better lifestyle for him and his wife reinforced his desire to do well on Australia's 1948 tour of England. He was not alone in this and as the 1948 tour drew near cricketers in every Australian state nurtured ambitions to make the trip.

The 1948 tour, the twentieth by an Australian team to England but only the eighth organised by the Australian Board of Control, brought Don Bradman's Test career to a dramatic conclusion in his 40th year. Thanks to Bradman's skill with the bat, and as a captain and a selector, Australia was at the top of the world's cricket nations. It held a respectable margin in its favour in Test wins and losses against England, South Africa, West Indies, and India. The great man would make it a memorable farewell.

Matched against the accomplishments of Australia's first-class players, the performance of the Board of Control from 1918 to 1948 was sadly inept. The Board had never been able to cast aside the strife and jealousy that brought about its formation. Success of the game had been despite the Board not because of it and after 35 years of feuding with players and handing out petty punishments it had failed to become fully representative of Australian cricket or of the players. The Board in 1948 represented the state associations, which in turn were run by the stronger clubs in the capital cities. The nation's Test players were not represented on the Board, nor were Aboriginals, and when they got to inter-state level the players found sympathetic friends on the

Board hard to find. The Board had never risen above the aim of its founders which was to take the control of Australia's international cricket out of the hands of the players, and most Board members had trouble recognising members of the Australian team.

Understandably, first-class players were not prepared to go through the laborious process of seeking election as suburban club delegates to the state associations and from that position winning appointment to the Board. Apart from Bradman, there were no Australian captains on the Board, no cricketers of distinction such as Sir Pelham Warner, Sir Stanley Jackson, Arthur Gilligan, Michael Falcon and Henry Leveson-Gower, who sat on the MCC committee in London. When the Bodyline affair was at its peak a players' committee was formed comprising Roger Hartigan, Monty Noble, Vic Richardson and Bill Woodfull to report on the problems of intimidatory bowling. Their report was largely ignored and the Board once again closed its doors to cricketers with intimate knowledge of the ethics and practicalities of the game. Australian cricket's great strength lay not in the committee rooms but in the nation's schools.

In the years leading up to the Second World War and immediately afterwards, schools cricket in Australia reached a very high standard, with hundreds of well coached, talented cricketers being channelled into district clubs from well organised competitions at private and public schools. Sportsmanlike behaviour was rated very highly by school masters, who gave freely of their time and enjoyed the success of their boys at higher levels. It was a production line no other cricket nation could equal and gave Australia a commanding lead over all other countries in terms of Test matches won and lost, but all too soon this schools' support for the game was to crumble.

Bibliography

Altham, H. S., *A History of Cricket*, Allen & Unwin, London, 1926

Arlott, John, *Gone To the Test Match*, Longmans Green, London, 1949
   The Great Ones, Pelham, London, 1967
   The Great Bowlers, Pelham, London, 1968
   The Great All-rounders, Pelham, London, 1969
   The Great Captains, Pelham, London, 1971

Armstrong, W. W., *The Art of Cricket*, Methuen, London, 1922

Bailey, Philip, Philip Thorn and Peter Wynne–Thomas, *Who's Who of Cricketers*, Newnes Books, London, 1984

Barker, Ralph, *Ten Great Innings*, Chatto & Windus, London, 1964
   Ten Great Bowlers, Chatto & Windus, London, 1967

Barker, Ralph and Irving Rosenwater, *England v. Australia 1877–1968*, Heinemann, London, 1969

Bowen, Rowland, *Cricket: A History*, Eyre & Spottiswood, London, 1970

Bradman, D. G., *The Don Bradman Cricket Book*, Hutchinson, London, 1930
   My Cricketing Life, Stanley Paul, London, 1938
   Farewell To Cricket, Hodder & Stoughton, London, 1950

Broadribb, Gerald, *Hit For Six*, Heinemann, London, 1960

Brooke, Robert, *The Collins Who's Who of English First-Class Cricket*, Collins, London, 1985

Canynge Caple, S., *The Cricketer's Who's Who*, Williams, London, 1934

Cardwell, Ronald, *The AIF Cricket Team*, privately printed, Sydney, 1980

Cardwell, Ronald, and Thomas Hodgson, *The Life and Times of H. S. T. L. Hendry*, privately printed, Sydney, 1984

Cashman, Richard, *'Ave a Go Yer Mug!*, Collins, Sydney, 1984

Darling, D. K., *Test Tussles On and Off the Field*, privately printed, Hobart, 1970

Derriman, Philip, *The Grand Old Ground*, Cassell, Melbourne, 1981
   Bodyline, Collins–Sydney Morning Herald, Sydney, 1984
   True To the Blue, Richard Smart Publishing, Sydney, 1985

Downer, Sidney, *100 Not Out*, Rigby, Adelaide, 1972

Dunstan, Keith, *The Paddock that Grew*, Cassell, Melbourne, 1962

Fender, P. G. H., *Kissing the Rod*, Chapman & Hall, London, 1934

Ferguson, W. H., *Mr Cricket*, Nicholas Kaye, London, 1957

Fingleton, Jack, *Cricket Crisis*, Cassell, London, 1946
   Masters of Cricket, Heinemann, London, 1958

Frindall, Bill, *The Wisden Book of Test Cricket*, MacDonald & Jane's, London, 1979

The Wisden Book of Cricket Records, Queen Anne Press, London, 1981

Frith, David, *The Archie Jackson Story*, The Cricketer, Tunbridge Wells, 1974

"*My Dear Victorious Stod*", privately printed, New Malden, 1970

England Versus Australia: A Pictorial History of the Test Matches Since 1877, Rigby, Adelaide, 1977

The Golden Age Of Cricket, 1890–1914, Angus & Robertson, Sydney, 1978

The Fast Men, Van Nostrand Reinhold, Wokingham, 1975

The Slow Men, Richard Smart Publishing, Sydney, 1984

Grace, Radcliffe, *Warwick Armstrong*, privately printed, Melbourne, 1975

Grimmett, C. V., *On Getting Wickets*, Hodder & Stoughton, London, 1930

Haygarth, A., *MCC Scores and Biographies*, Volumes I–IV, Lillywhite's, London, 1862

MCC Scores and Biographies, Volumes V–XV, Longmans Green, London, various years

Harris, Bruce, *Jardine Justified*, Chapman & Hall, London, 1933

Harte, Chris and Bernard Whimpress, *Adelaide Oval 1884–1984*, SACA, Adelaide, 1984

Hele, George and R. S. Whitington, *Bodyline Umpire*, Rigby, Adelaide, 1974

Hendren, "Patsy", *Big Cricket*, Hodder & Stoughton, London, 1934

Hobbs, J. B., *The Fight for the Ashes 1934*, Harrap & Co., London, 1934

Hutcheon, E. E., *A History of Queensland Cricket*, QCA, Brisbane, 1946

Iredale, Frank, *33 Years of Cricket*, Beatty & Richardson, Sydney, 1920

James, Alfred, *Averages and Results of Australian First-Class Cricket, 1850–51 to 1914–15*, A. B. M. James, Sydney, 1985

Jardine, D. R., *In Quest of the Ashes*, Hutchinson, London, 1933

Ashes—and Dust, Hutchinson, London, 1935

Larwood, Harold (with Kevin Perkins), *The Larwood Story*, W. H. Allen, London, 1965

Laver, Frank, *An Australian Cricketer on Tour*, Bell & Sons, London, 1907

Mailey, Arthur, *10 For 66 and All That*, Phoenix House, London, 1958

Martin-Jenkins, C. D. A., *Who's Who of Test Cricketers*, Rigby, Sydney, 1983

Moody, Clarence P., *Australian cricket and cricketers*, R. A. Thompson, Melbourne, 1894

Cricket album of noted Australian cricketers, Hussey & Gillingham, Adelaide, 1898

Moyes, A. G., *A Century of Cricketers*, Angus & Robertson, Sydney, 1950

Australian Bowlers, Angus & Robertson, Sydney, 1953

Australian Batsmen, Angus & Robertson, Sydney, 1954

Australian Cricket: A History, Angus & Robertson, Sydney, 1959

Mulvaney, D. J., *Cricket Walkabout*, Melbourne University Press, Melbourne, 1967

Noble, M. A., *Gilligan's Men*, Chapman & Hall, London, 1925

The Game's the Thing, Cassell, London, 1926

The Fight For the Ashes 1928–29, Harrap & Co., London, 1929

O'Reilly, Bill, *Tiger—Sixty Years of Cricket*, Collins, Sydney, 1985

Page, Michael, *Bradman*, Macmillan Australia, 1984

Page, Roger, *A History of Tasmanian Cricket*, Roger Page, Hobart, 1957

Parkin, Cecil, *Cricket Triumphs and Troubles*, C. Nichols & Co., London, 1936

Piesse, Ken, *Prahran Cricket Club Centenary History*, Prahran CC, Victoria, 1979

Pullin, A. W., *Talks With Old Yorkshire Cricketers*, Yorkshire Post, Leeds, 1898

Talks With Old English Cricketers, Blackwood, London, 1900

Richardson, Vic (with R. S. Whitington), *The Vic Richardson Story*, Rigby, Adelaide, 1967

Robertson-Glasgow, R. C., *Crusoe On Cricket*, Alan Ross, London, 1966

Robinson, Ray, *Between Wickets*, Collins, Sydney, 1949

   From the Boundary, Collins, Sydney, 1950

   The Wildest Tests, Pelham, London, 1972

   On Top Down Under, Cassell Australia, 1975

Rosenwater, Irving, *Sir Donald Bradman*, Batsford, London, 1978

Ross, Alan, *Ranji, Prince of Cricketers*, Collins, London, 1983

Sissons, R. and B. Stoddart, *Cricket and Empire*, Allen & Unwin, Sydney, 1984

Smith, Rick, *Prominent Tasmanian Cricketers*, Foot & Playstead, Launceston, 1985

Smith, Sydney, *History of the Tests*, Australasian Publishing Co., Sydney, 1946

Snow, E. E., *Sir Julien Cahn's XI*, Evington, Leicester, 1964

Swanton, E. W. and John Woodcock, *Barclay's World of Cricket*, Collins, London, 1966, 1980, 1986

Torrens, Warwick, *Queensland Cricket and Cricketers 1862–1981*, privately printed, Brisbane, 1982

Turner, C. T. B., *The Quest for Bowlers*, Cornstalk Publishing, Sydney, 1926

Verity, Hedley, *Bowling 'Em Out*, Hutchinson & Co. Ltd, London, 1936

Wakley, B. J., *Bradman the Great*, Nicholas Kaye, London, 1959

Warner, P. F., *Imperial Cricket*, London & Counties Press Association, London, 1912

   Cricket Reminiscences, G. Richards, London, 1920

   My Cricketing Life, Hodder & Stoughton, London, 1921

   The Fight for the Ashes 1926, George Harrap & Co., London, 1926

   The Fight for the Ashes 1930, Harrap & Co., London, 1930

   Long Innings, Harrap & Co., London, 1951

Webber, Roy, *The Book of Cricket Records*, Phoenix House, London, 1961

Wild, Roland, *Ranji*, Rich & Cowan Ltd, London, 1934

Williams, Marcus, *Double Century*, Willow Books, London, 1985

Wilmot, R. W.E., *Defending the Ashes*, Robertson & Mullens, Melbourne, 1933

Winning, Clifford, *Cricket Balmainia*, Balmain CC, Sydney, 1981

Wisden's Cricket Almanack, John Wisden & Co., London

Wynne-Thomas, Peter, *England On Tour*, Rigby, Adelaide, 1982

   "Give Me Arthur", Arthur Barker Ltd, London, 1985

Picture Credits

The author and publishers gratefully acknowledge the following people and organisations who gave permission to reproduce photographs and illustrations on the pages noted. Every effort has been made to trace copyright holders and apology is made for any unintended infringement. Pictures not listed come from the author's collection.

ABC Publicity Department, 392
G. O. Allen, 311
Australian War Memorial, 2–3, 7
Don Bradman, 339
Ronald Cardwell, 10, 26–7, 61, 68, 71, 87, 113, 124–5, 140
Central Press, 344
Courier Mail (Brisbane), 335, 376, 383
Cricketer, 41
J. C. Davis Collection (Mitchell Library), 5, 22–3, 24, 28, 29, 42, 56
John Fairfax & Sons, 394
Herbert Fishwick, 149, 152, 156, 159
Gray-Nicholls Collection, 266–7
Ken Kelly, 12, 117, 361
Mrs F. Lawry, 245

Melbourne Cricket Club, 15, 36, 56, 272, 309, 386
Mercury (Hobart), 351
New South Wales Cricket Association, 216–7
Bill O'Reilly, 332
Punch (London), 57
K. Piesse, 102
Ric Smith, 306
Sport and General, 298, 368
Thompson family album, 165
Topical Press, 369
West Australian Cricket Association, 262, 271
West Australian Newspapers Ltd, 395

Index

ANGUS & ROBERTSON PUBLISHERS

Unit 4, Eden Park, 31 Waterloo Road,
North Ryde, NSW, Australia 2113;
94 Newton Road, Auckland 1,
New Zealand; and
16 Golden Square, London W1R 4BN,
United Kingdom

First published in Australia
by Angus & Robertson Publishers in 1988
First published in the United Kingdom
by Angus & Robertson (UK) in 1989

Copyright © Jack Pollard 1988
National Library of Australia
Cataloguing-in-publication data.

Pollard, Jack, 1926–
    The Bradman years.

    Bibliography.
    Includes index.
    ISBN 0 207 15596 8.

    1. Bradman, Sir Donald, 1908–   .
    2. Cricket—Australia—History. 3. Cricket
    players—Australia. I. Title.

796.35'8'0994

Typeset in Bembo by Best-set Typesetter Ltd
Printed in Hong Kong